CW01082705

Preaching the Manifold Grace of God

Preaching
the Manifold Grace
of God

—— VOLUME 2 ——

Theologies of Preaching in the
Early Twenty-First Century

EDITED BY
Ronald J. Allen

CASCADE *Books* • Eugene, Oregon

PREACHING THE MANIFOLD GRACE OF GOD, VOLUME 2
Theologies of Preaching in the Early Twenty-First Century

Copyright © 2022 Wipf and Stock Publishers. All rights reserved. Except for brief quotations in critical publications or reviews, no part of this book may be reproduced in any manner without prior written permission from the publisher. Write: Permissions, Wipf and Stock Publishers, 199 W. 8th Ave., Suite 3, Eugene, OR 97401.

Cascade Books
An Imprint of Wipf and Stock Publishers
199 W. 8th Ave., Suite 3
Eugene, OR 97401

www.wipfandstock.com

PAPERBACK ISBN: 978-1-7252-5962-1
HARDCOVER ISBN: 978-1-7252-5963-8
EBOOK ISBN: 978-1-7252-5964-5

Cataloguing-in-Publication data:

Names: Allen, Ronald J., editor.

Title: Preaching the manifold grace of God, volume 2 : theologies of preaching in the early twenty-first century / edited by Ronald J. Allen.

Description: Eugene, OR: Cascade Books, 2022 | Includes bibliographical references.

Identifiers: ISBN 978-1-7252-5962-1 (paperback) | ISBN 978-1-7252-5963-8 (hardcover) | ISBN 978-1-7252-5964-5 (ebook)

Subjects: LCSH: Preaching. | Sermons.

Classification: BV411.2 P7377 2022 (print). | BV411.2 (ebook).

The excerpt from "Lookin' for Love in All the Wrong Places" is used by permission of Bluewater Music Services Corporation.

The excerpt from James McCauley, "An Art of Poetry," from his *Collected Poems* is used by permission of HarperCollins Australia Pty Limited.

The sermon by Karl Barth, "By Grace You Have Been Saved," is used by permission of Wipf and Stock Publishers.

The sermon by Gina Stewart, "God Is Doing a New Thing," is used by permission of the author.

The Gender Unicorn by Trans Student Education Resources (www.transstudent. org/gender). Illustrations by Anna Moore. Design by Landyn Pan, Eli Erlick, and many others. Licensed under Creative Commons.

Unless otherwise noted, Scripture quotations are taken from the New Revised Standard Version Bible, copyright 1989, Division of Christian Education of the National Council of the Churches of Christ in the United States of America. Used by permission. All rights reserved.

As indicated—marked (NIV)—Scripture quotations are taken from the Holy Bible, New International Version®, NIV®. Copyright © 1973, 1978, 1984, 2011 by Biblica, Inc.™ Used by permission of Zondervan. All rights reserved worldwide. www. zondervan.com/. The "NIV" and "New International Version" are trademarks registered in the United States Patent and Trademark Office by Biblica, Inc.™

As indicated—marked (CEV)—Scripture quotations are taken from the COMMON ENGLISH BIBLE. © Copyright 2011 COMMON ENGLISH BIBLE. All rights reserved. Used by permission.

To

Mason James Allen

Sparkling Blue Eyes

Overflowing Energy

Ever Eager for More

Contents

Introduction to the Two Volumes

Ronald J. Allen

PREACHING IS A THOROUGHLY theological act. Theological dimensions permeate every aspect of preaching from how the preacher understands God to how the preacher conceives the nature and purpose of the sermon, to the assumptions the preacher makes about the people who listen to the sermon, to how listeners process oral-aural communication, to the roles of the Bible and other authorities in the sermon, to how the preacher structures the sermon, and how the congregation and world respond to the sermon.

Diverse interpretations of the theology of preaching. This two-volume work is occasioned by the obvious fact that preachers, congregations, and Christian movements come to distinctive interpretations of the theological nature of preaching. There is no universal theology of preaching. Instead, there are multiple approaches to the theology of preaching. These differences are not arcane matters of interest only to scholars. Differences in theologies of preaching have practical outcomes for preachers and congregations in the respective ways in which they prepare sermons and listen to sermons.

When I step into the pulpit, I do not simply "preach," but I preach through the lens of a particular theological perspective along with the various lenses of social location (including such matters as race, gender, sexuality, class, political commitment, philosophical orientation). That *Gestalt* perspective shapes how I understand the issues named in the opening paragraph above. As a preacher I need to be as fully conscious as I can about the perspectives that I bring to the sermon so that I can work with their strengths and respond critically to their limitations.

On the one hand, approaches to preaching are distinctive enough that two preachers can sometimes use similar words but be saying and

doing rather different things. On the other hand, preachers from different theological families sometimes take diverse theological paths to sermons that are similar in theological analysis and homiletical content. The
contributors to these two volumes offer descriptions of a wide range of
theologies of preaching.

A *reference work*. In the first instance, this book aims to be a reference
work on the theology of preaching in historical and contemporary manifestations. Beyond that, the book displays a wide range of theological voices in
the hope that it can help preachers today better locate their own preaching
with respect to its roots in history and to the more contemporary theological viewpoints that may influence it.

A *different approach to each volume. A similar structure within each
volume*. Each volume has a slightly different approach. Volume 1 focuses
on several major historical families of preaching while Volume 2 turns to
contemporary perspectives. Within each volume, however, the chapters are
structured similarly, one structure for Volume 1 and another for Volume 2. I
hope these common structures will help readers engage in comparison and
contrast among the various theological households.

Volume 1. As noted just above, Volume 1 describes theologies of
preaching in several major historical theological families: Orthodox, Roman Catholic, Lutheran, Reformed, Anabaptist Anglican/Episcopalian,
Wesleyan, Baptist, African American, Stone-Campbell, Friends, and Pentecostal. Each essay includes a brief summary of the important historical
developments in the emergence of the theological household, the main
theological ideas of that theological family, the characteristics of preaching associated with that theological family, an indication of how the qualities of preaching associated with that historical family continue to appear
in preaching today, a consideration of themes that seem promising for the
twenty-first century church, and a brief evaluation of the strengths and
limitations of such preaching today. Each essay concludes with a short
bibliography for further reading.

Volume 1 includes an essay on African American preaching. African
American preaching is not a distinct historical-denominational theological
family in the same way as Reformed or Anglican preaching. Indeed, African American preaching occurs across many of the historical theological
households represented in Volume 1. Even more, African American preaching contains diverse streams. Yet, African American preaching does have a
particular history that transcends the boundaries of the other theological
families. Across denominations and movements, many African American
preachers participate in a distinct African American culture of preaching
even while manifesting elements of the theological family through which

they preach, ranging from groups such as Wesleyan through the many Baptist configurations to Pentecostalism. Eurocentric scholars of preaching have tended to give short shrift to African American preaching. The present work invites readers to honor African American preaching in its own right while paying attention to how it plays out in specific theological families. Volume 2 contains direct discussions of preaching through the lenses of African American liberation theology and womanist theology

A hundred years ago, the sermons of preachers in different historical theological families were often more distinct than they are today. Two things have happened to make preaching fairly homogenous among many congregations in the long-established churches. One factor is a growing ecumenical spirit. Indeed, at the high water mark of conciliar ecumenism, many people hoped for the end of denominationalism and the coming of a great united church. Caught up in ecumenical fervor, many preachers de-emphasized denominational particularities. The other factor is that the teaching of preaching in theological seminaries across the denominational spectrum has tended to come from textbooks that were written about preaching generally—and not about preaching in particular denominations or movements. Moreover, teachers of preaching increasingly tend to be trained in interdenominational graduate schools. The New Homiletic that took root in the 1970s, for instance, influenced preaching in similar ways in many different denominational settings.

However, the homiletical genetic code of preaching in many historical families is often deeply embedded. On a Sunday morning, one can still hear a "Presbyterian sermon" or a "Stone-Campbell preacher" or the echoes of Wesley. Sometimes the preacher intends such a resonance, though, increasingly in our world—afflicted by historical amnesia—such connections may not be conscious on the part of the preacher. I hope these volumes contribute to preachers becoming more aware of their distinct heritages and thinking critically about aspects to preserve as well as dimensions that are better set aside.

Volume 2. The chapters in Volume 2 consider theology and preaching in several contemporary theological movements. Of course, the theologies considered cannot include all contemporary theological movements. Nevertheless, these movements typically arise in response to issues experienced in particular communities. Early twenty-first preachers and theologians of preaching attempt to reformulate significant aspects of the theology and the work of preaching to take account of particular questions and social phenomena. The various liberation theologies, for instance, respond to particular social injustices.

The structure of the essays in Volume 2 differs somewhat from the structure of the contributions to Volume 1 by giving, proportionately, less attention to theological history and more attention to the practice of preaching by including a sermon. The reason for this shift is that I think many readers will be more familiar with actual preaching from the historical theological families than from the diverse array of contemporary theological perspectives. The sermons allow the reader to identify the particular characteristics of the perspective in homiletical action. Each chapter in Volume 2, then, includes a summary of the main theological ideas of the family, the purpose and characteristics of preaching associated with that family, a case study of the movement's approach to preaching in action (a sermon), a brief evaluation of the strengths and limitations of each theological family, and a short bibliography for further reading.

I have struggled with how to name several of the families in Volume 2. Two chapters each are devoted to theologies that focus on African American. Latinx, and Asian American communities. In each case one chapter considers the larger framework of preaching in that community with a title like "Preaching in the African American Liberation Theology Family" and a second chapter focuses on approaches focused particularly on women in the family with a title such as "Preaching in the Womanist Theological Family." This may sound like the first chapter sets out the normative approach and the second chapter accords women's experience a secondary role. That is certainly not the case in my mind, but I am not aware of more satisfactory ways of speaking.

Annotated Sermons. In Volume 2, the preachers have annotated the sample sermons to highlight points at which the sermon manifests important qualities of the theological family. The annotations are in *italics* in the bodies of the sermons.

Historical and contemporary families in the mix in a single preacher. As I have noted elsewhere, a complicating factor is that today's preacher often approaches the sermon from the viewpoints of both a historical theological tradition and a contemporary theological family.[1] For example, my own approach to preaching is informed by the Stone-Campbell movement (historical) as well as process theology (contemporary). From a theological point of view, I am a Stone-Campbell-Process preacher. Table One, "Bringing Historical and Contemporary Theological Families into Dialogue," illustrates many of the possibilities for the interaction of theological approaches

---

1. Allen, *Thinking Theologically*, 90.

to preaching from the past and the present.[2] Because of limited space, this book cannot explore these complicated relationships.

Diversity beyond the categories in these volumes. Given the many nuances in theological interpretations of preaching, two volumes cannot cover them all. Moreover, scholars and preachers often bring their own theological nuances into "*My* theology of preaching." I can easily imagine a preacher or theologian saying, "I do not fully recognize my approach here." But these two volumes do portray wide swaths of theological thinking about preaching that are central in both historical and contemporary communities.

Names for the Testaments. For almost two millennia the churches referred to the main parts of the protestant Bible as "Old Testament" and "New Testament." Following World War 2, a growing number of preachers and scholars have become aware of anti-Semitism at the heart of much Christian theology, including the part this prejudice played in justifying the Holocaust with its murder of six million Jewish people. From this point of view the word "old" is often associated with "worn out," "outdated," and "no longer functional," and the word "new" with "improved," "superior," and "replacing the old." In the ear of the conventional English hearer, then, the traditional names for the testaments can contribute to prejudice against the Jewish community, associated as it is with the *Old* Testament and to the superiority of the Christian community with its *New* Testament. Indeed, many churches have a supersessionist mindset, that is, they think Christianity has replaced Judaism.

Many voices in the church seek language that points to mutual respect and appropriate theological continuity between the two parts of the Bible as well as between Judaism and Christianity. Preachers and scholars posit the possible languages of First and Second Testament, Hebrew Bible, and Prime Testament. I prefer Torah, Prophets, Writings, Gospels, and Letters. However, this matter is undecided in the church at large. Preachers and scholars often have particular reasons for their language. With respect to the Testaments, the contributors to this volume use the language they prefer.

Thank you. Each contributor is a recognized scholar of preaching in the tradition for which she or he writes. The 30 scholars in this collection come from a wide range of theological orientations and social locations, embracing multiple genders and sexualities, racial and ethnic communities, and cultures. Many of the writers added this assignment to schedules that were already full. Furthermore, they worked during the great Covid–19 pandemic of 2020-21 when many theological libraries had limited access.

---

2. An earlier form of this table appeared in Allen, *Thinking Theologically,* 90.

This introduction gives me the opportunity to say thank you for doing such good work under difficult conditions.

I offer a particular word of thanks to five people who read and commented on parts of the manuscript or who engaged in meaning conversation about the book: O. Wesley Allen Jr., Kenyatta R. Gilbert, David M. Greenhaw, Helene Tallon Russell, and Mary Donovan Turner.

A prayer. This work appears as congregations are regathering after the traumatic disruption of community life caused by Covid–19 in 2020-21. As the churches reimagine our futures in the wake of the pandemic, my prayer is that these volumes can help preachers, congregations, denominations, and movements think afresh about qualities of preaching from the past and present that that have good chances to serve the renewal of God's transforming purposes through the church as well as those characteristics that may diminish that opportunity.

Abbreviations

Torah, Prophets, Writings

Gen	Genesis	Song	Song of Songs
Exod	Exodus	Isa	Isaiah
Lev	Leviticus	Jer	Jeremiah
Num	Numbers	Lam	Lamentations
Deut	Deuteronomy	Ezek	Ezekiel
Josh	Joshua	Dan	Daniel
Judg	Judges	Hos	Hosea
Ruth	Ruth	Joel	Joel
1–2 Sam	1–2 Samuel	Amos	Amos
1–2 Kgs	1–2 Kgs	Obad	Obadiah
1–2 Chr	1–2 Chronicles	Jonah	Jonah
Ezra	Ezra	Mic	Micah
Neh	Nehemiah	Nah	Nahum
Esth	Esther	Hab	Habakkuk
Job	Job	Zeph	Zephaniah
Ps/Pss	Psalms	Hag	Haggai
Prov	Proverbs	Zech	Zechariah
Eccl	Ecclesiastes	Mal	Malachi

Gospels and Letters

Matt	Matthew	1–2 Thess	1–2 Thessalonians
Mark	Mark	1–2 Tim	1–2 Timothy
Luke	Luke	Titus	
John	John	Phlm	Philemon
Acts	Acts	Heb	Hebrews
Rom	Romans	Jas	James
1–2 Cor	1–Corinthians	1–2 Pet	1–2 Peter
Gal	Galatians	1–2–3 John	1–2–3 John
Eph	Ephesians	Jude	Jude
Phil	Philippians	Rev	Revelation
Col	Colossians		

Contributors

Volume 2

Raymond C. Aldred. Director of Indigenous Studies, Vancouver School of Theology.

O. Wesley Allen Jr. Lois Craddock Perkins Professor of Homiletics, Perkins School of Theology, Southern Methodist University.

Ronald J. Allen. Professor of Preaching, and Gospels and Letters (Emeritus), Christian Theological Seminary.

Courtney V. Buggs. Assistant Professor of Preaching, Assistant Director of the PhD Program in African American Preaching and Sacred Rhetoric, Christian Theological Seminary.

Scott M. Gibson. Professor of Preaching, David E. Garland Chair of Preaching, Director of the PhD in Preaching Program, George W. Truett Theological Seminary, Baylor University.

David M. Greenhaw. President, Professor of Preaching and Worship (Emeritus), Eden Theological Seminary.

James Henry Harris. Distinguished Professor, Chair of Homiletics and Practical Theology, Research Scholar in Religion at the School of Theology, Virginia Union University; Pastor of Second Baptist Church (West End), Richmond, Virginia.

Pablo A. Jiménez. Associate Professor of Preaching, Associate Dean of the Latino and Global Ministries Program, Gordon-Conwell Theological Seminary.

Eunjoo Mary Kim. Professor of Homiletics and Liturgics, Iliff School of Theology.

Namjoong Kim. Associate Professor of the Practice of Ministry, Director of Korean Doctoral Programs, Claremont School of Theology.

Alison Milbank, Professor of Literature and Theology, University of Nottingham; Canon Theologian, Southwell Minster

Lance B. Pape. Granville and Erline Walker Associate Professor of Homiletics, Brite Divinity School.

Lis Valle-Ruiz. Assistant Professor of Homiletics, McCormick Theological Seminary.

Phil Snider. Senior Minister, Brentwood Christian Church (Disciples of Christ); Adjunct Professor, Drury University and Missouri State University.

Mary Donovan Turner. Carl Patten Professor of Preaching, Vice President for Academic Affairs, (Emeritus), Pacific School of Religion.

Karyn L. Wiseman. Herman G. Stuempfle Professor of Homiletics, United Lutheran Seminary; Minister of the Gloria Dei United Church of Christ, Huntington Valley, Pennsylvania.

Elizabeth J. A. Siwo-Okundi. Affiliated Faculty, Emerson College.

Casey T. Sigmon. Assistant Professor of Preaching and Worship, Director of Contextual Education, St. Paul School of Theology

1

Preaching in the Evangelical Theological Family

Scott M. Gibson

"Whatever evangelical meant, in other words, it did not mean closed minded."[1]

—Frederick Buechner

Evangelicalism is preaching. Preachers and their preaching have formed the backbone of the evangelical movement. In these days of politicism, defining the evangelical movement might be a little unclear, even difficult. However, what distinguishes evangelicalism is its historic commitment to the pulpit. The preaching of the Word is a distinctive mark of evangelicalism.[2]

Readers may not be clear about the term "evangelicalism." We begin with a definition and the circumstances that gave rise to this distinctive family of preaching. From there we will explore the purposes and characteristics of evangelical preaching by examining the contributions of evangelical preaching, provide a case study of an evangelical sermon, and conclude with an assessment of the movement.

---

1. Buechner, *Telling Secrets*, 79–80.

2. Portions of this essay were presented at the "God's Word and Our Words" preaching symposium at Baylor University in September 2017.

Circumstances That Gave Rise
to This Theological Family

Evangelicalism is not easy to define. Evangelicalism is a movement, not associated with any single group. One cannot point to a specific person or group and say, "that's evangelicalism," at least not in its entirety. Douglas Sweeney notes:

> Not only do evangelicals come in different shapes and sizes, but they also participate in hundreds of different denominations—some of which were founded in opposition to some of the others! The vast majority are Protestant, but even among the Protestants there are Lutheran, Reformed, and Anabaptist evangelicals. There are Anglicans, Methodists, Holiness people, and Pentecostals. There are Calvinists and Arminians.[3]

Sweeney continues, "There has never been—and there never will be—an evangelical denomination, despite the references one hears to the evangelical church."[4] The spectrum of evangelicals is wide which includes Peace-churches to Black Pentecostal churches, men, women, multi-ethnic, Native American, Latinx, Asian—a rich expression of evangelical ecumenism.[5]

Evangelicalism's roots are found over two hundred and fifty years ago in Great Britain, Germany, and America where the Wesleys and Whitfield, Edwards and Franke believed that one's Christian life was founded on the Bible, with personal rebirth through faith in Jesus Christ, the gift of the Holy Spirit, and the commitment to evangelism—persuading others to be born again.[6]

To define evangelicalism according to beliefs only, limits a fully contoured understanding of the movement. Social concern has been an

---

3. Sweeney, *The American Evangelical Story*, 19.

4. Sweeney, *The American Evangelical Story*, 10.

5. Smith, "A Shared Evangelical Heritage," 12. See also Dayton and Johnson, *The Variety of American Evangelicalism*; Naselli and Hansen, eds., *Four Views on the Spectrum of Evangelicalism*; Haykin and Stewart, eds., *The Advent of Evangelicalism*; Gerstner, "The Theological Boundaries of Evangelical Faith." For perspectives on Blacks and evangelicalism, see Pannell, "The Religious Heritage of Blacks"; Bentley, "Bible Believers in the Black Community"; Wilkens and Thorsen, *Everything You Know about Evangelicals is Wrong*. See also Salinas, *Taking Up the Mantle*; Kim and Wong, *Finding Our Voice*; Yong, *The Future of Evangelical Theology*.

6. Smith, "A Shared Evangelical Heritage." Smith considers these elements to be consistent in evangelical traditions. In *Evangelicalism in Modern Britain*, Bebbington states, "What we call cruicicentrism, conversionism, biblicism and activisim formed the enduring properties of the evangelical movement throughout the English-speaking world" (23).

important part of evangelical history. Timothy L. Smith notes, "the concern for social justice has been a major contribution of evangelical faith to modern culture."[7] Derek Tidball points out that evangelicals are realistic. "Recognizing that conversion does not always bring about long-term or wide-scale social transformation, and that sin is located in our fallen world not just in sinful individuals, they now generally believe there are two tasks to be accomplished, that is evangelism and social action."[8] The movement is global in its reach and influence.[9]

Evangelicals run the gamut on their positions and practices of education. Yet, not all evangelicals shy away from education. Evangelicals were on the forefront of establishing schools, led in inaugurating public education, and founded distinguished institutions of higher learning. From Wesley to Carl F. H. Henry to the present, evangelicals number among the graduates of some of the most elite universities in the world.[10] In the years following the Fundamentalist/Modernist Controversy in the United States there arose a "renaissance of conservative biblical scholarship."[11] Since then, evangelicals have found themselves on the faculties of departments of theology or biblical studies in major research universities and seminaries on both sides of the Atlantic.[12]

In the 1980s, mainline Presbyterian preacher and author Frederick Buechner was invited to teach a semester at Wheaton College in Wheaton, Illinois, a center of evangelicalism. In his memoir Buechner reflected, "I

---

7. Smith, "A Shared Evangelical Heritage," 16. See pages 16–28 where Smith details evangelical engagement with social justice. See also in the same volume, Wolterstorff, "Why Care about Justice?" Also see, for example, Spain, *At Ease in Zion*; Smith, *Revivalism and Social Reform*; Magnuson, *Salvation in the Slums*; Sweet, ed., *The Evangelical Tradition in America*; Lindner, "The Resurgence of Evangelical Social Concern (1925–75)."

8. Tidball, *Who Are the Evangelicals?*, 132.

9. See Hutchinson and Wolffe, *A Short History of Global Evangelicalism*; Lewis and Pierard, *Global Evangelicalism*. In *The Dominance of Evanglicalism*, Bebbington notes, "Evangelicals differed in theology, denomination, social characteristics and geographical location" (52).

10. Sweeney, *The American Evangelical Story*, 74.

11. Stanley, *The Global Diffusion of Evangelicalism*, 112.

12. Stanley, *The Global Diffusion of Evangelicalism*, 93–98. A casual internet search of universities and seminaries in North America and in Britain will demonstrate the place of evangelical scholars on these faculties. As for evangelical seminaries founded in North America in the twentieth century, these include Fuller Theological Seminary (in Pasadena, California), Gordon-Conwell Theological Seminary (in Hamilton, Massachusetts), and Trinity Evangelical Divinity School (in Deerfield, Illinois), and Regent College (in Vancouver, British Columbia), among others. In Great Britain, London School of Theology, among others, arose as a leading evangelical center of learning.

knew it was Billy Graham's alma mater. I knew it was evangelical though without any clear idea as to what that meant." He continued, "Whatever evangelical meant, in other words, it did not mean closed minded."[13] Buechner further pondered his brush with evangelicalism while at Wheaton. He wrote:

> The result was that to find myself at Wheaton among people who, although they spoke about it in different words from mine and expressed it in their lives differently, not only believed in Christ and his Kingdom more or less as I did but were also not ashamed or embarrassed to say so was like finding something which, only when I tasted it, I realized I had been starving for years.[14]

John H. Gerstner observed that in contrast to the rigidness of their fundamentalist forebears, evangelicals were "not militant, schismatic, or anti-scholarly . . . but who are, nonetheless, proponents of the fundamentals." He continued, "They call themselves evangelicals rather than fundamentalists, not because they repudiate the fundamentals, but because they reject the image which fundamentalists acquired."[15] Evangelicals have shared biblical commitments, many are socially aware, and many have an appreciation for education.

Purpose and Characteristics of Preaching in This Theological Family

Preaching is the mark of the evangelical's commitment to the Bible and the spread of the movement. Preaching arises as the unique feature of evangelicalism. The preachers of evangelicalism's first and second Great Awakenings, including Theodore Frelinghuysen, Jonathan Edwards, George Whitefield, Gilbert Tennent, Francis Asbury, Joseph Bellamy, Samuel Hopkins, Timothy Dwight, Lyman Beecher and later Charles Finney underscore the central role preaching played in the movement. Interestingly, although historians of evangelicalism have investigated various facets of the movement, the role and place of preaching appears to be an area yet to be explored.[16] For example, *The Oxford Handbook of Evangelical Theol-*

---

13. Buechner, *Telling Secrets*, 79, 80.

14. Buechner, *Telling Secrets*, 82.

15. Gerstner, "The Theological Boundaries of Evangelical Faith," 30–31.

16. The histories of evangelicalism seem to presume that preaching has had an impact on the movement, citing revivals and preachers. But no one has yet to connect the

ogy explores the Bible, theology, the church, and mission, yet none of the articles address the place of preaching in the movement.[17]

British evangelical preacher and author, John Stott begins his important book on preaching with the statement of the place of preaching, "Preaching is indispensable to Christianity."[18] Preaching is indispensable to evangelicalism.

The Neo-Evangelical movement reflected the same commitment to preaching. Clarence McCartney and Robert Lamont of First Presbyterian Church of Pittsburgh; A. Z. Conrad and Harold John Ockenga of Boston's Park Street Church;[19] Donald Gray Barnhouse and James Montgomery Boice at Tenth Presbyterian Church in Philadelphia; Gardner Taylor of Concord Baptist Church, Brooklyn; B. M. Nottage of Berean Chapel, Detroit; Shadrach Meshach Lockridge of Calvary Baptist Church, San Diego; and Lewis F. Evans of Hollywood Presbyterian Church, Hollywood, preached unwaveringly, many of whom were committed to systematic weekly exposition of different biblical books.[20] Evangelist Billy Graham, a key figure in the Neo-Evangelical movement, helped to solidify the place of present-day evangelicalism on the American and even world stage. On the other side of the Atlantic, John R. W. Stott of All Souls and Martin Lloyd-Jones of Westminster Chapel sounded the evangelical message. The pulpit was their platform. Preaching communicated their message. Preaching is inseparable from evangelicalism.

Derek Tidball observes, "By tradition, evangelicals have exalted two means of conversion as primary: preaching and personal work."[21] Preaching the gospel, preaching the Word, are simultaneous commitments: conversion and growth in Christ. Preaching being the primary means of conversion. As Tidball notes, "Whatever other methods of communication are employed, most evangelicals would agree that, at some stage, there must be a verbal explanation of the gospel for people to respond to it."[22]

What is evangelical preaching like? What are the features of an evangelical homiletic? Returning to Frederick Buechner, we read what someone from the outside perceives of the movement. Buechner writes:

---

dots to demonstrate the unique place of preaching in the movement.

17. McDermott, ed., *The Oxford Handbook of Evangelical Theology.*

18. Stott, *Between Two Worlds*, 1.

19. Rosell, *Boston's Historic Park Street Church.* See also Rosell, *The Surprising Work of God*, 55.

20. See Stanley, *The Global Diffusion of Evangelicalism*, 112–16; Old, *The Reading and Preaching of the Scriptures in the Worship of the Christian Church*, 7:88.

21. Tidball, *Who Are the Evangelicals?*, 122.

22. Tidball, *Who Are the Evangelicals?*, 123.

Most evangelical preaching that I have heard is seamless, hard sell, and heavily exhortatory. Men in business suits get up and proclaim the faith with the dynamic persuasiveness of insurance salesmen. If there are any evangelical women preachers, I have never happened to come across them. The churches these preachers get up in are apt to be large, packed full and so brilliantly lit that you feel there is no mystery there that has not been solved, no secrets that can escape detection. Their sermons couldn't be more different from the generally low-key ones that I am used to hearing in the sparsely attended churches in New England, but they give me the same sense of being official, public, godly utterances which the preacher stands behind but as a human being somehow does not stand in. Whatever passionate and private experience their sermons may have come from originally, you are given little or no sense of what that private experience was. At their best they bring many strengths with them into the pulpit but rarely, as I listened to them anyway, their real lives.[23]

As Buechner suggests, there are stereotypes of evangelical preaching, they differ depending on one's culture, region, and background. Today, the evangelical movement is world-wide, embracing the globe.[24] Preaching is at the center for evangelicals, persuading people to salvation in Christ and moving them to maturity.

Among the contributions and characteristics of evangelical preaching are a commitment to the Bible, a commitment to the high place of preaching, and a commitment to scholarship.

A Commitment to the Bible

Evangelical emphasis on the Bible as the authoritative Word of God is at the heart of preaching.[25] "It was part of the evangelical genius," says Hutchinson and Wolffe, that with "the Bible in hand and the Holy Spirit in mind, a reflected biblical vision of the future could be worked up out of the ground almost anywhere."[26] John Stott underscores the unique place the Bible has in the ministry of preaching. He urges:

---

23. Buechner, *Telling Secrets*, 84.
24. Hutchinson and Wolffe, *A Short History of Global Evangelicalism*.
25. Waltke, "Biblical Authority."
26. Hutchinson and Wolffe, *A Short History of Evangelicalism*, 76.

Since God's final deed and Word through Jesus were intended for all people of all ages, he inevitably made provision for a reliable record of them to be written and preserved. Without this he would have defeated his own purpose. As a result, today, although nearly 2000 years separate us from that deed and Word, Jesus Christ is accessible to us. We can reach him and know him. But he is accessible only through the Bible, as the Holy Spirit brings to life his own witness to him in its pages.[27]

Stott further notes:

It is certain that we cannot handle Scripture adequately in the pulpit if our doctrine of Scripture is inadequate. Conversely, evangelical Christians, who have the highest doctrine of Scripture in the church, should be conspicuously the most conscientious preachers.[28]

David L. Larsen emphasizes, "The history of preaching bears out the acute dangers of preaching out of a text rather than preaching the text." He continues, "Respect for authorial intention may be under siege currently, but it must be seen as the hermeneutical high ground which must not be surrendered."[29] The Bible is the foundation for evangelical preaching.

A Commitment to the High Place of Preaching

Evangelical ecclesiology is a "proclamatory ecclesiology," observes Leanne Van Dyk.[30] The Word is preached in the power of the Holy Spirit and people's lives are changed in conversion and in Christian growth. In his magisterial study of preaching, Hughes Oliphant Old devoted seven volumes to the study of preaching throughout the ages, focusing on preaching as worship as well as the place and practice of preaching in the theology of worship. He traces the contours of evangelical preaching while he explores the high place of preaching in individual preachers, suggesting the important role of preaching in the evangelical movement.[31]

27. Stott, *Between Two Worlds*, 68.

28. Stott, *Between Two Worlds*, 69.

29. Larsen, *The Company of the Preachers*, 14.

30. Van Dyk, "The Church in Evangelical Theology and Practice," 137. One can see in the various histories of evangelicalism that preaching is central to the movement. See for example, Noll, *The Rise of Evangelicalism*.

31. See Old, *The Reading and Preaching of the Scriptures*, 7 vols.

There has been an emphasis on expository preaching in evangelicalism. Forebears like Birmingham's R. W. Dale, advocated for systematic expository preaching.[32] G. Campbell Morgan of Westminster Chapel, London, influenced generations by his emphasis on the weekly exposition of the Bible.[33] He was followed by Lloyd-Jones, John Stott, and William Still in Britain, and Donald Grey Barnhouse and James Montgomery Boice in the United States. The practice of expository preaching remains a feature of evangelical preachers, including Calvin Thielman, Earl Palmer, William Pope Wood, Timothy Keller, Haddon Robinson, Bryan Chapell, and Tony Evans, among others.

Preaching is central to evangelicalism, despite its critics. "Preaching has stubbornly refused to acknowledge the validity of the charges against it," states Clyde Fant.[34] Preaching is here to stay.

A Commitment to Scholarship

Evangelical authors on the topic of preaching range from the popular to the scholarly. Over the years, publishers like Baker, Zondervan, Eerdmans, InterVarsity, and Moody, in addition to Crossway, Presbyterian & Reformed, Weaver, Christian Focus, and others, have devoted significant portions of their catalogs to the publication of evangelical preaching. The books range from popular to scholarly in content.

Several significant textbooks on preaching have emerged, including Haddon Robinson's *Biblical Preaching* (1980), Bryan Chapell's *Christ-Centered Preaching: Redeeming the Expository Sermon* (1994), and John Stott's *Between Two Worlds: The Art of Preaching Today* (1982).

In addition to scholarly publications, a professional guild, the Evangelical Homiletics Society, was founded in 1997 primarily for professors in seminaries and Bible Colleges who teach preaching. The society was established

> for the exchange of ideas related to the instruction of biblical preaching. The purpose of the Society is to advance the cause of biblical preaching through the promotion of a biblical-theological approach to preaching; to increase competence for teachers of preaching; to integrate the fields of communication, biblical

---

32. Old, *The Reading and Preaching of the Scriptures*, vol. 7, 451; vol. 6, 399.

33. Stanley, *The Global Diffusion of Evangelicalism*, 12.

34. Fant, *Preaching for Today*, 9.

studies, and theology; to make scholarly contributions to the field of homiletics.[35]

The society publishes *The Journal of the Evangelical Homiletics Society*, which is peer-reviewed, featuring research articles and book reviews.

Evangelical homileticians have gained important ground over the last fifty years and continue to make strides in writing, teaching and scholarship, including the establishment of several doctoral programs (Doctor of Philosophy) in preaching and the founding of centers for preaching for preaching research.[36]

The founding of the Evangelical Homiletics Society underscores a commitment to the teaching of preaching. As part of their purpose the Evangelical Homiletics Society encourages the development of pedagogy, has devoted conferences to the task of teaching preaching, and study groups as well. Some evangelical homileticians who have backgrounds in educational theory developed the book, *Training Preachers: The Use of Educational Theory and Christian Theology in Homiletics*, arising out of a Lilly Endowment grant. The book underscores the importance of informed educational pedagogy for evangelicals who teach preaching in Bible schools, colleges and seminaries.[37]

Case Study: Text and Sermon
(Colossians 1:28–29)

Evangelicals are committed to the belief in individual conversion to faith in Christ. Once one becomes a follower of Christ, a disciple of Christ, then the process of discipleship begins. This sermon is based on the Apostle Paul's statement that the result of proclaiming, admonishing and teaching about Jesus Christ the mystery now revealed as the hope of the Gentiles is that believers—disciples—might become perfect—mature—in Christ, which Paul does with all his energy.

35. The Evangelical Homiletics Society: http://ehomiletics.com.

36. See the websites of Southern Baptist Theological Seminary, Southeastern Baptist Theological Seminary, Southwestern Baptist Theological Seminary, Gordon-Conwell Theological Seminary (in cooperation with London School of Theology), and Baylor University's George W. Truett Theological Seminary. These schools, among others, have established Doctor of Philosophy in preaching programs. The Haddon W. Robinson Center for Preaching at Gordon-Conwell Theological Seminary, the Kyle Lake Center for Effective Preaching at George W. Truett Seminary at Baylor, and the Center for Expository Preaching at Southwestern Baptist Theological Seminary are among these newly established centers.

37. Gibson, ed., *On the Teaching of Preaching*.

This sermon is based on Haddon Robinson's philosophy of a sermon having one central idea. The idea for this sermon is: Our mission is to make mature believers in Christ.

"What's Your Mission Statement?"

[The introduction raises the need that whether as a business or church or even an individual, we operate with a spoken or unspoken mission statement. The sermon is structured in inductively, working through the text as reflected in the move sections/points of the sermon, leading up to the sermon idea.]

Introduction

What do you think of mission statements? Businesses have used mission statements to bring focus to the company, to unify its workers and to produce the kind of result that they intend to produce. A restaurant mission statement says, "Good food and good service don't just happen by accident." An internet company states, "Our goal is simply the best internet experience." A website design company crows, "Our goal is to provide the best products with the greatest service possible."

But what about churches? What is their mission statement?

Eagle River Church in Alaska states, "Our goal is to be a great place for your family." Mt. Zion Church in Alabama says, "Our goal is to preach, teach and baptize all who will heed The Word." One church I served developed this mission statement: "Harmony Baptist Church exists to glorify God, by communicating Christ to each other, our neighbors and the world."

Today we want to take a look at a mission statement of the early church, a statement found in one of Paul's letters—this one to the Christians at Colossae. The text is Colossians 1:28–29. As I read the text, try to figure out what the mission statement is. Try to see what the goal of being a follower of Jesus Christ is for all time.

We Have Someone to Tell about and Something to Teach

Paul says that we tell others about Christ and that we teach them his teaching. Evangelism was to give the good news about what Jesus Christ did for humanity. The word, "proclaim" is just that—to let others know about Jesus Christ. This was done in personal conversation, in lifestyle, in out-right preaching. Only Jesus is the above all other suggested ways of salvation. We want to tell others the full story, give them the whole truth.

> [Once the first move is established, that believers have someone to tell about (Christ) and something to teach (the doctrines of the faith), which has a claim on the lives of believers, the next important commitment is that of maturity, intentional growth in Christ.]

Our Goal Is Maturity

The biblical goal of the Christian life is to be mature in Christ. Paul wanted the Colossian believers to be confident that when they stood before the Father at the end of time that they would be seen as full, complete—mature in Christ. Here's this apostle, who never laid his eyes upon the Christians in this church, concerned about their spiritual well being. He was their spiritual father through the hand of his son in the faith Epaphras, who planted the church. Paul was concerned that these men and women not simply come to believe in Jesus but to grow in him. The central message was Jesus Christ but the goal of the Christian life is maturity. The NIV translates the word here as, "perfect." What it means is "mature, complete." Men and women aren't mature unless they grow in their faith—that they don't stay as an infant but mature into a full-grown Christian. The biblical goal of the Christian life is to be mature in Christ.

> [Growth is expected in a convert to Christianity—the believer personally apprehends commitment to growth, as does the church as they disciple this young believer. This leads inductively to the central idea of the sermon.]

Our Mission Is to Make Mature Believers in Christ

This was Paul's goal, the early church's goal—and ours, too. The task of the early church wasn't simply to convert people to faith in Christ. They knew that if the church was going to grow in depth, they were to do what Jesus had told them to do—make disciples and teach them everything he had commanded them. Combined with the collective wisdom of the Bible of the time—the Old Testament—they had a curriculum to teach. Converts, yes, and disciples, yes. That is why we have a letter like this one that Paul wrote to the Colossians—he wanted them to mature in their faith. All the other letters to the churches that are part of the New Testament have the maturity of the believer in mind. When a church has mature believers then the church has leaders. The expectation was that everyone would seek to grow, to mature, to be complete in Christ. No one is off the hook.

Conclusion

What is your mission statement? Do you intentionally want to deepen, mature, grow in your faith?

This is how the church is to be built—by men and women like you who move toward maturity.

This is our mission statement: Our mission is to make mature believers in Christ.

Assessment: Strengths and Limitations in This Theological Family

To be sure, there is a range of preaching in evangelicalism. The commitments listed above highlight the best of the movement. However, contemporary evangelical preaching is often driven by personality rather than the preacher having the ballast of education and maturity in the Scriptures. To evangelicalism's embarrassment, American pragmatism has distilled preaching to what works best. In his important study of evangelicalism, David Wells lamented:

> Where, then, has the church lost its vision? We can only surmise from the data we have. Perhaps the disaffection is grounded in the virtual collapse of biblical preaching in the contemporary church that some have noted or in the perception that even where biblical preaching is done, it is not always sufficiently nourishing.[38]

Wells wrote these words over twenty years ago as he surveyed the evangelical landscape of the late twentieth century—and, sadly, they can be reaffirmed to be the case today.

In spite of the detractions found within evangelicalism—the consumeristic tendencies, the threats of theological shallowness, the pervasiveness of the cult of personality—preaching drives the movement. Evangelicalism is made up of preaching and preachers. Preaching is of great significance

---

38. Wells, *God in the Wasteland*, 196. For another aspect of this concern, see Shelley and Shelley, *The Consumer Church*, 187–98 on "Pleasing Preaching."

for evangelicalism. We can say confidently that preaching is indispensable for evangelicalism.

For Further Reading

Bebbington, D. W. *Evangelicalism in Modern Britain: A History from the 1730s to the 1890s.* London: Routledge, 1989.

Loritts, Bryan, and John Ortberg. *Insider Outsider: My Journey as a Stranger in White Evangelicalism and My Hope for Us All.* Grand Rapids: Zondervan, 2018.

Marsden, George M. *Fundamentalism and American Culture.* New ed. New York: Oxford University Press, 2006.

———. *Reforming Fundamentalism: Fuller Seminary and the New Evangelicalism.* Grand Rapids: Eerdmans, 1995.

———. *Understanding Fundamentalism and Evangelicalism.* Grand Rapids Eerdmans, 1990.

Rosell, Garth M. *A Charge to Keep: Gordon-Conwell Theological Seminary and the Renewal of Evangelicalism.* Eugene, OR: Wipf & Stock, 2020.

———— 2 ————

Preaching in the Liberal Theological Family

David M. Greenhaw

A DENOMINATIONAL LEADER SHARED the following caricature: "Evangelicals think liberals don't believe in God and liberals think evangelicals don't have a brain."[1] As he noted, this quip is not true of either but holds just enough truth to be recognized by both. The near truth that liberals don't believe in God, is understandable, but could not be further from the actual truth. In fact, liberal preaching is animated by the problem of God and is part of a theological movement that has as a central task resisting the rejection of religion.

Circumstances That Gave Rise to This Theological Family

On the eve of the nineteeth century, Fredrich Schleiermacher published *On Religion: Addresses in Response to Its Cultured Critics.*[2] It attempted to redeem an essential element of religion for those whose adoption of the current rationalism led them to leave religion behind.[3] He urged his

---

1. Richard Land, Southern Baptist leader, responding to a question about obstacles to common cause between evangelicals and liberals. Evangelicals and U.S. Foreign Policy Symposium: Evangelicals and the Middle East: Session III Friday, November 30, 2007, at the Council on Foreign Relations.

2. Schleiermacher, *On Religion.*

3. By rationalism, I refer to a general confidence (born of the seventeenth- through nineteenth-century philosophical movements) in the power of knowledge—both of general principles and of inductive or empirical knowledge—to describe and explain

readers to look again, before they threw out religion, lest they miss out on its true value. Less than forty years after Schleiermacher addressed his audience in Germany, Ralph Waldo Emerson spoke to the graduating class at Harvard Divinity School. He said:

> I once heard a preacher who sorely tempted me to say I would go to church no more . . . He had not one word intimating that he had laughed or wept, was married or in love, had been commended, or cheated, or chagrined. If he had ever lived and acted, we were none the wiser for it. The capital secret of his profession, namely, to convert life into truth, he had not learned. Not one fact in all his experience, had he yet imported into his doctrine.[4]

Schleiermacher and Emerson, pioneers of liberal theology, both responded to prevalent intellectual reasons to reject religion. On the one hand, there was the rise of rationalism, science, evolution, and historical biblical criticism. These modern ways of interpreting the world and texts challenged traditional ways of knowing and the authority of inherited religion. How could one retain a Christian faith when an ancient worldview upon which it was constituted crumbles? On the other hand, there was the woodenness and increasing irrelevancy of arcane orthodoxy, doctrines of a church that failed to come face-to-face with the experiences of modern people.

Liberal theology drinks deeply of these reasons to reject religion. But it refuses to do so. Its theological construals, in one way or another, are efforts to redeem religion from modern reasons to reject it. Of course, an alternative is to reject evolution, science and historical criticism or to ignore a persistent call for relevance. This, however, is not an option for liberal theology. It both refuses to reject religion *and* refuses to reject the modern challenges to religion; instead, it seeks a "third way."

A Third Way

Gary Dorrien describes the agenda of liberal theology in this way: "to create a modern Christian third way between a regnant orthodoxy and an ascending 'infidelism.'"[5] There are many liberal theologies, but they have

---

the world.

4. Emerson, "Divinity School Address," 1–12. Emerson describes the scene with characteristic reference to nature: "A snowstorm was falling around us. The snowstorm was real; the preacher merely spectral; and the eye felt the sad contrast in looking at him, and then out of the window behind him, into the beautiful meteor of the snow."

5. Dorrien, *The Making of American Liberal Theology*, 1:xiv.

in common a commitment to traverse between these two poles: a regnant orthodoxy and infidelism. Understanding these two poles is key to understanding liberal theology.

Regnant orthodoxies are not necessarily doctrines of the church; they could be any theological formulation that captures the imagination of a culture and people. No doubt a reigning orthodoxy may hold sway because it effectively speaks to the circumstances and needs of its adherents. However, a reigning theology at some point can move from capturing the imagination of a people to holding it captive. For instance, verbal plenary inspiration, a view that every element of the Bible was divinely written, serves interests of its adherents, but strains in the face of the cacophonous and conflicting voices of biblical texts.[6] While it might be a way to find unity and inspiration in the Bible, it does so at the cost of intellectual credibility. Liberal theologians have tried to adhere to the principle that they can accept the best explanation, not the one they wanted.[7]

"Infidelism" is an antiquated term. A version of the word "infidel," it literally means without faith. While there are many people who do not have faith, liberal theology rejects the idea that it lacks faith. The term "infidel" has a negative connotation because it has been used as a condemning label for religious others, those who believe differently. Liberal theology rejects the notion that believing differently means not believing. For more than two centuries it has held that it could still believe, even if it rejected an orthodoxy that failed to adequately address the current context. A choice between believe "my way" or you don't believe, is a false choice.

In a variety of contexts and over an extended period of time, liberal theology has tried to find ways to connect theology to concrete experience, either that of the individual or the society. They have sought ways to incorporate intellectual trends into theology without loss of authentic piety.

Responding to the Current Context

What constitutes the current context changes over time. New contexts bring new challenges. What worked in one time, runs aground in a new context.

---

6. Dorrien poses the following questions: "Is it possible to be a faithful Christian without believing that God willed the annihilation of nearly the entire human race in a great flood, or that God commanded the genocidal extermination of the ancient enemies of Israel, or that God demanded the literal sacrifice of his Son as a substitutionary legal payment for sin? It is a good or true form of Christianity that teaches the doctrines of double predestination and biblical inerrancy?" Dorrien, *The Making of American Liberal Theology*, 1:xiii.

7. Clayton, *God and Contemporary Science*, 247.

For instance, the increasing acceptance of Darwin and evolutionary theory created a crisis for the forms of biblical interpretation of the reigning orthodoxies called for a response that helped form historical criticism. The problem of biblical interpretation occupied the attention of liberal theologians for a significant portion of the last two centuries, including such challenges as the fundamentalist controversies of the 1920s[8] and the inclusive language controversies of the 1980s.[9] Non-literal interpretation of the Bible remains a dominant characteristic of liberal theology and preaching.

As significant as interpretation of the Bible has been concern over theological orthodoxy's failure to address pressing social problems. In the late nineteenth and early twentieth century, the failure of theological orthodoxy to address the economic and personal costs of industrialization led Walter Rauschenbusch and others to assert a social gospel that was "effective" not just in saving individual souls, but in transforming the societies and institutions in which they lived.[10] By the mid-twentieth century, liberal theology began a project that responded to racism, sexism and homophobia in succession.[11] Martin Luther King Jr. raised a prophetic Christian voice calling out the injustice of racism and the complicity of religious leaders in perpetuating a horrific legacy.[12] Rosemary Ruether and others pointed to the social sin of sexism and looked for faith resources to transform the social order.[13] Awareness of complicity in the human oppressions[14] of racism and sexism soon gave rise to the challenge to heterosexism in church and society.[15]

By century end, the 'isms' of human and environmental oppression gave rise to concern with diversity. If an earlier era of liberal theology responded to the challenge of modernity, current liberalism is challenged by awareness of diverse experiences, cultures and perspectives long ignored or undervalued. Of course, such diversity was not in itself new, it had long been present; what was new was the acknowledgement and valuing of diversity. For liberal theology in the early decades of the twenty-first

8. Fosdick, "Shall the Fundamentalists Win?"

9. Throckmorton, "Why the Inclusive Language Lectionary?," 742.

10. Rauschenbusch, *A Theology for the Social Gospel*, 134–37.

11. Dean, "Can Liberal Theology Recover?," 25–32. Dean argues that each of these "isms" unfolded in succession and formed the backdrop for liberal theology in the last half of the twentieth century.

12. King, "Letter from the Birmingham Jail."

13. Reuther, *Sexism and God Talk*.

14. The question of theological orthodoxy's complicity in social ills became especially acute after the devastation of the Holocaust. See, Moltmann, *The Crucified God*.

15. Cheng, *Rainbow Theology*.

century, attending to the many voices long silenced or ignored is a central challenge, or as Dorrien names it: "appropriating multiple perspectives became the new *sine qua non*."[16]

Not Giving Up on God

Liberal theology has fought against theologies of oppression and sought more liberative modes of understanding God. And as it has done so, it has become aware that the very idea of God and theological discourse itself has been tainted by its complicity in restraining human freedom and fulfilling the demands of social justice. Nevertheless, as aware as liberal theology is of the problem of God, it has consistently remained a theology, that is, a discourse about God. It is as if liberal theology is "God-haunted."[17] Troubled by God, liberal theology nonetheless has tried to remain faithful to God.

Liberal theology's means of remaining faithful to God, of not giving up on God, cannot be exhaustively categorized, but fall into three main types. The first, dating from as early as Schleiermacher and continuing to more recent versions of mysticism, can be called a turn to subjectivism. Despite rational description or empirical evidence to the contrary, the reality of God is still 'known' in human subjective experience. For Schleiermacher, this was the "sense and taste of the infinite and divine," still able to be experienced immediately. A second type, found in the process theologies of followers of Alfred North Whitehead, might be called relationalism. In this approach, the radical relationality of the world is apprehended in the ultimate relationality of God. God is related to all of creation, and all of creation is related to each other and to God. Such relationality is evidenced in the insights of modern physics and the intricate ecologies of the natural order. A third type could be called pragmatic partnership. God is the guarantor of a just world that continually eludes the present but holds sway in a future yet to be made manifest. Thus, the phrase concerning "the arc of the moral universe bending toward justice," suggests God as ultimately concerned with this arc and as partner along the way.[18]

16. Dorrien, *Crisis, Irony & Postmodernity*, 529.

17. On reflecting on the character of religion in the South, she says, "I think it is safe to say that while the South is hardly Christ-centered, it is most certainly Christ-haunted" (O'Connor, "The Catholic Novelist," 861). In just this way, liberal theology is diverse in its renderings of God, but it is never able to escape God. It is "God-haunted."

18. This quote is often attributed to Martin Luther King Jr. While he made it popularly available, he was quoting a sermon from the nineteenth-century liberal preacher Theodore Parker. "Look at the facts of the world. You see a continual and progressive triumph of the right. I do not pretend to understand the moral universe, the arc a long

No Definitive Third Way

What constitutes liberal theology is not a singular and definitive way to fully embrace the scientific and rational approach to truth and hold fast to some notion of God, but rather a commitment to find this so-called "third way." Liberal theology believes that it is brave enough to pursue its inquiries as far as possible, even if it does not like the place it lands. It holds this courage, because at its base, liberal theology, like the liberal project itself, believes that when set free from the constraints of external authority, truth can be glimpsed, perhaps even finally found. Resolution of the tension between faith in God and pursuing truth no matter where it leads is not to be found in resolving the tension, but in continually maintaining and renewing it.

Purposes and Characteristics of Preaching in This Theological Family

Liberal preaching exemplifies the values and commitments of liberalism and especially the values of liberal theology. It is an important and distinctive preaching perspective that while changing over time, is still prevalent in many American pulpits. Like liberal theology, liberal preaching has as a central task resistance to the rejection of religion because of the challenges of modernity and the irrelevance of inherited orthodoxy.[19]

Rejecting religion is not something the liberal preacher brings to the congregation; it is something already there. In part, the task of liberal preaching is persuading the people of a congregation steeped in the secularism of the age that there is still reason to believe. Said another way, liberal preaching affirms the reality of God *and* seeks to make doctrines responsive to current contexts and circumstances.

It would seem obvious that affirming God is a purpose of all preaching, not just liberal preaching. While this is true, for liberal preaching the capacity to affirm faith in God is set in the context of the science that can as readily explain the warm spiritual feeling one has while looking at a sunset as a biochemical process within the brain and traceable on an MRI; or it can date the earth's origin in the millions of years and not the few thousand

---

one, my eye reaches just a little ways. I cannot calculate the curve and complete the figure by the experience of sight; I can divine it by conscience. But from what I see I am sure it bends towards justice" (Parker, "Of Justice and the Conscience," 84–85).

19. In the current climate of church decline, it is too easy a thing to see liberal preaching as resistance to the death of the church. While resisting church decline may be among the motivations for preaching, this is not what is meant here by resisting the rejection of religion.

accounted for in the Genesis narrative. In a similar fashion, the context of liberal preaching includes the challenges of psychological peril and social injustice. A credible faith in God cannot ignore the problems of the world and if possible, should open a path forward.

Building a Credibility Bridge

Liberal preaching aims to bear a responsibility to build a credibility bridge between faith in God and those the sermon addresses. This is especially true when it comes to interpreting the sayings and stories of the Bible. Many a liberal congregation brings a skepticism to the time of preaching. Stories of miraculous healings, pregnant octogenarians or wooden vessels large enough to repopulate the animals of the world, are rejected on their face. If these texts are to receive a contemporary hearing, the liberal preacher somehow will need to make them credible.

Liberal preaching, like liberal theology, has attempted to make credible what is not credible on its face through the tools of historical criticism of the Bible. Historical criticism's claim that the texts of the Bible have arisen from human communities responding to issues and challenges of their own context means that they may not be immediately transferable to the present context of the preacher and her community. The biblical text is alien, not addressing this time, without first being read in its own time. Questions of the authorship of texts, their intended audiences and historical referents place a burden on the liberal preacher to find ways to 'preach the Bible' with n authenticity that a liberal congregation finds credible.

The liberal preacher is embedded in a social context. By and large, liberal preaching, at least in the United States, involves a sermon or other speech delivered to an assembled Christian congregation during their weekly worship service. Usually the liberal preacher is theologically educated and has some form of ecclesial authorization. Like all preaching, liberal preaching has political implications, but it would be a mistake to affiliate it with the partisan binary of Democrat or Republican political parties in the United States. Research by Robert Putnam and David Campbell indicates a majority of religious people in the United States are aligned with the Republican Party,[20] but liberal preaching falls freely, or should one say "liberally," on the ears of Republicans and Democrats alike.

---

20. Putnam et al., *American Grace*, 369–442.

Changing the World

A foundational conviction of liberal preaching, and one shared by liberalism generally, is the power of freedom from external authority. The underlying conviction is that if one can be freed from the prejudices and constraints on knowledge common to oppressive regimes, it is possible to harness the power to change one's circumstances and the world. It is not an accident that higher education is called liberal education—by study one can gain the wisdom to contextualize oppressive powers and remove their totalitarian claims. Marry this general liberal perspective to a theology, and one has a formula for fomenting change.

Liberal preaching intends to energize the gathered community for changing the world. The ravages of poverty, racial or sexual oppression, the degradation of the environment, are among the many foci for application of the preached word. Not only will the hearer of the word be aware of oppressive forces, but they will also be enlisted to resist and to overthrow such regimes.

There are many forms and modes of liberal preaching. The vast majority is "from" the Bible.[21] Usually liberal preaching from the Bible involves an exegetical process informed by historical criticism.[22] A biblical text, from a verse or two in length to much longer, forms the basis of the sermon topic. The topic is informed by the *pericope* and in some fashion connects it to contemporary experience or contexts. Nearly always there is some call to action, either implicit or explicit. Nearly all liberal sermons share the same two purposes: affirming an experience of God and making some change in the world.

When Emerson challenged the preachers of his day to more honestly connect to the congregation, he believed there was a liveliness possible in liberal preaching, a possibility that it would be thoughtful and engaging. He complained that preaching had become dull and disconnected from things that really mattered to people. He observed: "It seemed strange that the people should come to church. It seemed as if their houses were very unentertaining, that they should prefer this thoughtless clamor."[23] Liberal

---

21. See especially the criticism of "preaching" on the Bible by Edward Farley: Farley, *Practicing Gospel,* 71–82.

22. "Historical criticism" is used here in the most general way. It assumes that other forms of biblical textual criticism are related to or derivative from historical criticism as such. Included would be critical reading of texts such as form criticism, literary criticism, rhetorical criticism, reader-response, etc.

23. Emerson, "Divinity School Address," 11–12.

preaching at its best is engaging—deeply thoughtful, "God haunted" and dedicated to the proposition that the world can be better.

Case Study: Text and Sermon
(Matthew 9:35—10:14)

The following sermon was preached in the 1990s to a United Church of Christ congregation in the United States, a denomination on the liberal end of American religion. The congregation, a middle-class, predominantly White suburban community, was disproportionally made up of college-educated professionals.

The text is Matthew 9:35—10:14. It narrates the calling of the twelve disciples, and begins with Jesus itinerating through cities and villages, "teaching in their synagogues, and proclaiming the good news of the kingdom, and curing every disease and every sickness." It describes Jesus seeing the crowds and having compassion (*esplanchnisthē)* for them, "because they were harassed and helpless, like sheep without a shepherd."

The disciples are called and given authority (*exousia*), or the power to act, over unclean spirits "and to cure every disease and every sickness." Tied to their calling in the generic sense the next three verses identify the disciples by name and often by affiliation. These are not just an anonymous group: they are James—you know, James who is the son of Zebedee; or Andrew—remember, he who is the brother of Simon, also known as Peter. This specificity contrasts with the nameless ones in the crowd. The disciples are given explicit direction on what they are to do and how they are to do it. They are warned that they will find some places where they are welcomed and places where they "will not welcome you or listen to your words."

Although they are given power to transform human life, it is not limitless power—it will not overcome all opposition, but it will work as the 'kingdom of heaven comes near.'

The transition from the unnamed crowd to the named disciples is the pivot point in the text for this sermon. The authority given the disciples by Jesus is an empowerment to transform human lives.

"Crowds into Communities"

[The opening of the sermon focuses on an encounter with bureaucracy common to many and the sense of futility experienced.]

I have a problem with automobile license plates. I have lived in several different states and in every state, I have had difficulty getting license plates.

The problem is, whatever I take with me to the Department of Motor Vehicles, I never have everything in order. If I bring the title, they want the registration. If I take the registration and the title, they want the emission control certificate, as well. Whatever I bring, I never have everything in order. I always have to make a couple of trips. It has gotten to the point that I set aside one whole day, declare it a waste, and dedicate it to getting my license plates. I set my alarm for early in the morning, get up, get dressed, grab the file called, "Car Stuff," and head out for a day of frustration.

The problem I have with license plates is that I am treated as just one in a crowd; I am a number and not a person. I am an 815 82 6841, a 4808, a 331 8618, or a 37211. The bureaucracy of Motor Vehicle Departments has the capacity to overwhelm me, to reduce me to just one in a crowd.

It seems that there are more and more crowds. One can hardly go to the grocery store without having to wait in a long line. Once peaceful country roads are becoming overcrowded highways. Everywhere you go there are crowds. Crowds, although filled with people, are amazingly lonely. To be just one in a crowd is to encounter a kind of helplessness and loneliness. You have an important story to tell; you are somebody—but when you are in a crowd, who you are gets buried, wiped out by the crowd.

[To this point, the sermon has tried to set up a connecting link between the contemporary experience of being "in a crowd" to the biblical text of Jesus encountering a crowd.]

In this Scripture reading from the Gospel of Matthew, it says Jesus "saw the crowds and he had compassion for them because they were harassed and helpless." Jesus saw the crowds and he knew what was going on with them. He knew that they were helpless and harassed, and he had compassion for them.

In what way were the crowds that Jesus saw harassed and helpless? To tell the truth, I don't know. The Bible doesn't say. It merely says that they were harassed and helpless. There were surely differences between today and back then, and being in a crowd could be very different, but I can't help but think that some things haven't changed that much. To be in a crowd is to be surrounded by people and still be alone. It is to be in relationships where you meet each other's expectations, but you never really meet. Crowds then and now have a certain momentum to them; to be in a crowd is to be carried along with the momentum with no way out.

There are surely differences between the crowds of then and now. But in our time at least, being in a crowd can feel helpless. Caught in the momentum, caught on the turning wheel, you do what everybody does. You punch the clock, or go to the office day after day after day, or drop the kids off here, pick up the cleaning there, stop at the market, pick the kids back up and get dinner ready by 6:30. Day after day after day after day, doing what everybody else is doing. But going nowhere, and through it all with that horrible feeling that all these things must be done, but may not matter or make any difference.

> *[The cultural distance between the time of Jesus and the current moment is acknowledged, while a common sense of being isolated and unimportant is presented as a credible connection between then and now.]*

We live in a world ruled by a crowd mentality. So much of life is the proverbial rat race. And you know what they say about the rat-race: You may win the race, but you are still a rat.

Jesus saw the crowds; he knew they were harassed and helpless, and he had compassion for them. Jesus had compassion.

It's a funny word, compassion. In the Greek New Testament, the word literally means to have one's bowels turned. It means to be so affected by the life of another that it wrenches your insides. Jesus sees the crowds; he sees their helplessness, their harassment and it tears him up inside. Today's Gospel reading says that Jesus went about all the cities and villages, teaching and preaching and healing because he had seen the pain and the emptiness of the people and it tore him up inside. He had compassion.

The problem with crowds is that there is so little compassion. All those people, but no one really makes a difference. But when there is compassion, when it is possible to have an impact on someone, when your life really matters to another, then you are no longer just a part of a crowd.

When there is compassion, crowds turn into communities. With compassion, nameless faces become real people with names and stories and feelings. Jesus has compassion, and the crowds that gather around him are no longer nameless faces, but people who make a difference, whose lives matter. The crowds who gather around Jesus become a community, the community we call the church.

> *[The key phrase, "turning crowds into communities," sets the stage of changing the world. The power is compassion.]*

In Matthew's Gospel, when Jesus calls the disciples, did you notice that he calls them all by name? They are not nameless faces; they have names, they are real people—they matter. When Jesus calls them together, he tells them that "the harvest is plentiful, but the laborers are few." We live in a world that is filled with crowds, but there are very few who have enough compassion to change crowds into communities.

And then Jesus gives them authority: he gives them the power to make a difference in the lives of others! He gives them authority to heal, to cleanse, to break the demonic forces, to bring life where there is death.

Those of us gathered here today, we are called by Jesus to be part of the community that is the church of Jesus Christ. We have received compassion. We have been able to make a difference, to be somebody, to not be bound to the endless return of the same. And because we have, we are in turn able to be compassionate toward others. And there is a huge need for compassion. Our is a world where the harvest is plentiful but the laborers few. There are many who are nameless faces, just part of a crowd.

> [The echo of the phrase "the harvest is plentiful but the laborers few" is interpreted here as the problem of crowds needing to be converted into communities through compassion.]

The call to be compassionate to others is not easy. Because when you have compassion, you see the pain and emptiness of others and it can tear you up inside. To have compassion is gut-wrenching. But there is no other way, there is no route from the emptiness of a crowd to the fullness of a community apart from compassion. It involves coming to know the ways in which your neighbor hurts, is harassed and helpless. It involves be so moved by the neighbor's pain that they quit being just a number, but a real human being worthy of love.

And although this is not easy, it is the way from crowds to communities. And it is a healing and powerful way. You do not go alone; like the disciples of old, you go as part of a called, empowered community.

Go in the name of the compassionate God, whose compassion changes crowds into communities and transforms the world. Amen.

Assessment: Strengths and Limitations
in This Theological Family

There are two prominent criticisms of liberal preaching. The first comes from the neo-orthodox movement in Protestant Christianity. Because liberalism attempts to resist the rejection of religion, it engages in what is called an apologetic task. That is, it seeks to make theology relevant in the terms of contemporary culture. Neo-orthodoxy criticizes such an attempt in a manner articulated well by Karl Barth. He says saying the "same thing in *other words*" is not the same as saying "*the same thing* in other words"[24] By this Barth suggests that the Christian gospel says something unique and on its own terms; efforts to translate it into terms other than the terms of the gospel misses the point. It is not just that there is something lost in translation, it is that the ability to interpret the meaning of the gospel requires entering the hermeneutical circle of the gospel. While it be might correct that orthodoxy is not relevant and out of touch with contemporary culture and experience, this criticism maintains that the correction is not to make the gospel speak in a contemporary idiom, but for the contemporary culture to accommodate the gospel.

The second prominent criticism of liberal theology and preaching comes from the postmodern movement. Here the problem is that liberalism is thoroughly shaped by the terms of modernity. Liberalism is so embedded in its culture that it fails to see it is in a culture. Its attempt to make a credible bridge assumes a set of universal meanings that are able to form the foundation for shared understanding. Justice, for instance, is taken to have a universal meaning that can be shared. Postmodernism can concede that there is something called justice, but it is completely conditioned by the particularity of the culture in which it is embedded. The liberal assertion of universal meaning is little more than the privileging of one culture over any other.

Both criticisms point to a danger in for liberal preaching—its driving desire to resist the rejection of religion can result in preservation of a religion that flattens genuine difference and reproduces itself. Or in the words of liberalism's neo-orthodox critics, the voice of God it hears is its own voice, raised aloud.

These criticisms have merit. They point to fundamental limits of liberalism. Despite these criticisms, liberal preaching continues to hold promise nonetheless. Its promise is in the two things that distinguish it. First, criticism is what has given birth to liberalism, and therefore attending to neo-orthodox or postmodernist criticism should not cause it to wither, but to respond and persist. Second, because liberal preaching is God-haunted, that is, because it not only attends to criticism but also refuses to give up on God, it can remain a theological enterprise fitting for the church and not devolve simply into an intellectual exercise.

---

24. Barth, *Church Dogmatics,* 1/1. 345.

For Further Reading

Campbell, Charles L. *Preaching Jesus: Hans Frei's Theology and the Contours of a Postliberal Homiletic.* 1997. Reprint, Eugene, OR: Wipf & Stock, 2005.

Dorrien, Gary J. *The Making of American Liberal Theology.* Vol. 3, *Crisis, Irony, and Postmodernity, 1950–2005.* Louisville: Westminster John Knox. 2006.

———. *The Making of American Liberal Theology.* Vol. 2, *Idealism, Realism, and Modernity 1900–1950.* Louisville: Westminster John Knox, 2003.

———. *The Making of American Liberal Theology.* Vol. 1, *Imagining Progressive Religion, 1805–1900.* Louisville: Westminster John Knox, 2003.

Farley, Edward. *Practicing Gospel: Unconventional Thoughts on the Church's Ministry.* Louisville: Westminster John Knox, 2003.

Meyers, Robin R. *Saving God from Religion: A Minister's Search for Faith in a Skeptical Age.* New York: Crown, 2020.

Mitchell, Ella Pearson, and Valerie Bridgeman Davis. *Those Preaching Women: A Multicultural Collection.* Valley Forge, PA: Judson, 2008.

Putnam, Robert D., et al. *American Grace: How Religion Divides and Unites Us.* New York: Simon & Schuster, 2012.

Preaching in the Neo-Orthodox
Theological Family

RONALD J. ALLEN[1]

NEO-ORTHODOXY BEGAN TO COME to expression shortly after World War 1 and was a dominant theological force in North America and Europe through the 1960s. While neo-orthodoxy has declined in the United States, it still has adherents, and many European theologians still follow its emphases, especially those associated with Karl Barth. Like most theological movements, neo-orthodoxy is not a singular pattern of thinking but contains voices that share certain perspectives while differing on others. Indeed, the theologians grouped in the neo-orthodox family could be quite contentious with one another.

This movement is also known as "dialectical theology," "Word of God theology," "crisis theology," and "Christian realism."[2] As the term

---

1. A note from the author: Most of the other chapters in this volume were written by authors who subscribe to the theological family about which they write. Because of a difficult situation, the author working on this chapter was not able to complete it. When I was unable to find a neo-orthodox theologian to write the chapter at the last minute, I did so. However, I am a process theologian. I attempt to write in a descriptive way, recognizing that I do not have the same "feel" for neo-orthodoxy as a member of that family. I have great respect the neo-orthodox movement.

2. While "neo-orthodoxy" is the most familiar designation for this movement, some of its proponents did not embrace that term. The expression "dialectical theology" calls attention to the "infinite qualitative distinction" between God and humankind, and to the notion of interchange taking place between two parties using logical methods of communication and argument. The expression "Word of God theology " calls attention to God revealing the divine Word to the human community. Human beings cannot discern this word on their own. The expression "crisis theology" refers to the facts that the theological movement birthed during crisis moments, and also to

"neo-orthodox" implies, this movement emphasizes aspects of traditional Christian doctrine in ways related to the new cultural situations in which the neo-orthodox theologians lived. Neo-orthodox theologians derived much their approach and language from Reformed and Lutheran Reformation perspectives, but preachers across a range of denominations embraced a dialectical approach. After neo-orthodoxy waned, many preachers and theologians with neo-orthodox roots—especially roots in Barth—made their way into postliberal theology, a movement that took root in the late twentieth century.[3]

Circumstances That Gave Rise to This Theological Family

The Enlightenment (1715–1789) discovery of science and reason as ways to improve life joined hands with the industrial revolution to create a widespread sense of optimism about the future.[4] The growth of factories making goods available, railroad travel, education becoming more available, the rise of medicine—such things gave rise to an optimistic spirit at the beginning of the twentieth century to those who benefitted from them. The world seemed to be getting better and better.

Prior to the Enlightenment, the church largely assumed that the Bible recounted factual events from the past. The church regarded doctrine as reliable. In response to the Enlightenment, many Christians sought to adapt their understandings of the Bible and theology to Modernity. Accepting as truth only that which is verifiable from a scientific point of view, Enlightenment thinkers came to regard history in the same way: people could regard stories and ideas from the past reliable only if they conformed to empirical verification. This perspective called into question the veracity of many things in the Bible and Christian doctrine. Biblical scholars noted the cultural conditioning of the Bible and Christian doctrine, including the presence of mythological elements. Biblical scholarship tended to explain biblical material in terms

---

the contention that the Word of God creates a crisis of judgement and decision when it speaks to the human community. The expression "Christian realism" is associated with Reinhold Niebuhr. Since only God can bring the world to its complete fulfillment, the church and world must operate "realistically," using power towards as many of God's purposes of love and justice as can be achieved at a given time. Inevitably, such actions lead to compromise.

3. On postliberal theology, see the excellent discussion by Lance Pape in Chapter 5 of this book.

4. David Greenhaw lucidly discusses the liberal movement in Chapter 2 of this book.

of historical development without discussing how biblical texts might be theologically significant for later generations. Many neo-orthodox thinkers described this approach as theologically sterile.

Since many Christians could no longer simply turn to the Bible and Christian tradition for authority, some theologians influenced by Enlightenment perspectives sought to find the authority for Christian faith in human experience in an ingrained sense of morality and feeling. Friedrich Schleiermacher (1768–1834) moved in this direction by claiming that the source for religion is "the feeling of absolute dependence." "Feeling" here refers to more than emotion. "The feeling of absolute dependence . . . is not to be explained as an awareness of the world's existence, but as an awareness of the existence of God, as the absolute undivided unity."[5] Authority was not "outside the self" in the Bible or doctrine but was "inside the self," that is, in intuitive levels of awareness. Moreover, many theologians influenced by the Enlightenment came to interpret Christian faith as an expression of universal religious truths and moral values.

This movement is often called "liberalism" or "Modernity." Many leaders in the Social Gospel assumed liberal tenents. Christians who adhered to this viewpoint anticipated progressive evolution in technology and spirituality until the realm [kingdom] of God would arrive.[6]

Neo-orthodoxy arose in response to these cultural and theological dynamics and is associated with theologians such as Karl Barth (1886–1968), Eduard Thurneysen (1888–1974), Emil Brunner (1899–1966), and Reinhold Niebuhr (1892–1971). Others of the same period, for example Rudolph Bultmann (1884–1976) and Paul Tillich (1886–1965), shared some neo-orthodox emphases while going in other directions.[7] While neo-orthodoxy was diverse in some theological respects, its thinkers shared several key perspectives.

5 Schleiermacher, *The Christian Faith*, 132.

6. Some groups today speak so dismissively about "liberalism" that it is important to remember that the word "liberal" was intended to invoke the notion of being liberated from superstition and falsehood. Furthermore, in theological discussion, the word "modern" often calls to mind not just "contemporary" but the worldview that grew out of the Enlightenment. Consequently, the expression "Modern theology" refers to theology that operates under the influence of the modern worldview.

7. Among others associated with this movement are Gustaf Aulén, Donald Baillie, John Baillie, Friedrich Gogarten, H. Richard Niebuhr, Anders Nygren, James D. Smart, and Thomas F. Torrance. Brevard Childs stresses the diversity among neo-orthodox theologians, concluding, "As we look back, it is difficult to imagine much theological consistency in either method or content, within a group that included Barth, Brunner, the Niebuhrs, and Tillich. The main element of commonality lay in their criticism of the extreme forms of Liberalism" (Childs, *Biblical Theology in Crisis*, 78).

Developments in the early twentieth century created a crisis for some liberal theologians: the carnage of World War 1, social chaos, the ruthless exploitation of labor, and the great depression. Later developments compounded their dismay, especially the rise of Naziism and World War 2. This suffering caused several theologians to lose confidence in the optimism of liberalism. The dream of progressive evolution was shattered. The technology that promised to benefit so many could be used for such destruction. Religious feeling and ingrained morality did not offer a satisfactory theological interpretation for such savagery. Modern religion did not offer a God who could prevent things. From the early neo-orthodox point of view, modern religion created a God who was little more than the image of the highest cultural values of the people who created that divinity. To the neo-orthodox, liberal Christianity was anthropocentric.

Karl Barth initially articulated what would become the neo-orthodox point of view. Disillusioned when many of his teachers—leading liberal theologians—endorsed the Kaiser taking Germany into World War 1, and traumatized by the war itself, Barth began to read the Bible in search of a more adequate theological interpretation. He found a "strange new world within the Bible,"[8] which reverses the flow of modern theology: instead of the human community trying to find a God acceptable to its world view, Barth's reading of Romans found a God who told the community what God makes possible through Jesus Christ.[9] Christianity is not about the human search for God but, about God's search for humankind.[10]

The neo-orthodox theologians did not completely abandon liberalism. They respected the scientific method and the historical-critical approach to the Bible, but they put those things under new theological management. These phenomena were useful to the neo-orthodox thinkers in so far they could help the church recognize the Word of God and respond to it appropriately. Nevertheless, several key perspectives emerged among neo-orthodox thinkers, though the different thinkers sometimes expressed such things in different degrees.

---

8. Barth, "The Strange New World within the Bible."

9. Barth, *The Epistle to the Romans*. In this commentary, Barth makes little use of critical biblical scholarship but, instead, reads Romans through the lens of his developing theological perspective. In the view of many biblical scholars today, *Romans* is not a reliable exegetical guide to Paul's thought, but Barth's *Romans* is a useful entry into Barth's world of thought. A more systematic overview of Barth's major ideas can be found in his *Dogmatics in Outline*. Barth's fully developed views are articulated in his thirteen-volume *Church Dogmatics*.

10. For a collection of sermons on this subject, see Barth and Thurneysen, *God's Search for Man*.

Neo-orthodox theology emphasizes *the otherness of God*, sometimes speaking of God as "wholly other" taking up Kierkegaard's notion of the "infinite qualitative distinction" between God and the created world.[11] To emphasize the differences between God and humankind, Barth spoke of the "Godness of God." The distance between God and humankind is so great that only God can overcome it. God is much more than a human being "writ large."[12] God is God.

For this theological family, the heart of *sin* is rebellion against God. Neo-orthodox theologians agree with historical criticism that Genesis 3:9–14 is not a literal story but does point to the human tendency to misuse the freedoms that God gave humankind in ways that are self-serving. Sin can take many forms, among the most damaging being idolatry, pride, greed, and sloth. Human beings hijack God's intentions and turn them to selfish ends.

Human beings can know God's nature and purposes as *God reveals them*.[13] The church cannot rely on human experience to point to God because human beings inevitably create idols, making god in our own image to serve our own limited aims. The Bible plays an important role in revelation but is not itself the revelation. The Bible is not itself the word; rather it witnesses to the word. God makes the word come alive when the community gathers around the Bible. Because God's word comes only from God, neither the church nor any other part of the human community can control that word. The word comes only from God.

In the neo-orthodox theological world. *Jesus Christ is the final authority*. Jesus is the Word of God. When the Bible points to the Word, it points to Jesus. For the neo-orthodox, Jesus Christ is not simply the Jesus of history but is the event in which God chooses to be God for the world and through whom God judges and saves. Through the word God speaks in two primary ways. First, God speaks a great No: God pronounces judgment on sin in all its forms including idolatry, pride, greed, sloth and the cultural captivity of the church. Second, God speaks a greater Yes: God reconciles the world to Godself and gives the world the opportunity to live towards God's covenantal

---

11. Kierkegaard, *Training in Christianity*, 13. For Barth on "Wholly Other," see his "Biblical Insights, Questions, and Vistas," 74. For Barth on the "Godness of God" see *Church Dogmatics* 1/1, 172.

12. Barth later softened this distinction in "The Humanity of God."

13. Neo-orthodox interpreters divided over the issue of how we receive knowledge about God. Barth holds that human beings gain knowledge of God only when God directly reveals it. Brunner holds that human beings can gain some knowledge of God through natural theology; that is, things that can be known about God through the ways in which God structured the world. Both Brunner's approach and Barth's inflamed response, titled "No!," can be found in Brunner and Barth, *Natural Theology*.

purposes. Barth famously envisions a threefold form of word of God: the revealed word, the written word, and the proclaimed word.

Whereas liberals believed people can work together in progressive actions to bring about the realm of God on earth, the neo-orthodox believe that the fulfillment of God's aims in history will come about only through God's eschatological action. Through the Word, God calls human beings (especially the church) to point to God and to urge the human community to repent.[14]

Reinhold Niebuhr, perhaps the most influential exponent of neo-orthodoxy in the United States, presumed many of these themes. On the one hand, Niebuhr considers liberal views of human nature and social progress to be naïve. On the other hand, he also considers conservative views of the Bible as simple record of fact to be naïve.[15]

Niebuhr, however, focuses less on matters related to the knowledge of God and turns more to sin and grace with an eye towards public life. Niebuhr calls attention to the social dimensions of sin.[16] Self-love, often manifest through pride, leads human beings to try to control their own lives at the expense of others. Sin is especially dangerous when people think they are exercising power for good when they are actually reinforcing their own interests. Self-love is the root of injustice. Sin is so intense that it can be

14. The neo-orthodox ethos helped launch the Biblical Theology Movement, which thrived from the 1940s through the 1960s. As noted above, critical biblical scholarship in the late nineteenth and early twentieth centuries tended to be descriptive: under the influence of the modern view of history as reporting on the facts that actually happened, biblical interpreters focused mainly on explaining the meaning of biblical texts in their historical and literary contexts, without giving theological attention to how the biblical material might inform the contemporary church. The rebirth of theological significance by neo-orthodox thinkers fostered a similar interest with specific respect to the Bible on the part of biblical scholars. Biblical scholars continued to not only attend to historical and literary matters but also to develop new interpretive methodologies for doing so. Scholars in the Movement went beyond such matters to identify the theological claims of texts and, typically, to regard those claims as normative for the contemporary congregation. The Biblical Theology Movement called attention to continuities that stretch from one part of the Bible through the other. Accompanying the idea of a unified Bible was the idea of a unified notion of revelation. A key book was Wright, *God Who Acts*. According to Wright, the actions of God described in the Bible reveal the nature and purposes of God. The Biblical Theology Movement also stressed the distinctiveness of the Hebrew way of thinking, which the interpreters saw in both testaments: they called attention to the differences between the Hebrew mindset (good) and mindsets of other ancient peoples, especially the Greeks (bad). Childs is especially good on the rise and fall of the Movement in Childs, *Biblical Theology in Crisis*, 13–89.

15. On Niebuhr as Preacher, see Scherer, "Reinhold Niebuhr–Preacher."

16. This motif is initially developed in Niebuhr, *Moral Man and Immoral Society*. He develops ideas and others in *An Interpretation of Christian Ethics* and the magisterial *The Nature and Destiny of Man*.

eliminated only by God's grace: God will bring about the eschatological age to restore creation. In the meantime, grace makes it possible for communities to take actions that limit the destructive effects of sin, though not to wipe it out. Niebuhr advocates "Christian realism": doing what a community can do to reduce the effects of sin and to promote justice, recognizing that many compromises may take place along the way.[17]

Neo-orthodoxy unraveled in the 1960s in response to a range of factors, including the emergence of new theological perspectives (such as the liberation theologies), the growing recognition of the diversity of the Bible, and the difficulty of speaking of God acting in history. Amid the cultural turmoil of the 1960s and 1970s many people lost confidence in the neo-orthodox interpretation of life. The eschatological focus gave way to the idea of the people and God in partnership bringing the realm.[18]

Purposes and Characteristics of Preaching in This Theological Family

Barth puts forward a distinctive view of preaching that is shared by many neo-orthodox preachers and scholars of preaching. Neo-orthodox preaching that does not follow Barth's schema in detail nevertheless often resonates with Barth's overarching concerns. Barth's view of preaching is rooted in his understanding of the word of God described earlier.[19] According to Barth, the word of God occurs in threefold form.

1. The revealed Word of God: the revelation of God that takes places through Jesus Christ.

2. The written Word of God, that is, Scripture as used by God for the purpose of revealing Jesus Christ.

3. The proclaimed Word of God: preaching as used by God to reveal Jesus Christ through modes, proclamation, especially the sermon.[20]

17. Niebuhr's work continues to influence people in public life into the present moment. Among public figures influenced by Niebuhr are Martin Luther King Jr., Barack Obama, James Comey, Hillary Clinton, and Madeleine Albright. Niebuhr himself had a robust public presence symbolized by the fact that he appeared on the cover of *Time* magazine on March 8, 1948.

18. In the process of locating Barth in theology in the last century, Gary Dorrien notes many criticisms of Barth in his *The Barthian Revolt in Modern Theology*.

19. For thoughtful discussions of Barth as preacher, see Willimon, "Barth on Preaching"; and Willimon, *Conversations with Barth on Preaching*.

20. Barth, *Church Dogmatics* 1/1, 88–122.

The same Word is revealed in threefold form.[21] God speaks only one word (the event of Jesus Christ) whom God sends to us in this threefold way. For Barth, when God animates a sermon, the sermon does not simply talk about the Word of God but becomes the Word of God As Elizabeth Achtemeier, a neo-orthodox biblical interpreter and scholar of preaching says:

> There is a miracle that takes place in preaching. It does not oc-
> cur every Sunday morning, no matter how skilled the preacher,
> and it cannot be produced by any wiles or will of [a human
> being]. Rather, it occurs when God wills it, and it is solely the
> product of [God's] working. It is the miracle whereby the words
> from the pulpit become the word of God for the congregation,
> the miracle of God's use of language to reveal [Godself] to the
> worshippers.[22]

In his *Homiletics*, Barth expands on what happens in preaching "from the top down" and "from the bottom up." For the "top down," Barth says, "Preaching is the Word of God which he himself speaks, claiming for the purpose the exposition of a biblical text in free human words that are relevant to contemporaries by those who are called to do this in a church that is obedient to its commission."[23] Two things are key in Barth's initial exposition of preaching. One is that God is the primary actor. The other is that preaching is an event. Something really happens. The "happening" did not just occur in history to people in the world of the Bible; it happens again, to people in the contemporary moment with the same force and power. As Elizabeth Achtemeier says, the miracle of preaching

> is of the most active and effective nature, for it is of the nature of
> the word of God that it always creates a new situation . . . So too

---

21. Barth shows the relationship within the threefold word of God by preceding the presentation of the threefold form of the word of God with a discussion of the Trinity. "There is only one analogy to this doctrine of the Word of God. Or, more accurately, the doctrine of the Word of God is itself the only analogy to the doctrine which will be our fundamental concern as we develop the concept of revelation. This is the doctrine of the triunity of God. In the fact that we can substitute for revelation, Scripture and proclamation the names of the divine persons Father, Son and Holy Spirit and *vice versa*, that in the one case as in the other we shall encounter the same basic determinations and mutual relationships, and that the decisive difficulty and also the decisive clarity is the same in both—in all this one may see specific support for the inner necessity and correctness of our present exposition of the Word of God" (Barth, *Church Dogmatics* 1/1, 120–21).

22. Achtemeier, *The Old Testament and the Proclamation of the Gospel*, 169.

23. Barth, *Homiletics*, 44.

is the case when the words of a biblical passage or sermon become the word of God for a congregation. Then a new situation is created and the word accomplishes that of which it speaks. The worshipers do not merely hear about judgment; they are in fact judged—set into the situation of separation from God which calls their entire existence into question. Or if the people hear a sermon that becomes God's word of forgiveness to them, they are in fact brought back into a new communion of life with their Lord. Or if they hear the biblical story of redemption, and God reveals [Godself] through that story, then the listening people are really redeemed from their slavery of the past and given a new freedom to act as God's sons.[24]

In the second part of the understanding of preaching, Barth calls attention to what happens "from the bottom up," by describing the role of the preacher. "Preaching is the attempt enjoined upon the church to serve God's own Word, through one who is called thereto, by expounding a biblical text in human words and making it relevant to contemporaries in intimation of what they have to hear from God himself.[25] Barth continues, "We humans must try to point to what is said in scripture."[26] The language of "point" calls to mind Barth's famous image of the work of theology he drew from the altarpiece painted by Matthias Grünewald at Isenheim in which the oversized finger of John the Baptist points at Jesus.[27] God designates the preacher, like John the Baptist, pointing to the event of Jesus Christ in the role of herald.

24. Achtemeier, *The Old Testament and the Proclamation of the Gospel*, 160–61. A number of scholars of preaching influenced by neo-orthodoxy speak similarly. For example, Farmer, *The Servant of the Word*, 8–9; Miller, *Fire in Thy Mouth*, 20. Paul Scott Wilson says that such thinking was part of a broader mover in preaching to think of the sermon as an event. Wilson, *Preaching and Homiletical Theory*, 60–69.

25. Barth, *Homiletics*, 44. While this book opens a window on Barth's thinking about preaching, this book does not present a comprehensive Barthian homiletic. Editors put it together in book form from notes from Barth's lectures. An earlier and smaller summary appear as Barth, *The Preaching of the Gospel*. *Homiletics* contains some material not available when *The Preaching of the Gospel* was assembled.

26. Barth, *Homiletics*, 45.

27. Barth, *Church Dogmatics* 1/1, 125. David Greenhaw notes that this image sets out "something of the Christian realism characteristic of neo-orthodoxy. Preaching points not to a world where all is getting better and better, but to a world of nearly unspeakable suffering, cruelty and despair." Between the World Wars, many people wanted to declare the scourge over and get back to normal, "But a few like Barth and Thurneysen, local church pastors, saw the suffering of the working people and later, joined by Reinhold Niebuhr in his own way, saw the church accommodate to the culture. They saw the dangerous hubris of the state, and saw in the gospel a critique of what they believed to be a culturally accommodating church." In this context, their preaching pointed to Jesus Christ as the great alternative (personal correspondence).

In the same way that a monarch sends a herald to precede the monarch and announce the coming of the monarch, so God sends the preacher to reveal God's coming.[28] The herald "has the task of proclaiming past and future revelation of God, the epiphany and Parousia of Jesus Christ."[29]

While God is the actor in the sermon, Elizabeth Achtemeier notes that many things that preachers do on the way to the sermon are "human skill, and some of it can be taught." While "the most accomplished of writers and orators cannot turn . . . human words in the word of God," the preacher can "*[remove] obstacles to hear the text; [the preacher] proclaims it and interprets it*" for the congregation to the best of the preacher's homiletical ability. "But then the preacher must wait for God to come and to use [the preacher's] human words as the channel of [God's] divine working. We preachers prepare the way of the Lord. We smooth out the road and get rid of the stumbling blocks. We announce the coming of God, and then we simply wait.[30]

Preachers are to avoid "declaiming their own systematic theology or expounding what they think they know about their own lives, or human life in general, or society or the state of the world."[31] The preacher begins with Scripture. Indeed, "preaching is exposition of Scripture." To be sure, the preacher needs to attend to Scripture with "exact philological and historical study."[32] But, the preacher does not simply preach the text. Careful exegesis and exposition from the standpoint of critical biblical interpretation is not the end. "Also needed is the attempt to read the Word of God in the text, in the self, and congregation."[33] This process calls for modesty on the part of the preacher. For if God speaks through the sermon, it is not the preacher's doing.

Barth does say the sermon should be "original." For Barth, originality refers not to the preacher's creativity but to preachers bringing their real selves to the text. For they have been called "as the persons they are."[34] At the same time, the preacher should approach the matter of application with caution. On the one hand, the preacher should keep the sermon close to the text and to life. On the other hand, the preacher can easily bring material into

28. Barth, *Homiletics*, 71. For an approach to preaching developed around the notion of herald, see Long, *The Witness of Preaching*.

29. Barth, *Homiletics*, 86.

30. Achtemeier, *The Old Testament and the Proclamation of the Gospel*, 165 (italics added).

31. Barth, *Homiletics*, 75.

32. Barth, *Homiletics*, 77. Barth points to the character of study for preparing the sermon on 93–101, esp. 96–101.

33. Barth, *Homiletics*, 77.

34. Barth, *Homiletics*, 81–84.

the sermon that draws the attention of the congregation away from the Word. The preacher should trust the power of the Word to create its own application.[35] The best application is the best explication of the text.[36]

Barth goes against both beginning the sermon with an introduction intended to engage the interest of the congregation and ending with conclusion aiming for a response. For Barth, the word creates its connections, whereas those engineered by preachers are distracting and waste valuable time. The most a preacher should do at the outset of the sermon is to provide a link from the reading of the Bible into the sermon. Similar things apply to the conclusion.[37] The sermon should end with the exposition. The word creates its own response. The preacher could end with word "Amen," which may be "a comfort to us after what has been said in weakness."[38]

Although Barth's general thinking about preaching guided much neo-orthodox preaching, some preachers took slightly other routes. Whereas Barth eschews referring to contemporary issues and events in preaching, Reinhold Niebuhr used the sermon as an occasion to reflect critically with the congregation on issues of the day. Some preachers who saw themselves in the neo-orthodox family did use introductions and conclusions. Moreover, some preachers in this tradition gave more attention to sermon design than Barth thought necessary.

Case Study: Text and Sermon
(Ephesians 2:5)

Karl Barth preached this sermon in a prison in Basel, Switzerland, in 1955. The focus is on a phrase in Ephesians 2:5: "By grace you have been saved." Barth interprets the text from the standpoint of his theology, emphasizing God's address to the congregation, Barth uses the expression "By grace you have been saved" as a theme line. He explores the phrase word by word, referring at times to the significance of salvation by grace to the imprisoned.

---

35. Barth, *Homiletics*, 111–19. In particular, Barth warns against adducing quotes or allusions to newspapers and similar things (117), the preacher's treasured perspectives (117–18), events and issues of the day (118–19), illustrations, references to contemporary events (119–120).

36. Barth says, "A sermon can often be more relevant when it does not seem relevant at all. Hence, we should never expressly state and affirm that this is what holy scripture means for us today. The meaning is to be presupposed as self-evident" (Barth, *Homiletics*, 128).

37. Barth, *Homiletics*, 127.

38. Barth, *Homiletics*, 127.

While the phrase is central to Ephesians 2:1–10, and, indeed, to the whole of Ephesians, Barth does not directly consider the possible meanings of the text in its historical or literary contexts. Barth never refers to the slight expansion of the phrase in Ephesians 2:8, "For by grace you have been saved through faith." From the point of view of today's historical and literary criticisms, Barth does not violate the fundamental functcions of the text, but never takes advantage of how awareness of ancient meanings might enrich the sermon.

"Saved by Grace"[39]

[Typical of Barth and many neo-orthodox preachers, Barth reads the text and then plunges directly into heart of the message without an introduction. Barth calls attention to the distinctiveness of the Word prompted by the text.]

My dear brothers and sisters: I now read a passage from the Letter of the Apostle Paul to the Ephesians (2:5): *By grace have you been saved.* This, I think, is brief enough for it to be remembered by all, for it to impress itself upon you and, if it be God's will, to be understood.

We are gathered here this Sunday morning to hear this word: *By grace you have been saved!* Whatever else we do, praying and singing, is but an answer to this word spoken to us by God himself. The prophets and apostles wrote a strange book, called the Bible, for the very purpose of testifying to this fact before mankind. The Bible alone contains this sentence. We do not read it in Kant or in Schopenhauer or in any book of natural or secular history, and certainly not in any novel, but in the Bible alone.

While the Bible is the instrument through which the Word comes, individuals do not hear it fully in isolation but in the community of the church. Barth clarifies the relationship of the Bible to the Word. Listening together "through it [the Bible]" the congregation encounters "the word of God."

In order to hear this word, we need what is called the church–the company of Christians, of human beings called and willing to listen together to the Bible and through it to the word of God. This is the word of God: *By grace you have been saved!* Someone once said to me: "I need not go to church. I need not read the Bible. I know already what the church teaches and what the Bible says: "Do what is right and fear no one!" Let

39. Barth, *Deliverance to the Captives*, 35–42.

me say this at this point: If this were the message at stake, I would most
certainly not have come here. My time is too precious and so is yours. To
say that neither prophets nor apostles, neither Bible, Jesus Christ nor God
are needed. Anybody is at liberty to say this to himself. By the same token
this saying is void of any new, of any very special and exciting message.
It does not help anyone. I have never seen a smile on the face of a person
reassuring himself with this kind of talk. As a rule, those who use it are a
sad-looking lot, revealing all too easily that this word does not help them,
does not comfort them, does not bring them joy.

Let us hear therefore what the Bible says and what we as Christians
are called to bear together: *By grace you have been saved!* No man can say
this to himself. Neither can he say it to someone else. This can only be said
by God to each one of us. It takes Jesus Christ to make this saying true. It
takes the apostles to communicate it. And our gathering here as Christians
is needed to spread it among us. This is why it is truly news, and very
special news, the most exciting news of all, the most helpful thing also,
indeed the only helpful thing.

> *In keeping with the neo-orthodox accent on sin, Barth urges the*
> *congregation to recognize that they are all sinners. As the entry into*
> *this discussion, Barth confesses that he is himself a sinner. Accord-*
> *ing to Barth, sin is a greater prison than the walls within which the*
> *congregation finds itself.*

"By grace *you* have been saved!" How strange to have this message addressed to us! Who are we, anyway? Let me tell you quite frankly: we are all
together great sinners. Please understand me: I include myself. I stand ready
to confess being the greatest sinner among you all; yet you may then not
exclude yourself from the group! Sinners are people who in the judgment of
God, and perhaps of their own consciences, missed and lost their way, who
are not just a little, but totally guilty, hopelessly indebted and lost not only
in time, but in eternity. We are such sinners. And we are prisoners. Believe
me, there is a captivity much worse than the captivity in this house. There are
walls much thicker and doors much heavier than those closed upon you. All
of us, the people without and you within, are prisoners of our own obstinacy,
of our greed, of our various anxieties, of our mistrust and in the last analysis
of our unbelief. We are all sufferers. Most of all we suffer from ourselves.
We each make life difficult for ourselves and in so doing for our fellowmen.
We suffer from life's lack of meaning. We suffer in the shadow of death and
of eternal judgment toward which we are moving. We spend our life in the
midst of a whole world of sin and captivity and suffering.

The word of grace comes not from the Bible per se but "from on high." Barth stresses that the community is saved by God's gracious work through Christ, "the word of God for us." Note the force with which Barth declares the certainty of salvation.

But now listen. Into the depth of our predicament the word is spoken from on high: *By grace you have been saved!* To be saved does not just mean to be a little encouraged, a little comforted, a little relieved. It means to be pulled out like a log from a burning fire. You have been saved! We are not told you may be saved sometimes, or a little bit. No, you *have been* saved, totally and for all times . You? Yes, we! Not just any other people, more pious and better than we are, no, we, each one of us.

This is so because Jesus Christ is our brother and, through his life and death, has become our Savior who has wrought our salvation. He is the word of God for us. And this word is: *By grace you have been saved!*

You probably all know the legend of the rider who crossed the frozen Lake of Constance by night without knowing it. When he reached the opposite shore and was told whence he came, he broke down, horrified.[40] This is the human situation when the sky opens and the earth is bright, when we may hear: *By grace you have been saved!* In such a moment we are like that terrified rider. When we hear this word we involuntarily look back, do we not, asking ourselves: Where have I been? Over an abyss, in mortal danger! What did I do? The most foolish thing I ever attempted! What happened? I was doomed and miraculously escaped and now I am safe!

Barth explains how God brought about salvation.

You ask: "Do we really live in such danger?" Yes, we live on the brink of death. But we have been saved. Look at our Savior and at our salvation! Look at Jesus Christ on the cross, accused, sentenced, and punished instead of us! Do you know for whose sake he is hanging there? For *our* sake—because of *our* sin—sharing *our* captivity—burdened with *our* suffering! He nails *our* life to the cross. This is how God had to deal with *us*. From this

40. Lake Constance borders Switzerland, Austria, and Germany. It is normally impassable in the winter, though once in a great while it freezes. Barth here recalls the story of a person who set out one winter day towards a village, planning to spend the night in a lodge and take a ferry across the river. According to Gustav Schwab's poetic retelling, the rider goes and goes, eventually asking a woman how far it is to the village, only to be told that he is in the town! The rider realizes he unknowingly crossed the lake on a very thin sheet of ice. He crossed the lake without evening realizing it. This sudden awareness fills him with such fear, he falls into the lake and disappears. See Gustav Schwab, "The Horseman and the Lake of Constance" (http://www.poetryatlas.com/poetry/poem/2981/the-horseman-and-the-lake-of-constance.ht).

darkness he has saved *us*. He who is not shattered after hearing this news may not yet have grasped the word of God: *By grace you have been saved!*

> *Barth calls attention to the immediate effects of salvation. The congregation is freed from the control of the past, even in prison walls "Our sin has no longer any power over us. Our prison door is open."*

But more important than the fear of sudden death is the knowledge of life imparted to us: *By grace you have been saved!* Therefore, we have reached the shore, the Lake of Constance is behind us, we may breathe freely, even though we still are in the grip of panic, and rightly so. This panic is but an aftermath. By virtue of the good news the sky truly opens, and the earth is bright. What a glorious relief to be told that there I was, in that darkness, over that abyss, on the brink of death, but there I am no longer. Through this folly I lived, but I cannot, and I will not do it again, never again. This happened, but it must not, and it will not happen again. My sin, my captivity, my suffering is yesterday's reality, not today's. They are things of my past, not of the present nor of the future.

I have been *saved!* Is this really so, is this the truth? Look once again to Jesus Christ in his death upon the cross. Look and try to understand that what he did and suffered he did and suffered for you, for me, for us all. He carried our sin, our captivity, and our suffering, and did not carry it in vain. *He carried* it *away*. He acted as the captain of us all. He broke through the ranks of our enemies. He has already won the battle, our battle. All we have to do is to follow him, to be victorious with him. Through him, in him we are saved. Our sin has no longer any power over us. Our prison door is open. Our suffering has come to an end. This is a great word indeed. The word of God *is* indeed a great word. And we would deny him, we would deny the Lord Jesus Christ, were we to deny the greatness of this word: He sets us free. When be, the Son of God, sets us free, we are *truly* free.

> *The preacher explains grace and emphasizes its priority in the work of salvation.*

Because we are saved by no other than Jesus Christ, we are saved *by grace* . This means that we did not deserve to be saved. What we deserved would be *quite* different . We cannot secure salvation for our selves. Did you read in the newspapers the other day that [human beings] will soon be able to produce an artificial moon? But we cannot produce our salvation. No one can be proud of being saved. Each one can only fold his hands in great lowliness of heart and be thankful like a child. Consequently, we shall never possess salvation as our property. We may only receive it as a gift over and over again, with hands out stretched. *"By grace* you have been saved!" This means constantly to look away from ourselves to God and to the man on the cross where this truth is revealed. This truth is ever anew to be believed and to be grasped by faith. To believe means to look to Jesus Christ and to God and to trust that there is truth for us, truth for our lives, and for the life of all men.

The preacher takes a neo-orthodox turn towards human rebellion against God. We rebel even against the notion that we are saved by grace.

Is it not a pity that we rebel against this very truth in the depth of our hearts? Indeed, we dislike hearing that we are saved by grace, and by grace alone. We do not appreciate that God does not owe us anything, that we are bound to live from his goodness alone, that we are left with nothing but the great humility, the thankfulness of a child presented with many gifts. For we do not like at all to look away from ourselves. We would much prefer to withdraw into our own inner circle, not unlike the snail into its shell, and to be with ourselves.

To put it bluntly: we do not like to believe. And yet grace and therefore faith as I just described it is the beginning of the true life of freedom, of a carefree heart, of joy deep within, of love of God and neighbor, of great and assured hope! And yet grace and faith would make things so very simple in our lives!

While salvation by grace is already accomplished, it can work more fully in behalf of the congregation when they believe. God has done God's part. The preacher now pleads with the congregation to do their parts.

Dear brothers and sisters, where do we stand now? One thing is certain: the bright day *has dawned,* the sun of God *does shine* into our dark lives, even though we may close our eyes to its radiance. His voice *does call* us from heaven, even though we may obstruct our ears. The bread of life *is offered* to us, even though we are inclined to clench our fists instead of opening our hands to take the bread and eat it. The door of our prison is *open,* even though, strangely enough, we prefer to remain within. God has put the house in order, even though we like to mess it up all over again. *By grace you have been saved!* This is true, even though we may not believe it, may not accept it as valid for ourselves and unfortunately in so doing may forego its benefits. *Why* should we want to forego the benefits? *Why* should we not want to believe? *Why* do we not go out through the open door? *Why* do we not open our clenched fists? *Why* do we obstruct our ears? *Why* are we blindfolded? Honestly, *why?*

> *Barth offers prayer as a practical way the congregation can accept the work of grace for salvation as the operative reality of their lives.*

One remark in reply must suffice. All this is so because perhaps we failed to pray fervently enough for a change within ourselves, on our part. That God is God, not only almighty, but merciful and good, that he wills and does what is best for us, that Jesus Christ died for us to set us free, that by grace, in him, we have been saved–all this need *not* be a concern of our prayers. All these things are true apart from our own deeds and prayers. But to believe, to accept, to let it be true for us, to begin to live with this truth, to believe it not only with our minds and with our lips, but also with our hearts and with all our life, so that our fellow men may sense it, and finally to let our total existence be immersed in the great divine truth, *by grace you have been saved,* this is to be the concern of our prayers. No human being has ever prayed for this in vain. If anyone asks for this, the answer is already being given and faith begins. And because no one has ever asked for this in vain, no one may omit praying like a little child for the assurance that God's truth, this terrible, this glorious truth, is shining even today, a small, yet increasingly bright light. *By grace you have been saved.* Ask and it will be given you; seek this, and you will find it; knock on this door and it will be opened to you.

This, my dear friends, is what I have been privileged and empowered to tell you of the good news as the word of God today. Amen.

Assessment: Strengths and Limitations in This Theological Family

Perhaps the greatest strength of neo-orthodoxy is its insistence that God is God. In every period of history this insistence is relevant. For human beings—including the church—are ever tempted to make idols of things that serve our interests at the expense of others.[41] Neo-orthodoxy criticizes

41 A potent example of the value of this perspective during the neo-orthodox era comes from Nazi Germany. Many individuals and congregations had become "German Christians," that is, Christians who believed that God approved of Adolf Hitler and the direction the Nazi Party was taking Germany. Barth and a group of pastors believed that the Nazis and German Christians had made an idol of the ideology of racial superiority and the wider network of Nazi values and behaviors. In a declaration made in 1934 in Barmen, the pastors affirmed that Jesus Christ alone is head of the church so that the church should never be subservient to a state.

culture from a theological point of view. This capacity is timely in early twenty-first century United States when many—including churches—use religion to justify making functional idols of race, gender, nation, social class, sexuality, and national origin.

The early twenty-first-century Eurocentric, historic churches in the United States are afflicted by biblical illiteracy and theological inadequacy. Neo-orthodoxy reminds such churches that biblical materials and critical reflection are fundamental to the identity of the church.

Neo-orthodox thinkers recognize that all perceptions of God and all speech about God is relative. At the same time, neo-orthodox theologians sometimes claim to think and speak about God as if they do so apart from cultural conditioning. Yet, every act of perception contains cultural conditioning, as does every use of language. We can never perceive God or speak of God in pure, uninterpreted ways; the best we can hope is to become as aware and critical as we can of such things.

Barth may think that the significance of a text is self-evident and does not require application or illustration. But observing congregations for more than fifty years, I have to say it is not self-evident that listeners come away from sermons having encountered revelation. Furthermore, with respect to leaving contemporary issues and events out of the sermon, David Buttrick provides a vivid rejoinder in his 1991 Foreword to Barth's *Homiletic*. "Are we willing to tell Allen Boesak or Bishop Tutu to stop referring to *apartheid* in preaching—particularly if we are white Reformed church people?"[42]

Although neo-orthodox theologians advocate the importance of the Bible, they seldom engage the Bible in exegetical depth. Indeed, neo-orthodox thinkers often read biblical materials through their interpretation of God's work through Jesus Christ without regard for the otherness of the text. On the positive side, the neo-orthodox preacher is not held theologically hostage by a text with troubling theological or moral elements, and the preacher has a resource in Jesus Christ for pointing the sermon in a renewing direction.[43]

---

42. Buttrick, "Foreward" to Barth, *Homiletics*, 9.

43 For its part, the Biblical Theology Movement does push the preacher towards paying more attention to historical contexts, literary features, and other exegetical matters. However, the sermon influenced by the Biblical Theology Movement often turns in the direction of an exegetical lecture with most of the focus on the past and only a brief connection to the contemporary world towards the end of the sermon. Preachers in the Biblical Theology Movement often have difficulty dealing with texts that put forward ideas and guidance for behavior that are theologically and ethically troubling. A good many preachers in the stream of the Biblical Theology Movement bring the sermon to a christological focus, even when preaching from texts from the Torah, Prophets, and Writings.

While Barth shuns using rhetoric to formulate sermons, he appears to use some rhetorical strategies, even if unintentionally. For example, Barth's the phrase "By grace you have been saved" as a theme line sounds a lot like rhetoric.

The neo-orthodox focus on sin as rebellion against God manifesting itself in idolatry, pride, idolatry, greed, and other attitudes and behaviors, seems true to the experience of many people. However, feminist theologians, beginning with Valerie Saiving, call attention to the fact that many women live not with rebellious pride but with its opposite—with a disempowering, negative view of themselves and of their possibilities.[44] Neo-orthodoxy has also been criticized for its extreme discontinuity between God and the created world, for Christomonism, for compromising Christian witness in the interest of pursuing ethical options that seem realistically possible, for retreating from social transformation in the present because of the expectation that God will act eschatologically to make things right, for ambiguous attitudes towards other religions, and for its identification with capitalism and Eurocentrism.[45]

For Further Reading

Achtemeier, Elizabeth. *The Old Testament and the Proclamation of the Gospel.* Philadelphia: Westminster, 1973.

Barth, Karl. *Dogmatics in Outline.* Translated by G. T. Thompson. New York: Philosophical Library, 1949.

———. *Homiletics.* Translated by Geoffrey W. Bromily and Donald E. Daniels. Louisville: Westminster John Knox, 1991.

Childs, Brevard S. *Biblical Theology in Crisis.* Philadelphia: Westminster, 1970.

Brunner, Emil. *Man in Revolt: A Christian Anthropology.* Translated by Olive Wyon. Philadelphia: Westminster, 1947.

Niebuhr, Reinhold. *Moral Man and Immoral Society.* New York: Scribner, 1932.

Smart, James D. *The Strange Silence of the Bible in the Church: A Study in Hermeneutics.* Philadelphia: Westminster, 1970.

Willimon, William H. *Conversations with Barth on Preaching.* Nashville: Abingdon, 2006.

44. Saiving, "The Human Situation: A Feminine View."

45 Gary Dorrien offers a judicious appraisal of neo-orthodoxy in *The Barthian Revolt in Modern Theology.*

4

Preaching in the Postliberal
Theological Family

LANCE B. PAPE

POSTLIBERALISM REPRESENTS A "THIRD way" in Christian theology in distinction from evangelical and liberal perspectives. In the wake of the Enlightenment, with its devastating critique of the Bible on the basis of reason and evidence as the sole arbiters of truth, Christian thinkers across the theological spectrum have sought to re-articulate the sense in which the Bible's claims about God are reliable and transformative for human life. Conserving Christians have focused on defending the Bible as literally true in the sense of reporting accurately about historical occurrences. Various liberal projects have argued that the Bible metaphorically encodes divine wisdom about morality, or the possibility of living authentically in the face of death. Postliberals practice a literary literalism that brackets, or suspends, questions of historical or ideational reference in order to let the "world" of the biblical text flourish in the imagination in ways that shape communal and personal identity.

Circumstances That Gave Rise
to This Theological Family

As its name suggests, postliberal theology is a response to theological liberalism. Chronologically, the story begins with Karl Barth's commentary on Romans, but it was Barth's interpreter, Yale theologian Hans Frei, who laid the theoretical groundwork for the movement. Frei wrote a dissertation (1956) on Barth's break with liberalism, and then spent the following decades

47

carefully tracing the influences behind that liberal approach to theology. His work culminated in *The Eclipse of Biblical Narrative* (1974),[1] which is the first of two key texts that shaped the movement.

On one level, *Eclipse* documented in minute detail Frei's painstaking historical reconstruction of the ways that Christian thinkers tried to respond to the emerging intellectual climate of early-modern Europe. The Enlightenment was an epistemological revolution. In other words, it broke radically from the past by introducing new rules for deciding what counts as true. Without getting too far into the weeds of parsing the meaning of words like empiricism and rationalism, we can say that the Bible was no longer granted special status as the arbiter of truth. Instead, it was treated like any other book, and its claims were subject to criticism according to a new historical sensibility shaped by reasoned consideration of evidence and experience.

So, if the Bible claims that a flood destroyed the world, but that every species was rescued by being loaded onto a huge boat, the Enlightenment approach might begin to ask questions about that. Is there independent evidence from other sources pointing to the existence of such a universal flood? How big was that boat, and, cross-referenced with a growing catalogue of biodiversity in various parts of the world, does the math check out in terms of payload? What about the plants? Based on ordinary experience with feeding and caring for animals, does this scenario seem possible (never-mind likely)?

If this process strikes the reader (and the author of this chapter!) as rather obvious, that only proves that we are both products of the Enlightenment. Our world is characterized by a shared historical perspective, respect for physical and documentary evidence extrinsic to the Bible, and an implicit trust in a set of rational procedures for testing everything that claims to be true. For us, it would be absurd to do anything other than try to fit a story from the Bible into the world as we already understand it. That is what makes us modern. It is hard for us even to imagine the pre-modern assumption: that every human experience and idea should be judged by whether *it could be fit into the world given and described by the Bible*. It may be that there is no way to put the modern genie back in the pre-modern bottle. But Frei invites readers to consider what is lost in such a sweeping hermeneutical reversal. If we allow modernity to dictate how we read the Bible, can we be sure that we are not "eclipsing" what the Bible is talking about in its own distinctive way?

---

1. Frei, *The Eclipse of Biblical Narrative*.

Frei's point in *Eclipse* is that once an interpreter starts marshaling evidence extrinsic to the Bible to argue that a story from the Bible is true, "the great reversal" has already taken place: it is now the Bible that must be explained, defended, and justified in light of another, more total and convincing, account of reality.[2] As the eighteenth century unfolded, Christian thinkers engaged in good faith efforts to rearticulate the truth, significance, and usefulness of the Bible in terms of this reversal. Some, the predecessors of contemporary conservatives, tried to put the pieces back together through ever more elaborate, and at times, tortured defenses of the historical veracity of the narratives. Others, the precursors to contemporary liberals, let go the historical project, and began to frame the meaning of biblical stories in terms of their capacity to disclose moral and religious truth. Conservatives argued that the Bible was true because it accurately referenced truth "behind" the text in history; liberals argued that the Bible was true because it faithfully referenced moral and religious wisdom "above" the text.

But on another level, *Eclipse* was a vehicle for Frei the theologian to propose that both those modern approaches do a kind of hermeneutical violence to the text, and to offer a counterproposal about how to read the Bible in the wake of the Enlightenment in the way that is most sensitive to and cooperative with its distinctive genre. Frei argued that before the Enlightenment there was a consensus that privileged the literal sense. It is crucial to distinguish this premodern literal sense from the literalism practiced by conserving modern readers. Pre-Enlightenment theologians certainly assumed that the events depicted in biblical narrative happened as described, but that assumption did not drive the interpretation of the text's meaning, nor did the truth value of the biblical text hinge upon it first being ratified as a reliable historical source. To put it a bit differently, for the premodern reader, the literal sense as the appropriate vehicle of meaning was not logically entangled with historical reference in the same way it is for a modern conservative.[3] Frei's proposal was that it is possible to break those two aspects of literalism apart, and to read biblical narrative in a way that enjoys continuity with the long and generative tradition of the *sensus literalis* without committing the interpreter to the distracting and doomed task of defending the Bible's historical accuracy at every turn.

2. "It is no exaggeration to say that all across the theological spectrum the great reversal had taken place; interpretation was a matter of fitting the biblical story into another world with another story rather than incorporating that world into the biblical story" (Frei, *The Eclipse of Biblical Narrative*, 130).

3. For a discussion of contemporary conservative hermeneutics as distinctively early–modern (as opposed to a continuation of premodern reading strategies), see Marsden, *Understanding Fundamentalism and Evangelicalism*, 117.

Rather than arguing that the Bible is meaningful because it points beyond itself "back" to history, or "up" to moral ideas, Frei claims that the meaning of the Bible is "within" the text itself: "There really is an analogy between the Bible and a novel writer who says something like this: I mean what I say whether or not anything took place. I mean what I say. It's as simple as that: the text means what it says."[4] On this reading, the genre of the Bible is neither accurate historical report, nor encoded moral myth, but rather adequate poetic testimony. It is literal in the sense that it really is about what it seems to be about (the nature of God, the unsubstitutable identity of Jesus as God's unique agent, and so on), but its stories are closer in form to narrative theological poems, than factually rigorous chronicles.

This "literary literalism" (for lack of a better term) is a bid to suspend questions of historical and ideational reference so that questions of textual meaning can flourish unapologetically. It is an approach well-represented by the oft-repeated legend about Barth's paradoxical response to the challenger who questioned the plausibility of the story about the speaking serpent in the garden of Eden: "It doesn't matter whether the serpent spoke. What matters is what the serpent said." Ultimately, of course, the issue of correspondence to reality must resurface, but in the meantime, the postliberal interpreter is unencumbered by such concerns judged foreign to the genre of the biblical text, and free to explore other questions deemed more appropriate: What exactly is the nature of this world that is displayed by the words of this narrative? Who is the God depicted here, and who are people in relation to that God? What kind of person do I become, or rather, what kind of community do we become, if we accept this world and this God as our reality, and live together in a manner that is consistent with it?

The hermeneutical implications of this approach to biblical narrative were summed up most memorably by Frei's Yale colleague George Lindbeck in the movement's other classic text, *The Nature of Doctrine*: "It is the [biblical] text, so to speak, which absorbs the world, rather than the world the text."[5] The stories of the Bible are not best understood as reliable or unreliable descriptions of the world we already know, but as a proposal about a possible world that is available to those who trust their testimony. According to this way of thinking, the question about truth and correspondence to reality comes only after such reading practices run their course. Only after suspending disbelief and embracing the world proposed by the text can we find out whether the text is a reliable witness to the true nature of God and the blessed

---

4. Frei, "Response," 208.

5. Lindbeck, *The Nature of Doctrine*, 118.

life: the faithful flourishing of the community produced by such reading practices becomes the test of all that the Bible claims.

Purposes and Characteristics of Preaching in This Theological Family

The preaching that grows out of the postliberal theological project described above is intensely focused on the biblical text. Such preaching does not view the Bible primarily as a window into the past, either in terms of the events depicted in its stories, or in terms of using those stories as clues to aid in the speculative historical reconstruction of the communities that produced them. This is because it does not consider the meaning of the biblical text to be constrained by or synonymous with the conditions of its production. Nor does postliberal preaching approach biblical narrative as a primitive form of moral or existential discourse that needs to be translated into categories that are less taxing to a late-modern plausibility structure. This is because it does not understand the biblical text as a naive or veiled attempt to talk about something other than what it seems, on its surface, to be talking about. Rather, postliberal preaching is an attempt to take the biblical text seriously, to cooperate with its distinctive mode of discourse, to follow its literal itinerary of meaning, to display its world, to trust its surprising testimony, and to faithfully and imaginatively narrate the contemporary congregation's experience in light of that testimony.

Although its method is literary, postliberal preaching is interested in and indebted to the historical-critical project on which so much of the church's intellectual resources have been lavished over the last 200+ years. In the first place, postliberalism is interested in that project because exploring the history of the church, even from its earliest days, is a fascinating and valuable discipline. Postliberalism is not a bid to obviate that project, nor does it question the legitimacy of employing the biblical text (like any text) as a resource for historical inquiry, even as it distinguishes between historical and properly theological uses. More importantly, postliberal preaching is indebted to historical criticism because it supplies the necessary linguistic resources for becoming a competent literary-theological interpreter of the biblical text. (Indeed, most preachers rely upon such expertise implicitly due to their dependence upon translation.) Literary literalism prioritizes a close reading that displays the world projected by the biblical text, and although the textual world is not reducible to the world that produced it, the linguistic competence to display and engage the textual world is resourced by historical criticism. Language emerges symbiotically in relation to culture, and there is no such thing as an expert in an ancient language that is not also an expert in the cultural context from which it emerged. The preacher who wants to display and explore the world of a story that talks about Jesus in conflict with Sadducees, for example, will be helped by the expertise manifested in a critically informed essay about the Sadducees of history, even as she appreciates that the primary agenda of the biblical text is not to refer back to the Sadducees of history. Indeed, the slippage between the Sadducees of history and the character "the Sadducees," a literary construct of Matthew's narration, may offer an important clue to that Gospel's distinctive testimony to the identity and mission of its protagonist.

Postliberal theology and preaching has a special interest in narrative. Narrative is the primary mode of biblical testimony, supplying the skeletal structure around which the other and diverse sub-genres gather and organize themselves. Frei's original argument was focused on the proper interpretation of biblical narrative, and postliberal theology has often been described as "narrative theology." At about the same time that Frei's *Eclipse* was creating a groundswell of interest in narrative, Fred Craddock's *As One Without Authority* was energizing the field of homiletics with its proposal for inductive sermon form, emphasis on biblical and sermonic language as experiential meaning event, and appreciation for the hearer as an active participant in sermonic meaning. Perhaps even more than his influential books about preaching, Craddock's own practice as a preacher whose sermons turned on extraordinarily engaging and winsome storytelling had a profound effect on preaching. Craddock's work both as a theorist and a practitioner is widely understood as one of the foundations for the "New" or "Narrative" homiletic that dominated the last decades of the twentieth century and continues to be influential even to the present day. So, during the 1970s, narrative became an emerging concern for theology generally, and homiletics in particular.

In an important text that carefully works out the homiletical implications of Frei's thought,[6] Charles Campbell has drawn a sharp distinction between the affinity for storytelling of the New Homiletic and postliberal narrative interpretation: "We are narrative preachers only to the extent that Jesus is what he does and undergoes. In a postliberal homiletic, narrative is important neither because it provides a 'homiletical plot' for sermons nor because preaching should consist of telling stories. Rather, narrative is important because it is the vehicle through which the Gospels render the identity of Jesus of Nazareth, who has been raised from the dead and seeks today to form

---

6. Campbell, *Preaching Jesus.*

a people to follow his way."[7] In other words, for Campbell Christian procla-mation is interested in these particular stories because of who they are about (God and Jesus), not in story generally. It may be that stories are rhetorically engaging, that they are able to evoke powerful emotional experiences, and draw the hearer into an active role in the meaning-making process, but none of these qualities qualifies a sermon as distinctively Christian. For Campbell, the essential task of Christian preaching is to keep the emphasis on the unique identity of Jesus, and to explore how that identity shapes the practices of the community that gathers in his name.

My own work on postliberal homiletics has drawn upon the narrative theory of philosopher Paul Ricoeur to try to think more about the distinc-tive nature of biblical narrative testimony, the narrative quality of all human experience, and the way human identity is worked out at the intersection of multiple competing narratives.[8] While I share Campbell's interest in the distinctiveness of the Christian narrative tradition and the importance of the literal sense of Scripture, my approach is more sympathetic to the New Homi-letic's intuition that narrative form itself is fundamental to the preaching task. If a person's self-understanding is organized and expressed as an unfolding story of which they are the protagonist, and if new experiences are integrated into that identity narrative under the guidance of paradigmatic narratives that we take seriously, then the sermon can be understood as an attempt to facilitate as a collective experience an encounter within the world of the biblical text that comes through a close and cooperative reading. In this way, the preacher helps the congregation explore the new array of contemporary possibilities proffered by the biblical text and demonstrates how to faithfully narrate contemporary experience under its guidance.

An open question within postliberal homiletics is how much attention to give to the contemporary context in preaching. Does fidelity to the biblical narrative exclude taking seriously the many compelling new narratives that shape our lives? Is it better to think in terms of the biblical world absorb-ing our experience completely, or should we imagine preaching as a kind of negotiation and interweaving between the many narratives that shape our self-understanding—albeit a negotiation and interweaving that strives self-consciously to privilege the biblical vision as authoritative?

7. Campbell, *Preaching Jesus*, 189–90.

8. Pape, *The Scandal of Having Something to Say.*

Case Study: Text and Sermon
(Psalm 74:1–11)

The following sermon was offered November 24, 2020, via Zoom as part of a Brite Divinity School chapel service themed "A Gathering of Grief and Gratitude." I was assigned the first of two short homilies for the service, and I was given the theme of "grief." I chose Psalm 74:1–11, the complaint section that is a typical structural feature of a psalm of communal lament. I felt free to focus exclusively on complaint and disorientation because I understood that other aspects of the chapel service, including a second short sermon, would attempt to perform and interpret God's presence.

My goal for the sermon was to harness the tone and energy of the psalmist's shockingly frank and assertive relationship with God, and then to narrate our collective experiences of the past several months in the same mode.

"Direct Your Steps to the Perpetual Ruins"

[After preliminary remarks encouraging self-care for listeners especially vulnerable to certain intense descriptions that would follow, I began with a description of the psalm's "author."]

We begin with a poet in exile, sitting in tortured meditation. Her body is in Babylon—of course it is—carried there against her will along with all the rest, all those years ago. But in moments of solitude, her thoughts are her own. Her body is captive, but her heart, at least, is free to roam; it flees, it flies, across all those miles of wilderness. Like a migrating bird that somehow knows the way in its DNA, knows the way back to where it began—her heart knows the way back to Zion. Over vast sand and waterless wadi she wings her way, returns west, descending through memory and cloud to look down upon the Temple mount.

[The situation described draws upon historical background information, but it is less about precisely establishing the exilic context of the psalm, and more about introducing the author of the psalm as a character in my own sermonic plot.]

It is a painful descent, for each wingbeat draws her heart closer to that place of loss. She sees it all again in her mind's eye: the emblems of the invading army arrayed before the Temple entrance, its beautiful wooden trellis hacked to splintered bits, its lovingly crafted carved work, crushed by hammer, split by axe. It was a building, but more than a building. It was their life, love, and devotion shaped in stone, metal, and wood. It was their history, their hope, the architecture of their identity, given expression through the skill of their hands, and the sacrifice of their economy. And it was ruined. Burned, desecrated, mocked, destroyed.

> *[We have now followed her back through memory to the events the psalm laments. The disturbing images she sees in her mind's eye become the occasion to incorporate details from the psalm's complaint into the narration. (Six weeks later in our world, these images of a violent mob desecrating a national sacred place will resonate differently and more directly, but in the sermon's original context they serve as a proxy for other griefs.)]*

And in the midst of it all, in the despair and grief of this return to the site of Israel's ruin, she has one desire. Not a hope, for "there is no longer any prophet." Not an expectation, for "there is no one among [them] who knows how long" they must wait. It is not a longing for rescue or a cry for vindication, for such things belong to another time. Her desire is simply to be seen. She longs for God to look upon their despair and feel what they feel. "O God why do you cast us off forever? Remember us! Remember Zion! Direct your steps to the perpetual ruins." Walk amongst our shattered hopes, prod our grief with your toe. See us broken and ruined. Be among the destruction you allowed. Let our despair settle upon you like dust.

> *[The sermon's first move is now completed. Its task was to narrate into consciousness Israel's national tragedy—its experience of loss and its sense of total abandonment by God. The world of this text does not ask us to solve that experience, but it does demonstrate where we should turn when we are utterly abandoned by God.]*

I don't know about you, but I feel like this grief is playing the long game with us. All those years ago back in March, as I set up a room for lecturing via Zoom, I remember thinking: "This could be a long spring." That thought seems almost adorable to me now. Like the thought of a child. Because this grief waits us out. It outlasts all our theodicies, positive thinking strategies, and self-care regimens. It grinds us down on the mill of time, and leaves us grist—a gristle of our former selves. The long grief. The perpetual ruins.

If we were to beg God to direct her steps to our perpetual ruins, I sincerely don't know where I would tell her to go first. There are so many places to go and see! Where to begin?

[Four episodic sketches will now try to reframe our experience in light of the psalm's disposition of assertive and brutally honest lament.]

God, stumble through Breonna Taylor's apartment in the dark. Step on the shell casings—so many! Smell the smoke and the fear, and wait for someone to turn on the lights at last. Turn on the lights to show clearly what we have become, what we surely were all along. Direct your steps to the perpetual ruins.

God, watch our democracy come unhinged, unmoored, unmasked. Move as only you can among the algorithms on the social networks. Feel the cold equations as they do the inhuman math that calculates the value of our attention. Pay attention as the capitalists release the machines like hounds, tearing through the digital detritus of our 8 billion lives to arrive at an answer that only a billionaire could love: the discovery that we are worth more to the advertisers when we are divided, hating, lusting, marinating in fake news, grievance, and distrust. Direct your steps to the perpetual ruins.

God, put on your mask and walk the urine-scented hallways of the nursing facility where she will die alone. Gasping for breath now stolen by a virus that spread through the air, sure, but mostly through the incompetence of our government, and the indifference of our neighbors, and, let's face it, through the simple fact that we are frail and can be felled by something too small to be seen, and too inert to know or care whether we live or die. Direct your steps to the perpetual ruins.

God, ride in the patrol car they sent to his tiny house in rural New Mexico. Isolated by pandemic. Job lost to economic shutdown. A history of depression. Walk up the cracked cement steps and knock to no answer. Find him there in the drab bedroom. Take the gun from his lifeless hand. Direct your steps to the perpetual ruins.

[The stage is now set for the final appeal which will name our need and beg for God's presence.]

Look upon our ruin, God. There is no prophet among us. We do not know how long. But, God, please, please, see us. See us, and do not leave us alone.

☙ ☙ ☙

Rather than beginning with our experiences of crisis and alienation, and then asking whether talk of God has any comfort to offer in their midst, the sermon invites the hearer to enter the world of the text and experience its frame, assumptions, and possibilities. Within that world, God is a given for us; even in our experience of God's absence we have no where else to turn in our grief. Emboldened by the text, we articulately insist that God look full upon us in our abandonment, bear witness to our loss, and accompany us in our godforsakeness. The sermon does not ask how useful the text can be in making sense of our experience framed in contemporary non-theological terms; it presumes and performs the almost tyrannical power of the textual world to shape our interpretation of experience.

Assessment: Strengths and Limitations in This Theological Family

> When I wrote *The Eclipse of Biblical Narrative*, I had liberals much more than conservatives in mind. And what I had in mind was the fact that if something didn't seem to suit the world view of the day, then liberals quickly reinterpreted it, or as we say today, "revised" it. And my sense of the matter though I'm not antiliberal, was that you can revise the text to suit yourself only just so far.[9]

Both the great strength and the great weakness—perhaps we should say "risk"—of postliberal theology and preaching are hinted at in the uncharacteristically unguarded quote, above.

The strength of the approach is that it shows the way forward for preaching that engages the biblical text with maximal seriousness and deference. And, as I have tried to show, this approach allows textual meaning to flourish without the distortions that impinge when an interpreter capitulates to the prevailing insistence that the Bible offer its fragile and all-important testimony in modes that (1) conform to the (early) modern obsession with verifiable facts, certitude, and mastery, or (2) can be translated into categories deemed more plausible to (late) modern sensibilities.

The weakness or "risk" of the approach has to do with what Paul Ricoeur has called the devastating possibility of "a lie in the heart of the witness."[10] Is biblical testimony faithful to the surprising and transformative truth about God and the blessed life, or is it—at least at certain points—corrupted by human idolatry, and guilty of perpetuating an unjust lie about God? Is the Bible misogynistic, racist, homophobic, and cisheteronormative, or is it ultimately the source of our awareness of and concern about all those things? Is it the voice of the past, incapable of addressing a radically connected and pluralistic emerging super-culture that seems

9. Frei, "Response," 208.
10. Ricoeur, "The Hermeneutics of Testimony," 128.

to be accelerating at an astonishing rate into a future so different we can scarcely imagine it? Or is it the harbinger of God's good future? If we give so little weight to other stories and their power to elucidate experience, if we surrender the independent analytical prowess that is our Enlightenment birthright, if we harness our reason and discipline our imaginations to work mostly within the logic and possibilities of the world proffered by the biblical text, will we become dangerous fools?

These are serious questions and they are not offered merely as a rhetorical foil for an answer that I will pretend to know. We cannot have real access to the Bible's momentous testimony without granting the text tremendous power over our imaginations. Granting such power is always a wager.

For Further Reading

Brueggemann, Walter. *The Practice of Prophetic Imagination: Preaching an Emancipating Word*. Minneapolis: Fortress, 2012.

Frei, Hans W. *The Eclipse of Biblical Narrative: A Study in Eighteenth and Nineteenth Century Hermeneutics*. New Haven: Yale University Press, 1974.

Lindbeck, George A. *The Nature of Doctrine: Religion and Theology in a Postliberal Age*. Philadelphia: Westminster, 1984.

Wallace, Mark. *The Second Naiveté: Barth, Ricoeur, and the New Yale Theology*. 2nd ed. Studies in American Biblical Hermeneutics. Macon: Mercer University Press, 1995.

5

Preaching in the Existentialist
Theological Family

O. WESLEY ALLEN JR.

EXISTENTIALIST THEOLOGY GROWS OUT of themes promoted by a range of philosophical thinkers (not all of whom embraced the label of "existentialists"). These thinkers examine human existence and ethics through various lenses of freedom and authenticity. Christian theologians who were influenced by existentialism examine human existence through these same lenses but shape and expand the thought in different directions as they related it to a theistic worldview. Christian preaching in this mode, then, invites hearers to live authentically in the face of finite freedom, as proclaimed and made possible through the gospel, rooted in a hermeneutic for interpreting ancient biblical texts in light of contemporary existentialist thought. A question to be asked of this movement is this: "What does it mean to live authentically?"

Circumstances That Gave Rise
to This Theological Family

The Enlightenment world view, which developed in the late 1700s and early 1800s, regarded reason as the source of truth. Enlightenment (or rationalist) thinkers turned to empirical observation from the senses, and especially from science, to establish truth. The results of these approaches caused advocates of the Enlightenment to question much of traditional Christian doctrine based on supernatural revelation that could not be empirically verified, and even sometimes drifted towards superstition.

In the nineteenth century, Friedrich Schleiermacher (1768–1834) laid the foundation for liberal theology by seeking to reconcile Enlightenment perspectives with traditional Christianity. He did this by claiming that core to Christian faith is religious "feeling," utter dependence on God, not some literal understanding of ancient dogmatic expressions found in Scripture and church teaching (e.g., the creeds) that do not make sense in a rationalist worldview. Much of Protestant thought in the nineteenth century (especially in the academic fields of biblical scholarship and theology), then, focused on making Christianity reasonable and palatable to the modern mind, erasing it of ancient superstitious claims the got in the way of true apprehension of eternal Christian claims.

From the point of view of many later theologians, however, the liberal movement mistranslated much of Christian thought into terms of Enlightenment-based humanism, an outlook that places the weight of concern on the human rather than the divine and has confidence in human reason's ability to solve the world's problems. Christianity was understood as a sort of modern moral disposition more than a set of doctrines.[1] Emphasizing human experience and thinking (over against divine revelation) as the primary source of knowledge and ethics, liberal theology valued the power of human reason to solve human problems to the exclusion of other resources for working at such issues. This optimism was sparked in part by new technological developments that were part and parcel of the Industrial Revolution, giving evidence, so they argued, of human ability to eventually overcome problems such as poverty and hunger. This thinking led a number of Christian thinkers in Germany (along with many other scholars, scientists, and artists) to support the kaiser as the world entered its first world war, associating support of the state with the moral obligation of humans to solve its problems. Immediately, however, this association lead many scholars who had been influenced by liberal theology to recognize its problems and reject it.[2]

Karl Barth (1886–1968) announced his perception of the failure of liberal theology most explicitly in his commentary on Paul's *Epistle to the Romans* (1919). Over against liberal theology, Barth emphasized the revelation of God as the source of Christian faith and theology, stressing

---

1. Indeed, many attempts during this period to research the historical Jesus characterized him in terms of a liberal theologian calling for inner transformation that leads to such a moral disposition.

2. In truth, many people held on to the nineteenth-century approach to liberal theology until World War II and the Holocaust showed that the very technology in which they had placed hope to solve the world's problems could be turned to the purposes of such horrific evil.

the transcendence of God to the point that it is impossible for humans to reason their way to God on the basis of philosophical and empirical observations or analogies.

Others who joined Barth in rejecting the place that nineteenth century theology had ended up saw his move as too extreme, as throwing out the baby with the bathwater. They still saw the need to connect ancient Scripture and tradition with contemporary reason, but they sought to do so without making the ancient a servant of the contemporary. They sought a focus on human potentiality being shaped by Christian faith that does not give in to an idolatry of that very human potentiality as seen in some forms of humanism.

One way some tried to do this was to draw on existentialist philosophy as a bridge between the ancient, supernatural, superstitious sources of Christian faith, thought, and practice and a contemporary, scientific view of the world and life in it. This theological approach was in line with the earlier thinking of Søren Kierkegaard (1813–1855) and contemporaneous philosophies of people like Jean-Paul Sartre (1905–1980) and Simone de Beauvoir (1908–1986). Especially influential in Germany was Martin Heidegger (1889–1976).

Existentialist thought flips philosophical methodology on its head with the assertion that existence precedes essence.[3] Instead of assuming that the inherent nature of something determines its existence (that is, the mere fact of its being), existentialists assert that humans determine or create their value and the meaning of their lives by the choices they make.

In this view, then, philosophy properly begins with problems and questions that arise out of my personal experience and being. Whatever knowledge we have grows out of our existing in concrete situations that force us to make concrete choices and reveal to us the limits of our finitude, with death being the ultimate limit. Angst is the natural response to this situation of finitude—the recognition that our freedom to determine our own existence is limited. While troubling, this anxiety is necessary in that without it we do not face the crisis that leads us to break free from inauthentic existence—living in the world of the ordinary as defined by the ordinary bondage of concern for the ordinary. Authentic existence, in contrast, looks in the face of finitude, recognizing that death can come at any moment, and realizes that every moment is one of great consequence and potential. Every moment has the potential to be *kairos* and not just *chronos*, because in every moment we choose who we are and what our

---

3. The following summary of key themes of existentialism is dependent upon Livingston et al., *Modern Christian Thought*, 133–38.

existence means. To live authentically is to decide to embrace the potential of the moment, courageously choosing not to be overwhelmed by the limits of finitude and follow the herd mentality of the inauthentic. As I point out further below, Christian existentialists think of the potential of the moment in theological terms.

Christian theologians who, in the mid-twentieth century, were unwilling to go as far as Barth in rejecting liberal theology's aims and drew instead on elements of existentialist thought to reform liberal theology range wide and include Teilhard de Chardin (1881–1955), Gabriel Marcel (1889–1973), Karl Rahner (1904–84), and John Macquarrie (1919–2007). By far, however, the two most influential voices in the conversation were Rudolf Bultmann (1884–1976) and Paul Tillich (1886–1965).

Bultmann was a New Testament scholar who drew on existentialism for the sake of hermeneutics.[4] He came to be influenced by the existentialist thought of his philosophical colleague Heidegger when they both taught at the University of Marburg. He argued that the modern mind could not accept the stories and beliefs of the ancient Scripture that explained phenomena in supernatural terms. Today, he contended, we view the world in terms of natural cause and effect, with scientific explanations for phenomena that were not available to ancient communities of faith. Moreover, we know that the universe is not physically structured with three tiers of heaven above, earth in the middle, and hell below.

Instead of rejecting ancient supernatural claims as unreasonable and thus dismissible in the way a Deist might, for instance, Bultmann argues that we should value them as myths, that is, as traditional stories explaining some natural phenomenon in supernatural terms in order to convey a deeper theological import not dependent on the historical or scientific factuality of the claim. In other words, using an existentialist perspective about human potentiality as a Rosetta Stone of sorts, interpreters are to translate the cosmological and supernatural elements of the Bible into anthropological, theological claims. In short, Bultmann argued that supernatural claims in the Bible were mythological ways of talking about the meaning of human existence before God and the potential of human existence in Christ.

Instead of a biblical scholar, Tillich was a theologian who drew on existentialist thought to shape his systematic theology.[5] In this attempt he argued for an ontology for God as Being-itself. As such, God does not

---

4. Bultmann's most accessible work that argues for a program of demythologization is *Jesus Christ and Mythology* (1958); his essay introducing the idea, however, was first published in 1941 and is titled "The New Testament and Mythology," available in *The New Testament and Mythology and Other Basic Writings*, 1–44.

5. Tillich, *Systematic Theology*.

exist alongside other beings, but is the source of all existence. Humans, dependent on God for their being, are filled with angst over their finitude unto death, leading to an estrangement from God and one's best self as dependent on God. The result of such angst is that we idolatrously place something other than—that is, less than—God as our ultimate concern (faith). Christ is the New Being that offers us life out of death, authentic existence in the face of our finitude.

Like Bultmann's, Tillich's theology was shaped apologetically to translate the Christian message into terminology and concepts acceptable to the modern age. He spoke of the claims and imagery of the Bible and church tradition more in terms of symbols than myths. Tillich's hermeneutics was a method of correlation in which he argued that the existential questions of modern (or any) culture could find their answers in the ancient symbols of the faith, so long as those symbols were not reduced by a literal interpretation. The symbols, again, represent ways of talking about the meaning of human existence before God and the potential of human existence in Christ.

Purposes and Characteristics of Preaching in This Theological Family

Bultmann and Tillich were both greatly concerned with preaching.[6] They wanted their students, readers, and the church broadly to be able to draw on biblical interpretation and theology to help proclaim the gospel of Jesus Christ in ways that the modern mind would find meaningful from the perspective of modern canons of truth. Both, in true Protestant fashion, thought of preaching as the Word of God through which Christ is present to listeners and offers to them authentic existence in Christ.

Preaching in the North American context has been shaped by these two existentialist thinkers in ways many preachers who are indebted to them are unaware, especially in the influence that the New Homiletic has had on the pulpit and the study of preaching.

Two students of Bultmann, Ernst Fuchs (1903–2015) and Gerhard Ebeling (1912–2001) took elements of Bultmann's existentialist hermeneutic and concerned themselves with contemporary interpretation as an *event* in which readers/hearers can experience the Bible as a word addressed to them today. Fred B. Craddock (1928–2015) studied Bultmann in his training as a New Testament scholar, spent a sabbatical studying under Ebeling, and drew on Kierkegaard in shaping his approach in what is often considered

---

6. For examples of their own preaching, see Bultmann, *This World and Beyond*; and Tillich, *The Shaking of the Foundations, The New Being,* and *The Eternal Now.*

the most important homiletical work of the twentieth century, *As One Without Authority*, and his later work *Overhearing the Gospel*. Craddock's existentialist bent is present for the reader looking for it, but it is covert and can be missed by those who only read him for method. Craddock's approach utilizes an inductive movement and evocative language and imagery that can fit with many different theological orientations. The goal of his approach, however, is existentialist in orientation: to create a sermonic event that offers the hearers an experience of the gospel found in the biblical text. This experience has the potential to effect transformation in the hearers (translation: the sermon as event can invite hearers to experience authentic existence). Indeed, in true existentialist fashion, Craddock argues for open-ended sermons that hearers must finish in the sense that they must choose how to respond authentically for themselves.

In a similar but more overt fashion, Charles L. Rice (1936–2018) drew on Tillich's hermeneutics to fund a homiletic anchored in story. In his 1970 work, *Interpretation and Imagination: The Preacher and Contemporary Literature*, Rice begins with Tillich's view that religion is the substance of culture and culture is the form of religion. Thus, says Rice, biblical preaching consists of translating the faith from the language system of an ancient culture into a contemporary cultural language system. Preachers seek a sort of resonance between the experience found in the ancient text and the experiences constitutive in contemporary culture (expressed best through the modern period's art and literature). Story interprets story in the sense that the colliding of ancient and contemporary stories transforms the stories of the hearers.[7]

While not all homileticians or preachers who were part of the New Homiletic were as shaped by existentialist thought as were Craddock and Rice, existentialist hermeneutics, understanding of language, and theology certainly found a home in this movement. And while few preachers in the early twenty-first century may consciously think in existentialist terms, many in the historically "mainline" tradition certainly reside in the broader liberal theological camp as it manifests itself today, rejecting the mythosymbolic character of the ancient stories of the Bible as being historically or scientifically factual, and translating the claims of the texts in terms of the contemporary culture and concerns of their congregations.

Indeed, hermeneutically speaking, preaching influenced by existentialist thought today has built on but also moved beyond methods of demythologization and correlation. Although a process thinker, Ronald J. Allen,

---

7. See also the book Rice coauthored with Edmund A. Steimle and Morris J. Niedenthal: Steimle et al., *Preaching the Story*.

has drawn on David Tracy's revisionist hermeneutic in arguing for mutual critical correlation in preaching.[8] Tracy expands the method of correlation to place contemporary experience and ancient Christian texts more in conversation with each other than Tillich allowed. Instead of the ancient texts providing symbolic answers for contemporary questions, both the ancient and contemporary can provide questions and answers, the contemporary religious dimension can challenge ancient religious claims.

But the potential of existentialist preaching in today's setting lies not only in its hermeneutic. In a postmodern era in which authority is held in suspicion and meaning-making is viewed as a local, relative endeavor, existentialism's view of the human condition as characterized by finite freedom that leads to both angst and possibility is spot on. Many today reject traditional truth claims for a self-constructed worldview. The secular existentialist philosophers of the mid twentieth century might well view elements of their proposals being fulfilled. In truth, however, people who reject traditional truth claims for a self-constructed world view are more often than not still shaped by cultural tides of which they are unaware and end up with worldviews that lack the consistency or depth to sustain and guide them in making meaning in the worst (or best) of times. A theist approach to existentialism can meld the individual approach to making meaning with a grounding in something bigger than one's own ability to construct a meaningful life and world.

When I started as dean of the chapel at a university, the college radio station thought it would be good programing to set me up against the outspoken atheist biology professor on campus. The twenty-year-old interviewer imagined throwing a bone between us and sitting back to watch us fight. So, her first question was about where the universe and specifically life on earth came from: big bang and evolution, or six days of creation by God? The biologist jumped in arguing for millions of years natural selection shaping life on earth as we know it. When I was given a chance to respond, I said, "I agree." He went on talking about the expansion of the universe going back billions of years to a natural "explosion" of all energy and matter, and I said, "I agree."

At this point the poor student looked despondent because the battle between science and religion she had set up seemed doomed to consensus. But the biologist would have none of it.

"What about the creation stories in Genesis, then?" I responded that at the literal level that I viewed them as the perspective of an ancient

---

8. See Allen, "Preaching as Mutual Critical Correlation."

mindset that could no longer be maintained, but that I saw them as speaking theologically at a metaphorical level.[9]

He would have none of this and accused me of exactly what Christian existentialists have often been accused: "That's a cop-out. You are just like me. You are an atheist but you just throw around a little religious language here and there."

But I argued that was not the case and asked him a question: "Am I correct in assuming that you think all meaning is internally or socially constructed?"

His answer was a simple yes.

I continued, "I do not. Without denying the importance of individual freedom or social systems for determining much of the boundary and potentiality of human existence, I ultimately believe that there is meaning external to me. And I believe that when life is oriented toward this external meaning, we find an authenticity and potentiality that we could not have imagined own our own. I call that external meaning God and believe I come to understand that meaning through Jesus Christ and through the Scriptures understood metaphorically."

He jumped in and interrupted me, "You are right we are different." And it is that salvific difference that existentialist preachers strive to offer their hearers over against the voices of the world telling us our meaning is small enough that we can control and create it all by ourselves.

Case Study: Text and Sermon
(Mark 5:25–34)

The following sermon is based on Mark 5:25–34, the story of the woman with a twelve-year hemorrhage seeking healing from Jesus. Mark intercalates the story with that of Jesus healing Jairus's daughter (5:22–24, 35–43), so that the two should be interpreted together. Christologically speaking, in both, Jesus's supernatural power is emphasized: he can raise the dead with a word and heal the chronically ill simply by being touched.

A modern, scientifically grounded theology, however, is not satisfied with such stories as worthy of an expression of ultimate reality when understood as a literal claim. Read mythologically, the stories' Christology serves anthropology, highlighting the effect experienced by the ones healed.

---

9. Sallie McFague (1933–2019) draws on but moves beyond Bultmann's understanding of biblical language as mythological and Tillich's understanding of it as symbolic to speak of *all* theological language (ancient and contemporary) as metaphorical in ways I think are more helpful today; see McFague, *Metaphorical Theology*.

The woman with the hemorrhage is an especially appealing character with whom to invite a congregation to identity in an existentialist, homiletical approach. Her actions of reaching out to touch Jesus signify the epitome of human freedom and authenticity. Yet, her freedom is finite, not extending to the point of being able to heal herself. For wholeness, she is utterly dependent on Jesus.

"FOMO"

[I begin the sermon with a contemporary experience of angst with which I hope listeners can identify.]

Some of you here may be old enough to remember a song from my childhood. It was the country music, crossover hit sung by Johnny Lee that was part of the soundtrack for the 1980 movie *Urban Cowboy*:

> I was lookin' for love in all the wrong places,
> Lookin' for love in too many faces,
> searchin' their eyes and lookin' for traces
> of what I'm dreamin' of.
> Hopin' to find a friend and a lover;
> I'll bless the day I discover
> another heart lookin' for love.

In addition to the obvious romantic intentions of the one speaking in the song, the lyrics became a metaphor for looking for fulfillment, satisfaction, etc., in all the wrong places. I'll bet many a preacher back in the early eighties talked about sin as looking for love in all the wrong places instead of finding it in God.

A more contemporary expression of a similar idea is that of FOMO. I must admit the first time I heard my teenage daughter mention this, I had a little dyslexia and almost washed her mouth out with soap. But FOMO is the Fear Of Missing Out. This anxiety is the birthchild of 9/11 and digital media. As one article that traces the origin of the term puts it, after terrorist crashed planes into the World Trade Center and the Pentagon, young people, especially those geographically close to the attacks, "felt the need to do everything all the time because [they'd] seen [their] own mortality."[10] Out of this grew a "sometimes all-consuming feeling that something's happening and they're not a part of it." So people would wait for the last minute to

---

10. Schrekneringer, "The Home of FOMO."

commit to a social opportunity, constantly checking their texts, Facebook, Instagram, in case something better might come along.

> *[Having named FOMO as a cultural phenomenon, I deepen the diagnosis, demonstrating that it is a manifestation of existential angst. That is, FOMO serves as a lens for seeing the difficulty with living authentically.]*

But this fear has grown beyond concerns about what young people are going to do for entertainment on the weekend. Psychological and sociological studies have been written on FOMO as a defining phenomenon of our age. It is the anxiety that "Wherever you deposited yourself at any moment, you were setting yourself up for failure, relatively speaking." We cannot live in the moment because whatever we are doing at the moment might be setting us up to miss what could be possible in the next.

FOMO is more than the stuff of memes making fun of young people so focused on looking for a good time that they never have one. It expresses a core element of the human condition of people of all ages in which we are so focused on looking for others to provide us with a life worth living that we, well, never chose a life worth living for ourselves. We try to fight off a sense of meaningless, a fear of our own mortality, by unconsciously striving to be a part of the right crowd at the right time: the right social class, the right neighborhood, the right school district, the right groups of friends at school, the right political party, attending the right school, rooting for the right sports team, getting the right job, watching the right news station, even being a member of the right church.

It's not that caring about some of these things are wrong in and of themselves. In fact, participating in community that stands for good things is a good thing. The point is that, in the end, following the crowd, any crowd, will not provide the ultimate meaning and salvation we all seek.

> *[The exposition of Mark 5:25–34 that follows exhibits the two sides of existentialist hermeneutics. First, it acknowledges the problem with reading the story of a supernatural miracle literally. Second, it translates the story in soteriological-anthropological terms.]*

In our Scripture reading for today, we find a woman who is following the crowd. Now on the surface level, this scene presents a story in which the woman is healed by a supernatural miracle, something that is hard to relate to today. But underneath the surface, Mark constructs the story to offer more. It is an ancient metaphor for FOMO.

Mark characterizes the woman as having had a perpetual menstrual period for twelve years. She has been suffering physically and socially. The constant flow of blood would have rendered her ritually unclean by ancient standards. This would have led to some serious restrictions on her social and religious life. She had gone to doctor after doctor after doctor, but healing alluded her. Even though she spent every cent she had on the doctors, she grew worse. She was searching for wholeness in all the wrong places.

Now she finds herself in a crowd. Just one among many. Faceless, meaningless, just moving with the flow of the herd. But making an appearance in the crowd is Jesus. Just before this scene, Mark has told of Jairus approaching Jesus to ask him to come heal his daughter. Right after this scene, Jesus will find that she has already died, but he will raise her from the dead. This technique Mark uses of framing one story with another is a way to make us see the stories as having a shared interpretation. It is clear, then: while the woman with hemorrhage is not on the verge of dying from her ailment, the issue is one of life and death for her. To be stuck in the crowd, viewed as unclean, is surely to be dead.

But then Mark portrays the woman as doing something extraordinary. Most women in the Bible are stock characters with little agency. But this woman, weakened by the constant loss of blood, exhibits extraordinary strength. She makes a choice. She chooses not to simply stay stuck in the crowd. She chooses to act independently of the herd. So, she reaches out and touches Jesus's robe to get the healing she needs. The crowd and its doctors can't bring her wholeness. She can't make herself whole. But when she chooses so, Jesus can and does.

Mark paints a picture of Jesus as one who know when power leaves him, and he asks, "Who touched me?" The disciples can only see the crowd of which they are a part, a crowd bumping into Jesus but not intentionally, authentically reaching out to place a finger on Jesus's robe. But the woman confesses. When Jesus hears what she has done, does he get angry that a woman didn't know her place in the crowd and reached out and touched him? No, he calls her choice "faith," and says that it saved her.

If we read this story at the surface level, we might think it argues that we don't need doctors and nurses and vaccines and bandages, and surgeries. We just need to turn to Jesus and we will be healed of physical ailments. But I have attended too many funerals in life to be willing to reduce this story to that kind of nonsense. At a deeper level, Mark offers us a story that shows that only when we are willing to break from the herd and choose to place our full dependence on Jesus are we resurrected from death to new life, here and now.

[At this point, the sermon transitions from the ancient back to the contemporary. As FOMO served as a lens for inauthentic existence, the woman's choice to reach out and touch Jesus to find wholeness serves as a lens for viewing transformative moments of choosing to live authentically today.]

As surely as you experience times of FOMO in your life, I'll bet you experience moments like this as well. Times when in the midst of the death-dealing world you know life in its fullness, life that comes not from being part of the crowd, but from standing out from the crowd exactly where and how God wants you to be.

I hear stories about these kinds of moments all the time from my seminary students. Life seemed fine for the most part. Family life. Work life. Even church life. Fine. But not right. They had a sense of calling that they had ignored, denied, maybe even fought. Until finally they reached out and touched Jesus's robe. Gave up a good-paying job and struggling to get by with school bills. Family pressures have increased. Studies are hard, especially for those who haven't been in school for a long time. But life . . . life is not just fine. It is good, it is right, it is now whole.

In 2012 Ken Parker joined the Ku Klux Klan in Georgia. He rose to the ranks of grand dragon. The crowd he was following was not radical enough for him so he joined a neo-Nazi group. He followed this crowd to Charlottesville, Virginia, in 2017 to stand up for the White race. While he was there, however, just hours before Heather Heyer was run down and killed, Parker bumped into to a brown-skinned Muslim woman who was a filmmaker. He was experiencing heat exhaustion, and she showed him kindness in spite of the alt-right group he was with and his swastika tattoos.

Parker puzzled over her actions—actions that went completely against his own hate and his stereotype of her—that one day not long after, out of the blue he approached an African American man having a cookout at his apartment complex. The man let him ask whatever he wanted. It ended up that the man was a pastor, and after several conversations, he invited Parker to his church for Easter worship. He experienced a little resurrection that day and soon he stood up before the congregation, the Black congregation, and confessed who he was. The congregation was stunned but instead of shunning him, they all came forward and hugged him. That summer, just a little less than a year after Charlottesville, Parker traded in his KKK robe for a baptismal robe. It was slow, but he found the strength to step out from the crowd, reach out, and grab hold of Jesus's jacket. And he walked out of his tomb of racism and hate and experienced resurrection in a God of love and justice.

Every choice we have is one between following the crowd into death or stepping from the crowd to follow Christ into wholeness of life. Every choice can be driven by the fear of missing out on who the world says we ought to be and faith in God's claim on who we are. But you already knew that. You may not be called into ministry and I certainly don't imagine you are neo-Nazi, but you make smaller, but just as real, life and death choices a hundred times each day. Every time you choose what to post on Facebook, every time you choose what to say to the classmate who made fun of you, every time you choose what kind of company to invest in, every time you choose how to respond to the person asking for money at the intersection, every time you choose how to approach a task at work, every time you choose to take a stance on a political issue, every time you decide what to do with your leisure time, every time you make any choice at all you are choosing who you are. You know that with each and every choice you can either shuffle along with the crowd or you can reach out and take hold of Jesus's robe and see where Life takes you instead.

Assesment: Strengths and Limitations in This Theological Family

The interest in existentialist philosophy seen in the early and mid-twentieth century has greatly diminished in the late twentieth and early twenty-first centuries. Yet existentialist themes, such as authentic selfhood of the individual, has significant resonance with the evolving postmodern culture. Preachers can find in existentialist theology an approach to offer postmoderns meaning when they may be inclined to see the world as meaningless without forcing them to forsake the whole of their worldview.

Yet one reason many have seen existentialism as falling short of the full breadth of the gospel is its emphasis on the individual over the social. By placing existence (of the individual) before essence (of all), concern for the common good can be displaced. What does individual authentic existence have to do with social justice?

In response to this concern, we should first recognize that Bultmann and especially Tillich drew on existentialist thought to argue against Nazism in Germany.[11] (Of course, like most philosophies and theologies, this

---

11. Tillich delivered hundreds of radio addresses condemning Nazism, collected in Stone and Weaver, eds., *Against the Third Reich*; Bultmann's public response was not as strong as Tillich's, but, especially after Heidegger publicly supported the Nazi Party, Bultmann joined the Confessing Church and preached that Aryanism was unchristian.

can cut both ways. Heidegger used existentialism as a basis for his support of the Nazi regime).

Second, existentialist thought does offer insight into systemic forms of violence and oppression but simply comes at the issue from a different angle than other approaches. For the existentialist, the root of the human dilemma is the estrangement of the self. This inner brokenness, then, leads to individuals harming their neighbors, which in turn leads to corporate forms of inequity and injustice.[12] The problem, however, is that existentialist theology does not then provide a clear answer to that corporate sin. It neither clearly explains how it is addressed by God or how it should be addressed by human communities. This means, at least for this author, any appropriation of existentialism today must be supplemented by thought from other schools, especially the various strands of liberation theologies, to be able to preach the fullness of the gospel found in Christian Scripture and tradition.

For Further Reading

Flynn, Thomas R. *Existentialism: A Very Short Introduction.* Very Short Introductions 153. Oxford: Oxford University Press, 2006.

Kelsey, David H. "Paul Tillich." In *The Modern Theologians: An Introduction to Christian Theology in the Twentieth Century,* edited by David F. Ford, 87–102. 2nd ed. Malden, MA: Blackwell, 1997.

Livingston, James C., et al. "Christian Existentialism." In *Modern Christian Thought.* Vol. 2, *The Twentieth Century,* 133–64. 2nd ed. Minneapolis: Fortress, 2006.

Morgan, Robert. "Rudolf Bultmann." In *The Modern Theologians: An Introduction to Christian Theology in the Twentieth Century,* edited by David F. Ford. 68–86. 2nd ed. Malden, MA: Blackwell, 1997.

Wicks, Robert L. *Introduction to Existentialism: From Kierkegaard to the Seventh Seal.* New York: Bloomsbury Academic, 2019.

12. See Allen, *Preaching and the Human Condition,* 99–118.

6

Preaching in the Radical Orthodox Theological Family

ALISON MILBANK

SERENDIPITY WAS THE CAUSE of the now worldwide theological sensibility called Radical Orthodoxy (RO). John Milbank, Catherine Pickstock, and Graham Ward, the editors of the original volume of essays that launched this movement, happened to be teaching and studying at the University of Cambridge in the 1990s. Five other contributors to the collection were graduate students in the same faculty of Divinity, although it also contained contributions by American scholars such as William T. Cavanaugh. RO quickly became thoroughly ecumenical, with adherents in Orthodox, Catholic, Lutheran, Reformed, and even Pentecostal churches, but the original editorial triad was not only high church Anglican but worshiped at the same parish church, Little St Mary's. Place, particularity, and community are central to this theology, so this "local habitation" is appropriate to mention. The movement also continues: a number of the sermon contributors to the more recent *Preaching Radical and Orthodox* collection who have been at it some time, are members of this congregation and/or its sister Anglo-Catholic church in Oxford, St Mary Magdalene.[1] RO has attracted young theologians who are concentrated in the United Kingdom in these two universities but is now global, with adherents everywhere from South Africa to Hong Kong.

The original Cambridge focus indicates the highly intellectual nature of this movement, which has enormously ambitious aims that have provoked much controversy from ecclesial conservatives and liberals alike. As

1. Milbank et al., eds., *Preaching Radical and Orthodox*, ix–xiii. Over twenty of the contributors and all three editors have this association.

73

Simon Oliver argues, RO is neither neo-orthodox in seeking to "shore up theology's identity or legitimacy by defining a peculiar subject matter, usually revelation," nor is it liberal in allowing other discourses to position it. Instead, it seeks to restore theology as the queen of the sciences. It is radical in the literal sense of going back to roots and it offers a complete reinterpretation of the usual account of the onset of secularism.

Although sometimes criticized as too intellectual, this is quite unfair. In order to make a new argument about Western intellectual history, RO must speak the languages of philosophy, postmodernism, literary and political theory. It has been applied to everything from the history of science to the genealogy of law. In this short summary, I shall indeed argue that RO offers a theological history, but equally that it offers a real praxis as well as politics, and to demonstrate its practical implications for the Christian life, to make ready for its hermeneutics of preaching.

Circumstances That Gave Rise to This Theological Family

"Imagine," commands John Lennon, and rather tiresomely invites his hearers to imagine removing experiential realities such as religion. One originating text of the RO movement, John Milbank's *Theology and Social Theory* of 1991, invites us to do the opposite. It begins in the manner of a fairy tale, "Once there was no secular," but as in Tolkien's account of the Incarnation, this is a fairy-tale that is true.[2] We are invited to reimagine the history of the last five hundred years away from the narrative of progress and secularization that dominates our usual cultural story and squeezes religion nearly out of existence. This is a narrative that matters because it affects the ordinary lay Christian. Secularism runs through the church as well as society at large. As Charles Taylor points out, we have moved from "a society in which it was virtually impossible not to believe in God, to one in which faith, even for the staunchest believer, is one human possibility among others."[3]

RO argues that secularism was not a natural removal of the superstitious elements of religion towards a value-free, enlightened public space, but a competing ideology and bad theology. Its narrative here is parallel to that of Charles Taylor's magisterial *A Secular Age*, as he acknowledges, and it shares the ascription of the origin of secularism in medieval metaphysical debates, in which increasingly, God's otherness, which guarantees human participation in the divine life (see below) is compromised by a univocity of

2. Milbank, *Theology and Social Theory*, 1.
3. Taylor, *A Secular Age*, 3.

being, in which human beings and the divine come to be conceived as upon a continuum. Paradoxically, Catharine Pickstock argues, this pushes God further away, across infinity, and opens up a flattened space between God and humankind, in which revelation must intervene, thus, in the end, separating faith and reason.[4] The RO critique of nominalism is highly technical and complex, and there is little room to articulate it here. Taylor's *Secular Age* demonstrates its effects on what it is to be human and to its role in disenchanting the cosmos, making way for the mechanistic understanding of nature and the withdrawal of God from creation. Australian theologian Tracey Rowlands has discussed the importance of a nondualist account of grace and nature in contemporary theological debate and how a concept of pure nature accompanies an autonomous secular sphere.

This history matters because it has strong implications for the mystical practice of RO, the heart of which is an understanding of our calling as Christians to share in the life of God himself through participation (*methexis*) and deification (*theosis*). This opens up a communality between RO and Eastern Orthodox theology, since this tradition has cherished these ancient Christian mystical ideas, which declined in the West due to the increasing separation between nature and grace. RO is a form of Christian Platonism, which does not denigrate the material but believes that it can be itself raised to participation in God, as Christ did in his incarnation. RO views participation as sharing in God's own creativity and is expressed in poetry, music, and making of all kinds.

Such a theology depends upon a classic idea of God not as a Being or even Being but its source. God creates ex nihilo, freely and out of his own overflowing life and love. Creation is sheer gift, a gifting that is within the life of the Trinity itself. We are not in competition with God but share in his life analogically. God's otherness as our cause enables intimacy with him, as in a lover's touch. As Thomas Aquinas writes, "because in all things God Himself is properly the cause of universal being which is innermost in things; it follows that in all things God works intimately."[5] The Aquinas of RO is the Thomas who preserves the mystery of God, who questions how we can speak of God at all, but is equally the Aquinas who demonstrates that we can glimpse in the radiance of every creature a sign of its divine createdness, its origin. RO therefore combines a negative and a positive theology rather in the manner of the sixth-century Syrian theologian Dionysius the Areopagite, in whose letters particularly, positive statements about God reveal their inadequacy and are negated but are later retrieved at a new level

---

4. Pickstock, "Duns Scotus."
5. Thomas Aquinas, *Summa Theologica* 1a, 105.1.

in an interplay of assertion and denial. The incarnation of God himself is 'hidden even amid the revelation."[6]

RO thus offers a mystical quest into the divine. Its strong hold on God's otherness and creation ex nihilo denies the primacy of evil and embraces the traditional idea of the privation theory, whereby evil is but parasitic upon the good. In this nondualist theology, difference is peaceable, as it is within the Trinity itself. In this way, the devotional praxis opens on to politics and ecclesiology. RO denies the nihilism in competitive modes of economic theory, arguing for mutuality, reciprocity, and virtue in markets and economic practice. Its politics varies between adherents but is always radical. It crosses political divides, standing for the importance of the family, local community and subsidiarity and tradition in ways that would be thought conservative, even valuing virtuous hierarchy, while severely and radically critiquing capitalism. It is highly committed to ecology, as in the work of Michael Northcott.

As for Stanley Hauerwas, an influence on the movement, Christianity is itself a political praxis, a peaceable kingdom of reconciliation and mutual forgiveness. The sacraments of baptism and the eucharist embody a politics in which Christians live out their faith in non-identical repetition or "repetition with variety" of Christ.[7] We enter a realm of gift, receiving the Spirit in baptism and confirmation in order to pass on the gift. In the eucharist we are part of the offering of Christ, as his body on earth.

RO is also viewed scandalously for its positive and hopeful view of the church, which it takes some heroism to hold to in these dark and degenerate times. This mystical understanding is, however, wholly biblical, the theology of the Pauline epistles. RO embraces and has contributed to the new philosophical interpretation of Saint Paul. RO sympathizer David Bentley Hart has gone so far as to translate the New Testament, stressing against Protestant extrinsic understandings of justification, the synergistic union of our spirit with the Holy Spirit, and the strong emphasis on the participation of the whole creation in salvation.

RO scandalizes because it looks back to roots at a time in which the past, and institutions with histories, are universally judged negatively. And yet it is far from nostalgic, believing that only as we look back can we imagine doing things differently in the future. RO scholars such as Conor Cunningham and Michael Hanby engage evolutionary theory and modern physics. Many RO theologians engage contemporary philosophical attempts at materialist metaphysics. RO is both orthodox, in rejoicing in the Christian creeds, and

6. Pseudo-Dionysius, *Complete Works*, 264.
7. Milbank, *The Word Made Strange*, 64; Pickstock. *Repetition*.

postmodern in its critique of Enlightenment rationalism, believing that the only power Christianity has is the compelling truth of its story. Our writings range widely from Angel Mendez Montoya's theology of food to John Hughes on daily work because as for C. S. Lewis, theology is not one subject among many, but through Christ offers a lens through which everything and every subject matter can be viewed and understood.

I began this brief outline with three young theologians at church in a university town. Above all RO is rooted in particularity and liturgical participation, in which we learn to live in Paradise, where we model ethics, politics and friendship and mutual forgiveness. In the parochial setting, people of different ages, races, cultures and classes learn peaceable difference and the tools to transform the world. And it is within this setting that the sermon finds its place.

Purposes and Characteristics of Preaching in This Theological Family

Preaching in RO circles is most usually in the context of the eucharist. Even when it occurs at a service of the word it is always divine worship, a movement in the action of the liturgy and never seen as a separate element. For the purposes of this article, I shall describe the character of preaching in a eucharistic context.

Every aspect of such preaching has the purpose of enabling participation, our key feature of theological aim and practice. Indeed, we might describe our homilies as mystagogic in the manner of early church proclamation, in which congregations were being initiated into the mysteries of the sacraments. As with the Barthians, for us preaching makes something happen: it is an event in that sense in which the gospel is proclaimed. It is, however, a part of a larger action or event, in which it nourishes its hearers on the Word, and prepares them to lift up their hearts in eucharistic thanksgiving. It is then one part of a movement that gathers a group of people into Christ's body, ready to be part of the offering, to be transformed. One image I find powerful is Mary of Bethany's jar of precious ointment in John 12:3, which is broken open to anoint Christ, revealing his role as Messianic king and pointing to his death. The preacher opens the Scriptures like a jar, and the whole people are bathed in its scent. That visceral sense of smell is so important to the Bethany sequence: Christ, the resurrection and the life will turn the stench of the corpse in John 11:39 to the sweet perfume of new life, which fills the whole house.

Another Mary models the second feature of RO preaching: Mary Magdalene, the apostle to the apostles. She is the first Christian preacher, sent by Christ himself in John 20.17 to "go to my brothers and say to them: 'I am ascending to my Father and your Father, to my God and your God.'" In later implicitly feminist legend, she takes the gospel to the South of France, where her preaching is so persuasive that the local people destroy their idols and become Christians. Any act of preaching must similarly be prophetic in revealing the constructedness of idols and questioning the secular, both as an autonomous realm apart from God and in all its injustice. In the legend Mary Magdalene appears in a dream to the queen to denounce her for ignoring the needs of the poor. There are various ways in which this breaking open of the secular can be achieved, whether by preaching from the prophets, or by calling attention to our assumption of the secular as the lens by which we understand our experience: showing the outline of what Charles Taylor calls the "immanent frame" of a naturalistic account of human life and thereby questioning its limit.[8] A third way may be by reenchanting and deepening the mystery of our daily lives and seemingly secular arenas, to demonstrate that there is no "outside."

What directs and constrains the manner of the prophetic witness for RO preaching is the lectionary. It is shaped by the liturgical year and therefore decenters us from secular time and births us within sacred time. Many mainline denominations share a common lectionary, which gives three readings for a eucharist: from the Old Testament (often the prophets), the New Testament epistles or other writings, and the gospel. The value of this approach for preaching is that it forces the preacher to address the whole of salvation history, and to understand how the Old and New Testaments interpret each other. It prevents preachers from selecting the parts of the Bible they prefer and teaches humility as preachers submit themselves to the Word. If Christians are called to repeat the life of Christ with variety, as asserted above, then the sermon is the site of productive mimesis, situated within the tensions and challenges of interpreting these diverse readings. The triad of readings enacts a narrative ontology, by which the hearers are woven within the text and the texts into their lives.

The gospel procession expresses this truth. In the Anglican/Episcopal tradition, an extensive version of this procession has evolved, in which the Gospel book is taken from east to west, right down into the middle of the people, raised to show its holiness. On its return, it is not raised, as the Word has entered the people, who will similarly move east to offer the gifts and then themselves in the act of communion, finally sent out, the Word in their hearts

---

8. Taylor, *A Secular Age*, 542–57.

and minds. As we wrote in *Preaching Radical and Orthodox,* "the interpretation of Scripture by the people of God is part of the Bible's inspiration, by which it continues to be breathed upon by the Spirit."[9]

Unsurprisingly, the theology of participation lies at the heart of RO preaching, which aims to be performative: to flood the church with the perfume of Mary's jar and raise us to unite with angels and archangels at the heavenly altar. To use the language of Christian mystical ascent, if the idol-breaking is purification, the use of the lectionary illumination, participation models the ecstatic action of union. Teaching within liturgical homiletics is not so much discursive as formative, shaping and directing the soul like a stone flung from a catapult. It should awaken desire for God, and it may do that through connecting with experiences people may already have but not name or by engendering that longing which is the opening to faith. The Christian Platonism of RO allows the erotic in its broadest sense to lead the soul to God, and beauty, widely and cruciformly understood, is the lure. Christ "hung deformed upon the cross. But his deformity was our beauty: as Saint Augustine wrote.[10] "Beauty," writes Dionysius, "'bids all things to itself,' 'like a light it flashes onto everything the beauty-causing impartations of its own well-spring ray."[11] It causes beauty in us and in everything, so the beauty of the gospel proclamation both draws our desire and makes us its reflective mirror, to shine beauty out upon the world of people and creatures.

For, as Elaine Scarry has taught us, beauty is distributive: it causes us to be just.[12] It makes us aware of the irreplaceable particularity of things, their value and vulnerability. The vision of beauty makes the viewer vulnerable too. And the turning of the self back to God from sinful self-alienation is part of the action of participation. There must be purification and a decentering from the self in an act of *metanoia,* so that we may become porous to the light and love of God. It is the charism of RO that the lure of what Augustine called "beauty so old and so new" can provoke this turning. RO preaching in that sense is thoroughly orthodox, in the literal sense of that word as "right praise," which comes from a sense of being drawn into self-offering and self-forgetfulness in the sea of God's mystery.

Scarry also says that "beauty brings copies of itself into being."[13] This is the RO idea that we are called to act as Christ in repetition with variety. A

9. Milbank, *Preaching Radical and Orthodox,* 3.

10. Augustine, *Sermons,* sermon 27 (page 107).

11. Pseudo-Dionysius, *Complete Works,* 76.

12. Scarry, *On Beauty and Being Just.*

13. Scarry, *On Beauty and Being Just,* 21.

homily should so move the hearers that they become part of its gospel as gifts to the world. A Christian life-story in all its failures and quest for holiness can be engendering of story. So, the last element of RO preaching lies in its use of the lives of the saints, broadly understood, so that this encompasses anyone whose life has this production of story, whether it is Mary Magdalene, the potential of whose preaching to the disciples is realized in later legends of active ministry, or a person encountered the week before. These are people whose lives offer a cruciform beauty and offer a fit with the life of Christ, illuminating the gospel and our own quest to embody a life shaped by the beauty of holiness. Just as the gospel book returns lowered as the good news is embodied in the hearers, so the story of holiness must be beautiful, so that it is welcomed and relived in retellings and incorporation.

An example told to me in a homily comes from a Quaker home where a little girl asks to spend time with her baby sister alone. The parents peep in to check. The little girl makes not too hearty an attempt to pick up her sister from the cot, only to hear the child on the cot whisper: "Can you tell me what heaven is like? Because I've forgotten." This is not just an example of a charming child narrative but offers real truth. The little girl's faith and understanding of her divine origin takes the breath away. Young children do, as psychological experiments have verified, have a truly metaphysical understanding of reality.

This story is truly memorable because it reestablishes a life as one lived from God that engenders productive story. The narrative makes the Christian doctrine of creation strange—it defamiliarizes it—so that we can receive it back freshly as true, made doubly so by the child's experience. It is beautiful and distributive in that it sheds on all lives the luster of eternity. Here Christianity out-narrates the atheist account of reality. You only have to look at a baby to see its truth, that we are more than we seem.

I have thus described some key elements of RO preaching. RO's articulation as philosophical theology might be intellectually expressed, but its preaching embodiment reveals its theurgic heart, that the lowest is raised liturgically to the highest, to divine union. First, preaching is part of this movement, not an event in itself but part of a performative action. Secondly, it humbly accords itself to the lectionary, and situates its hearers in sacred time. Thirdly, it has a prophetic element, calling into question the limits secularism puts on Christian witness, and the idols we accept as real. Fourthly, it is participatory, in provoking desire for God and a longing for union; and fifthly, it offers Christian lives as nonidentical repetitions, improvisations on Christ's example, which are generative and gift-giving as they are themselves responses to God's initiating gift of himself. RO is a sensibility and a charism, and we all do it differently, but this is my own understanding. If readers say:

"but this is just how I preach!" that is part of the point of RO, to call us back to our roots, to take account of contemporary philosophical challenges, and to re-found our orthodoxy on generous and life-giving foundations. Even what is written in this section assumes quite complex theological assumptions but can be incorporated into a children's catechetical program.

Case Study: Text and Sermon
(Matthew 13:31–33, 44–52; Romans 8:26–39)

This sermon aims to open the experience of union with the divine and embody participation, the third RO homiletic feature, and to do so quite openly by discussing religious experience. It has the task of discussing three eucharistic readings set for the fifth Sunday after Trinity, and unite Jacob's marriage to Leah and Rachel, St Paul's great passage on nothing separating us from the love of Christ, and a group of parables. That day I certainly had a task submitting humbly to the lectionary, as in our second principle of preaching.

The phrase that started me off was Jesus's comparison of his own teaching practice to a householder bringing out "treasures old and new." It made me think of the wonder of our local ironmonger's (hardware) store and offered a lure to provoke desire for God in an example that would speak to us all. For me, there is unacknowledged beauty in the hardware store, which offered an opportunity to reveal the sacred nature of the seemingly mundane, and question the separation of the secular, as in the second RO principle. The theological account of RO above discusses the interweaving of positive and negative theology and that is made the subject of this sermon, with reference to Dionysius. The way of images is contrasted with Paul fighting off anything that separates us from God as an example of the negative way.

While there is no individual example here for mimetic appropriation, the sermon aims to make each hearer an example by examining their experiences of particularity and the beyond and making those generative, folding them into the gospel paradigm of the parable as something thrown down to open up our understanding of reality. A poem is brought in at the end to draw together the threads of the way of images and its ascesis with the Christian poet as an example of the scribe of the kingdom, but without analyzing it. The aim is to leave the images open to the imagination of the hearers—"Give every image space and air / To grow"—like the mustard seed of the parable, so that the words become generative in the manner of the parables themselves. The poem is then reinterpreted in the context of eucharistic thanksgiving and reception, in which the congregation itself becomes the offering and the image.

"Treasures Old and New"

I offer you some words from our Gospel reading: "Therefore every scribe who has been trained for the kingdom of heaven is like the master of a household who brings out of his treasure what is old and what is new" (Matt 13:52). Whenever I hear these words my thoughts conjure up the paraffin smell and Aladdin's cave complexity of an ironmonger's shop, like the Handicenter here in Southwell. Do you want tap washers, cake icing funnels, rivets, clothes dye, radiator keys, bird food or light-bulbs? One of the many expert staff will disappear into the back and return quietly triumphant with treasures as old as a piece of iron for a Victorian fender or as new as the latest power-hose. They have it all. Fine pearls possibly not: but the nets and mustard seed of the parables quite certainly.

[Here I establish the lure: a shared experience of specificity and abundance which I want to reveal as beautiful and use to demonstrate the theurgic raising of the lowest to presence and meaning.]

Like me, the Victorian Jesuit poet Gerard Manley Hopkins found spiritual value in this kind of stuff—he writes lyrically of "all trades, their gear and tackle and trim" in his poem, "Pied Beauty." In the twenty-first century, so much of our technology hides its working; perfectly good cell phones are discarded for the latest model, but in the hardware store all the various objects that mend things and keep our houses and gardens together are given their due importance, as are the tools of the trades of plumber, joiner and builder. I stand bemused in a trance of wonder before the fifty different sizes of brass screw, each of which serves a particular purpose, and only one of which will fit the hinge in my cupboard door. The array of brush-heads makes me long to sweep something, and who can resist the rope as thick as your arm or as narrow as a baby's finger? These objects are full of presence: they speak of a world of great richness and particularity. For me the kingdom of heaven is like a heaving hardware store.

[The theological grounding of this experience is asserted and the Incarnation introduced as justifying the sacrality of any person or object.]

This approach to reality is utterly Christian in being incarnational. In a world in which God himself took flesh, objects like those in the parables and their surprising behaviour speak to a depth of meaning in the physical world, which materialism cannot capture. Nails can only reveal their full naily quality when we see them as participating in a divine cosmos, in which each nail proclaims its thisness and particularity in a blaze of being. In this positive way, love of nails or flowers or people can be a path to God, because they each reveal something of Him in their own particular way and have a specific role to play.

> [The negative way is introduced by a particular reading of the Romans passage and as an experiential reality for some people.]

But there is another equally important spiritual emphasis in Christianity, represented by St Paul's concluding words in our epistle, often used to powerful effect at funeral services: "For I am convinced that neither death, nor life, nor angels, nor rulers, nor things present, nor things to come, nor powers, nor height, nor depth, nor anything else in all creation will be able to separate us from the love of God in Christ Jesus our Lord." (Rom 8:38) Here, the powers and objects of the created order are viewed as obstacles—possibly opponents—to our access to the divine love. St Paul is metaphorically fighting them off to stress a direct relation with Christ. Here, other mediators are all rejected and, to quote John Henry Newman, "heart speaks to heart." There are some people, and you may be one of them, to whom God speaks directly "heart to heart," who are what are called mystics. You may feel Christ holding you, or, like John of the Cross, sometimes reach a state in which you do not feel a separate person at all but one with God—in a kind of intimate darkness.

> [RO stresses "ressourcement," the French twentieth-century movement of recuperating origins and here the Old Testament reading is brought in as a unifying trope for positive and negative ways in the manner of early and medieval modes of allegorical exegesis.]

In Christian tradition, this second path is called the negative or apophatic way; the first the positive or kataphatic. Early Christian writers called the first Leah and the second Rachel, those wives of Jacob whom we heard of. In our first reading. Leah with the lovely eyes was the active life, in which one used one's eyes to encounter God and bless Him in the nails, bricks, cakes and babies of the life of work or family. Beloved Rachel was the contemplative life in which the soul seeks to ascend to God directly. Putting our epistle and gospel side by side, however, we can see that, like Jacob, we do not have to choose between Leah and Rachel. Indeed, as in the Genesis story, Leah can actually lead to Rachel. Attending to the world—watching swallows swooping round the eaves of a house, making parabolas of delight and freedom—you too may find yourself part of their ecstatic action, and go beyond images. Listening to music you may touch the quick of reality; in a beloved person you may catch the beauty of God; in the eyes of a dying person enter the infinite. And the holiest contemplative hermit—there are surprisingly many of them out there—needs images of some sort. Even our Lord himself is the image of God, and we all need the mediation of the Holy Spirit, who intercedes "with sighs too deep for words" (Rom 8:26).

[The negative way is linked back to Dionysius but the interplay of both asserted and again related to people's own experience, to draw them into participation.]

The way of negation or mystical theology owes a great deal to the writings of a Syrian priest of the sixth century, who called himself Dionysius after Paul's convert at Athens. But he did not give up using images; rather his procedure was to meditate on the images of Scripture, until he was aware of their limitations, and went beyond them. Yet he writes, there would come a time when he would return to these same images and find in them a deeper meaning on the other side of their negation. If you have ever had a moment of union, of self-forgetfulness, you will know that when you come to yourself, the environment around you seems suddenly brighter, more vivid, sharper and more defined. For Christian mysticism returns us to the world, to the yeast and the nets and the mustard seeds of the parables: so simple, so obvious in a way, and yet so profound. St Paul, indeed, has a vision of the whole created order being liberated by the resurrection, when nothing, from nail to plant to people, will be lost in the heavenly hardware store.

[Recapitulation of the theme and return to where we started]

So if you want a truly mystical experience this coming week, I invite you to the Handicentre, to meditate on paint-brushes and spanners; I invite you to caress the mug of your breakfast coffee, to hold a beech-nut in your hand, as we can't manage mustard trees in the Midlands, and to contemplate the silky bronze richness of the spreading beech-tree cover, knowing that you are as close to our Lord at that moment as in any mystical flight. For, did he not walk our dusty earth, plane wood and hammer in nails, leaving his blood and sweat to be part of our earth as long as it lasts?

[Sermons at a Eucharist are short. In a longer exposition one could have applied the positive and negative ways in a more extended way to the parables and how they work. Instead, I gesture towards these ideas by quoting McAuley's poem.]

I give the last words on the power of physical images to the Australian poet James McAuley. His subject is the art of writing poetry, but his

words are also descriptive of our religious experience in which positive
and negative ways to God, loss and gain, begin in the treasures old and
new of Christ's parables:

> Give every image space and air
> To grow, or as bird to fly;
> So shall one grain of mustard-seed
> Quite overspread the sky.

> Let your literal figures shine
> With pure transparency:
> Not in opaque but limpid wells
> Lie truth and mystery.

> And universal meanings spring
> From what the proud pass by:
> Only the simplest forms can hold
> A vast complexity.

> We know where Christ has set his hand
> Only the real remains:
> I am impatient for that loss
> By which the spirit gains.[14]

*[A sermon at the Eucharist ends by moving the action towards the
act of thanksgiving and communion, the participation in the life of
God, understood here by becoming ourselves signs, and thus generative, as in the fifth element of RO homiletics.]*

Treasures old and new await us here at the altar this morning. A crumb
of bread like the grain of mustard seed which overspread the sky will be
enough to feed us all, to feed the world. The simplest forms of bread and wine
will hold 'a vast complexity'. Through the Holy Spirit, Christ's hand blesses
bread and wine and offers the world back to the Father, all the people, the
creatures, the plants and seeds, and the spanners, nails and made things. And
we too are part of the offering, the tools and nails of God's making, to be signs
of God's transforming power that will make us shine with all the wonderful
particularity of the items in the hardware store, offering images to others of
the variety, abundance and holiness of God's creative power.

14. McAuley, *Collected Poems*, 70.

Assessment: Strengths and Limitations
in This Theological Family

One key feature that characterizes RO preaching is its substantive biblical and theological character, which is particularly evident in the British context, where sermons have become quite thin, as preachers seek to align their message with contemporary secular insights. In evangelical circles, the sermon is often densely concentrated around one verse, or passage, without much contextualization. RO preaching is always highly biblical but not in the manner of biblical critical readings so much as by a theological use of Scripture. Following a lectionary, it always involves hermeneutics and even, on occasion, displays and discusses its hermeneutic of charity or Christ as the key episteme. The case study sermon was offered to a parish community at a rural cathedral but sought to introduce a number of theological concepts in an embodied and personal way. RO preaching delights in creedal orthodoxy and finds it adventurous, not constricting and negative. Like G. K. Chesterton, we try to show that "there never was anything so perilous or so exciting as orthodoxy."[15] There is an energy about RO preaching and a confidence in faith that can be engaging, especially to those from outside the faith.

A second strength of much RO preaching is its poetic quality, which seeks to vividly and materially embody its ideas and unite form and content. RO sermons not only make much use of quoted poetry but seek a more poetic style than is usual today. Similarly, if a visual image is used, it will not be merely illustrative but used to create an *ekphrasis* or living picture in words that will draw the viewers and listeners to unite with the image. RO preaching engages cultural productions at all levels but does so carefully and with methodological rigor. Images or literary texts are taken up into the action of liturgical movement.

RO adherents tend to be strongly engaged in political, cultural and social debates and to be comfortable engaging them at an authoritative level. They will often be more confident in opening up subjects such as contemporary science or current affairs from an ecclesial perspective, able to give a theological reading of any public discourse. This is a strength and is a key skill among RO preachers in university settings, for example.

The faithfulness of RO to the lectionary can, on occasion, be seen as a weakness, not least because of the drawbacks of the limited selection of Old Testament material in the Revised Common Lectionary. Use of three eucharistic readings can mean not being able to go into the exegetical detail

---

15. Chesterton, *Orthodoxy*, 167.

one might like, as all the texts have to be addressed. If one is not careful, one can make them all agree in ways they do not. Sermons at evensong or vespers do not have quite such lectionary constraints and with a different mode of liturgical progression can be more discursive in style. The emphasis on participation does not always work so easily in such circumstances. *Preaching Radical and Orthodox* contains examples of this more discursive pedagogy, showing that RO preaching can be adapted to a single reading and offer deep engagement with text and context.

The accusation made against RO preaching as against its theology generally is that of elitism. RO preaching tends to be unabashed in making reference to high culture—opera as well as jazz, Dante as well as *The Simpsons*. This would be a weakness were such reference used to exclude participants, make them feel small, or not address people's experience. RO believes that these are resources for everyone, precisely not for an elite, and that it is patronising to believe that people cannot respond to beauty and truth wherever they are found if presented compellingly. We can only judge sermons by how they are received and the energy of young RO preachers, lay and clerical, is a strength and positively received.

For Further Reading

Burrell, David. "Radical Orthodoxy: An Appreciation." *Philosophy and Theology* 16 (2004) 73–76.

Davison, Andrew. *Participation in God: A Study in Christian Doctrine and Metaphysics.* Cambridge: Cambridge University Press, 2019.

Milbank, Alison, et al., eds. *Preaching Radical and Orthodox.* London: SCM, 2017.

Milbank, John, and Simon Oliver, eds. *The Radical Orthodoxy Reader.* Radical Orthodoxy Series. London: Routledge, 2009.

Milbank, John, et al., eds. *Radical Orthodoxy: A New Theology.* London: Routledge, 1999.

Montag, John. "Radical Orthodoxy and Christian Theology." *Philosophy and Theology* 16 (2004) 89–100.

Pabst, Adrian, and Christoph Schneider, eds. *Encounter between Eastern Orthodoxy and Radical Orthodoxy: Transfiguring the World through the Word.* Farnham, UK: Ashgate, 2009.

Smith, James K. A. *Introducing Radical Orthodoxy: Mapping a Post-Secular Theology.* Grand Rapids: Baker Academic, 2005.

7

Preaching in the Deconstruction and Weak Theology Theological Family

PHIL SNIDER

WHILE IT IS IMPOSSIBLE to trace the advent of deconstruction to any singular voice, its prominence is closely tied to the work of Jacques Derrida (1930–2004), who was born to a French-speaking Jewish family in Algeria. Deconstruction took the academic world by storm in the latter half of the twentieth century and was a driving force in what came to be known as postmodernism. The development of weak theology is primarily associated with John D. Caputo (b. 1940); it emerged out of his engagement with deconstruction and radical theology. From a homiletical perspective, deconstruction and weak theology provide frameworks for celebrating the unconditional call of the gospel—and responding to it—in ways not reduced to the limitations imposed by the Enlightenment and its counterpart, liberal theology.[1]

Circumstances That Gave Rise to This Theological Family

In its most basic sense, deconstruction is a way of reading texts; it can be viewed as a resource for hermeneutics. It is associated with linguistic claims that challenge the possibility of definitively determining the meaning of texts. Words do not point to anything outside of themselves (they are not

1. Derrida was not anti-Enlightenment; he described himself as a person of the Enlightenment, "albeit of a new Enlightenment, one that is enlightened about the Enlightenment and resists letting the spirit of the Enlightenment freeze over into dogma." (Caputo and Scanlon, *God, the Gift, and Postmodernism*, 2).

representational); words only make sense in relationship to other words. This view of language, called poststructuralism, describes the ways that meaning is not fixed according to some pre-determined structure of meaning but is different according to the different contexts and ways in which words appear: words as signifiers refer only to other words. Language, like meaning, is viewed as an open system, not a closed one; language is endlessly evocative, performative and inventive.[2]

While Derrida's insights related to poststructuralism built upon the structural linguistics of Ferdinand de Saussure (1857–1913), his philosophical insights are best understood in proximity to the continental philosophers who deeply shaped his work, including Friedrich Nietzsche (1844–1900), Martin Heidegger (1889–1976) and Emmanuel Levinas (1906–1995). Each of these thinkers challenged basic assumptions about the ability of the Western metaphysical enterprise to arrive at totalizing truth claims, that is, truth claims that are true in every time and place.

In the 1960s, Derrida gained particular notoriety for exposing the ways that dominant texts in the Western philosophical tradition constructed meaning by privileging certain items over and above others (e.g., masculine over feminine, presence over absence, speech over writing, etc.), thus creating false binaries predicated on socially constructed hierarchies.[3] Homiletician Anna Carter Florence compares deconstruction to therapy because it "permits us to uncover the masked priorities and power dynamics of a text that may warp its authority structures, and so create ingrown systems that lead to oppression and suffering."[4] For these reasons and more, deconstruction became enormously useful in various fields, including postcolonial criticism, feminism, critical race theory and gender studies.[5]

When something is subject to deconstruction, readers or listeners often assumed the process is entirely negative and is designed to disparage, denigrate and destroy. A more critical examination shows that deconstruction is not an act of destruction; rather, it harbors a promise of affirmation and possibility: beyond deconstruction, something constructive could emerge.[6] In Derrida's own words, "Deconstruction . . . is not

---

2. As Myers clarifies, "This doesn't mean that there is no such thing as reality, or that all is language. Rather, it means that language, as a constant movement of differences in which we find no stable resting point, makes it impossible to appeal to reality as a refuge independent of language. Everything acquires the instability and ambiguity that is inherent in language." See Myers, *Preaching Must Die!*, 43.

3. See Taylor, "What Derrida Really Meant."

4. Florence, *Preaching as Testimony*, xv.

5. See Wilson, *Preaching as Poetry*, 64.

6. Of course, the positive "something" itself becomes a candidate for deconstructive

negative, even though it has often been interpreted as such despite all warnings. For me, it always accompanies an affirmative exigency. I would even say that it never proceeds without love."[7]

In a dynamic sense, deconstruction is expressive of a vocative call stirring in texts and traditions, highlighting the ways in which texts and traditions (including biblical texts and theological traditions) "contain what they cannot contain."[8] Take the word love, for example. All of the categories and conceptions we have for love (which includes language about love) fall short of all that is trying to be expressed in the name of love. The word love contains what it cannot contain, for the experiences of love—and all that is called forth in the name of love—exceed the understanding of love (Here is where preachers might notice how this parallels theological language, wherein experiences of the Holy exceed the understanding of the Holy). As such, deconstruction is not something one does to a text or a tradition; it constitutes what is already happening in texts and traditions, including in language itself.

This phenomenon is similar to the way Christians recognize that the actually existing churches never live up to all that is called forth in the name of the church. This recognition emerges not out of a disdain for the church, but because of a love for all that is harbored in the name of the church, and a longing for the dream of the church—as the presence of Christ in this world—to come true. In the same way that no actually existing democracy (to use one of Derrida's favorite examples) lives up to all that is called forth in the name of democracy, no actually existing institutional church lives up to all that is called forth in the name of the church. What is stirring in religious texts and traditions (e.g., God, justice, the reign of God, etc.) can never catch up to all they evoke. This is not due to their lack of meaning, but to their excess of meaning. They contain what they cannot contain.

By the 1990s, Derrida's work focused on the tension between the law (what exists) and justice (what does not exist).[9] Derrida's reversal of the Western "metaphysics of presence" challenged the idea that truth and action must be solely predicated on what exists (i.e., what is present). This became incredibly important for postmodern theologians. As Derrida demonstrated, the very absence of justice (what does not exist) creates the urgency for justice to exist. This is similar to the messianic structure, wherein the hope of the coming of the messiah is based on the realization

---

analysis.

7. Derrida, *Points . . . Interviews, 1974–1994*, 83.

8. See especially Caputo, *Deconstruction in a Nutshell*.

9. See especially Derrida, "The Force of Law."

that all that is called forth in the name of the messiah does not exist (i.e., is not present). The very condition in which people of faith long for the messiah to arrive is directly tied to the degree in which people of faith experience the absence of the messiah. If the time of the messiah had already arrived in full, then people of faith would not be praying for the messiah to come (once or for a second time).[10]

This may sound simple enough, but it is easily complicated. There are all kinds of things that do not exist that someone might like to see come true. For example, a ruling despot might desire to have all power and authority. Or religious zealots may desire a coming messiah to wipe out their enemies. This is where, as in all things, deconstruction's rigorous ethical analysis is at work. Derrida did not abandon claims to truth; he did not think that, in the words of Mark C. Taylor,

> We must forsake the cognitive categories and moral principles without which we cannot live: equality and justice, generosity and friendship. Rather, it is necessary to recognize the unavoidable limitations and inherent contradictions in the ideas and norms that guide our actions, and do so in a way that keeps them open to constant questioning and continual revision. There can be no ethical action without critical reflection.[11]

Caputo stresses this point at length. The very notion of the justice-to-come in deconstruction refers structurally to the vulnerable, to the victim, "to the one who is not being heard, who is silenced, victimized by the existing structures. It will always be the case that someone is being injured by the present order, so that the worst injustice would be to say that present order represents perfect justice."[12]

There is no such thing as deconstructive theology or poststructuralist theology; this movement is about what deconstruction and poststructuralism bring to bear on already existing institutions, texts and traditions.[13]

---

10. This approach serves as a reversal of the privileging of a metaphysics of presence, but deconstruction does not just repeat binaries in an inverted form. Here absence is inhabited and haunted with a spectral presence; we only know absence and presence in relation to the trace of its other. It is not-quite-present and not-quite-absent, like the already/not yet experience of the kin-dom of God. To return to the idea of love: we long for all that is evoked in the name of love because we catch a glimpse, a trace, of all that love evokes; we yearn for its fullness in its absence, thus it carries a sort of hyper-presence, which is often expressed in weak theology as a haunting.

11. Taylor, "What Derrida Really Meant."

12. As a response to Kearney's essay "Desire of God," 131.

13. Technically, deconstruction is not a "thing." It does not exist on the plane of being; it haunts ontology but does not repeat it. This is why it is common to see

Deconstruction does not operate outside the context of texts and traditions; it operates within them. It does not function as a critique happening outside of religion, but as a spectral "haunting" taking place within it. From the vantage point of Christianity, deconstruction takes place not out of a disregard for Christianity but because of all that stirs in the name of Christianity.

As apophatic and radical orthodox theologians engaged Derrida and deconstruction in their own respective ways, postmodern theologians remained focused on deconstruction's emphasis on the justice-to-come and the structure of the messianic, which became staples of Caputo's seminal work in weak theology.[14] When Caputo develops what he calls "the weakness of God," he is using tropes borrowed from deconstruction. It is "weak" because (in contrast to the dominant Western metaphysical traditions) it does not turn on a God of omnipotence, presence or being. Caputo translates Derrida's writing on justice with an eye toward Jesus and the proclamation of the reign of God. In the same way that the lack of justice in the world is the condition of the desire for justice in the world, so too is the lack of the reign of God in the world the condition of the desire for the reign of God in the world. From this vantage point, the vocative call of God, or, in Caputo's phrasing, the unconditional call of the event harbored in the name of God, can be understood in terms of what W. E. B. Du Bois expressed as "the unvoiced longing toward a truer world."[15]

Purposes and Characteristics of Preaching
in This Theological Family

Proponents of deconstruction and weak theology have sought to help preaching overcome the challenges posed by modernism, particularly in terms of the apotheosis of the Enlightenment, in which religion was reinscribed within the limits of reason alone, faith was reduced to morality and the infinite qualitative distinction between God and humanity had collapsed. At the same time, it has sought to move preaching beyond the limits of representational language by incorporating the insights of poststructuralism. To adapt the words of Mary-Jane Rubenstein, deconstruction and weak theology are "only at odds with [preaching] if theology is entirely

deconstruction referenced with scare quotes, or disclaimers like the French *s'il y en a*, "if there is such a thing."

14. For a brief introduction to weak theology, see especially Caputo and Vattimo, *After the Death of God*.

15. Du Bois, *The Souls of Black Folk*, 253. Caputo's language related to the event is highly influenced by Gilles Deleuze.

reducible to a 'metaphysics of presence.'"[16] While Ron Allen is right in noting that the "respect for diversity and Otherness that is inherent in the heart of postmodernism undercuts any suggestion of a single postmodern way of preaching,"[17] here are a few interrelated characteristics of preaching from the perspective of deconstruction and weak theology.

Transcendence

With the modern milieu in mind, the first sustained homiletical engagement with deconstruction, offered by John S. McClure, became known as "other-wise" preaching. McClure's method focused on Derrida's teacher, Emmanuel Levinas, who worked out of the conviction that the history of Western philosophy could be viewed as a destruction of transcendence.[18] "Levinas makes it clear that fullness of life is found only in our openness to the absolute mystery of the other. In the neighbor's face (*visage*), we experience an absolute obligation towards compassion, resistance, justice, and hope that grips our lives and holds us to a new vision for all humanity."[19] In the words of Jacob Myers, "Preaching must be exposed to a certain haunting, an exposure of the radically o/Other irreducible to sameness."[20]

Plurality

Other-wise preaching is heavily influenced by what Caputo calls "radical hermeneutics," which relates to interpreting from the perspectives of deconstruction and poststructuralism. For preaching, this includes not just the interpretation of the Bible and various traditions (religious, economic, political, etc.), but also how they're interpreted in a given community, and by whom. In being open to preaching's "others," it asks questions like, Which voices are lifted up in a given text or tradition? Which are ignored? How is power structured and shared? This is generative of collaborative, contextual models for preaching, as in Lucy Atkinson Rose's *Sharing the Word* and McClure's

16. See Rubenstein, "Unknow Thyself."

17. See Allen, *Preaching and the Other*, 2.

18. Levinas, *Of God Who Comes to Mind*, 56. It should be noted that for Caputo et al., transcendence is a weak transcendence; what's stirring in the event "is not an ontico-ontological episode on the plane of being but a disturbance within the heart of being, within the names for being, that makes being restless." See esp. Caputo, *The Weakness of God*, 5–11.

19. McClure, *Other-wise Preaching*, 133–34.

20. Myers, *Preaching Must Die!*, 165.

roundtable pulpit. Instead of assuming a common, universal experience among listeners (as is typical in dominant modes of modern preaching), it became vital "to analyze sermonic texts in terms of their socioecclesial locations and theological interests."[21] Meaning-making is a shared, collaborative, open-ended endeavor. It consists not of some ahistorical universal truth that comes from on high but a truth that rises up from below, with meaning that disseminates in different directions.

Disturbance

In weak theology, God is not a projection of humanity's highest impulses (*pace* Feuerbach), but rather a projectile, "a provocation, an insistent disturbance, a solicitation, a visitation."[22] For Derrida, like the prophets of old, transcendence is in relationship to the future. What *exists* is disturbed by, and exposed to, what *insists* (depending upon a variety of factors this may or may not be cause for comfort). We may pass much of our time within the quotidian realm of the mundane and foreseeable, but the very thing that constitutes experience as experience is when the unforeseeable future comes over us, shattering the horizon of our present and opening up a new way of being.[23] This is what Derrida and Caputo call the impossible, which for them is "the least bad definition of deconstruction." The impossible refers to the moments in time when that which *insists* upon our lives becomes that which *exists* in our lives, thus transforming the very ways in which we live and move and have our being. In weak theology, this is the time of the messiah, the event that groans to be born, the truth-event stirring in Christianity. This serves as the subject matter of the sermon's affirmation and desire. As Caputo notes, "the scriptures are filled with narratives in which the power of the present is broken and the full length and breadth of the real open like a flower, unfolding the power of the possible, the power of the impossible beyond the possible."[24] The gospel experienced in these moments is not the event per se, but the coming true of what the event harbors, the coming true of what is stirring in the name of God (e.g., forgiveness,

---

21. Cannon, *Katie's Canon*, 113.

22. Caputo, *The Insistence of God*, 28.

23. Here we notice that "deconstruction is structured like a religion. Like a prayer and tear for the coming of the wholly other (*tout autre*), for something impossible, like a messianic prayer in a messianic religion, *viens*, like a vast and sweeping amen, *viens, oui, oui*. Like a faith in the coming of something we cannot quite make out, a blind faith where knowledge fails and faith is all we have to go on, which even believes in ghosts or specters" (Caputo and Scanlon, *God, the Gift, and Postmodernism*, 4).

24. Caputo, *On Religion*, 15.

hospitality, justice, love, etc.).[25] Mary Donovan Turner captures this beautifully. She asks, "Aren't we as preachers always hoping and/or longing that something will be *different*?"[26]

Celebration

The impossible, as described by Derrida and Caputo, lends itself well to sermons in which listeners might be lost in wonder, love and praise, which is very different from modern sermons reduced to—in the words of the venerable Fred Craddock—grand ethical exhortations that lead preachers to "fill the air with ought and must and should until the church just becomes a pile of dark cinder blocks where a few good people meet every week to make each other miserable."[27] Caputo frequently reminds his readers that weak theology should not be mistaken for anemic theology. While the transcendent truth of the event (the justice-to-come) turns on absence rather than presence, this doesn't inhibit its movement toward sermons shaped by celebration and praise, but increases and amplifies it. It makes sermons all the more affective and evocative, especially in terms of celebrating the inexpressible, unconditional truth stirring in the gospel. Weak theology proceeds with passion and conviction; It is the subject matter of unconditional desire and longing, with hopes and sighs and tears too deep for words.[28]

Prayer and Praise

Preaching, like theology, runs up against the limitations of speech. This leads Myers to ask, "Is not preaching both impossible and that which transgresses (upon) the impossible?"[29] Words like justice, love and hospitality

25. Because the event that is stirring in the name of God is infinite and unconditional, there's always more to-come. We never get to the end of it; It is bottomless in its affirmation and appeal. "The unfulfilled does not mean the loss of an ideal but the never finished production of the idea to come." See Caputo, "The Return of Anti-Religion," 30.

26. See Turner, "Disrupting a Ruptured World," 135 (italics added). See also Jacobsen, ed., *Homiletical Theology in Action*, 115.

27. Craddock, *Tell It*, chapter 4.

28. As an example, consider Martin Luther King Jr.'s iconic speech, "I Have a Dream." The longing for Dr. King's dream to come true in the world is set into motion precisely because it does not exist in the world. By virtue of not existing, it becomes all the more insistent. All that is evoked in Dr. King's dream makes a claim that demands to come true.

29. Myers, *Preaching Must Die!*, 43.

(what is stirring in the name of God) exceed all actually existing instantiations of justice, love and hospitality. When it comes to the name of God, preachers run up against a limit concept. "The name of God is a name that we learn at our mothers' breast, a word that is deeply embedded in our language," Caputo writes. "We seem never to get to the end of this word, never to finish probing this word and its work on us, what it is done to us. In that sense, this word contains a deeper provocation than anything else, and what it means always lies before us."[30] There is so much resonating in the name of God, so much stirring, so much that is called forth, so much evoked, yet none of our actually existing concepts and categories for understanding can contain all that is harbored in the name of God. "The good which we can neither picture nor define is a void," Simone Weil writes, "but it is a void fuller than all fullness."[31]

Paradoxically, the preacher's very inability to speak of God is what makes preaching possible. As Karl Barth famously wrote: "As ministers we ought to speak of God. We are human, however, and so cannot speak of God. We ought therefore to recognize both our obligation and our inability and by that very recognition give God the glory."[32] Myers expresses appreciation to Herbert McCabe's insights. Through our words as preachers about God we do not access the Word as such, but we access "a mystery beyond our understanding which we do not create, but which rather creates us and our understanding and our whole world."[33] From the vantage point of weak theology, sermons are preached in restless pursuit of the event that is harbored in the name of God (the hope and desire that stirs in the name of God). At the limits of language preachers stumble upon the impossibility of expressing the inexpressible, where words can only give way to proclamations of praise and prayer.

Call and Response

In weak theology, preaching celebrates the provocation of the call to love, to do justice, to love mercy, to open oneself to the reign of God, but it does not confuse the actually existing instantiations of love, hospitality, justice and so forth for the unconditional call and solicitation that provokes

30. See Caputo and Vattimo, *After the Death of God*, 146.

31. Weil, *Gravity and Grace*, 58.

32. Barth, "The Word of God and the Task of the Ministry," 186.

33. As quoted in Myers, *Preaching Must Die!*, 90. In relationship to proclamations of prayer and praise, it is notable that Myers calls attention to Luke Powery's emphasis on imagining preaching within the context of gift, prayer, and song.

them. All of this speaks to the theory of truth at work in weak theology, which consists of both call and response. While the truth of the event can never be captured in language, the vocative call beyond the plane of being still insists. For Caputo, "truth means what is trying to come true, which points to our responsibility to make it actually come true."[34] The truth stirring in the gospel (what groans to be born; to exist; to come true) carries an affective appeal; it empowers listeners to respond, to do the truth, to make the truth happen.

For weak theology, the purpose of preaching, in a word, is transformation. As a materialist homiletic, the primary concern for preaching is not simply trying to interpret the world but rather changing the world. With both James Cone's figure of the lynching tree and Catherine Keller's figure of planetary entanglement in mind, Caputo distinguishes between the name of God not as the name of a causal power that solves our problems but as the call for resolution so that the reconciliation is not a matter of existence but of insistence.

> The call does not alter the world. It calls for the alteration. The call does not call off the difficulty; it calls it out. The insistent call for justice does not come from afar but rises up from the existence of an unjust and brutal world. . . The reconciliation refers to the call that is made upon us by the world to seize and savor this passing cosmic moment in all its transient glory."[35]

Within the context of Christianity, the body of Jesus, and the memory of Jesus, is not disentangled from the bodies of this world. Nor should Christian proclamation be. "The name (of) 'God' is the name of call to which we are supposed to be the response," Caputo writes. "Without the response the name is a dead letter. The real death of God is to ignore the call, to let the specter expire, to let it draw its (really) last breath. For all the world, the only thing anyone can see, and the only thing that exists, is the response." He then turns his attention to the Christian Scriptures, as Christian preachers must do, and speaks of the theopoetic truth they harbor:

> Truth here does not mean what it means in the departments of (modern) philosophy, propositions inside our head picking out objects in the world outside our heads. Instead, truth means *facere veritatem,* making the truth, doing the truth, making our lives into a work of truth . . . When Paul said we are to fill up what is lacking in the body of Christ, he got the whole idea.

34. See Caputo, *What Would Jesus Deconstruct?*, 61.

35. Caputo, *Cross and Cosmos*, xiv.

The earthly body of Jesus had taken its leave of the world, and now it was up to us to heal the sick he left behind and proclaim the year of the Jubilee. When the author of the Fourth Gospel said the Word must become flesh, he got the whole idea. The disembodied spectrality of the call must be incarnated in the world of flesh and blood. The call must become a response. The word must take the form of transformed flesh.[36]

In some of its finest moments, the power of preaching allows listeners to experience another reality altogether, ushering forth experiences of the impossible. This can be an embodied "Third Space" that is not colonized by oppressive powers,[37] as Kwok Pui-lan has described, or perhaps a place in which those complicit in perpetuating oppression experience the truth of being born again. Such preaching harbors the potential to resist the intrusive impositions of death-dealing power structures in order to make room for the transforming realm of God. "To say that something will 'preach' means it can touch lives, issue in action."[38]

Myers builds on a theopoetics by offering his own *cosmopoetics*. Here preaching shifts from "words about God to a burning desire to see God's love made manifest in the world." In adapting Caputo's felicitous phrasing, preaching exists so that God may insist. "The preacher is not here to teach us about God but to draw us *into* God," Myers writes. Such preaching "draws us into the insistence of God so that we may join in God's liberative, life-giving work in the world. Herein we discover our identity."[39] This is preaching as poetics. "We might say that a poetics is a discourse with a heart, supplying the heart of a heartless world," Caputo explains. "Unlike logic, it is a discourse with *pathos*, with a passion and a desire, with an imaginative sweep and a flare, touched by that of madness, hence more of an a-logic or even a patho-logic, one that is, however, not sick but healing and salvific."[40]

Case Study: Text and Sermon
(Revelation 22:12–21)

This sermon is based on Revelation 22:12–21, which consists of the closing verses of the book of Revelation. The identity of the speaker in each verse is not entirely clear, but the various voices (John, the Alpha and Omega,

36. See Caputo, *In Search of Radical Theology*, 91–93.
37. See Kwok, "Postcolonial Preaching in Intercultural Contexts."
38. Caputo, *In Search of Radical Theology*, 95.
39. Myers, *Preaching Must Die!*, 86–87.
40. Caputo, *The Weakness of God*, 104.

and Jesus) work together to modulate the call stirring in the name of God. While this passage includes a prayer for the final coming of Jesus, it was also used as a prayer for the presence of Christ experienced in the Eucharist.[41] In order to highlight the tension expressed in the structure of the messianic hope, I supplemented this text with Mark 1:1–15. While the lectionary texts for this sermon can be found in Year C (Seventh Sunday of Easter), I adapted them for use on the tenth anniversary of 9/11.

"Nourished by Our Hunger"

[I begin the sermon by introducing a popular trope in the Bible Belt that privileges a metaphysics of presence, and then I express interest in its (deconstructive) reversal.]

Have you ever heard the expression, "There is a hole in our heart that can only be filled by God?" That expression is pretty popular here in the Ozarks. The hole in our heart usually refers to our lack, our hunger, our thirst—that which we don't have—and we think about God's arrival as that which fills this void, satisfies it, quenches it. It's a nice image and all, but this morning, I'm more interested in reversing this image, turning it inside out, setting it upside down.

[Here I introduce the structure of the messianic hope and then turn to the biblical texts.]

I'd like to reflect on this God-shaped hole in our heart—this image of lack, of hunger, of thirst—within the context of the coming of the messiah. Most messianic language is structured around the hunger and longing of things to come. When we pray for the messiah's arrival, we're praying for that time and place that we don't have words for yet deeply long for; we're praying for that indescribable realm of love and justice, compassion and peace; we're praying for God's kin-dom to come, for God's will to be done, on earth as it is in heaven.

We have to acknowledge, of course, that one of the oddities surrounding Christian belief in the messiah is that no sooner than we Christians proclaim that the messiah has come, we're praying for the messiah to come again. The book of Mark begins by proclaiming the messiah's arrival ("The time is fulfilled; the kingdom of God is at hand"), yet the book of Revelation—and thus the end of the entire Bible—concludes by praying for the messiah to come yet again. It's like the messiah was present and had arrived, yet now the messiah

41. See Boring and Craddock, *The People's New Testament Commentary,* 817.

has gone missing, AWOL, absent (Jesus has left the building). Christians celebrate the messiah's presence yet at the same time mourn the messiah's absence. It's like Christianity needs to make up its mind already: Has the messiah arrived—as in the book of Mark's proclamation—or is the messiah still "to come," as in the book of Revelation's prayer?

> *[This part of the sermon challenges binary thinking and opens the door for understanding the way that absence drives the longing for presence.]*

One of the problems is that we tend to think about these things along either/or lines: Either the messiah has arrived, or the messiah has not arrived. Either the kin-dom is here, or the kin-dom is not here. And if it's not here yet, then—depending upon one's perspective—it will either come one day in the future, or it will not come at all. It will appear one grand and glorious day, or it will never appear at all. It's messiah or no messiah. Kin-dom or no kin-dom. This or that. Now or later. Either/or.

But what if in the Bible we encounter a much more radical approach to all of this? What if Mark's proclamation of the messiah, and Revelation's prayer for the messiah, what if they somehow depend upon one other? What if the trace left in the aftermath of the messiah leaves our hearts forever hungry to catch glimpses of the messiah yet again?

> *[At this point the sermon shifts gears. The tenth anniversary of 9/11 was on the hearts and minds of listeners. The sermon recalls these events and expresses sadness and loss that the kin-dom of God was not fully present.]*

Today we pause to remember that tragic September morning ten years ago, when airplanes were flown into the twin towers, when the World Trade Center came crumbling down. I don't know where you were on September the 11th—I remember turning on the news just as the second plane hit the south tower—and I can't remember all that went through my mind. But as I watched the sky fall that day, I thought one thing for sure, and that's that the kin-dom of God was not here; God's will was not being done on earth as it is in heaven; the indescribable realm of love and justice, compassion and peace, was nowhere to be found. If the coming of the messiah meant that the time had been fulfilled and the kin-dom was at hand, then I had picked the wrong messiah.

[Now I provide examples of those who responded to the call of the gospel (that which does not exist on the plane of being) in order to help transform that which does exist.]

Yet at the same time, on that same day, amidst the wreckage and ruins of Ground Zero, there were cups of cold water given and received; there were warm blankets placed on damp, ashen bodies; there were perfectly good lives lost so that others could be saved. In the midst of the wreckage, on the site of the ruins, where the kind-om was absent ("my God, my God, why have you forsaken me?")—it was precisely there, in that place, that the kin-dom somehow emerged, like a flower growing through broken, cracked cement; like a small tree springing forth out of the trunk of a hollowed out old oak tree; like a stone being rolled away from a tomb.

[The concluding sections offer theological analysis that builds to the celebration of the event stirring in the name of the messiah, as expressed in Revelation's closing prayer. The sermon interprets the text theopoetically; it does not describe the event but expresses longing for the event.]

Walter Benjamin says that praying for the messiah to come is not about praying for an arrival way off in the future, at the end of time or even outside of time, because, he says, the heart of every moment—the heart of every moment—contains the little door through which the Messiah may enter.[42]

When we hope for the kindom to arrive and for the messiah "to come," it's not so much a prayer for what might arrive one day way off in the distant future, something that none of us will live to see, but it's rather about praying for the kin-dom to come now, in the midst of our lives and in the midst of our world; even—perhaps especially—in the midst of the ruins. It's a prayer that does not require our patience as much as it requires our passion. As John Caputo says, "the call for the messiah to-come goes hand-in-hand with the urgency of justice now, with the absolute intolerance with anything in the present that would pass itself off as justice or that would make us complacent with the sorry state of the present."

All of which gets us back to the God-shaped hole in our heart. What if the hole in our heart is a void; a void that, instead of being filled, puts us in pursuit of God all the more? What if the glimpses and traces of the kin-dom that we so fleetingly saw in Jesus, glimpses and traces so beautiful that many could not help but see in him the Messiah, the incarnation of their hopes

---

42. This is a sermonic mashup alluding to Caputo's commentary on Benjamin in *The Weakness of God*, 95. "The 'now-time' *(Jetztzeit)* is a door through which at any moment the Messiah may pass."

and dreams, the embodiment of the kin-dom—what if these glimpses and traces (which we locate in Jesus but do not confine to Jesus), what if they don't so much fill the God-shaped hole in our heart but instead make it bigger and bigger, larger and larger, expressing that which we most deeply long for, yearn for, hunger for, even if we don't have words for, and want to see come into our lives and our world again, and again, and again, infinitely, ceaselessly? What if we imagine the hole in our heart not so much as what gets filled, but rather as the void left in the aftermath of the messiah, the void that compels us to call upon the messiah time and again?

What if, as Richard Kearney suggests, this hunger for God is no mere deficiency or lack, as we've often been led to believe, but instead is its own reward?[43] As the Psalmist says, "Those who seek the Lord lack no good thing." What if such desire is not some gaping emptiness or negation but an affirmative "yes" to the summons of that which we know not what, that which we desire beyond desire; that which we pray for, long for, hope for? What if this hole in our heart is not a symptom of deficiency but of excess; what if it is not to be mourned but to be celebrated? What if we are nourished by our hunger?

Such a desire leads to an odd paradox at the heart of Mark's proclamation of the messiah and Revelation's prayer for the messiah: On the one hand, it's like the messiah had to come—otherwise we would not know what we are waiting for. But on the other hand, the messiah can't possibly be here—otherwise we would not still be waiting.

Many of us have caught traces of our heart's longing in the kin-dom inaugurated by Jesus—in sharing and receiving cups of cold water, in breaking bread with friends and strangers, in loving our neighbors and maybe even our enemies—and as we catch these glimpses, these traces, we become dissatisfied with anything less; these glimpses keep us hoping and praying and dreaming and weeping for the messiah to come not once but again, and again, and again; not to come way down the road in the far off future, at the end of time or beyond time, but today, this week, now. In the aftermath of the messiah, in the trace that tears our hearts and leaves a void, we are forever left inviting, calling and longing; hoping, sighing and dreaming.

The God-shaped void in our hearts leaves us forever after God; forever restless; forever weeping and praying for the messiah to come again and again and again. When our world is shattered and hope seems lost, we pray for the messiah to enter, not just once, but a thousand times:

Into a world where religion is marked more by hatred than by love, we pray Come, Lord Jesus. Into a world where heartache and sorrow is all

---

43. See Kearney, "Desire of God," 114–16.

too often the norm, we pray Come, Lord Jesus. Into a world where fear drives more decisions than clarity of thought, we pray Come, Lord Jesus. Into a world where the rush to violence silences calls for peace, we pray Come, Lord Jesus. Into a world where justice seems impossible, we pray Come, Lord Jesus.

"The Spirit and the bride say, 'Come.' Let everyone who hears say, 'Come.' Let everyone who is thirsty say come. 'Surely I am coming soon,' says the Lord, 'Surely I am coming soon.'"

In moments of our lives when hope feels lost, when our ways have worn thin, and we are in need of a different world to be born: "Come, Lord Jesus, come!" Amen.

Assessment: Strengths and Limitations in This Theological Family

Caputo's radical hermeneutics have helped many a preacher find their voice. As a pastor, I count myself among them. But there are still a number of matters to consider.

First, if other-wise preaching wishes to overcome the limitations imposed by modernism, including the domestication of transcendence, it must be mindful of Marlene Ringgaard Lorensen's observation: "A significant theological critique of other-wise preaching practices is that the collaborative coauthorship of the congregation threatens to dismiss divine agency."[44] In being open to preaching's "others," how does sermonic discourse differentiate between the more determinate others (entities on the plane of being) from the wholly other (the event stirring in the name of God, which is not on the plane of being)? Sermons that turn on the insistence of God bend an ear not simply to others that already exist (entities), but to the spectral lure of the wholly other that does not exist. In my view, the event that is stirring in the name of God should be the subject matter of the sermon's affirmation and desire, not the more determinate others that are already on the plane of being.

Second, if an "event cuts across the distinctions among the various confessions, and even across the distinction between the confessional faiths and secular unbelief, in order to touch upon a more elemental, if ambiguous quality of our lives, however this quality is given words or formulated, with or without what is conventionally called religion or theology,"[45] how are commitments to other-wise sensibilities, particularly those that resist

44. Lorensen, "Carnivalized Preaching," 11.
45. Caputo, *The Weakness of God*, 4.

sameness, maintained? Given postmodernism's emphasis on context and social location, how does the preacher avoid speaking of the "royal we"? In referencing the "hoping and sighing and dreaming and weeping" experienced by listeners in the wake of all that is stirring in the name of God, how are these experiences, and this call, not reduced to an oppressive sameness that repeats the problems of modernism? Eunjoo Mary Kim's "transcontextual hermeneutic" is helpful here.[46]

Third, preachers engaging radical hermeneutics should recognize that deconstruction is not an anything goes type of relativism. Contrary to popular assumptions, what Derrida's critics have not recognized—and this is one of the reasons Derrida said toward the end of his life that he has been read less and less well for over twenty years—is "that the destabilizing agency in his work is not a reckless relativism or an acidic scepticism but rather an affirmation, a love of what in later years he would call the undeconstructible."[47] Caputo stresses this point throughout his work: "Derrida does not advocate outright chaos. He does not favor a simple-minded street-corner anarchy (nothing is ever simple) that would let lawlessness sweep over the land, although that is just what his most simplistic and anxious critics take him to say . . . [D]econstruction is not a matter of leveling laws in order to produce a lawless society, but of deconstructing laws in order to produce a just society."[48]

Perhaps most importantly, it is worth noting that it did not take a twentieth century philosophical celebrity to discover (or invent) what's going on in deconstruction. It has a long history in biblical traditions; it has as much to do with Aaron and the golden calf as with anything that happened in Paris in the 1960s. Just as Dale Andrews shows that the "New Homiletic" has deep roots in African American preaching traditions that stretch much further back than the mid-to late-twentieth century,[49] there is a long history in preaching wherein the weight of all the doesn't exist makes the present tremble. In an article in the *Boston Globe*, Caputo asks: "What would it be like if there really were a politics of the bodies of flesh that proliferate in the New Testament, a politics of mercy and compassion, of lifting up the weakest and most defenseless people at home, a politics of welcoming the stranger and of loving one's enemies abroad? What would it be like if there were a politics of and for the children, who are the future; a politics not of sovereignty, of top-down power, but a politics that builds from the bottom up, where *ta me onta* [lit. "the nothings"] enjoy pride of place and a special

46. See Kim, *Preaching in an Age of Globalization.*

47. Caputo, "Jacques Derrida (1930–2004)."

48. Caputo, *The Weakness of God*, 27. See also his *What Would Jesus Deconstruct?*, 63–69.

49. See esp. Andrews, "Response to Narrative," 96.

privilege?"[50] He raises these questions in recognition of the work that has long been done in Black, liberation, queer, womanist and feminist spaces, and claims that this must also be the work at the heart of deconstruction and radical theology, if it is to have a heart. Otherwise, it is not the gospel of the poetics expressed in the figure of Christ.[51]

To be sure, a weak homiletic will not receive universal approval. It does not turn on strong power or presence or being, but on the spectral call beyond being, which may or may not come true, to which people may or may not respond. It is a homiletic of the perhaps, of the may-be.[52] Preachers who want a strong God, with all of the guarantees of might and strength and privilege and presence, will be disappointed. The weakness of God is not a bug in weak theology, but a feature. There's no guarantee that everything will end well. Preaching is a risk. It's an act of—what's the word?—*faith*. Weak homiletics hitches a ride with Jesus and the reign of God, which is risky business of the highest degree. If preaching is even possible, Caputo says, it "must dare to make its way out into the deep, where the land is no longer in sight, risking the perils of being lost at sea, daring to preach the kingdom of God without rewards."[53]

Preaching from the perspective of deconstruction and weak theology means preaching about something that does not exist and may not come true. This is the promise and the threat, the hope and the fear. It also just so happens to be the very structure of faith, in which one hopes against hope for the insistence of God to come true, to-be, perhaps.

Homiletics is haunted by a very holy ghost.

For Further Reading

Caputo, John D. *The Insistence of God: A Theology of Perhaps.* Bloomington: Indiana University Press, 2013.

Florence, Anna Carter. *Preaching as Testimony.* Louisville: Westminster John Knox, 2007.

McClure, John S. "Deconstruction." In *The New Interpreter's Handbook of Preaching*, edited by Paul Scott Wilson, 146–49. Nashville: Abingdon Press, 2008.

Moody, Katharine Sarah. *Radical Theology and Emerging Christianity: Deconstruction, Materialism and Religious Practices.* New York: Routledge, 2016.

Myers, Jacob. *Preaching Must Die! Troubling Homiletical Theology.* Minneapolis: Fortress 2017.

50. As quoted in Ambrosino. "Jesus' Radical Politics," 33.

51. See especially Caputo, *Cross and Cosmos*, 86–105.

52. See Caputo, *The Insistence of God*; and Kearney, *The God Who May Be.*

53. Caputo, *In Search of Radical Theology*, 95.

8

Preaching in the Black Liberation Theological Family

James Henry Harris

INTERPRETING THE WORD OF God with the aim and goal that privileges the context and reality or the condition of Black existence is the *prima facie* reason for preaching the message of liberation and freedom. There are all kinds of messages, but *the message* that the Black church needs to hear and heed is not the message of the media. It is not the message of movies or billboards. This message is not the message of rap, or reggae, not the message of rhythm and blues, pop or soul. It is not even the message of any music or melody. No, there is only one basic, essential, liberating, transforming message that has power in season and out of season, that can convince, convict, convert, rebuke, rekindle and revive, teach and inspire, one message that can console and comfort, that can heal and help persons who are poor and distressed. This is the message of Jesus Christ. Jesus is the essence of the gospel message. This message is the preaching of the gospel. Jesus came with a message–a message from God and the power of the Holy Spirit. It was not a flowery message, and it did not titillate the ears or massage the egos of the power elites. It was not a message laced with pretty words or empty phrases. But it was a liberation message, a message of transformation that needed to be heard and heeded by kings and princes, young and old, rich and poor. The gospel needs to be heard by all who sought to understand that the kingdom of God is manifested in Jesus Christ.[1]

The existence of Black people in a world that defines human existence in Eurocentric terms is traditionally confounding and oppressive.[2]

1. Harris, *Preaching Liberation*, 18.
2. Harris, *Preaching Liberation*, 67.

However, when the Black preacher communicates the gospel in light of his or her existence to those with the same skin color, socioeconomic condition, experience of oppression and injustice, and racial hatred, a message of hope and liberation creates the possibility for a new world. These are the workings of preaching from the perspective of Black Liberation Theology. This thoroughly biblical perspective gives rise to the language and process of communication which conveys the idea that God works alongside Black people in the struggle for freedom. Sometimes this is hard because it appears more evident that "the wicked seem to prosper" and Black folk continue to struggle and suffer. Preaching a message of liberation is the precondition of transformation,[3] which is intended to effect change in the nature and structure of persons and society.[4] It thereby constrains the preacher to have a view of God and the world that enables him or her to try to reconcile the real contradictions of life. The preacher in this sense is a vicarious teacher–one constantly engaged in reflection on the practice of Christianity to inform and help Black people to deal with the issues and troubles of the existing world.[5]

For this chapter, Black Liberation Theology informs my preaching as the bedrock of transformative preaching, stands as a homiletical exercise in Biblical, theological, and sociocultural interpretation through the lens of the oppressed, analyzes the dialectics within humanity, discourse, and consciousness, and seeks to provide a continuum of pragmatic reflection on everyday issues of racism and injustice. This approach to preaching is critical because liberation of the oppressed and the oppressor is a necessity for genuine Christian community.[6]

Circumstances That Gave Rise to This Theological Family

As a pastor and to my chagrin, I have always recognized that the language and behavior of the Black church is too synchronous with that of white conservative evangelicals. The emphasis continues to be on personal salvation at the expense of the liberation and transformation of communities. Additionally, there has been historically too much time spent on issues of division between husbands and wives (Col 3:13–14), head coverings, what one should wear, etc. These are all ancillary to the meaning of the gospel, to

3. Harris, *Preaching Liberation*, 8.
4. Harris, *Preaching Liberation*, 8.
5. Harris, *Preaching Liberation*, 2.
6. Harris, *No Longer Bound*, 166.

church life, and the Christian practice of liberation and freedom. And yet, they remain front and center.

The Black church where I serve is often times much more interested in tradition and ritual, (priestly activities, visiting the sick, baptism) than social justice activities (protests, advocacy for the poor, preaching liberation). More particularly, the commitment to preaching liberation is a very costly and dangerous action in the Black church and is virtually non-existent in the white evangelical church, which has a history of supporting slavery and segregation and white supremacist ideology. One of my former graduate students, Tony Baugh, says that "white supremacy is a religion." This normative ethical action of "going along to get along" often characterizes the Black church leadership from top to bottom. The complexity of this issue is grounded in a desire to be popular and accepted by both congregational and ministerial peers in the practice of Black Religion.

The lure of the "call and response," the applause, the energy and "entertainment" often come at the expense of sermonic discourse that challenges and confronts racism, sexism, white supremacy, injustice, patriarchy, etc. In other words, liberation theology still has an uphill battle in making its way into the consciousness and practices of the Black preacher and congregation.

The blatant acts of evil grounded in chattel slavery continue to manifest themselves four hundred years later in the systematic and ubiquitous killing of Black males and females throughout the United States. Not even the murder of George Floyd in Minneapolis and Breonna Taylor in Louisville by the police vis-à-vis the persistent protests around the world have been able to codify a message of liberation bursting forth univocally from the mouths of preachers in every Black church and white pulpit in America. There is a severe lack of interest in espousing a message of liberation for fear of being ostracized or challenged to remain politically correct to the members of one's particular congregation and community. Preaching liberation has to be a deliberate act of rebellion against the powers of empire within and without the walls of the church. This rebellion is burdensome and often lonely because there is a tendency to conform to the expectations of the greatest number of supporters in order to remain in the pastoral position by any means necessary. This utilitarian approach is highly correlative with popularity and the rule of the majority. Newsflash: Preaching liberation is a minority point of view.

Preaching liberation and working to liberate oppressed people is not only a minority view and practice, but it is a view from the underbelly of society and many in the Black church are no longer interested in struggle and hardship. This is a very natural and understandably practical position on many levels because suffering and struggle is endemic to being Black—creating a rapid and insipid contrast to the joys of life. It is indeed an everyday struggle to maintain some semblance of sapidity and zest for life. The legacy of the evils of slavery continues. It is an existential reality, a constant threat to Black life. But liberation theology is not about maintaining the status quo or the hegemony inside or outside the Black church or in society. At its core, liberation theology is about teaching and preaching with the goal of helping folk understand the insidious evil of racism and injustice embedded in the fabric of American democracy, business, politics, economic disparities, and white religion as practiced in private schools, seminaries, and churches. The only practical yet dangerous antidote to this reality is Black preaching that takes the liberation motifs emblazoned in Scripture (Luke 4:18) seriously.

Purposes and Characteristics of Preaching in This Theological Family

The purpose of preaching from the perspective of Black Liberation Theology has its impetus within the context of Blacks suffering under white supremacy. The reason for this type of preaching evolved out of the social, political, and economic reality of oppression. The history of the Black church confirms that Black preachers did what was necessary to survive and encourage the congregation in the midst of segregation, Jim Crow laws, and other forms of degradation and discrimination. Black folk did not want to continue worshipping God under the dominant hand of whites, so they liberated themselves from the hypocrisy and oppressive rule of the white church. My church, Second Baptist Church in Richmond, Virginia came out of a white church by the same name in 1846 because of the reality of oppression, racism, and injustice inherent to the slavocracy. In this sense, the establishment of independent Black churches was an act of resistance and liberation. This resistance reflects the African American people's unwillingness to believe that God intended that they be slaves, even in worship. It seems that there is little systematic effort to address ills that plague African Americans. Historically, their preaching, however, was quasi-liberationist to the extent that it focused on integration, uplift, and education, but not to the point of advocating or constructing a new social order or a new kingdom in the radical and transformative sense that Jesus presented and proclaimed.[7]

African American preaching has traditionally related Scripture to the social and cultural condition of oppressed people and has sought to correlate this condition with the presence of sin and evil in the world. The preacher tells it like it is, believing that God has told him or her what to say

---

7. Harris, *Preaching Liberation*, 16.

and he or she is compelled to tell it to the congregation and community, because the truth can and does indeed provide a hope that can potentially set us free. The preached language of liberation and freedom starts with the words of Jesus, whose language was radical and bold, often shocking to those who listened. Joseph Johnson reminds us that "the radicalness of the humanity of Jesus is not only expressed in his service but also in his speech. We must permit his speech to address, probe, disturb, and challenge us."[8] In reading the Synoptic Gospels, we readily sense the radical and liberationist tone of the language Jesus used. Let us seek to emulate Jesus, not his disciples and other detractors.

The preacher, like the theologian, is very much concerned with telling people about Jesus as the liberator and transformer of individuals and society in a way as passionate as Jesus' own.[9] Preaching from the perspective of Black Theology demands a passionate conviction about the proclaimed word, and I believe that the message of Jesus is intended to create a new world view, that is, a new understanding of self and world in order that the manifold grace of God can be actualized. In their book *Jesus and the Ethics of Kingdom*, Bruce Chilton and J. I. H. McDonald say, "In Luke, this liberation motif is expounded with particular force (cf. 4:18–19). Jesus' proclamation and ministry signal the time of fulfillment (4:21): the time when Scripture was fulfilled, the Kingdom was actualized . . . and when welcome news is given to the poor, release to the captives, sight to the blind and freedom to the oppressed." The kingdom of God then, is about understanding liberation because Jesus symbolizes the essence of the kingdom and preaching liberation is in effect preaching the kingdom of God, as Justo and Catherine Gonzalez describe in *Liberation Preaching: The Pulpit and the Oppressed:*

> A theology of liberation is a theology of the Kingdom. The goal toward which we move is the fulfillment of the promises of the Kingdom . . . Since in Christ the Kingdom has come, we can now live out of that new order. But since he is also still to come, we are not yet liberated, but in the process of being liberated.[10]

The centrality of Black Liberation Theology necessitates another purpose for preaching from this perspective, which is the specific and consistent message of hope, justice, and freedom coming to the oppressed. To be able and willing to preach this type of message is the embodiment of the manifold grace of God. This family of preaching is purposed to

---

8. Harris, *Preaching Liberation*, 14.

9. Harris, *Preaching Liberation*, 15.

10. González and González, *Liberation Preaching*, 111–13.

encourage during the present moments of oppression for survival, but it is equally important to convey a message of hope for the present and future–that one day and as soon as today, justice will come to Black people's front door. The Black preacher has traditionally believed that God is a God of justice, ultimately concerned with the freedom of the oppressed. Moreover, whether preaching survivalism, integration, separation, or transformation, the preacher grounded his or her perspective in the word of God and in the existential reality of Black pain and suffering. In the Bible, God is "all in all," the "I am that I am." God is Father, Son, and Holy Spirit, possessing all divine attributes.

Certainly, the God of history is not limited to the experience of Abraham, Isaac, and Jacob. The concept of God as a focal point for reverence and worship is inherent in all religions. For example, we know that the Babylonians' God was Marduk, who acquired the status that Zeus would later hold in the Greek Parthenon. For Socrates, that teacher of teachers, known as a gadfly, God was to be obeyed. Although the Western church has often talked about God in many wonderful and alluring ways, it has not thought of God as a friend and liberator to those who are objects of sneers or victims of systematic oppression and injustice.[11] Preaching about the power of God in the life and history of the Black church experience is a *sine qua non* to action and reflection. Here is where the preacher, through his or her communicative skills and the help of the Holy Spirit, is able to help the congregation experience the meaning and power of God. To the Black preacher and to those who live in poverty and in the constant presence of humiliation and degradation, God is not confined to classical arguments about cosmology and metaphysics. God is not limited to the traditional hegemonic understanding of history and theology. God is not only friend and comforter but is the architect of justice and righteousness. God is the one who troubles the waters of hatred, injustice, and oppression. Few can describe God with the eloquence and imagination of the Black preacher. The preacher is able to talk of God in terms that engender faith and fear, strength and power. When the Black preacher speaks of God, people cry and shout, weep and moan, believing that God is able to do all things–even to liberate people from sin and oppression.[12]

A major characteristic of preaching in this family is the polyvalence of language. African American preaching is creative and imaginative–fusing and finding a liberative voice in the biblical text amid all other voices that are integral to the text. Traditional white theologians have presumed

11. Harris, *Preaching Liberation*, 21–22.

12. Harris, *Preaching Liberation*, 22.

interpretative authority such that a text means this or that—nothing more and nothing less. However, in preaching from the perspective of Black Liberation Theology, meaning is often determined by the preacher/interpreter and the hearer/interpreter in dialogue with each other based on the context. The Black preacher who focuses on liberation is always trying to get in front of the text in order to create a new world where "justice rolls down like waters and righteousness like a mighty stream." The Black preacher uses language that extols God's grace, freedom, justice, repentance, and salvation, while at the same time is similarly speaking with a multivalent univocity, not of meaning but of purpose and intent. This is a type of "homiletical heteroglossia," or a multi-voiced perspective.[13] The spokenness of African American preaching has a dialogical character, which means that the sermon has many voices. These many voices often rise from the scriptural text (a postmodern notion), the preacher as text, the congregation as text, and the sermon itself as text.[14]

Language is a symbol for understanding and clarification and the preacher's use of language or words of liberation and freedom, when spoken, constitutes the most effective symbolic reference of the sermon. The uttered, spoken word has new world creating meaning each time it is spoken. This means that the sermon is never the same, even if the written words are the same, because each time the words are spoken, they create a new world (a more just and free world) by the nature of their meaning and the context in which they are spoken. Preaching from the perspective of Black Liberation Theology is to use language of love and hope, grace and mercy, life and death, faith and perseverance with the preacher being open to the multiplicity of voices that emanate from and surround the Scripture text. This means that not only is the uttered instance of the word creating new possible worlds, understanding, and meaning, but the word itself is different each time it is uttered. It sounds and feels different and is therefore internalized differently by the hearer as well as the preacher. As symbols, words engender reflection and thought, causing the hearer to use other words that create connections between the words by the preacher and the words these preached words have given rise to. The most important aspect of this characteristic is that the word is a symbol of freedom embodied by the preacher who speaks a word of hope to the congregation.[15]

In African American preaching, there is evidence that the actions— that is body movement, facial expressions, gestures, tonality, syncopation,

---

13. Harris, *The Word Made Plain*, 53.

14. Harris, *The Word Made Plain*, 51.

15. Harris, *The Word Made Plain*, 53–55.

verbal eloquence, etc.—serve to project meaning in the sermon. This is an embodied hermeneutic,[16] correlating to another characteristic of preaching from a perspective of Black Liberation Theology which is that of aesthetic style. The aesthetic elements within this family of preaching contribute to the sermon's content. Cleophus J. LaRue adds, "the power of Black preaching is not uniquely derivative of style or technique but of how Blacks perceive God as a result of their experiences and their interpretation of Scripture based on those experiences."[17] And that perception of God manifests itself in the amalgamation of substance and style, creating a beautiful fusion of horizons The aesthetic and art of Black Liberation preaching is correlated with the lived experience in such a way that it can be viewed as a culminating expression of the unique phenomenon of Black life. Preaching from the perspective of Black Liberation Theology is an intersectional reverberation of joy and pain. Interweaving biblical interpretation and hope into the ontological dialectic of oppression and freedom, the preacher performs this task with rhythm, cadence, body movement, and tonality. Black liberation preaching is a unique melding of experience and practicing the art of scriptural interpretation, thereby resulting in an embodied hermeneutic that reflects particularly the Black encounter with God.[18] The concomitants of gesture as symbolic language, aurality and orality, and sermonic imagination humanize and contextualize the God who "woke me up this morning and started me on my way."[19] The essence of the sermon in this case, is an unparalleled amalgamation of its constituent parts—including its delivery in the pulpit of the Black church.

Case Study: Text and Sermon
(1 Peter 4:7–11)

Exegeting biblical texts for the liberation of Blacks requires my five-part method of reading as a requirement for Black preaching. These steps are reading, re-reading, *unreading*, writing, and rewriting. This methodology utilizes creativity and vision as a way toward understanding Scripture texts for the purpose of developing sermonic discourse.

The first book of Peter was written to the exiles within the provinces of Pontus, Galatia, Cappadocia, Asia, and Bithynia. The addressees were aliens in the communities in which they lived, that is, that they were persons who

16. Harris, *The Word Made Plain*, 86.

17. Harris, *The Word Made Plain*, 87.

18. Harris, *The Word Made Plain*, 87.

19. Harris, *The Word Made Plain*, 75.

had moved to new communities but were not fully integrated into those communities. In the Roman world, such "resident aliens" stood on the margins of society much like Blacks in America.[20] These Christian believers were dealing with suffering which is always difficult and discouraging.

Suffering is seared in the pages of this short letter; but nevertheless, I claim that there is a symbiotic and semiotic relationship between love, hope, and suffering. Hope is not simply an eschatological phenomenon. It is a "newness" that sustains Black people in the middle of hopelessness. From a Black Liberation perspective, this text is inspirational because its main focus is grounded in the power of love and kindness which is highly correlative with the hope that sustains oppressed people. Verse 7 urges the believers consider the urgency and time constraint of the world ending to motivate them to heed the writer's words. Verses 8 and 9 implore the actions of love and kindness, which are significant identifiers of Christians. Verses 10 and 11 acknowledge the giftedness within each believer that should be utilized to glorify and honor God.

The Hope of Love and Hospitality (1 Peter 4:7–11)

[The sermon begins by calling attention to conditions of repression of African American communities that are manifest today.]

I have been thinking that the spirit of American chattel slavery lives on; not just in the South, but across this country, from sea to shining sea. The murders by police of Ahmaud Arbery in Georgia, and Breonna Taylor in Louisville, and George Floyd in Minneapolis have helped some people to acknowledge and understand the fact that racism is alive and well and living everywhere we breathe. It is dominant and ever-present, and as deadly as the coronavirus. Indeed, it too is a pandemic that traumatizes Black folk.

Now, I have been saying this in sermons and classrooms for thirty years and I've had difficulty in getting our people to understand this. Some Black people have said to me that they did not want to hear any more about Black suffering. Yet, it cannot be avoided, and it cannot be swept under the rug any longer.

The continued senseless murders of Black people by police is a national crime, a continuation of the slaveocracy. The Minneapolis police officer, Derek Chauvin's facial expression, appeared to suggest that he actually got a "charge," i.e., a satisfaction, from killing, murdering, a Black man. This was done in broad daylight while the cameras were rolling and

20. Ehrman, *The New Testament*, 432–33.

people in the street were yelling for him to stop the strangulation. This blatant police brutality which caused a forty-six-year-old Black man to call on his mama and to say "I can't breathe" troubles and saddens me to the point of traumatic speechlessness. All four of the police officers were complicit in this murder in the public square.

> *[The sermon seeks to help listeners recognize that while the Euro-centric community is the leading actor in oppression, some people in the African American community are complicit in maintaining racism by not actively resisting it. Sometimes we need to be liberated from our own reticence.]*

For too long Black people have been docile and silent while the smoldering embers of anguish and anger continue to burn and the rage against racism has been quelled by our abiding love for whites. Well, no longer can the top be held on the pot; the pressure cooker cannot contain the heat, so the only language we can speak is one of revolt, protest, and riots. This is the language of the poor and oppressed as Martin Luther King Jr. said over sixty years ago. Nobody will listen to the calm and rational pleas of our people who are dying at alarming rates from the pandemics of racism and the coronavirus. They are the ones working and laboring in places where these is no protection, no personal protective equipment, no social distancing, no regard for their poverty, their struggles as grocery store workers, warehouse workers, custodians, and on the front lines.

Again, for purpose of the redundancy this Black man, George Floyd, was emotionally and spiritually beaten down, had lost his job, and simply wanted a pack of cigarettes purchased with a "so called" counterfeit $20 bill. Four cops responded to a call about $20, and he is killed, murdered on the spot. This is crazy because his death is clearly about something else. It is about a persistent evil. It is about power and violence and it is about white supremacy and racism. It is about systemic injustice and hatred toward Black people.

> *[When turning towards the Scriptures for help in interpreting what needs to happen in liberation, the sermon seeks to invite listeners to identify positively with the text by pointing to the loving nature of the Black community but also to ways in which that nature sometimes works against the urge to participate in liberating activity. The sermon encourages the congregation to un-read the text.]*

While the Scripture text encourages us to "maintain constant love for one another because love covers a multitude of sins," I can only think that

Black people have been and remain a loving people. Frantz Fanon says that "Black people love white people, and whites struggle to be human." And, unfortunately, we have allowed our love for this country and our extraordinary love for whites to keep us quiet and docile for too long. We have allowed our Sunday school religion, the slave masters' religion, and conservative evangelicals to keep us quiet and content, suffering more and more and comparing it to the suffering of Jesus Christ. All Black people are Christ-figures. Crucified daily.

Well, it is time to re-examine and raise our consciousness because our love has covered the sins of our oppressors for too long. And they have been multitudinous. Black people know how it feels to be discriminated against, to be harassed, to be second guessed and overlooked. We have borne the cold fears and blazing flames of the night and the scorching heat and sting-ing sunlight of the day. We have felt and seen sorrow and sadness. Yes, in the language of the Negro spiritual, "We've been 'buked and we've been scorned." And still there was something about the expression of "pleasure" on the face and in the body language of the murderous police officer that made me realize again that this white man sees himself as a "sovereign" god-like figure who can take the life of a grown suffering Black man at will, without trepidation, and with religious fervor and determination. This im-age of evil is forever etched in my consciousness and everyday it haunts me like the ghosts in Toni Morrison's novel *Beloved*.

> *[The sermon now weeks to help the congregation re-read the text from the perspective of how the text can empower the congrega-tion to participate in actions that may seem confrontive but whose purpose is ultimately liberative. The text has two important and related foci: love and hospitality. The sermon focuses first on love. In the language of the text, liberative efforts are ultimately loving not only for African Americans but for white Americans also.]*

This powerful and lofty language in the text "above all maintain con-stant love for one another" should help us understand that Black protest is in fact an act of love for one another. No longer can Black folk be docile and sit back in silence while our people are treated more inhuman than animals. The protest against police murders of Black people can only be seen as a demonstration of the spirit of love for one another in a way that we haven't done before. The pain and suffering can no longer be con-tained. We know by experiential evidence that Black people love whites as seen in the language of forgiveness by the families of those murdered by a white man in Bethel Church in Charleston and as written about by the

Black Martinican Psychiatrist Frantz Fanon in his book, *Black Skin, White Masks*. But now the marches and the protests exclaiming that Black Lives Matter demonstrate that Blacks' love for one another is also connected to morality, justice, and social action.

Police violence is a cancerous, hateful disease that not only affects Black men, but unfortunately, Black women are equally oppressed and victimized. It is a public health threat to Black life. For example, Louisville police officers shot Breonna Taylor in her home at least eight times during a "no knock" drug search warrant in March 2020. There were no drugs found on the premises. Miss Taylor was a twenty-six-year-old former EMT who aspired to become a nurse. This horrific murder by the police is made worse by the fact that it took several months for the media and the world to notice that yet another innocent Black woman was murdered by the police–an arm of the state.

This is another vivid and vicious example of Black suffering and pain that is causing me to hold back tears even as I write these words. This reality of Black existence is exhausting and hurtful because there seems to be no end to the governments' and societies' violence and hatred perpetuated against Black females and males. The mentality of the slavocracy lives on and the cries of Black people continue to be unheard and unheeded because there is no consciousness of Black suffering in the church and society.

[The sermon personalizes the issue by drawing on the preacher's own experience.]

For almost thirty years now, I have sought to speak about these pervasive issues to our people in Second Baptist Church. Some have gotten mad at me and stopped coming to church because I dared to point out the obvious. I have consistently preached liberation, justice, and freedom and instead of the church welcoming the liberating word and crowding out the sanctuary, as they do for evangelical sermons, the numbers have dwindled with people saying, believing, and preferring that I focus not on liberation and freedom, but on "priestly duties" instead. This is the influence of evangelical television religion as practiced by Black and white preachers throughout the United States and the world. It is also the irony of Black life and the struggle of the Black Liberation preacher.

Well, all is not well. Police brutality and evil toward Blacks has been a long-standing staple of American democracy and white racism. I have been preaching and theologizing about this all my adult life and some Black people in my own congregation have actually called me racist; saying that I don't like white people. Like most Black people, I do not hate white people, but let it be known that my disdain is against white supremacy and racism which is ingrained in the fabric of America, in the laws, in the politics and policies, and in the practices of government and American corporate and economic culture. The United States is a culture of racism and brutality; not just police brutality, but brutality rather than hospitality. This is a nation founded on violence, nourished on violence, and sustained by violence. Slavery was the most violent enterprise known to humans, yet it is the basis upon which America has operated for the past 400 years.

> [While the need for liberation—and for liberation preaching—has existed in this country since the first settlements, recent events have dramatically renewed attention and given a fresh sense of urgency to the movement for liberation.]

This means that slavery and its principles have never ended. Not even a war could end the hatred and bring about the dawn of hospitality when it comes to Black people in this country. The recent "straw that broke the camel's back" was indeed the white police officer training police recruits how to be inhumane to Blacks; how to be evil and aggressive towards Black people. He was demonstrating how to criminalize and animalize Black men and women. George Floyd, a Black man, was used as a demonstration to his recruits and comrades in arms. The lead police officer was saying "this is how you arrest, approach, treat, and murder a Black man." You have to break his neck or strangle and choke him to death with the full weight of your knee for nearly nine minutes while he pleads for mercy and calls on his momma, or until he can no longer breathe.

For Blacks in America, the police are considered state-sponsored terrorists. For example, in Buffalo they are abusers of senior citizens, especially if you are protesting in support of Black people, and in Maryland on the bike trail, even off-duty, the police are harassers and abusers of children if those children are passing out flyers that support Black lives. The lack of hospitality is ingrained, ensconced, and embedded in society when it comes to how Black people are treated.

It has taken how many years, how many murders, how many lynchings, how many lawsuits, how many marches and how many Black bodies dead and gone for Blacks and/or whites to acknowledge that Black lives, Black children, Black youth, Black men and Black women matter? What will it take for people to realize that the Black body is sacred, and no organization or arm of the state has a right to dehumanize or destroy it?

[The sermon turns to the second major focus in the text: hospitality. As in the case of love, the sermon urges the listening community to consider ways in which the United States is inhospitable to Black people. The sermon also invites the listener to reread (reunderstand) the notion of hospitality from the perspective of how hospitality towards white people by blacks is normative and can actually allow the conditions that call for liberation to go unchallenged. Black people have an unrequited love for White people that manifests itself in an exorbitant amount of hospitality, however, they have never been able to sit at the table with White people or enter through their front door. The historical record is replete with examples like this.]

This Scripture text is not only about love, but it is about hospitality which is a necessary human trait and a precondition to being Christian and human for that matter. We see it from Abraham to Jesus. From Genesis to Revelation. We see it in our text today. It is related to the love and hope we have been talking about for a while now. "Be hospitable to one another without complaining." I have catalogued the lack of hospitality that America has shown for Black people for hundreds of years. So, despite their cocktail parties, the speeches, and writings about "liberty and justice for all," despite the crumbs given to Blacks for welfare and social security; despite the pretense toward "equal opportunity," equal justice, and equal housing, there is still no equality for most Black people.

The economy purportedly gained 2.5 million jobs in May 2020 and Blacks are still forty percent unemployed. There is no hospitality, no kindness towards Black people by the Democrats or the Republicans, by the United States House of Representatives, or by the Senate, by the president or by the Supreme Court. They all have been unkind and inhospitable toward Black people for over four hundred years– rom 1619 to 2020.

And, Black people have adhered to the word, "be hospitable." We are the poster children of hospitality, kindness, warm welcome, kindheartedness, congeniality, sociableness, cordiality, amiable behavior, generosity, and friendliness. That is the meaning and practice of hospitality.

Growing up in Central Virginia, my parents were poor, but you would have never known it because they were kind-hearted and generous. My father and my mother were the embodiment of this part of our Scripture text: Be hospitable to one another without complaining and I learned this as child–not in church, but at home.

We practice hospitality among and towards ourselves. And sometimes we practice it towards white communities in ways that leave them overlooking the savage actions and conditions of oppression.

Notice that hospitality must be accompanied by "no complaining." We think we cannot be kind and generous to folk and then complain about it. The complaining nullifies the hospitality. This is an "undoing" of the good you have done. We think that if we do good and complain about it, we might as well not do it. But I am here this morning to tell you that when it comes to oppression, "complaining" about it is not inhospitable. Complaining about it is the first step towards re-creating our nation as a community that is hospitable for all. Because complaining about it in protest marches, in city council meetings, at school board meetings, in the neighborhood associations, in short in all the places where we live, work, and play, and, yes, in sermons. Without complaining does not mean without critique. Black people are compelled to critique white America and each other, not as an obviation of hospitality, but in tandem with what it means to be hospitable. Hospitality is the act of expending considerable effort and exerting oneself for the sake and needs of others. Black people have unrequitedly been this way towards whites for centuries and it is illogical to think there would be no complaining, which is grounded in a rebuke of injustice and hatred. I am complaining by getting in front of the text and getting in front of the issue by interpreting what the text means for Black people today. In this context, complaining is giving voice to the victims of white supremacy, and is integral to hospitality, not asynchronous and not to be interpreted as a prohibitive action suggested by the text of grumbling and whispering under one's breath. Getting in front of the text is critical for Black people because getting behind the text is death. Here is where Ricoeur's notion that the sense of the text is in front of it applies because it takes on a new meaning and therefore, creates the possibility of a new world, one that operates within a system of justice and freedom for all.

Until this nation becomes loving and hospitable to Black people, until this nation becomes kind-hearted to Black people, until this nation becomes friendly and generous to Blacks, it will not truly be loving and hospitable, or kind-hearted, or friendly and generous in a complete way for white people or anyone else. Until the social world embodies these things, everyone will live in degrees of inhospitality, some (Blacks) more serious than others (many whites). Living in a culture of inhospitality degrades the quality of life for all. Until our whole nation becomes a culture of hospitality to all people, our text warns us: Do not be surprised by the fiery ordeal that is taking place among [us] . . . (v. 12).

Assessment: Strengths and Limitations in This Theological Family

There are at least three strengths and three weaknesses in this theological family and its approach to preaching. Here are strengths:

1. There is a strong social justice emphasis that characterizes this family.

2. This perspective recognizes that humanity is sacred and Black people are human.

3. God's manifold grace is demonstrated in human love and hospitality.

And here are two potential weaknesses:

1. A weakness is that this family has to always justify itself because of the refusal of the church to embrace it without a deep-seated historical struggle.

2. It may lead to inaction towards liberation on the part of the hearer as he or she "waits on Jesus to fix it."

It is a binding fact that preaching is a complex dialectical enterprise, much like life itself. Preaching is a joy and a sorrow, a high and a low, a constant struggle and a thankless achievement.[21] This enterprise has both its strengths and weaknesses. Strengths that have propelled an ever-increasing zeal to share the good news of the gospel: "The spirit of the Lord is upon me, because he has anointed me to bring good news to the poor. He has sent me to proclaim release to the captives and recovery of sight to the blind, to let the oppressed to free." (Luke 4:18) The pledge to put the full puissance of preaching for the sake of not only the gospel, but more importantly, for the liberation of Black people's suffering under the hands of white supremacy and racism in all of its manifestations is a moral and ethical action of utmost urgency. The weightiness of preaching liberation in the face of abject hatred intensifies the importance of Black Liberation and how "Liberation is not deliverance from all suffering but only from that suffering which lies at the core of oppression."[22] As such, "Black theology must become "public theology."[23] A public theology based on the importance that both Blacks and Whites cognize the effects of suffering for both the sufferer and the advocates of the same.

---

21. Harris, *Black Suffering*, 148–49.

22. Ware, *Methodologies of Black Theology*, 88.

23. Ware, *Methodologies of Black Theology*, 147.

Blackness and Black suffering are the poster child(ren) of "absolute power corrupts absolutely." Considering this reality, "Pastoral theology is liberation theology because it is grounded in praxis."[24] Therefore, the practical application of Black preaching on the platform of myriad social issues, i.e., racial, economic, and political injustices, gives rise to what Hans-Georg Gadamer calls a fusion of horizons. From a Black Liberation aspect, the horizon of [Black] suffering is fused with the horizon of the Black preacher to cultivate, encourage, and inaugurate new horizons heretofore never achieved.

For Further Reading

Cone, James H. *The Cross and the Lynching Tree*. Maryknoll, NY: Orbis, 2011.

Freire, Paulo. *Pedagogy of the Oppressed*. Translated by Myra Bergman Ramos. 30th anniversary ed. New York: Continuum, 2000.

Hegel, Georg Wilhelm Friedrich. *Phenomenology of Spirit*. Translated by A. V. Miller. Edited by John N. Findlay. Oxford Paperbacks. Oxford: Oxford University Press, 2013.

Hopkins, Dwight N. *Down, Up, and Over: Slave Religion and Black Theology*. Minneapolis: Fortress, 1999.

Painter, Nell Irvin. *Sojourner Truth: A Life, A Symbol*. Rev. ed. New York: Norton, 1997.

Reddie, Anthony. *Working against the Grain: Re-Imaging Black Theology in the Twenty-First Century*. Cross Cultural Theologies. London: Equinox, 2008.

Ricoeur, Paul. *Interpretation Theory: Discourse and the Surplus of Meaning*. Fort Worth: Texas Christian University Press, 1976.

———. *The Symbolism of Evil*. Translated by Emerson Buchanan. Boston: Beacon, 1986.

Thurman, Howard. *Jesus and the Disinherited*. Boston: Beacon, 1996.

West, Cornel, and Eddie S. Glaude, eds. *African American Religious Thought: An Anthology*. Louisville: Westminster John Knox, 2003.

24. Harris, *Pastoral Theology*, ix.

Preaching in the Feminist Theological Family

MARY DONOVAN TURNER

I want to posit the possibility that there is a word, that there are so many words, awaiting woman speech. And perhaps there is a word that has not yet come to sound—a word that once we begin to speak out will round out, and create deeper experience for us, and put us in touch with sources of power, energy of which we are just beginning to become aware.[1]—Nelle Morton

ALTHOUGH THE ROOTS OF feminist theology are much older, this movement began to come to the attention of growing numbers of women and men in the 1970s in liberating, ife-giving ways. Distinctive feminist approaches to preaching soon emerged and have been developing ever since. This essay explores the history of feminist theology, articulates a feminist approach to preaching and offers a brief exegesis and sermon on Numbers 27:1–11, the daughters of Zelophehad.

Circumstances That Gave Rise to This Theological Family

It is not possible to pinpoint the precise beginning of the long and circuitous relationship between feminist theology and preaching. This is in part because feminist theology raises not one, but at least two, overarching and essential questions related to the homiletic conversation: *What* should be preached? And *who* is allowed to preach it? While a definitive beginning to this vital

---

1. Morton, *The Journey Is Home*, 87.

and dynamic conversation cannot be clearly identified, it is possible to take a snapshot of a particular place and time, and then identify both the important tributaries to this western world, contextualized feminist theology/homiletic moment and the rivers that rush downstream from it.

For our purposes the snapshot in time is the publication of Frances Willard's *Woman in the Pulpit* in 1888. While to start here with this volume, and the publication of *The Woman's Bible* by Elizabeth Cady Stanton which quickly follows, is a somewhat arbitrary decision, it has proven to be a fruitful one. The tributaries to this moment are many and unmistakable and were flowing in ancient as well as contemporary times. In the early days of the Hebrew women, in the early church, the Middle Ages and beyond, women spoke up and spoke out, spurred on by conscience and inspiration.

The preaching women on the frontier of the United States included groups such as the Quaker women (between 1,300 and 1,500 of them) who came from Europe to preach the gospel in the colonies in the early 1700s.[2] There were also individuals like Jarena Lee, an African American woman born to free parents who was licensed to preach in the AME church in the early 1800s,[3] and Louisa Woosley who preached on horseback from Kentucky to the West Coast in the late 1800s,[4] both of whom wrote autobiographies/memoirs that give us a glimpse of their preaching lives. Though the names of these two women and others are known to us, we can be sure that we only know the names of a small percentage of these courageous female preachers.[5] History has not been kind to women's contributions to this conversation; women have been silenced and forgotten, making each new movement, such as that in the late 1800s, somewhat orphaned from the historic voices that preceded it.[6]

What happened that brought forth the voices of evangelical women preachers in the 1700 and 1800s? In these early days of the United States, in small towns and on the prairies along well traveled stage coach paths and eventually the transcontinental railroad, women and men devalued hierarchies and authorities that dictated values and life styles. In a climate that valued rugged personal independence instead, denominational polities and

---

2. Larson, *Daughters of Light*, 63.

3. Lee, *The Religious Experiences and Journal of Mrs. Jarena Lee.*

4. Woosley, *Shall Women Preach?*

5. Brekus, *Strangers & Pilgrims*, 7. Brekus estimates that there were as many as one hundred African American and White women preachers from the mid-eighteenth to the mid-nineteenth century on the US frontier.

6. There are strong efforts to recover and help us remember the names of these women. See for instance Florence, *Preaching as Testimony*; Simmons and Thomas, eds. *Preaching and Sacred Fire.*

authorizations were not as important as the personal and spiritual lives of the preachers who brought forth spirit filled, extemporaneous words. The First Great Awakening (ca. 1730–1740) and the Second Great Awakening (ca. 1790s–1830s) provided the landscape on which women began to preach and fashion a foundation for subsequent feminist theology/preaching conversations. Women, though denied theological training, brought words based on their own life experiences, particularly in new denominations and sects.[7] As women were caught up by the spirit and began to pray publicly and find voice in revivals and camp meetings, the nineteenth century women became one of the greatest *tributaries* to the first wave of feminist theological thinking. Women who felt a call to ministry found places to spread the word–school houses and public squares.[8]

Feminist Theology: The First Wave (1880–1920)

As women, then, began (at great cost to their personal lives, families and health) to preach, by circuit riding around territories and communities, it became *imperative* for the clergy and professors of theology and the women themselves to reflect on the practice of these preaching women. Should these women be preaching? By what authority do they do so? Is their preaching consistent with Scripture and church tradition? Answers to these questions were varied, of course, and saturated denominational publications, articles, and volumes. Some made apologetic appeals to accept the preaching of women while others cited New Testament quotations that were thought to forbid it. Women began writing their own autobiographies to recount their experiences of call and inspiration. Feminist theology in its embryonic stages began addressing the question of women and preaching by reconsidering and evaluating the traditions, Scriptures, theologies, and practices of the church. This is feminist theology's task.

Frances E. Willard, president of the Women's Christian Temperance Union (WCTU), in 1888 published *Woman in the Pulpit* to build the scaffolding for the argument that women had an inherent right to preach. At the time she wrote, she knew thousands of women who, on behalf of the WCTU,

7. Tisdale names the development of new denominations and cults (ecclesial transitions), as one of the primary variables leading to the rise in the number of women preachers. She also delineates geopolitical transitions and personal transitions as other important factors. See *How Women Transform Preaching*, 31–35.

8. For a more complete listing of the early groups and individual women preachers in the early centuries of the United States, see Tisdale, *How Women Transform Preaching*, 23–47.

were teaching and expounding on Scripture.[9] Other women brought the gospel to east coast and west. These women were the impetus for her writing; her theology grew out of women's lived experience. While not a trained theologian or biblical scholar, but, emphasizing the need for common sense when interpreting Scripture,[10] she reasoned that:

- women were gifted lecturers in other contexts (primarily places calling for social change in relation to voting rights, etc.), and the church could rightfully use those gifts;

- male translators and interpreters who believed in the subjugation of women, translated and interpreted according to their biases (this she demonstrated with clarity and much humor). Exegesis, she said, is one of the most manmade of all sciences, and one of the most misleading of all arts.[11]

- there were thirty to forty examples of women prophesying and preaching and leading in the Old and New Testaments; texts that *appear* to speak against women's leadership, rightly interpreted, do not;

- to keep women from preaching results in a monolithic understanding of Scriptures;

- men's preaching was catechetical, deductive, focused on doctrine, "of the mind," argumentative, abstract, and often confusing. Religion, Willard says, is an affair of the heart. Women connected with those who were struggling because women knew what it is like to be silenced and live under the burden of society's crushing pyramid. Men preach a creed; women declare a life.[12]

For Willard, it is the interpreters of the text and not the text itself who have oppressed women; male interpreters engage in "word-wrangle" to keep women silent.[13]

As the country grew larger, poverty, mental health, women's right to vote, abolition, prison reform, and temperance became more imperative, and women came to believe that these problems, as well as those related to family and home, were theirs to solve. Elizabeth Cady Stanton, well known suffragist and activist in the United States,[14] and a group of over 20 women,

9. Willard, *Woman in the Pulpit*, 57.
10. Willard, *Woman in the Pulpit*, 26.
11. Willard, *Woman in the Pulpit*, 23.
12. Willard, *Woman in the Pulpit*, 26–47.
13. Willard, *Woman in the Pulpit*, 60.
14. For a discussion of the women who were preachers and suffragists, see

published *The Woman's Bible* (*TWB*) in 1895. (The accompanying volume II was published in 1898.) The legacy of *TWB* is ambiguous to be sure. The women authors were not biblical scholars, but they commented on all women's stories or texts in the Old and New Testaments where women were present or where they were conspicuously absent. The women attacked male bias and, importantly, the misogynistic tendencies of text itself. In other words, Stanton sought to correct the overt sexism of the Bible itself. In contrast to those who called the Bible "the word of God," Stanton argued that the Bible was written by men who had never really seen or talked with God. She viewed it as fallible and androcentric.[15]

The Woman's Bible volumes were criticized by scholars but were wildly popular; the volumes were important for at least two reasons. First, women realized that they could not successfully argue for equality and the right to vote unless they dealt with Scripture. Interpretations of Scripture that argued for submission and the inadequacy of women were one of the most important variables, if not the most important variable, keeping attitudes of the inferiority of women and rigid gender roles in place. Second, Stanton's fundamental understanding of the Scriptures being patriarchal and androcentric, brought to the forefront the essential, critical question women themselves had to answer. Frances Willard, insisted that the Bible correctly understood, did not preach women's subordination and argued that the true message of the Bible was obstructed by faulty translations and biased interpretations. Stanton, on the other hand, insisted that the Bible had not just been misinterpreted but that *Scripture itself was androcentric and biased in the interest of men.* She addressed the issues of biblical authority; an ambivalent relationship to Scripture is created for women when they are marginalized in it.[16] In the work of Willard and Stanton, issues identified and strategies subsequently used by second wave feminists, were already firmly in place though in basic, raw, and uncritical form.

Feminist Theology: The Second Wave (1960–1980) and Beyond[17]

In 1920 women, at least White women, were granted the right to vote in the United States. The struggle to gain equality in the life of the church

---

Zink-Sawyer, *From Preachers to Suffragists*.

15. Schüssler Fiorenza, "A Feminist Introduction," x.

16. Schüssler Fiorenza with Matthews, "Preface," 4.

17. The dates of the second-wave of feminism are generally defined as 1960–1980. In the theological world, the boundary between the 1980s and the decades that followed

sadly remained, and ushered in the second wave of feminism around 1960. The flood waters of the second wave, finding their genesis in the work of the first wave feminists (also movements for civil rights and the secular feminist movement in the United States) were strong, torrential. This is amazing since the second wave feminists were writing almost exactly one century later than the first! The external challenges related to women and preaching were answered: Yes. Women can go to seminary and receive a theological education. Yes. In most denominations women can be ordained. And slowly they were. Understandings of scriptural interpretation, polities, and women's leadership were thoroughly researched, and women became proactive, resistant scholars and clergy.

Acknowledging the work of the feminists of the late nineteenth century but armed with new and growing critical methodologies, feminist theologians and feminist biblical scholars authored seminal works that called out for inclusive language, explored the depths of the patriarchal bias of sacred texts, re-interpreted through contextual and critical methodologies Scriptures that had been used through the centuries to subjugate women, and recovered biblical stories of women, those that spoke of strong female leadership and those that described the tragedies experienced by our Hebrew and Christian foremothers.[18]

Many scholarly volumes deserve acknowledgment, but we mention here only two; in each, there is clear and intentional expressed appreciation for first wave feminists, Willard and Stanton. In 1992, Carol Newsom and Sharon Ringe published the first edition of *The Women's Bible Commentary* (*TWBC*), the first comprehensive attempt to gather some of the fruits of feminist biblical scholarship on each book of the Bible. The title pays tribute

---

were permeable. Advances were enormous, and the movement between the second wave and the third which followed, seamless. In its nascent forms, feminist thinking was "too small." Some feminists assumed that they were talking for all women when, in reality, if context is taken seriously, that cannot be the case. In what is sometimes called third-wave feminism, feminists sought out diverse groups of women for insight. Some groups split off from the feminist camp, rightfully needing their own development of thought (womanist, Latina, Asian and Asian American, queer, and so forth). These fields of study had their own tributaries, women who began the conversations and courageously helped them develop. Intersections between feminism and other theologies (postcolonial, liberation, and others) were sought. Feminists began to understand that their oppression as women was inextricably tied to other oppressions which deserved their attention. The fruits of this expanded vision can be witnessed in the feminist homiletic described below.

18. We pay tribute to second-wave feminist theologians and biblical scholars: Mary Daly, Rosemary Radford Reuther, Phyllis Trible, Letty Russell, Sallie McFague, and so many others whose work broached new topics and explored the yet-unexplored implications of patriarchal language and systems.

to the work of Elizabeth Cady Stanton and her volume *The Woman's Bible* but changes the word *woman* to *women*, acknowledging the diversity of women's experiences reflected in those chosen to contribute to the volume. *TWBC* continues the tradition of Stanton's volume not only mining the Scriptures for stories about women but also uplifting the importance of having women read the biblical text consciously as women. In the first edition of *TWBC*, and also the editions that have followed, critical method and theory enhance the understandings of canonical women.[19] In the introduction Newsom and Ringe give tribute to the work of first-wave feminist Frances Willard who says in *Woman in the Pulpit*, "We need women commentators to bring out the women's side of the book; we need the stereoscopic view of truth in general, which can only be had when woman's eye and man's eye together shall discern the perspective of the Bible's full-orbed revelation."[20]

In 1993 and 1994, Elisabeth Schüssler Fiorenza published two companion volumes: *Searching the Scriptures I and II*. Acknowledging the work of Elizabeth Cady Stanton, and also seeking to transform it, Schüssler Fiorenza first recognizes and underlines the political nature of biblical interpretation and its effects on women's lives. Unlike Stanton, whose collaborators were mostly Protestant, white women from the United States, the author gathers together many of the best feminist scholars from around the world, bringing to the edited volume diverse thought and challenge. Primarily the author discusses in the three parts of Volume 1, the importance of recognizing that biblical interpretation changes with the perspectives of different sociohistorical locations, the rethinking of the critical methods used in biblical interpretation from a feminist perspective, and finally, the delineation of the effects that feminist biblical study has on worship, proclamation, and Bible study.[21]

Schüssler Fiorenza's first volume calls feminists to analyze and evaluate processes of canonization and interpretation that have silenced women. Yet, she says, there is inherent in the Word a liberating impulse that can disrupt the patriarchal text. Borrowing and refashioning words from Adrienne Rich regarding Marie Curie: the Bible "is at one and the same time a source for women's religious power and for women's suffering."[22]

Questions of biblical authority inherited from the first wave of feminism took center stage. *Is the Bible a liberating document that can lay claim to the lives of women? Or, is it fundamentally so patriarchal that it, along with*

19. Newsom and Ringe, Introduction, xiii.

20. Willard, *Woman in the Pulpit*, 21 as quoted in Newsom and Ringe, Introduction, xiii.

21. Schüssler Fiorenza, "A Feminist Introduction," v–x.

22. Schüssler Fiorenza with Matthews, "Preface," 6.

the church that claims it as sacred, must be rejected? On the one hand, the Bible is written in androcentric language, has its origin in the patriarchal cultures of antiquity, and has functioned throughout its history to inculcate androcentric values. On the other hand, the Bible has also served to inspire and authorize women and other nonpersons in their struggles against patriarchy. *Women's biblical studies in one way or another presuppose and seek to address this dual problematic.*[23] For some during the second wave of the feminist movement the answer was that the Bible was so inherently patriarchal, it could not lay claim to women's lives. An example of this perspective is Mary Daly who publicly made a statement that she was leaving the church. She and others left the church, and some found other alternative spiritual communities and practices to nurture their lives.

Purposes and Characteristics of Preaching in This Theological Family

In so many ways, feminist homileticians are indebted to and dependent upon the feminist theologians and feminist biblical scholars of the first, second, and third waves of feminism. By definition, homileticians have addressed the dual problematic framed above, and have made the decision to work from within the church. That is, they struggle and fight for the women's right to be ordained and preach. The text, they believe, can be a redemptive force not only for women, but also for all groups of people who are "othered" and marginalized, oppressed.

In 1985, Nelle Morton, a beloved feminist foremother, published a series of lectures she had delivered in different places and contexts throughout the 1970s. The volume in entitled *The Journey is Home*; many budding feminists found a "home" in her words. She addresses women who have left the church (or organized religion) because they have been excluded, experienced male domination or violence from the patriarchal institutions. The volume, she wrote, is also for feminists who were enrolling in great numbers in seminaries and who were already in ministry taking a bold look at the imagery and language that had for centuries oppressed women. She names the divide between feminists who stayed in the church and those who could not; the divide often severed relationships between those who chose differently.[24]

The first essay in the volume was a recounting of a public address Morton gave in 1970 on the fiftieth anniversary of the ratifying of the

23. Schüssler Fiorenza with Matthews, "Preface," 4.
24. Morton, *The Journey Is Home*, xxvii–xxv.

Nineteenth Amendment granting women the right to vote. She discusses how church women fought for this right–their interests not just religious, but also the social, political, cultural constructs of their day.[25] The third essay entitled "Preaching the Word" was written in 1971 just when a developed feminist hermeneutic was in its infancy. Morton calls for the shattering of patriarchal images and symbols within the church that derail our thinking about women and preaching. She says, "In the beginning was not the Word. In the beginning was the hearing." The essay frames God as one who listens, who hears us into speech. She goes on, "If the style of a woman's preaching was not to deliver (or proclaim) the Word but to place her ear close to the pulse of the people, then a new kind of Pentecost would be possible." And she asks: How is it that the Word of God has become identified with a deep voice? What kind of theology is it that requires male hands for a sacrament to have efficacy?[26]

In 1989 Christine M. Smith published the first full volume to focus exclusively on a feminist homiletic.[27] *Weaving the Sermon: Preaching in a Feminist Perspective*, uses the metaphor of weaving to define the loom and essential threads of a feminist homiletic. She advocates for:

- an understanding of power and authority that is woven with authenticity and mutuality, not driven by role, position, and status;

- an extended and profound rethinking and revisioning of ecclesial language, images, and metaphors;

- an enlarged feminist vision that sees all forms of oppression interconnected; is committed to peace, non-violence and living in harmony with all creation; understands the linkage between spirituality, social transformation, and political action; appreciates the human body; and appreciates in a profound way the diversity in different women's ways of knowing and being.[28]

Smith follows this volume with two others that embody elements of her feminist homiletic. In *Weeping, Confession and Resistance* she asks: How can a person preach a word of hope and faith in a world filled with

25. Morton, *The Journey Is Home*, 1.

26. Morton, *The Journey Is Home*, 41.

27. She drew upon the insights of second-wave feminist theologians and biblical scholars such as Letty Russell, Nelle Morton, Elisabeth Schüssler Fiorenza, Beverly Wildung Harrison, Mary Daly, Rosemary Radford Ruether, and Sallie McFague to name only a few.

28. Smith, *Weaving the Sermon*, 43, 59, 105.

violence and suffering?[29] In *Preaching Justice,* her third volume, Smith brings together eight very diverse voices from eight distinct cultural/ ethnic communities, challenging them to articulate the specific justice concerns, issues, and passions that give rise to a preaching ministry within their own community and beyond.[30]

In 1993 Marjorie Procter-Smith contributed an article in *Searching the Scriptures,* edited by Elisabeth Schüssler Fiorenza, titled "Feminist Interpretation and Liturgical Proclamation." In it she outlines major components of what she calls Feminist Emancipatory Proclamation. She begins with the assertion that to read and interpret Scripture in a liturgical context adds layers of complexity.[31] Underscoring feminists before her, she advocates that the patriarchal and androcentric character of the Bible must be acknowledged. She outlines the guiding values of feminist proclamation: Women must claim their power to speak. Feminists must be committed to change. *The commitment to women must take precedence over the commitment to Scripture.* And, feminists acknowledge that the biblical text recounts not only the silencing and oppression of women, but also their struggle for emancipation, their courage and their hope. Proctor-Smith outlines a homiletic that is contextual, embodied, dialogical, communal, and participatory. It seeks not only to speak but to empower others to speak. This proclamation is fluid growing out of ongoing conversations with a diverse group of women.[32] In the end, she tackled the thorny issues of biblical authority stating clearly that violation of people is more insidious than violation of text.[33]

Mary Lin Hudson and Mary Donovan Turner in *Saved from Silence: Finding Women's Voice in Preaching* (1999) delineate five elements of voice (physical and metaphorical) that relate to women and preaching. Voice is, or can be, distinctive, authoritative, authentic, resistant, and relational.[34] Through exploration of the Hebrew Bible and the New Testament, a theology of voice develops, one that, like feminists in both the first and second waves of feminism,[35] searches for and acknowledges women's stories in text and tradition, appreciates voices' diversity, redefines theological categories,

29. Smith, *Weeping, Confession, and Resistance.*

30. Smith, *Preaching Justice.*

31. Procter-Smith, "Liturgical Proclamation," 313.

32. Procter-Smith, "Liturgical Proclamation," 313–14.

33. Procter-Smith, "Liturgical Proclamation," 319.

34. Hudson and Turner, *Saved from Silence,* 9–16.

35. Hudson and Turner acknowledge their appreciation for and dependence on feminists Nelle Morton, Frances Willard, Adrienne Rich, Rebecca Chopp, Anna Julia Cooper, Patricia Hill Collins, Mary Tolbert, Audre Lord, Beverly Harrison, Alice Walker, and others.

laments the ways the church has colluded with women's oppression (both within the church and beyond),[36] and advocates for a Theology of the Voice that replaces or enhances the Theology of Word. Word is static. On a page. It needs a voice to contextualize it. It needs women and men to read it, study it, pray with it to disrupt, or liberate, the Word on the page and to bring it to life so that it can engage the contemporary sufferings and injustices that many in the world are experiencing.[37] Rather than getting self "out of the way" in preaching, *Saved from Silence* calls feminist preachers to bring all that they are and experience, their memories, their education, their context and social location, in other words unapologetically to read, interpret, and preach as women. It is a more vulnerable kind of preaching, one that is more accessible to the listener and life. The volume recognizes the challenges of the woman preacher who has internalized the pervasive external forces that have long sought to silence her.

The concept of a Theology of Voice arises in part out of the work of Anna Julia Cooper, an African American theologian who first entered the public arena as a speaker for women's rights in 1886.[38] Born in 1838 to a mother who was in slavery, Cooper went on to get an education and received her PhD at the Sorbonne; she wrote about slavery and about voice from a theological perspective. Biblical principles and the life of Jesus were foundational for her beliefs. Cooper calls God the "Singing Something," a movement toward freedom and equality. The Singing Something works within to help those who are mute about their suffering, whose external oppressions have been internalized. She maintained that the Black woman's "little voice" could be brought into the human chorus by the working of God in them. Thus. she said, we should not talk about being created in the *image* of God, but in the *sound* of God which asserts the sacredness of *all* humanity.[39] Sound is active; image is not.

Feminists had named the ways that women had been silenced and marginalized in the processes of canonization, biblical interpretation, and in the development of polities and doctrine. Feminist homileticians also mined the ways women were silenced in liturgical practices such as in the development of the lectionary.

In 1996 Ruth Fox wrote an article evaluating the Roman Catholic lectionary, and found that a disproportionate number of passages about women had been omitted, for instance Shiphrah and Puah, Deborah, and Huldah

---

36. Hudson and Turner, *Saved from Silence*, 87–91.

37. Hudson and Turner, *Saved from Silence*, 92–93.

38. Baker-Fletcher, "Anna Julia Cooper and Sojourner Truth," 41–42.

39. Baker-Fletcher, "'Soprano Obligato.'"

from the Hebrew Bible. Mary's Magnificat was never read during Sunday worship, and the lection for Easter stopped before the story of Jesus appearing to Mary Magdalene and his commission to her. A somewhat humorous, but blatant, example of the way women were diminished in the lectionary is related to Proverbs 31. In the text that describes the "good wife," the lectionary leaves out vv. 14–18 and vv. 21–29 that describe the good woman's initiative, business acumen, dignity, and wisdom. The lectionary includes, however, the ways she should support her husband.[40]

Protestant communities realized the same omissions in their own lectionary and when the Revised Common Lectionary was published in 1992, several women's stories were added—the promise of God to Sarah for her faithfulness, the story of Hagar, the Hebrew midwives, the encounter of the Syro-Phoenician woman with Jesus, and the ministry of Lydia. For centuries, the stories of these women had been omitted from the proclamation and preaching of the church.[41]

Even these changes, however, did not fully satisfy the hunger for women's stories and feminine imagery. Westminster John Knox Press will soon publish *A Woman's Lectionary* which focuses on passages about women in the Bible and on feminine imagery for God. It reimagines the calendar of preaching for one year.[42] And *National Geographic* published an edition in 2020 entitled "Women of the Bible," which recounts the stories of about fifteen biblical women and shows how they were depicted in classical art.[43] Feminists have often used the metaphor of a wall to describe the patriarchal stronghold on text and tradition, and they advocate for taking the wall down stone by stone so that new insights and liberating understandings for women can be seen and accessed.[44] Feminists for a century and a half have done that, but not just that. They have redefined, reimagined, rethought, reengaged to build new feminist understandings of language, text, authority, and of preaching. Two examples are Lucy Rose's[45] reimagining of a preaching world where everyone is invited to speak, and Sally Brown who redefines the theology of the cross, redemption, and suffering.[46] It is important and would be helpful, then, to glean the insights of the past generations and formulate a constructive feminist homiletic contextualized to this place

---

40. Fox, "Women in the Bible and Lectionary."
41. Consultation on Common Texts, *The Revised Common Lectionary*, 12.
42. Wilcox, *The Women's Lectionary*.
43. Isbouts, *Women of the Bible*.
44. Morton, *The Journey Is Home*, xxiv.
45. Rose, *Sharing the Word*.
46. Brown, *Cross Talk*.

and time but dependent upon the insights of feminist theologians, feminist biblical scholars, and feminist homileticians, historic and contemporary. Below is a beginning, preliminary proposal for fundamental ideas/understandings/strategies for a feminist homiletic. A feminist preacher:

1. advocates for women in ministry, women's ordination, and women preaching;

2. deconstructs the patriarchal politics of otherness, the patriarchal bias and misogynistic tendencies of text and tradition that not only are inscribed on pages of the Bible but also modern discussions related to biblical normativity and authority; understands both the oppressive and liberative natures of Scripture;

3. uses inclusive language for God and humanity, building a wide umbrella under which all can be welcomed and included; reflects and re-defines the major theological categories (Christ, salvation and redemption, sin, etc.) from a women's perspective;

4. understands the importance for women to read intentionally as women, out of their own life experiences and understandings, so that church communities receive a more balanced, nuanced, and comprehensive understanding of the text;

5. turns her attention in her exegesis and interpretation to characters in the narrative that are *not* the narrator's attention or focus and thus usually not deemed important. That includes those who are silent, not named, or who even may be absent. This practice is incarnated in the feminist preacher's life as she looks to the margins for those who have been forgotten, those who have been silenced or rendered invisible, seeking to bring them to voice;

6. engages the suffering in and of the world, of women and others, so the disparity dissipates between Sunday conversation and the world's realities;

7. maintains dialogue with others who have different understandings— about life, community, and about the sermon, choosing interpretive partners, (in conversations or through written word as in commentaries, etc.), who know different social locations and cultural contexts. A feminist preacher understands contextuality and how it shapes and forms us to have different priorities, values, and ideas; she holds a cultural humility about her own;

8. understands that women's oppression is woven tightly with other oppressions, so that the feminist preachers' work is seeking justice for all who long for it;

9. moves beyond lectionary, beyond text, and even beyond canon to find the narratives that are redemptive and that bring life and hope to the global woman's search for freedom. Feminist preachers understand that these stories can subvert or disrupt the androcentric nature of the biblical text. They break the text open to find the stories that speak a different and inspiring word about women, combing sacred texts for women's stories that have been forgotten or silenced. granting to these women life and legacy.

10. acknowledges the distinctive gifts women bring to preaching;

11. understands that biblical interpretation is political, and as such, directly and indirectly informs the answers to questions related to the *who* and *what* of preaching.

Case Study: Text and Sermon
(Numbers 27:1–11)

Numbers 27:1–11 was chosen for this sermon because it illustrates so clearly several of the important influences feminist theology had upon preaching. First, it brings to the community one story, nearly completely forgotten; Numbers 27:1–11 has not been a part of church/tradition lectionaries. The story introduces five women, sisters, who surprisingly are named for the reader. The women address the community, and those in power, requesting that a law be changed, one that is oppressive and unfair; it addresses gender bias. The sermon contextualizes the need for prophetic voices that challenge a harmful political and social climate. More substantively, the sermon addresses how we are called to disrupt law, even canonized law, that is harmful or not equitable for all God's creatures. Beneath any canonized word, the interpreter must seek to determine the will of "the Good Spirit," the one who is constantly at work to overcome the efforts of fallible men and women to bring liberation and freedom. The sermon advocates a certain understanding of biblical authority, the need for a theology of voice rather than word, an eye toward those oppressed by texts and traditions which suppress the liberating impulse of God.

"Disrupting the Word"

[I began working on this sermon, the week following the death of Congressman John Lewis (July 2020). His death was felt strongly among members of my congregation. He was a strong icon and symbol of hope; there was a real desire on the part of the community that his legacy be acknowledged, that he be remembered.]

Speak up! Speak Out! Get in the way! These words spoken by the late U.S. congressman John Lewis succinctly capture his philosophy of what he called good trouble, necessary trouble. Dedicating himself to a lifetime of activism, of striving for justice and equity in a world that often denies it, Lewis encouraged others to join the fight by speaking, walking, voting, rallying, protesting–doing whatever it took to create change. He not only advocated for racial equality but also for gender equality and for the rights of the LGBTQAI+ community. His vision was broad, not narrow and confined. Freedom is not a state, he said, it is an action. It took work, a lot of work, with hands, feet, heart, and voice to combat the pervasive forces of oppression and prejudice. It took a willingness for each of us to get into "good trouble," stirring the pot of status quo.

When reading the Exodus story of the calling of Moses, the deliverance of the Israelites from Egypt and their journey through the wilderness to the promised land, I am overwhelmed by the women in the story who, risking imprisonment or death, were willing to get into "good trouble." Staring into the faces of the powerful, those who could decide if they lived or died, they did what they knew was right, and without thought of their own security or safety, they spoke in word and deed. The church has forgotten many of their stories, omitting them from lectionaries and congregational preaching cycles. Such a shame. Some of the most valiant and courageous women have been left out of the church's preaching.

The Exodus story is one of several pivotal stories in the history of the Hebrew people who were enslaved and oppressed in Egypt. Many of us have known since childhood the story of Moses, the shepherd, who was called at the site of the burning bush to deliver the people from slavery and oppression. God had heard their cries. And Moses leads them out from Egypt and following a miraculous crossing of the Red Sea, he leads them through the wilderness to the land God had promised. What is not so well known in the church are the stories of the courageous women who defied power, stared it down, and living by their own conscience and what they thought to be right, saved Moses in his infancy and allowed the great hero to live and eventually become one of God's great deliverers. *Shiphrah and Puah*–Hebrew midwives

who defied the king and allowed Hebrew male babies to live. *Moses' mother*–
who feared for his life and took him to the water's edge to hide him from
the Egyptians. His sister *Miriam* who watched over him. *Pharaoh's daughter*
who took the child in and raised him.

Without these brave women there would be no story of deliverance by
Moses. But Moses was saved. He led the Israelites out of Egypt and through
the wilderness, a journey of forty years. As that journey ends we find the
amazing story of the daughters of Zelophehad.

It is interesting that the story of the five women is remembered.
Not only the story but also each of their names: Mahlah. Noah. Hoglah.
Milcah. Tirzah. Five sisters. They passed along courage to one another,
courage they had because they were united. The five sisters go hand in
hand to ask for a change to a God given law–the one that said only sons
could inherit their father's property–in front of the whole congregation
and its leaders, Eleazar the priest and the great Moses. Imagine their fear.
Feel their beating hearts, their shaking knees. Perhaps they had never
seen a woman challenge the law. Or maybe they had watched Miriam who
challenged Moses and who was smitten with leprosy! Our father has died
in the wilderness, they said, and he had no sons. *We* should inherit his
possessions, his property since there is no male heir. *We* need a place to
call our home, and there is no one else to carry on his name. Give *us* our
father's inheritance. What an audacious request!

*[Jewish midrash often provides interesting, insightful thinking about
stories in the Hebrew Bible that can become the heart of the sermon.]*

When Jewish rabbis wrote about this story centuries ago, they did so
with amazing insight. Listen to what they said: The mercies of men are not
like the mercies of [Him} who is everywhere. Men are more apt to be more
merciful to males than to females. But [He], who spoke and the world came
into being, is different. [His] mercies are for males as well as females. His
mercies are for all.[47] In other words, we cannot expect humans to be just and
act with equity, but God will because God values *all* people. The daughters
asked for a change to the law; they shook the written word out of its complacency and set it loose to do its disruptive, liberating work. Moses took the
sisters' request to God, and *God said yes*, just as the sisters hoped or maybe
even expected. The sisters spoke up. They spoke out. Good trouble.

---

47. Bialik and Ravnitzky, eds., *The Book of Legends*, 97–98.

[I included the following story about the passport to reinforce the importance of Anna Julia Cooper in our history, even though many may have never heard of her.]

Not long ago, I was looking through my passport because I needed it for identification to receive what is being called in California "The Real ID." The passport is an interesting document—following the first page with identifying information, there are pages that are stamped when you enter and leave non-native countries. At the top of each of these pages there is a quotation from a famous historical person who called the United States home or from a document that was formative in the country's formation. George Washington, words from the Declaration of Independence, Martin Luther King, Jr., John Kennedy, Theodore Roosevelt, Dwight Eisenhower, Lyndon Johnson. Words from a Mohawk Thanksgiving Address, and words spoken when the trans-continental railroad connecting the Atlantic and Pacific Oceans was finally completed. But then, on the last page: woman words–the only woman words! I was astonished. I was elated. I wondered who knew to add the words of Anna Julia Cooper to a United States passport.

Anna Julia Cooper was born in the southern part of the United States during the mid-1800s. Though her mother was a slave, she got an education and received her PhD in France at the Sorbonne. She wrote about slavery and theology. In seeking the best metaphor for God, Cooper came to understand God as the Singing Something. She said there is a singing something within me that brings me to voice–that allows to speak up and out through my pain and suffering and that of others. God brings me to voice, and I have begun thinking not that I was created in the image of God but in the sound of God. I can cry out for freedom and redemption.

[This last section of the sermon is intended to remind the listeners that the best way to honor Lewis's legacy and Cooper's legacy is to follow in their footsteps.]

Can you imagine a conversation between Anna Julia Cooper and John Lewis? I think he would say to her—Yes! Yes! Yes! There is something inside us, something that allows us to speak courageous words, words of liberation and hope and change. The words are God given. The courage to speak up for change. God given. The liberation and freedom is God given; it is what God longs for. God is waiting for us to liberate God's word from the confines of its ancient pages and to recover the dynamic and ever changing, new ways that God wishes to be at work in the world. That's our commission; that is our charge! Disrupt what oppresses. Speak up. Speak out. Go forth . . . and create some good trouble.

Assessment: Strengths and Limitations in This Theological Family

Barbara Brown Zikmund, Adair Lummis, and Patricia Chang in *Clergy Women: An Uphill Calling*, researching primarily white, Protestant clergy women, and Delores Carpenter in *A Time for Honor: A Portrait of African American Clergywomen*, described the state of clergywomen in this country about two decades ago. Both found that clergy women were significantly underpaid in relation to men and that denominational hiring processes consistently placed women at a disadvantage. Women were tracked into positions with less status and into ministries like chaplaincy and nonprofit work that were not preaching ministries. There was an especially strong resistance to preaching women in historic black congregations. A statistical update to these studies was published by Eileen Campbell-Reed in 2018.[48] While much improvement in the numbers of women who had been ordained and were preaching in many denominations/traditions was noted, Campbell-Reed indicated that there was still much work to do.[49] *Who* can preach? It would be naïve to think that after centuries of denying women access to leadership in the church, even with a burgeoning theological feminist movement in play, women would easily and quickly be welcomed into the preaching ministry and all questions about women preaching, biblical authority, and androcentric language would be answered. Biblical messages about the inferiority of women have been ingrained in hearts and minds for too long to be quickly dispelled.

What should be preached? As seen above, feminist biblical scholars and feminist theologians, provided for the homiletic community a wealth of information about the biblical text, women, authority, inclusive language and the redefining of theological categories that has directly or indirectly informed the homiletic conversation. It has been up to the feminist homileticians, then, to take the *most difficult* step–contextualizing feminist insights into local contexts. During the '90s and early 2000s women's preaching garnered attention through published volumes of women's sermons (and

---

48 Campbell-Reed, "State of the Clergywomen."

49. Zikmund, *Clergy Women*; Carpenter, *A Time for Honor*; Campbell-Reed, "State of the Clergywomen." See Tisdale, *How Women Transform Preaching*, for a comparison of the statistics explicated by each (Zikmund, 1–3; Carpenter, 3–4; Campbell-Reed, 4–6).

the exegetical work on which they were based) and feminist worship resources. These were helpful in highlighting women's gifts in preaching and normalizing women's liturgical leadership.[50] Still questions linger. Where in the seminary homiletic curriculum in our seminaries are the fundamental questions raised about biblical authority and the patriarchal nature of the biblical text? When should the preacher preach against the text, prioritizing women's rights over Scripture? When are realities raised about what it means for women to intentionally read texts as women? Not in most basic preaching texts, I think. Perhaps that is because these questions are raised elsewhere in the seminary curriculum. Or perhaps it is because most questions related to biblical and personal authority have been sufficiently wrestled to the ground, and answers are assumed. Yet, the questions and their implications seem endless even still.

Frances Willard ends *Woman in the Pulpit* with a biographical notation. In her earlier life she felt called to a preaching ministry but confesses she was "too timid" to follow it. She encourages young women to be braver, and she encourages communities to support them.[51] This seems a fine way to finish any essay about feminist theology and preaching.

For Further Reading

Brown, Sally A. *Cross Talk: Preaching Redemption Here and Now.* Louisville: Westminster John Knox, 2008.

Hudson, Mary Lin, and Mary Donovan Turner. *Saved from Silence: Finding Women's Voice in Preaching.* St. Louis: Chalice, 1999.

Rose, Lucy Atkinson. *Sharing the Word: Preaching in the Roundtable Church.* Louisville: Westminster John Knox, 1997.

Smith, Christine M. *Weaving the Sermon: Preaching in a Feminist Perspective.* Louisville: Westminster John Knox. 1989.

Tisdale, Leonora Tubbs. *How Women Transform Preaching.* Nashville: Abingdon, 2021. (Lyman Beecher Lectures, Yale Divinity School, Fall 2019).

---

50. See Winter, *Woman Word*; Childers, ed., *Birthing the Sermon*; Tisdale, *Abingdon Women's Preaching Annual* as examples of the editions in this series.

51. Willard, *Woman in the Pulpit*, 62.

10

Preaching in the Womanist
Theological Family

Courtney V. Buggs

The term *womanist* may be traced to Alice Walker's 1979 essay "Coming Apart" in which she writes, "the wife never considered herself a feminist—though she is, of course, a 'womanist.' A 'womanist' is a feminist, only more common."[1] In the notes of the essay Walker explains how the use of the term womanist comes from her own culture and is implicitly Black. Womanist is a word Black mothers used to describe "strong, outrageous, or outspoken behavior."[2] The use of the term gained wider usage after Walker's explicit description in *In Search of Our Mothers' Gardens* (1983):

Womanist

1. From *womanish* (Opp. Of "girlish," i.e., frivolous, irresponsible, not serious). A black feminist or feminist of color. From the black folk expression of mothers to female children, "You acting womanish," i.e., like a woman. Usually referring to outrageous, audacious, courageous or *willful* behavior. Wanting to know more and in greater depth than is considered "good" for one. Interested in grown-up doings. Acting grown up. Being grown up. Interchangeable with another black folk expression: "You trying to be grown." Responsible. In charge. *Serious.*

2. *Also*: A woman who loves other women, sexually and/ or nonsexually. Appreciates and prefers women's culture,

1. Walker, "Alice Walker's Womanism," 7.
2. Walker, "Alice Walker's Womanism," 7.

women's emotional flexibility (values tears as natural coun-
terbalance of laughter), and women's strength. Sometimes
loves individual men, sexually and/or nonsexually. Committed to survival and wholeness of entire people, male
and female. Not a separatist, except periodically, for health.
Traditionally universalist, as in: "Mama, why are we brown,
pink, and yellow and our cousins are white, beige, and black?
Ans: "Well, you know the colored race is just like a flower
garden, with every color flower represented." Traditionally
capable, as in: "Mama, I'm walking to Canada and I'm taking
you and a bunch of other slaves with me." Reply: "It wouldn't
be the first time."

3. Loves music. Loves dance. Loves the moon. *Loves* the Spirit.
    Loves love and food and roundness. Loves struggle. Loves
    the Folk. Loves herself. *Regardless.*

4. Womanist is to feminist as purple to lavender.[3]

Thus, the field of womanism emerged as Black women scholars across
academic disciplines resonated with the various expressions of womanist
ways of being. Black women scholars in religion analyzed how Walker's
language functioned in exploring notions of the Divine.[4] More specifically,
this essay explores womanist preaching as sacred proclamation informed
by particular theological, ethical, hermeneutical, and homiletical reinter-
pretations and expansions of Walker womanism. Womanist preaching
begins with theology that takes seriously the lived experiences of Black
women. The convergence of womanist scholars in ethics, interpretation,
and theology, and the everyday practices of preaching women, is expressed
in womanist preaching.

Circumstances that Gave Rise to This Theological Family

What characterizes womanist discourse is that black women
are engaged in the process of knowledge production that is
most necessary for their own flourishing rather than being
exploited for the enlightenment and entertainment of white
psyches and male egos.[5]

3. Walker, *In Search of Our Mothers' Gardens*, xii (italics original).

4. This writing refers to womanism in the North American context. It does not address Africana Womanism and Muslim Womanism.

5. See Floyd-Thomas, ed., *Deeper Shades of Purple*, 2.

In the context of Black liberation theology and feminist theology, Black women theologians noted the absence of attention to race, class, and gender as a tripartite source of oppression in the study of theology. Whereas as Black male theologians raised questions about the prevalence of white supremacy and white dominance in theological studies, and [white] feminists interrogated issues of patriarchy and gender equality, Black women theologians located themselves at the intersections of race and class and gender–and void of theological discussions that interrogated the impacts of this positionality. While Black women in religion shared with Black men the tasks of deconstructing whiteness in Christianity, they resisted doing so in ways that disregarded their own gendered-raced experiences of faith. Womanist theology critiques perpetuation of both white supremacy and Black male dominance.

Womanist theology emerged in the academy as a theological enterprise by Black women theologians to express God and the activities of God in the world from Black women's perspectives, rather than through the lenses of theologies that ignore or denigrate Black feminine embodiment. "Womanist theology is the systematic, faith-based exploration of the many facets of African American women's religiosity . . . based on the complex realities of black women's lives."[6] By valuing the ontologies and epistemologies of Black women, and women of color, womanist theology reimages Black women as real beings, rather than stereotypical caricatures of the white imagination. Womanist theology seeks to reclaim marginalized epistemologies of Black women and to take seriously the ways in which Black women engage God and religion.

Delores Williams' *Sisters in the Wilderness: The Challenge of Womanist God-Talk*, a classic text in womanist theological scholarship, critiques liberative theologies that fail to seriously consider the situatedness of Black women. "Womanist theology attempts to help Black women see, affirm and have confidence in the importance of their experience and faith," writes Williams, "for determining the character of the Christian religion in the African American community."[7] In the tradition of womanist theological thought, the life of the biblical Hagar is raised as a prism through which to demonstrate the operative motif of survival and quality of life for Black women.[8] Hagar personifies the ability to endure and thrive against and in spite of the odds, an enduring characteristic that typifies the experience of enslaved and emancipated Black women in North America.

6. Mitchem, *Introducing Womanist Theology*, ix.

7. Williams, *Sisters in the Wilderness*, 6.

8. Williams, *Sisters in the Wilderness*, 6.

Additionally, womanist theology appropriates the life of Christ (as opposed to his death) as an ethical imperative. Jesus' ministerial vision of life is one that resists domination, marginalization, and oppression.[9] This theological view necessitated new analytical categories and methods to interrogate validation of Empire in the biblical world and how Empire-like systems impact contemporary Black women and religious experiences in Black communities. Womanist theologians reread religious histories and interpretations of the Divine with suspicion, reading and reclaiming the lives of Black women and girls as historically valuable rather than extinguishable, inconsequential or disposable. This rereading involves naming and disrupting the contradictions of theologies that privilege an all loving, all knowing, all powerful God, who passively observes systemic and institutional injustices.

Womanist theologians refuse to allow the histories of Black women to be subsumed by a totalizing Black or Eurocentric experience. Rather, womanists critique themselves, their communities, and society, for the ways in which Black women are ignored, devalued, and marginalized. Moreover, womanists deconstruct hegemonic practices and structures that maintain and perpetuate the cultural production of evil against black women's bodies.[10] Considering the centrality of faith and spirituality to many Black women, womanist scholars interrogate faith communities, particularly the Black church as an institution, concerning traditional church doctrines that restrict, control, and silence Black women under the guise of Divine mandate and Black male authority.

In addition to Williams, Jacquelyn Grant and Katie G. Cannon are known as matriarchs of womanism in religion. In *White Women's Christ and Black Women's Jesus*, Grant critiques early [white] feminists/feminist theologians for participating in oppression and racism.[11] Claiming to appeal to "women's experience" is to do what oppressors do.[12] Feminism presumes commonality with oppressed women, commonality that does not exist. Grant shifts attention from the traditional white male Christ to the Jesus who aligns with the "stranger, the outcast, the hungry, the weak, the poor."[13] Like Williams, Grant centers the tridimensional experiences of Black women as the center of gravity for theological reflection.

---

9. Williams, *Sisters in the Wilderness*, 22.

10. Townes, *Womanist Ethics*.

11. Grant, *White Women's Christ and Black Women's Jesus*.

12. Grant, *White Women's Christ and Black Women's Jesus*, 218.

13. Grant, *White Women's Christ and Black Women's Jesus*, 219.

Cannon's revolutionary *Black Womanist Ethics* interrogates established moral approaches to ethics, which do not take into account those living under oppression. Cannon investigates the ways in which "racism, gender discrimination and economic exploitation" necessitate Black communities, more specifically, Black women, to cultivate ethical standards that enable them to survive and thrive against the odds.[14] Drawing on analysis of the work of literary folklorist Zora Neale Hurston, Cannon contends for the moral vision used by Black women that is cultivated in the difficulties of everyday life.

These works were among the first publications of womanism in religion and proved foundational to establishing womanism as a field of study in the American Academy of Religion and seminaries and divinity schools. Since then, second and third wave womanists (and beyond) in the fields of theology, ethics, biblical interpretation, ecology and homiletics continue to expand on the ways in which sacred texts are reinterpreted and proclaimed, not only for Black women, but for all persons who resist relegation to the edges of society.

Purposes and Characteristics of Preaching in This Theological Family

> A womanist critique of homiletics challenges conventional biblical interpretations that characterize African American women as "sin-bringing Eve," "wilderness-whimpering Hagar," "henpecking Jezebel," "whoring Gomer," "prostituting Mary-Magdalene," and "conspiring Sapphira."[15]

In the context of homiletics, womanist theology, womanist ethics, and womanist interpretation, converge to inform womanist preaching. It is preaching that critically examines the world of the text, the text, the contemporary world, and the condition of humanity, with particular attention to Black women's experiences, to interrupt practices of proclamation that reinforce discrimination and marginalization. Womanist preaching contains the core elements raised in Black preaching,[16] but it is distinguished by commitment to Black women and girls and redemption of women in sacred proclamation. While womanist preaching takes form and structure similar to other

14. Cannon, *Black Womanist Ethics*, 8.

15. Cannon, *Katie's Canon*, 114.

16. For more on Black preaching see: Mitchell, *Black Preaching*; Crawford and Troger, *The Hum*; Simmons and Thomas, eds., *Preaching with Sacred Fire*; Gilbert, *The Journey and Promise*; and Thomas, *Introduction to the Practice.*

preaching methods, it necessarily orients around Black women's engagement with the world and texts of various forms.

While womanist thought maintains its origins with Walker, subsequent scholarship "has been adapted to more effectively address the interest and exigencies of Black women but also to broaden the limited scope of religious discourse in the academy."[17] Womanist scholars in religion expand and reinterpret Walker's work, further mining what it means to critically appreciate Black womanhood and Black women's contributions to a better world. The womanist tenets described in Stacey Floyd-Thomas's edited volume provide a useful framework for womanist homiletical analysis. The tenets of radical subjectivity, traditional communalism, redemptive self-love, critical engagement, and appropriation and reciprocity, are briefly described below.[18]

The first tenet, radical subjectivity, refers to a "process that emerges as Black females in the nascent phase of their identity development come to understand agency as the ability to defy a forced naiveté in an effort to influence the choices made in one's life and how conscientization incites resistance against marginality."[19] It is naming and claiming one's own identity, or as Debra Majeed writes, "the empowering assertion of the Black woman's voice or the voice that speaks when others fear to."[20] Radical subjectivity is unapologetically showing up as ones whole self, resisting the isms that cause self-fragmentation, partitioning, and multiple consciousness.

The second tenet, traditional communalism, is described as "The affirmation of the loving connections and relational bonds formed by Black women—including familial, maternal, platonic, religious, sexual, and spiritual ties. Black women's ability to create, re-member, nurture, protect, sustain, and liberate communities which are marked and measured . . . by the acts of inclusivity, mutuality, reciprocity, and self-care practiced within it."[21] This expansive tenet includes notions of hospitality, solidarity and cross generational values. At the same time, traditional communalism pointedly resists "the biological deterministic assumption that a woman's role is to serve as nurturer and protector."[22]

---

17. Floyd-Thomas, "Introduction," 5.

18. Four of the tenets align with Walker's four-part definition. Floyd-Thomas et al. add one additional tenet, critical engagement, to emphasize the critical dialogue between womanist scholars and womanist allies.

19. Floyd-Thomas, "Introduction," 16.

20. Floyd-Thomas, "Introduction," 16.

21. Hayes, "Standing in My Mother's Shoes," 78.

22. Hayes, "Standing in My Mother's Shoes," 78.

Generously loving oneself as a Black woman is the essence of the third tenet, redemptive self-love. It is "an assertion of the humanity, customs, and aesthetic value in contradistinction to the commonly held stereotypes characteristic of white solipsism."[23] Kelly Brown Douglas expresses redemptive self-love this way: "the ability and permission to know that it is alright to be Black and female."[24] Redemptive self-love is both reclamation of self and active resistance to social "norms" that diminish the beautiful beingness of being Black and woman . . . woman and Black.

The epistemological privilege of Black women is central to the fourth tenet, that is, critical engagement. It is the "conscious and intentional appropriation of one's knowing and the orientation of that knowledge," writes M. Shawn Copeland, "toward the achievement of authentic and moral human living . . . and the internal requirement toward excellence."[25] Critical engagement takes seriously the multiple oppressions experienced by Black women and the ways in which Black women strategically challenge and dismantle them. Simply put, critical engagement empowers Black women to embrace their knowledges as valid, viable, and significant, independent of Eurocentric systems of validation.

Finally, Floyd-Thomas offers a fifth tenet—appropriation and reciprocity—as a "postscript to womanist allies."[26] While it does not directly correlate with Walker's four-part definition, it invites practices of solidarity and shared intentionality for liberation of all who are oppressed and pushed to the margins. Ada Maria Isasi-Díaz cautions allies against romanticizing the mutual struggle, yet embraces epistemological tasks raised in womanist work—the work of knowing and naming and renaming and defining and redefining from the perspectives of one's lived experiences.[27]

In terms of womanist preaching, these tenets provide an ethical framework in which preachers may engage the text, the local and larger community, and the life of the preacher. For example, using the tenet traditional communalism, womanist informed sermons may explore the richness of Black culture alongside the culture of the ancient biblical world, dismantling notions of uncivility, barbarism, and heathenism that have been associated with historical Africa. The values with which one approaches practices of engagement with the Divine; exegesis of self, text, and community; and preaching itself, are critical to womanist preaching.

23. Westfield, "'Mama Why . . . ?,'" 142.

24 Westfield, "'Mama Why . . . ?,'" 142.

25. Copeland, "A Thinking Margin," 208.

26. Townes, "The Womanist Dancing Mind," 50.

27. Isasi-Díaz, "Womanists and *Mujeristas*," 269.

Stated differently, womanist preaching is an intentionally liberative resistive sacred speech act, that takes seriously the lived experiences of Black women, and other marginalized populations, in conversation with the Divine and Spirit world, sacred texts, and the political, social, economic realities of everyday life. Moreover, womanist preaching embodies epistemological privilege exercised by Black women proclaimers, both in the realm of the academy and everyday life.

Womanist preaching practices include interrogation of homiletical practices that include "homiletical othering" (that is, using language to stigmatize others, creating distance between oneself, the congregation and others in the world) which can even go so far as insulting and demeaning others.[28] The sanctity of life for all persons is critical to a womanist homiletic. The womanist tenets inform the how the preacher might engage written texts hermeneutically and the language the preacher uses to convey reflections on the texts; and the embodied sensibilities used during the preachment. Preaching from a womanist perspective need not encompass every element of womanism in every sermon; womanist preaching is pliable and expandable, even as it is grounded by commitment to the agency and vocal expression of the lived experiences of Black women and girls. "A Womanist homiletic for twenty-first century proclaimers," writes Fry Brown, "means utilization of a liberative discourse with God's people with *metamorphic boldness*, stepping out of the status quo and seeking language and content that shakes dungeons and makes chains fall off."[29]

Preaching from a womanist perspective is not a new form or endeavor; rather, the ethical considerations of womanist preaching are evident in nineteenth and twentieth century Black preaching women such as Julia A. J. Foote, Maria W. Stewart, Sojourner Truth, and Prathia L. Hall, to name a few. Rhetorical analysis enables us to look back at sermons using the language of womanism to then classify preachments as womanist preaching.

It is important to note that proclamation by Black women preachers is not necessarily *womanist*, in the same way that not all Black women are necessarily womanists.[30] Womanism, and by extension womanist preaching, is not contained by strict lines of demarcation for what/who is and what/who is not expressly womanist. Proclaimers and practitioners engage womanism

28. Brown, "A Womanist Model," 6.

29. Brown, "A Womanist Model," 9.

30. For a fuller discussion on naming oneself and claiming womanism, see the essays in the section called "Radical Subjectivity" in Floyd-Thomas, ed., *Deeper Shades of Purple*: these pieces include Cannon, "Structured Academic Amnesia"; Duncan, "From 'Force-Ripe' to 'Womanish/ist'"; Majeed, "Womanism Encounters Islam"; and Hayes, "Standing in the Shoes My Mother Made."

from their own points of entry, adopting, expanding, interrogating, and building upon a foundation of preaching that attends holistically to Black women in particular, and all persons, in general.

Case Study: Text and Sermon
(Luke 1:46–59; Isaiah 43:18–19)

The following sermon is based on Luke 1:46–59 and Isa 43:18–19. The context of the sermon is the pastoral installation service of the first woman elected as senior pastor in the one-hundred–year history of the Allen Temple Baptist Church in Oakland, California, Jaqueline A. Thompson. The preacher, Gina M. Stewart, is also a Black woman senior pastor, who was elected to the senior pastorate as the first woman in her congregation' twenty-eight-year history. Homiletically, context matters. Attentiveness to the social and local context enables the preacher to ground the sermon in ways that resonate with both the community and the larger audience. Moreover, this particular Black woman preaching this particular pastoral installation in this particular church allows the event of the preachment to be a progressive message that speaks to Black religious traditions. The sermon title itself, "God is Doing A New Thing," functions on cultural, social, and local levels to convey that times are changing, and the changes are God's doing. Throughout the sermon, the preacher engages the community with vernacular and the pastoral authoritativeness often found Black churches.

Theologically, the preacher offers a vision of Jesus that is countercultural: Jesus is a revolutionary rabble rouser. This womanist reading of Jesus, that is, Divinity enfleshed, resists christological views of a passive Savior of the world, even in and of an unjust world. This Jesus upends unjust systems of the world that do harm. Womanist interpretation–reading against the text and interrogating historical readings that do not account for the lived experiences of Black women–enables the preacher to excavate meaning from the text that is life giving for Black women, in particular, and Black communities more generally. The sermon moves listeners from a romanticized view of a submissive peasant girl to the praise speech of a young girl who dares to sing.

When turning to the sermon itself, we note that the printed version is reduced somewhat from the complete sermon as preached.[31] The sermon

---

31. This sermon manuscript was approved for use by the author and preacher, Rev. Dr. Gina M. Stewart. The choice to examine a sermon other than my own is one of the ways in which I embody Walker's phrase, "Mama, I'm walking to Canada and I'm taking you and a bunch of other slaves with me." It is meant to demonstrate my capacity

has an introduction and four moves that culminate in the claim of a "new day" in the life of the local church and the lives of the listening audience.[32] The new day is from God, and is not just for the pastor-elect, but it is for all Black women in ministry, all black women interested in ministry, and all those who support Black women in ministry. More broadly, it is for all women, and persons interested in gender justice in local churches.

"God Is Doing a New Thing"

[Introduction. The sermon begins by naming the situatedness of women in the biblical world, contemporary society, and the church. The preacher brings into view the conundrum of Black women and the church, meaning, traditional Black Baptist churches. Radical subjectivity is the visible womanist ethic.]

When women appear in the Bible, they are often among the extras in the story. Sometimes they have supporting roles, but very rarely are they the stars. Like extras in a movie, even when they are the topic of discussion, they are often in the background. This is because the stories of the Bible often reflect what theologian Lisa Wilson Davison calls a "patriarchal, patrilineal and patrilocal society."[33] This means in practical and societal terms that the culture is dominated by men, wives live with their husbands' and/or families, and land is passed down through male heirs.

The larger implication is that in the biblical text most of the primary concerns are male concerns. The storyline revolves around men. Even when women appear in the story, they are most often presented from a man's perspective. "Thus, while holding the belief that all Scripture is given by inspiration of God, it cannot be denied that the Bible is a male production."[34]

This is not just true for the Bible it is also true in society. In her book *Lean In*, Sheryl Sandberg states, "The blunt truth is that men still run the world. Despite significant strides made by women over the years, women often lag behind their male counterparts in most arenas of leadership and in compensation."[35] And James Brown put it this way: it's a man's world.[36]

---

for the work, coupled with my desire to bring other capable Black women into the work.

32. The sermon is structured by moves, following the suggestion of Buttrick, *Homiletic: Moves and Structures.*

33. Davison, *Preaching the Women of the Bible* (Kindle locations 186–87).

34. Davison, *Preaching the Women of the Bible* (Kindle location 184).

35. Sandberg, *Lean In*, 5.

36. Brown, "It's a Man's Man's World," track 5 on Brown, perf., *The Best of James*

It doesn't stop with society, in many instances it is true in (although there are exceptions), the church. While the Black church has been a source of strength and empowerment for Black women; some of us learned to speak in the church and to serve in the church and lead in church, but it is also the place where the invisibility of women particularly in positions of leadership is most pronounced.

> [Move 1. Having framed the context in which women operate in the world and in ministry, the sermon pivots with "Nevertheless . . . ." The preacher strings together instances in which God does something on behalf of a woman in the biblical text, rather than in the interest of men. Critical engagement (with the text) is the womanist ethical tenet at work here.]

Nevertheless, there are times when despite patriarchy, despite misogyny, and despite sexism, racism, precedent and in some cases tradition, God steps into history and intervenes in such a way that it turns the world upside down. Every now and then God steps in and redirects/reroutes the course of history.

Consider the Daughters of Zelophehad: the daughters of Zelophehad who, after the death of their father came to the door of the tent of meeting, where judgments were issued, to talk to Moses, Eleazar, the leaders, and the congregation. Their father had died in the wilderness, and he had no sons. They said to Moses, "Why should our father's name disappear from his clan because he had no son? Give us property among our father's relatives" (Num 27:4). And in an unprecedented decision, God ruled in favor of the daughters.

Consider Deborah: in the violent and turbulent aftermath of Joshua's conquest of Canaan and against the backdrop of a culture steeped in patriarchy, against the backdrop of a patrilineal and patrilocal society, Debra was called and gifted by God to lead in a man's world. God stepped in and Called Debra, a prophetess, the wife of Lappidoth and a judge to lead God's people to victory and provide leadership to the kingless people.

> [Move 2. Next, exegesis of the text is articulated in plain language that paints a picture of God's interruption and intervention in the life of a young girl who would likely otherwise be ignored.]

And although we have often read this text as a Christmas story there is more to this story than what meets the eye. For it is against the backdrop

---

Brown (CD).

of the dark night of oppression and hopeful waiting, that God step in and sends the angel Gabriel to deliver a life-altering message to Mary, a teen-age girl from the wrong side of the tracks. Mary was not wealthy or powerful.

Gabriel appears to her in a private home in Nazareth-an insignificant village likely made of nothing more than a handful of simple homes around a common well. In a culture where women were barely even noticed except as a wife and mother or in reference to the man they were in relationship with, Mary at around the age of 15 who has been betrothed to marry Joseph, the carpenter of Nazareth is told that she has found favor with God.

But it is not the kind of favor that has been highjacked by contemporary church vernacular that declares we're blessed and highly favored. This would be a different kind of favor. A favor that could mean ridicule, shame and isolation because of the assignment.

And this young girl (who from a sociological perspective would have never made the short list for the assignment because of her position and location) meets with her cousin Elizabeth (who had been barren for years but is now also pregnant in her old age) for consultation, confirmation and celebration. She realizes that the Spirit is on her, in her and with her. Mary's first response is reminiscent of the song that Hannah sang when she found out that the Lord had opened her barren womb. Mary opened her mouth and sang a song of praise.

[Move 3. The third move of the sermon is to illuminate Mary's agency, vividly demonstrated in the Magnificat. Radical subjectivity and Redemptive Self-Love (of Mary, and by extension, other women) are central to womanist ethical values.]

It is called The Magnificat which literally means "my soul magnifies. She sang, "My soul magnifies the Lord and my spirit rejoices in God my Savior." Women receive special attention in Luke's Gospel. Only Luke gives the full speeches of Mary and her cousin Elizabeth prior to the birth of Jesus. Only Luke mentions Anna the prophetess. Only Luke tells that women traveled with Jesus and actually supported Jesus financially. Only Luke mentions the occasion at the home of Mary and Martha where Jesus taught Mary as a rabbi teaching a disciple. Luke frequently puts together a parable with a man as the central character with a woman as the central character to teach about the realm of God.

Not only does Luke record this song that is our text, but he displays rhetorical proficiency by using epideictic speech or praise speech, the Magnificat, on the lips of a woman. And thereby Luke portrays her, not just as the pregnant woman who is the mother of Jesus, but a woman with a prophetic voice announcing the coming reign of God's redemptive justice. Notice what she says: "For the Mighty One has done great things for me, / and holy is his name. / His mercy is for those who fear him / from generation to generation. / He has shown strength with his arm; / he has scattered the proud in the thoughts of their hearts. / He has brought down the powerful from their thrones, / and lifted up the lowly; / he has filled the hungry with good things / and sent the rich away empty."

Praise speech is attributed to a woman, a member of a typically voiceless or marginalized population-specifically an unmarried peasant girl, subjected to economic exploitation by oppressive rulers, living in an economically depressed and militarily occupied country. She sings in revolutionary language, the language of reversal is on the lips of a woman who describes the revolutionary acts of God that will result in an upheaval of the social hierarchy of power, wealth and poverty. Mary's song signals that a change is coming.

The incarnation is not just about babies and mangers and swaddling clothes, but incarnation is revolution. The incarnation is about revolution, good news for all people. A baby will grow up to be a rebel rabbi, and a rabble-rousing preacher who will proclaim good news to the captives, the recovery of sight to the blind, the year of the Lord's favor. Holy work in the world has always been like this: messy, earthy, physical, touchable." God is stepping in to turn the world upside down.

> *[Move 4. In the final move, the sermon shifts to what happens when God steps in—new things. The reason of the occasion for this preachment is a new thing. It is a call to celebration and a critique of religious systems that marginalize women's leadership. Traditional communalism surfaces as the preacher articulates a communal call to new beginnings.]*

While many have focused on what God does with Mary's body as the mother of Jesus (which is significant), I wish to suggest that we do not need to "sleep on" what God does with her voice. Mary's song offers an unmistakable clue that Luke's message is not just for a select few but it is intended for a wider and more diverse audience. In a culture of materialistic values and beliefs, shame and honor, the proclamation of salvation included those that society typically excluded. And so, Luke begins this Gospel with Mary's song of exaltation extolling a divine reversal. And Mary sang. "My soul does magnify the Lord and my spirit rejoices in God my savior." All because God stepped in . . . and did a new thing.

And we rejoice today because God has done a new thing! Isaiah prophesied that God would do a new thing. And God has done a new thing here at Allen Temple Baptist Church. After 100 years, more than 2,000 parishioners stood patiently to cast more than 90% of their votes for Rev. Dr. Jacqueline A. Thompson as your ninth Senior Pastor. On April 7, 2019, Allen Temple, a Baptist Church made a pioneering move and broke with tradition and precedent and shattered the glass ceiling by electing the woman who was arrested by the preaching and ministry of Dr. J. Alfred Smith, Sr. at the age of 12.

In its centennial year of existence. In its 100 year of existence, as you celebrate the faithfulness of God, the decision to call the Rev. Dr. Jacqueline Thompson is a revolutionary act. This is a revolution. At a time when some churches' nostalgic relationships with tradition threatens to tie the people to their past and repress alertness to present realities, repress responsiveness to new, and repress the potential for growth into yet-unrealized possibilities, God has stepped in again and done something to shake Christendom, Baptists and the Black Church out of its complacency and its complicity.

God is doing a new thing. Not only did Isaiah hear God but Allen Temple heard this same God whose presence was not limited to the past but who was active in contemporary events. And this God says to Israel, "I am about to do a new thing; now it springs forth, do you not perceive it? God's past actions provide the foundation for his present and future works because his nature is unchanging. And so God says forget the former things so that they can perceive the new thing God is about to do. Knowledge of the past can limit the imagination, and God's capacity to act knows no limits.

This text invites the community to see beyond the obvious: to see what God creates anew. New, refreshing experiences of faith are the reason for a community to praise God. Faith is restored as we see differently. The world is never as we perceive it: God's creative power, always active in the world, becomes a source of hope: "I will make a way in the wilderness and rivers in the desert" (v. 19b). This verse invites a foretaste of the fruits of "something new," something beyond the obvious, something beyond what we have been programmed to see. But not only did God step in back then, God keeps stepping in, despite the sexism, despite the racism, despite the classism and all of the other systems that would impede our ability to flourish, God keeps stepping in, despite disappointment, betrayal, hardship, opposition, satanic harassment, and the powers of darkness, despite disorientation and fragmentation God keeps stepping in!

[The sermon ends with inspired ad-lib celebration. It is homiletics on its feet as the Spirit gives utterance. This practice of "closing" is

*common in Black preaching traditions. The preacher moves from
what is written on paper to what is written on her heart.]*

Assessment: Strengths and Limitations
in This Theological Family

One of the most significant contributions of womanist preaching to the
field of homiletics is that it takes seriously the voices and contributions
of persons who have been undervalued and ignored as sources for critical
theological reflection: Black women. That said, the short history of scholarship on womanist thought is not indicative of the ways in which Black
women have participated in sacred speech acts, both in the local church
and the local community. The particular lens of Black women who have
been ignored, discounted, and marginalized in the North American context, enables a bottom-up view from which to engage sacred texts and a
vision of hope and wholeness for humankind.

Second, womanist preaching brings to the fore embedded theologies that ignore systematic forms of oppression such as racism, classism,
sexism, ableism, and heteronormativity. While it may be considered in
the family of other liberative preaching methods, womanist preaching is
distinguished by theological and ethical commitments that intentionally
privilege the quotidian experiences of Black women as authoritatively relevant for engaging the activity of the Divine in the world. Stated differently, preaching from a womanist perspective is accessing, even honoring,
the divinely inspired epistemological capacity of women, Black women, to
call forth and proclaim a hope for the world.

While lived experience is a factor in how one engages the Divine,
the cultural and social histories associated with Black women in North
America make it difficult for some to envision Black women as sources of
religious authority. Proponents of biblical authority privilege the Bible as
the primary sacred text, rather than a sacred text among other texts, such
as, for instance, raced-gender-sexed bodies as sacred texts. Womanists
insist that particular embodiment—Black women's bodies—offers critical
insights for redemption for those persons deemed 'the least of the least'.
Womanist preaching holds space for viewpoints that resist homogeneity,
preferring particularity as a Divine good.

While womanist preaching offers critical engagement that interrogates
oppressions, public proclamation in support of lesbian, queer and transgender women. In many Black religious communities, heteronormativity takes
precedent over claims of inclusion for all women, and open conversations

about sexuality and gender fluidity remain unaddressed. Third wave womanists advocate for more visible support of gay, lesbian, bisexual, transgender and queer women in the quest for equal treatment and access.[37] Arguably, early womanists engaged the major theological questions of their generation, leaving subsequent womanists to continue the work of making space at the table for all voices. Twenty-first century womanists (preachers or otherwise) take up the challenge of inclusive religious practices and proclamation. To this end, womanist preaching in necessarily informed by academic scholarship and the witness of Black women in the pews and the public square. The convergence of the two enables possibilities for solidarity with and wholeness for all women animated in sacred proclamation.

For Further Reading

Allen, Donna E. *Toward a Womanist Homiletic: Katie Cannon, Alice Walker, and Emancipatory Proclamation*. Martin Luther King, Jr. Memorial Studies in Religion. Culture, and Social Development 13. New York: Lang, 2013.

Brown, Teresa L. Fry. "Prophetic Truth-Telling in a Season of Fatigue and Fragmentation." In *Questions Preachers Ask: Essays in Honor of Thomas G. Long*, edited by Scott Black Johnston et al., 126–39. Louisville: Westminster John Knox, 2016.

———. "A Womanist Model for Proclamation of the Good News." http://www.theafricanamericanlectionary.org/pdf/preaching/WomanistPreaching.

Cannon, Katie Geneva. *Katie's Canon: Womanism and the Soul of the Black Community*. New York: Continuum, 1996.

Crawford, A. Elaine Brown. *Hope in the Holler: A Womanist Theology*. Louisville: Westminster John Knox, 2002.

Floyd-Thomas, Stacey M., ed. *Deeper Shades of Purple: Womanism in Religion and Society*. Religion, Race, and Ethnicity. New York: New York University Press, 2006.

Johnson, Kimberly P. *The Womanist Preacher: Proclaiming Womanist Rhetoric from the Pulpit*. Rhetoric, Race, and Religion. Lanham, MD: Lexington, 2017.

Mitchem, Stephanie Y. *Introducing Womanist Theology*. Maryknoll: Orbis, 2002

37. See Coleman, ed., *Ain't I A Womanist, Too?*

11

Preaching in the Latinx Liberation Theological Family

PABLO A. JIMÉNEZ

THE RELATIONSHIP BETWEEN LATIN American liberation theology with homiletics as a theological discipline, and preaching as a pastoral practice, has always been difficult. These controversies have several historical roots.

Circumstances That Gave Rise to This Theological Family

We may identify three important roots that give rise to the tensions among Latin American liberation theology and homiletics we well as the pastoral practice of preaching. First, Latin American Liberation Theology emerged in the context of the Roman Catholic Church in South America. Preaching in the Roman Catholic Church in Latin America is rather limited, for the parish priest rarely offers a full sermon in a Sunday Mass, opting for short homilies instead. These meditations comment on some aspects of the text and provide some theological insights, but they seldom explore topics in depth.

Second, evangelization of the Americas was intertwined with colonial enterprises. For this reason, both Catholic and Protestant preaching in Latin American has been mostly politically conservative. On the one hand, until recently the Roman Catholic Church was recognized as the official religion of many Latin American countries. Of course, the Catholic Church largely legitimized the conquest of America, disguising indentured servitude as evangelism. Case in point are the "Encomiendas," a system by which the church placed groups of indigenous people under the care of hacienda owners. The system forced indigenous individuals to work for the *encomenderos*, to whom they had been "entrusted" to be evangelized. Some priests, like Antonio de Montesinos, preached against this practice. However, such priests were soon removed from their positions and substituted with priests who were compliant to the Spanish Crown.

Notice that I said "compliant to the Crown" and not to the Church. The Catholic Church entered into an agreement with Spain that gave the Crown the right to manage the affairs of the Church in the newly discovered lands. The *Patronato Real* ("Royal Patronage"—also called the "Indian Patronage") gave the Spanish monarchy the authority to select and send missionaries to America, collect tithes and ecclesiastical taxes, fix and modify the boundaries of the dioceses in America and to veto the election of bishops and archbishops. The *Patronato*, which expanded through a series of bulls issued from 1486 to 1539, allowed the Crown act on behalf of the Pope and even to filter communication between Rome and the nascent Church in the Americas. The end result is clear: The Roman Catholic Church in Latin America depended on the Spanish Crown and, therefore, represented its interests.

On the other hand, Protestantism arrived in Latin America during the nineteenth century, affirming many of the values and practices of the European countries that asserted colonial power over different parts of the world. The missionary agencies that evangelized Latin America were also very theologically and politically conservative. Given that Latin America was mostly Catholic, the region was largely excluded from the ecumenical councils held in Europe in the nineteenth century. This explains why most of the early Protestant missionaries were sponsored by independent missionary agencies, not by mainline denominations.

The Cold War further entrenched conservative political views in both the Catholic and the Protestant church, which rejected Communism, an ideology that defined itself as atheist. Therefore, sermons condemning communism and atheism were common at the time. The conservative political ideas of pastors priests and preachers were transparent at the pulpit.

Latin American Protestantism was also largely as politically conservative as the Catholic Church. The main difference between their outlooks was that Catholics looked to Spain, representing the past colonial heritage; while Protestants looked mostly to the United States, representing the future neocolonial interests of the nation that soon became a superpower.

Third, the hermeneutics used to interpret Scripture tended to spiritualize the Biblical text, rendering the biblical stories into allegories about salvation. I remember clearly when my pastor, who was a learned man, taught me this interpretation technique. Taking as point of departure the story of the multiplication of the loaves and the fishes, he told me that the needy people represented the multitudes who "hunger" for salvation. The bread and the fishes represented the message of the gospel. Of course, the disciples represented the church, for Jesus commands them to feed the crowd. According to this interpretation, the main point of this miracle story is that Jesus commands the Church to evangelize, addressing the spiritual needs of the crowds who have not accepted Jesus as personal savior, nor confess that Jesus is Lord.

At the time, many interpreters also emphasized that biblical texts had only one possible correct interpretation. Proponents of the allegorical interpretation of Scripture denied all other approaches, particularly those "political" readings that paid attention to the social context of the Bible. While no one denies the command to evangelize, forced allegorical interpretations like the one described above overlook not only the social and political implications of the text, but also the historical setting, the sociological condition and the economic situation of the people of God, as depicted in the Bible.

Church leaders weened on biblical interpretation that overlooks the social and political needs of the people, tend to develop pastoral practices that also overlook the social and political needs of their parishioners. Even though some Protestant churches and denominations opened hospitals, orphanages and schools, most congregations concentrated their efforts on saving souls, not on feeding the hungry.

These conditions explain why the emergent Latin American liberation theology saw preaching and homiletics with suspicion as vehicles to support the political and economic systems that created and sustained poverty in the region.

The Emergence of Latin American Theology

The aftermath of the First World War changed the world of theology. One of the main consequences was the development of Theologies of Action, particularly in French-speaking countries. These theologies, also called Theologies of Human Action, called the church to reflect upon the reality faced by the people. However, the reflection had to be critical, using the emergent social sciences as instruments of analysis. Theologies of action also analyzed critically the church's ministerial practice. Furthermore, they called the Christian community to transcend practice, developing instead a praxis. What is the difference between practice and praxis? A praxis is based on an ideology, while practice is not. Praxis guides the pastoral action of the church, seeking the transformation of society.

While many critics affirm that praxis is anti-biblical, both the Theologies of Action and their many derivatives assert that praxis is based on the Bible, particularly on Jesus' ministry. Jesus engaged in praxis, for his point of departure was ideological: The "gospel of the kingdom." Given that Jesus had the goal of transforming society according to the values of the kingdom of God, his message was ideological and his ministry was praxis.

While Theologies of Action emerged after the First World War, the decolonization movement emerged after the Second World War. The United Nations, founded in 1945, affirmed in Article 1(2) of its charter the principle of "equal rights and self-determination of peoples." In 1945, 750 million people (about a third of the world's population) lived in territories controlled by colonial powers. Since then, more than 80 countries have obtained their independence. The UN General Assembly adopted the Resolution 1514 (XV) in 1960, titled *Declaration on the Granting of Independence to Colonial Countries and Peoples* calling for the end of colonialism in all its forms.

The struggle for the independence of Algiers, a French colony in Africa, stoked the fires of anti colonialism. Soon, the literature on the subject proliferated, particularly in French. It is no coincidence that one of the key figures in the development of Latin American Liberation Theology, Gustavo Gutierrez, studied philosophy and psychology in Belgium and France.

It is rather easy to envision how these trends coincided in Latin America. The Cold War divided the world between pro-western and pro-soviet countries. This ideological polarization gave Europe and the United States of America an excuse to tolerate right-wing dictatorships in Latin America and the Caribbean. Since 1945, over 40 dictators and military juntas have ruled different countries in the region, at different times.

Soon Catholic theologians, most of whom had studied in Europe, blended principles from the French Theologies of Action with anticolonial theory and Marxist social analysis, birthing, thus, Latin American Liberation Theology. Although the movement grew during the sixties, it received its name from a series of lectures titled "Toward a Theology of Liberation," presented by Gustavo Gutierrez in a regional meeting in Peru 1968. Gutierrez published the book that launched the movement, *Teología de la Liberación: Perspectivas* (English Translation: *A Theology of Liberation: History, Politics and Salvation*), in 1971.

Catholic Liberation Theology proliferated in structures called *Comunidades eclesiales de base* or CEBs (in English, ecclesial base communities). These were communities of 30 or more persons who shared both faith and work. Although they usually gathered around a religious leader, such as a priest, a deacon or a nun, every member of the community had a vote on important matters. They shared crops, profits and worship. CEBs, which were similar to the Kibbutz movement in Israel, were usually seen with suspicion by both the traditional Catholic hierarchy and the military juntas, and consequently suffered much persecution.

On the Protestant camp, Liberation Theology also had a decisive impact. Evangelical theologians, like Carlos René Padilla, created the Fraternidad Teológica Latinoamericana or FTL (in English: Latin American Theological Fraternity) in 1970, with the commitment to respond to the social and political challenges the people of God faced in Latin America and the Caribbean. To this day, the FTL pursues the development of a *Misión Integral* that transcends the otherworldly spiritual perspective inherited from the missionaries.

Also in the Protestant camp, the *Concilio Latinoamericano de Iglesias* or CLAI (in English, the Latin American Council of Churches) entered into a deeper dialogue with Latin American Theology, developing an approach that was more openly political than the FTL. CLAI leaders even supported CEBs, tending ecumenical ties with their catholic counterparts. Protestant liberation theologians paid a high price, being persecuted by totalitarian governments, banned by their denominations and forced into exile.

Purposes and Characteristics of Preaching in This Theological Family

Orlando E. Costas, a Puerto Rican theologian, became a key figure in liberation theology. In 1983, during my sole exchange with him, I asked him: Why did he define himself as an "Evangelical Liberation Theologian"? His answer was forceful: "Evangelical, because we cannot compromise the Reformation, Luther and Sola Escritura; Liberation because they are killing us."

Costas, who wrote two important books on homiletics, described the situation accurately. Two years later, I moved to Costa Rica to teach homiletics. Interestingly, a few of my colleagues told me that my position was superfluous. They thought traditional sermons were so compromised that they had to be substituted by dialogues with the congregation, following the *lectio divina* model that Ernesto Cardenal used in his CEB, in an archipelago called Solentiname, located in the southern part of Lake Nicaragua. This modality of sharing the word spread in both Catholic and Protestant communities.

All this points to a key question: Is it possible to develop a Homiletic of Liberation? Justo and Catherine González were the first authors to tackle this issue in a significant manner, publishing *Liberation Preaching* in 1980.

Their thoughtful perspective affirmed that all interpreters approach with the Bible and the practice of preaching from their own social location. More than a choice, this is simply inevitable, for no preacher can shed his or her gender or ethnicity. Therefore, instead of blindly affirming that our particular perspective is universal or denying our ethnicity, we must acknowledge that our gender, class and ethnicity color the way we read, interpret and proclaim both the Bible and Christian theology.

According to Justo and Catherine Gonzalez, "The distinguishing characteristics of liberation preaching is not its content but its hermeneutics."[1] A hermeneutics of liberation presupposes that:[2]

- The interpreter approaches the Bible from a perspective of liberation looking, for the power of the God manifest in the message of the gospel liberates humanity from bondage to the forces of evil, sin and death, both at a personal and corporate level.

- The interpreter suspects that the traditional readings of the Bible reflect the perspective of the hegemonic powers and, thus, seek to preserve the prevailing power structures. This is an "ideological suspicion," for it suspects that topics and perspectives related to some oppressed constituencies have been excluded for ideological reasons. This approach calls the interpreter to read the Bible anew, engaging on a *relectura* or "rereading" of the text.

- The interpreter reads the Bible from the perspective of, or in solidarity with the "poor," understanding "poverty" as a category that includes all disenfranchised people. Therefore, a liberation perspective will also be in solidarity with women, immigrants, people of color, disabled people and any other person or constituency systematically excluded from the structures of power. Furthermore, a hermeneutics of liberation should consider the situation of society, as a whole, not only of those who defined themselves as part of particular communities of faith.

- The interpreter examines what the biblical text and Christian theology teaches about the use and abuse of power in society. In other words, liberation preaching recognizes the political implications of the Bible. Of course, this means that the historical, social and economic backgrounds of the biblical text come to the forefront, using sociological and even postcolonial theory to understand the setting of the text. The interpreter must identify who are powerful and who are the powerless,

1. Gonzalez and Gonsalus Gonzalez, "Liberation Preaching," 307.

2. The ideas are developed in Jiménez, "In Search of a Hispanic Model of Biblical Interpretation."

discerning whether their relationship is one of empowerment or oppression.

- Finally, the interpreter must incorporate the findings of his or her research to the homiletic process, proceeding, thus, to design, prepare and deliver a sermon that proclaims the liberating gospel.

Justo and Catherine Gonzalez peppered their book with anecdotes about how they discovered this perspective. In particular, Justo recalls the time when he was preparing a sermon about Peter's denial of Jesus. During his childhood, he had heard a sermon on the subject in which the preacher affirmed that those who know Jesus "looked" different from non-believers. However, in this occasion he realized that Peter was identified by his accent: "Surely you are one of them; your accent gives you away" (Matt 26:73b). This led Justo and Catherine to the realization that he had learned to overlook issues or race, gender and ethnicity whenever he read the Bible. This was his first step on the way to read the Bible "in Spanish," i.e., from a perspective that took seriously race, gender and ethnicity.

Notice that Justo and Catherine Gonzalez did not call for abandoning the sermon in favor of group *lectio divina* sessions. On the contrary, they incorporated the liberation perspective to the sermon preparation process. In time, their perspective gained the day in both Latin America and in the United States. In this sense, the news about the demise of the sermon as a vehicle for the proclamation of the gospel proved to be premature.

This does not mean, though, that the traditional deductive sermon continues to be king. In particular, I have called attention to the relationship between the form and the content of the sermon, which are irrevocably intertwined.[3] I have denounced the traditional deductive sermon, inherited from the British rationalistic homiletic tradition, as a colonial vestige that presents the minister as an authority who shares truths that the congregation must simply accept and apply. In my writings, I present the inductive sermon as an option that includes parishioners in the homiletics process, guiding them to discover biblical truths and pondering how to apply them to their personal situations and social settings. I call the preacher to present him or herself as a fellow believer who shares his experience of faith; as someone who is still growing in the faith, traveling a spiritual path might just be slightly ahead of the congregation. Seen from this perspective, a preacher is someone who shares more questions than answers about the faith. The preacher is a fellow seeker, not an authoritarian figure.

---

3. Jiménez, *La predicación en el siglo XXI*.

While I asserted earlier that liberation preaching focuses on herme-neutics, this approach to the Bible and theology transforms our theologi-cal perspectives. From a perspective of liberation, the living God reveals an entire theology of life through the history of Israel and the life and ministry of Jesus Christ.

Leonardo Boff has summarized the key question that Latin American liberation theology asks from homiletic theory and practice: How to preach the message of the cross in a continent populated mainly by "crucified" people?[4] That is the unanswerable question that guides our reflection below.

God shows preferential option for the "poor," i.e., for the disen-franchised, because they have been excluded from participation in the structures of power. We can see such preferences in biblical texts such as "Blessed are the poor in spirit, for theirs is the kingdom of heaven" (Matt 5:3) and "The blind receive sight, the lame walk, those who have leprosy are cleansed, the deaf hear, the dead are raised, and the good news is pro-claimed to the poor" (Matt 11:5).

The "gospel of the kingdom" affirms that power belongs ultimately to God. Therefore, the gospel judges all exercise of human power according to the values of the kingdom. God. Judgement seeks the liberation of both the oppressor and the oppressed. The aim of divine judgement is not punish-ment, but repentance, conversion and transformation.

Jesus, as God incarnated, reveals the human face of God to humanity. In Jesus, God shows his solidarity with the poor, for "the Son of Man did not come to be served, but to serve, and to give his life as a ransom for many" (Mark 10:45).

Jesus suffered the death to end all death. He struggled against the forces of sin, death, and evil, defeating them in the cross: "He forgave us all our sins, having canceled the charge of our legal indebtedness, which stood against us and condemned us; he has taken it away, nailing it to the cross. And having disarmed the powers and authorities, he made a public spectacle of them, triumphing over them by the cross" (Col 2:13b–15).

The resurrection is, thus, the victory of life over death, which "has been swallowed up in victory" (1 Cor 15:54b). Through baptism, Christians af-firm solidarity with Jesus and participation in the resurrection (Rom 6:5b).

Yet, *la lucha sigue* (in English: "the struggle continues"). People of faith have to face individual and corporate sin, which manifest itself in spiritual and social structures. In the language of the New Testament, believers fight against "principalities and powers" (Eph 6:11).

---

4. Boff, "Como Pregar a Cruz Hoje numa Sociedade de Crucificados?"

The Holy Spirit is our ally (Greek: *parakletos*, John 16:7) in *la lucha por la vida* (the struggle for life). The Holy Spirit unmasks sin (John 16:8–11.) Furthermore, the Holy Spirit empowers believers to resist oppression. Elsa Tamez calls us to translate the Greek word *hupomoné* as "militant resistance," not as "patience" as it has been traditionally rendered. Literally, the Greek term means "to be steadfast under pressure," i.e., to resist oppression. The power of God empowers believers to confront the principalities and powers (Eph 6:10–11).

God calls the Church to be a community of faith that lives according to the values of the Kingdom, in hope, solidarity and love. The Church must reach out to the world, preaching the liberating gospel and incarnated God's love for "the least of these" (see Matt 25:31–46). Believers must demonstrate solidarity with one another, addressing their mutual needs (see Acts 4:34).

Holiness transcends the personal and engages the social ethics. "Social Holiness" summons us to heed the prophetic call "to act justly and to love mercy and to walk humbly with your God" (Mic 6:8).

In terms of theological anthropology, a theology of liberation affirms that God created humanity to live and live in freedom. It sees humans in a holistic way, denying dichotomies between body and soul, the religious and the secular. Life, as a whole, occurs in the presence of God. For this reason, a spirituality of liberation affirms that God is with us *en lo cotidiano* (in the small details of our daily life). The presence of God fills even those spaces that others find trivial, such as taking the bus to go to work. Why? Because God manifests divine love and power in our life, in *this* life. God is with us *en la lucha por la vida*, for Jesus has promised to be always with us (Matt 28:20).

Turning our gaze to eschatology, we come full circle. The goal of the gospel is the kingdom of God. The church yearns and creation groans for the full manifestation of God's authority and power over the world. Believers, who by faith have become children of God (John 1:2), expect to "inherit" the kingdom of God (see Matt 25:34; Col 1:12; Jas 2:5). However, people who become instruments of the forces of evil, sin and death will not inherit the kingdom (see 1 Cor 6:9–10; Gal 5:21; Eph 5:5).

Finally, while the kingdom is in our "midst" (Luke 17:21), it will fully manifest itself at the end of time. Therefore, the kingdom still does not have a "place" in our word. Given that the Greek word for place is *topos*," something that still has not taken place is a "utopia." Therefore, the kingdom of God is the "utopia" that guides our dreams of liberation. As the sermon shared below states, the Church longs for "another place," for an "alternate place" of peace with love and justice. The prophetic imagination that spans from the beginning to the end of the Bible leads us to affirm that the "utopia" of the kingdom someday will have a *topos*, a place among us.

Case Study: Text and Sermon
(John 14:1–3)

The main idea of this sermon, based on John 14:1–3, is: "Jesus Christ is building an alternate place for the oppressed communities of the world." This sermon is a prophetic challenge that calls the congregation to read Hispanic reality in a different way. This expository sermon was originally preached at the Biennial Assembly of the Association for Hispanic Theological Education (AETH) held in August 2002 at Austin Presbyterian Theological Seminary.

"Another Place"

I. Introduction

[The sermon, preached originally in 2002, begins commenting on the crises that ushered the twenty-first century. It also explores the meaning of the concept "postmodernity."]

The twenty-first century began in an ominous way with the Y2K false promise of chaos. Soon came terrorism, war and economic crisis wreaking havoc around the world.

Our world faces the challenges posed by the end of modernity and the colonialism that made it possible. One of the consequences of the emergence of the Postmodern Era—or the Crisis of Modernity, according to Jameson[5]—is a profound crisis of values. The new generations believe that there are no absolute values, that all values are contextual and relative. In a world without fundamental values, personal and social ethics are forgotten. The rampant individualism of the Modern Era has given birth to a postmodern society obsessed with the pursuit of personal pleasure and prosperity, motivated by a radical sense of individual freedom. This society is one in which "me," "mine" and "I" are the most important things, explains how and why moral and financial crises have arisen.

Postcolonial movements present an even deeper and more dangerous challenge than postmodernity. Suffice it to say that those who planned the crimes of September 11, 2001, were originally trained by US security

5. Jameson "Postmodernism, or the Cultural Logic of Late Capitalism."

agencies. Radical Islamic movements have rebelled against the United States in response to our nation's neo-colonial policies in the Middle East. These groups are the cultural heirs of the movements that liberated the Arab countries from British control; their violent actions are motivated by hundreds of years of colonialism, oppression and exploitation.

The beginning of the twenty-first century has been violent. I fear that the crisis we are experiencing today is only the beginning of the birth pains of postmodern societies and the postcolonial world.

II. Faith in Times of Crisis

[This section approaches the biblical text from a postcolonial standpoint, introducing the concept of "liminality."]

As believers, we turn to the Bible for direction in times of crisis. The most logical move is to try to discern what our brothers and sisters in faith did in times of crisis; in "liminal" times,[6] when one era is ending while another one emerges. We could turn to various texts, both from the Hebrew Bible and the New Testament, since humanity has always found itself between faith and a crisis of faith. However, on this occasion I suggest a text that describes the attitude of the disciples of Jesus before the crisis brought about by the departure of their beloved teacher.

The Gospel of John teaches us that, by the end of Jesus' ministry, governmental authorities and security forces were eager to assassinate him. They saw Jesus as a dangerous person, who agitated the people. They thought that his ideas could incite the poor masses to banditry, social resistance and even revolution. John describes the cynicism of the religious and political leadership of the time, when Caiaphas justified before the Sanhedrin the plot against Jesus by saying: "It is better for you that one man die for the people than that the whole nation perish"(John 11:50).

Like all good prophets, Jesus had a great ability to read the signs of the times. He understood that his death was imminent. For this reason, Jesus decided to prepare his disciples to live without him.

Jesus' farewell speech begins in John 13 and runs until the end of chapter 17. The narratives in chapters 12 and 13 prepare the listeners for the speech. After the speech, we find the story of Jesus' execution. Therefore, almost half of the Gospel according to Saint John is focused on Jesus's farewell.

The speech begins immediately after Judas leaves the group to search for the security forces who will assassinate his teacher. While awaiting the

---

6. See Ashcroft et al., "Liminality," 130–31.

arrival of the Jerusalem temple police, Jesus tells the rest of the disciples that the authorities were going to arrest, prosecute and torture him before finally executing him. The speech is very long. So, I invite you to meditate only on the first three verses of chapter 14.

> Do not let your hearts be troubled. You believe in God; believe also in me. My Father's house has many rooms; if that were not so, would I have told you that I am going there to prepare a place for you? And if I go and prepare a place for you, I will come back and take you to be with me that you also may be where I am. (John 14:1–3)

Jesus encourages his defeated disciples, whose world was collapsing. They had left everything to follow Jesus, abandoning land, work, and family. After so much sacrifice, Jesus announced a sudden departure that threatened everything they had built.

As usual, Jesus' words of encouragement sound strange; they are not like the inane phrases you and I use to comfort our friends and family. No! Jesus does not deny his departure or minimize his impact. On the contrary, Jesus affirms that his departure is an integral part of his mission.

Jesus uses an enigmatic and interesting phrase: "I am going there to prepare a place for you" (John 14:2b). Jesus is going to prepare a "place" for us.

III. Jesus Prepares a "Place"

[The sermon introduces the concept of "place" as its main metaphor, understood from a Latin American liberation theology perspective.]

The word "place"[7] is extremely important for our reflection. As we know, the Roman colonial power oppressed the Jewish people during the time of Jesus. One of the consequences of colonialism is a deep sense of dislocation in the colonized peoples. Colonial "places" are redefined by the influence of the colonial metropolis. Colonizers make maps that change known borders, give old places new names, and impose a foreign tongue as the official language. With military strength and economic might, the colonial powers downplay the importance of our social places, indicating that the only truly important "place" is the metropolitan capital.

---

7. See Ashcroft et al., "Place."

The issue of citizenship is a clear example of the sense of dislocation produced by Roman hegemony. Jesus, who was born and lived his entire life in Palestine, was not a "citizen" of his own country. He was hung on a cross—the torture reserved for resident aliens. Despite being in his own land, Jesus was a "foreigner" who did not have full civil rights.

Hispanics who live permanently in the United States experience a similar sense of dislocation. Some of us are "foreigners" in the land in which we were born. We do not have access to the centers of power where the decisions that define our lives are made, even though geographically we live next to them. As Fernando F. Segovia has wisely said, we are permanently the "others" in our own society.[8]

John 14:1–3 proclaims good news for all peoples and individuals who do not find a "place" in the world: Jesus has gone to prepare a "place" for us.

IV. Jesus Prepares "Another Place"

[Using prophetic imagination,[9] the sermon expands the definition of "place" and correlates it the alternative "place" that Jesus promises to prepare for the faithful.]

Jesus has decided to go and build a space for the oppressed, marginalized and colonized peoples. Jesus affirms that he will build "another place" for those people who come to be part of God's project. I say "another" because it is evident that the place that Jesus promises us is different from the one we occupy today. It is an alternate place, free from the oppressive realities that define the colonial "place" occupied by the Jewish people of yesterday and the Hispanic people of today.

To visualize that place, we must use prophetic and apocalyptic imagination. This was precisely why the Early Church envisioned the "new heaven and new earth" with which the book of Revelation, and therefore the New Testament, concludes.

> Then I saw "a new heaven and a new earth," for the first heaven and the first earth had passed away, and there was no longer any sea. I saw the Holy City, the new Jerusalem, coming down out of heaven from God, prepared as a bride beautifully dressed for her husband. And I heard a loud voice from the throne saying, "Look! God's dwelling place is now among the people, and he will dwell with them. They will be his people, and God himself

8. Segovia, "Two Places," 31.

9. Brueggeman, *The Prophetic Imagination*.

will be with them and be their God. He will wipe every tear from their eyes. There will be no more death or mourning or crying or pain, for the old order of things has passed away (Rev 21:1–4).

At the end of the first century of the Christian era, the Early Church faced painful repression at the hands of the Emperor Domitian. Such repression brought tears, death, pain, and outcry—the same elements that do not exist in the new heaven and new earth. Following this example, Hispanic communities must also use prophetic and apocalyptic imagination to envision "a new heaven and a new earth" free of poverty, illegal drugs, gangs, police brutality, prostitution, AIDS, and of the repression of the *migra*,[10] because in the "alternate place" that Jesus went to build, "the first things are past" (Rev 21:4b).

Before proclaiming the coming kingdom, you must imagine it. We must imagine it in a contextual way that is relevant to our people. That alternate place will be the criterion that will allow us to critique today's society. That place feeds the hope that prevents us from conforming to the painful reality of today.

V. Conclusion

[The sermon ends calling the congregation to show its commitment with the God's project of liberation, the kingdom of God.]

Let us go back to verse 3, where Jesus tells us: "And if I go and prepare a place for you, I will come back and take you to be with me that you also may be where I am." This promise is one of the tenents of the Christian faith: Jesus will return to take us to the "other place" that he is building for us.

What worries me is whether we are willing to go with him, for some of us have become comfortable in this place: While our people are starving, some of us have good wages; While our people cry and suffer, some of us go to meetings in luxurious hotels to talk about their poverty. While our people are crushed by an oppressive system, some of us have become its brokers.

Are we eager to go with Jesus to that alternate place? Or, are we so comfortable in "this place" we wish that Jesus would delay his return? Are we truly committed and committed to the project of God as revealed by Christ Jesus.

This is an important question, for those radically committed to the alternate future that Jesus is preparing will go with him. But those people

---

10. *Migra* refers to immigration law enforcement agencies.

invested in the current system that benefits the few and oppresses the many, will have no part in the Kingdom.

May God bless us. May God awaken in our hearts the first love that once led us to take the arduous path of Christian ministry. May our commitment with God lead us to shout: "Come Lord Jesus" (Rev 22.20b).

Strengths and Limitations in This Theological Family

The strengths of a liberation approach to preaching are evident, for this theology unleashes the powerful message of the gospel. Sermons preached from this perspective analyze the social context of the Biblical text, correlating it with the context of the congregation. Of course, a relatable sermon will be more engaging than a speech with little or no points of contact with the lives of the congregation.

Congregations confronted with this homiletic approach respond with a mix of surprise and indignation. Surprise, because they suddenly discover that the many points of contact among the biblical text, its context, and their own lives. Indignation, because they realize that they have been hearing sermons that overlook the social setting of the Bible.

Liberation preaching is inherently prophetic. It invites the congregation to exert prophetic imagination; to envision alternate futures free from the oppressive elements that hinder our lives today. It also confronts the "powers that be" with the Word of God that affirms the values of the Kingdom. Furthermore, it calls oppressors to repentance and conversion, so that they may attain salvation. This cannot be more biblical, for Scripture says: "Let the wicked forsake their ways and the unrighteous their thoughts. Let them turn to the Lord, and he will have mercy on them, and to our God, for he will freely pardon" (Isa 55:7).

Paradoxically, Liberation preaching's prophetic stance is simultaneously its greatest strength and its main limitation. Lazy hermeneutics and strained correlations of social contexts can yield sermons that trivialize the concept of oppression, finding it everywhere. We have all heard our share of sermons that aim to liberate "suburban captives" from the "burden" of being upper middle class and invite them to engage in modest actions of justice. However, Liberation preaching must aim higher, addressing the pressing needs of society, such as economic justice and racial reconciliation.

Finally, we must remember if a preacher only preaches prophetic sermons that confront the congregation, all the sermons will have a similar tone, leading part of the congregation to think that sermons all sound alike. Variety in sermon approach is needed. Furthermore, liberation preaching does not berate the congregation. On the contrary, it builds up and empowers the community, calling the congregation to keep hope alive "because our salvation is nearer now than when we first believed" (Rom 13:11b).

For Further Reading

Boff, Leonardo. *Passion of Christ, Passion of the World*. Translated by Robert R. Barr. Maryknoll, NY: Orbis, 2011.

González, Justo L., and Catherine González. *The Liberating Pulpit*. 1994. Reprint, Eugene, OR: Wipf & Stock, 2003.

González, Justo L., and Pablo A. Jiménez. *Púlpito: An Introduction to Hispanic Preaching*. Nashville: Abingdon, 2005.

Jiménez, Pablo. "If You Just Close Your Eyes: Postcolonial Perspectives on Preaching from the Caribbean," *Homiletic* 40 (2015) 22–28.

———. "Toward a Postcolonial Homiletic: Justo L. González's Contribution to Homiletics." In *Hispanic Christian Thought At the Dawn of the 21st Century: Apuntes in Honor of Justo L. González*, edited by Alvin Padilla et al., 159–67. Nashville: Abingdon, 2006.

12

Preaching in the Mujerista Theological Family

LIS VALLE-RUIZ

GOD'S MANIFOLD GRACE IS revealed in the everyday lives of Latin-American womyn living in the struggle facing racism, sexism, and poverty in the United States of America.[1] Many of these Latinas proclaim salvation/liberation from pulpits and through their everyday lives through *mujerista* praxis. Their praxis and theological insights inform *mujerista* biblical interpretation, the purpose of preaching from the perspective of *mujerista* theology and the content of sermons, all aligned to actualize liberation for Latinas and their communities.

Circumstances That Gave Rise to This Theological Family

The impetus for Latina activists and theologians to name themselves emerged in the late '80s as a further development of the Latin-American liberation theology that focused around a preferential option for the [male] poor. The dire social conditions in which poor Latin-American communities live in the western hemisphere find root causes that began or worsened upon the arrival of Conquistadors from Europe. The Conquistadors enslaved both the indigenous communities they found in what today we know as the Americas, and also the people that they brought from west

1. I use the term "womyn" to include all persons who self-identify as women, whether cis- or transgender, or who were socialized to become women, even if they do not any longer self-identify as such. When referring to the work of other Latina scholars, I will use the term "women" because that is the term they used.

African countries through the transatlantic slave trade.[2] After centuries of colonization, assimilation, and interbreeding, womyn in the Americas continue to survive, resist, and thrive under multiple and interlocked layers of oppression.

More recently, social and political conditions in many countries in Latin America and the Caribbean that were under authoritarian military dictatorships between the 1930s and the 1980s produced fertile ground for the development of Latin-American liberation theology in the 1960s.[3] Responding to political oppression and economic injustice Latin-American liberation theologies advanced the notion that the Christian church is called to exercise a preferential option for the poor and to actively engage in changing the social and political conditions, perceived as systemic sin, so that the poor may experience liberation. Liberation theology affirmed the rights of the poor and the ability of *comunidades de base* (base communities), to think theologically and to work towards their own social, political, and economic liberation. Latin-American liberation theology eventually migrated to the USA and evolved into Hispanic/Latino theology.

Latin-American liberation theology and Hispanic/Latino theology paid great attention to political and economic oppression but, for the most part, ignored the role of gender and the lived experience of women oppressed under the same political and economic conditions but suffering it differently. In the '70s, women in the liberation movements in the Americas and the United States brought attention to the multilayered oppression that Latin-American women suffer. Beyond the issues of economic justice at the center of the attention of Latin-American [male] liberation theologies, Latina activists and theologians espoused the indivisibility of class, race, and gender in their lived experience of marginalization and oppression.[4] One of these theologians was Ada María Isasi-Díaz, whose work providing a platform for the voices of grassroots Latinas popularized the concept of *mujerista* theology.

Born in a diasporic context along with Hispanic/Latino [male] theology, the circumstances that gave rise to *mujerista* theology are slightly different than those that gave rise to Latin-American [male] Roman

2. For a succinct version of an analysis of this history as it relates to the importation of Christianity and to Latin American spirituality, see the Medina and Gonzáles, Introduction to *Voices from the Ancestors*. For a thorough and detailed analysis of this history, see, Rivera Pagán, *A Violent Evangelism*.

3. A significant event in the development of this liberation theology was the second Latin American Bishops' Conference, which was held in Medellín, Colombia, in 1968.

4. Two other manifestations of Latina theologies exist beside *mujerista* theology: Latina feminist theology and Latina *evangélica* theology.

Catholic liberation theologies.[5] Location and political conditions are the most evident differences. *Mujerista* theology emerges in the USA. This is something it has in common with Hispanic/Latino [male] theology, as both of those expand the liberation theology born in Latin America. Also, *mujerista* theology emerges under a democratic government rather than under military dictatorships. Finally, gender is the most important difference, as *mujerista* theology pays attention to the lived experience of poor Latinas and the triple oppression of race, class, and gender. *Mujerista* theology affirms the same commitments that Latin American liberation theology has to a preferential option for the oppressed and to the capacity that base communities have to produce theology.

Mujerista theology also emerges alongside third wave [white] feminism and womanist theology. Third wave feminism is characterized by intersectionality, paying attention to the interconnections of race, class, and gender, and including the feminist movement more intentionally as well as the plights of women of color and transwomen. Womanist theology also centers the intersection of racism and sexism. It evolves from the work of Alice Walker, who first coined a definition for the term womanist in her classic text, *In Search of Our Mothers' Gardens*. The parallel development of third wave feminism, womanist, and *mujerista* theologies matches the racial classification of humans in the USA risking essentializing white, black, and Latina women, each as a separate and monolithic group. Additionally, there is a risk to perceive a linear development in which one emerges after the other as an expansion of the prior. These risks result in making invisible the diversity of thought and theology among white, black and Latina women and the genealogies particular to feminism, womanism, and *mujerismo*.[6]

Ada María Isasi-Díaz began elaborating a *mujerista* theology working *en conjunto* (together) with Yolanda Tarango and using the terms Hispanic and *Mujerista* to make space for Latin-American women to name themselves.[7] Isasi-Díaz conducted ethnographic research, interviewing grassroots Latinas, focusing on Mexican, Cuban and Puerto Rican women living in the USA, to elaborate a *mujerista* theology, which she shares in *En La Lucha = In the Struggle: Elaborating a Mujerista Theology*.

---

5. For a great example of doing Hispanic/Latino and Latina theology *en conjunto* see Isasi-Díaz and Segovia, eds., *Hispanic/Latino Theology*.

6. Consider that the body of work from womanist theory is distinct from Black feminist theory.

7. See, Isasi-Díaz and Tarango. *Hispanic Women, Prophetic Voice in the Church = Mujer hispana, voz profética en la iglesia* (1988) and by the same authors, *Hispanic Women, Prophetic Voice in the Church = Mujer hispana, Voz profética en la iglesia* (1992).

In *En La Lucha*, Isasi-Díaz explains the nuances of the lived experiences of Hispanic/Latina women that make necessary the development of *mujerista* theology. She rejects the single focus of feminist theology on sexism as the only oppression experienced by women and insists that the combined discrimination based on race and gender as well as the economic situation of Latina women result in a multilayered system of oppression particular to them. Isasi-Díaz identifies as one main identity trait of Latina women their socioeconomic location in which their bodies have been exploited sexually and with hard and long labor hours. Latina's daily experience is characterized with oppression and injustice due to sexism, racism, and poverty. These sources of oppression operate together in such a way that Latinas experience marginalization and oppression as one factor.[8] Living under these conditions is living in the struggle, *en la lucha*.

Isasi-Díaz also found other main identity traits that characterize Latinas, which include their creative survival skills, their *mestizaje* and *mulataje* that manifest their Amerindian and African heritage, their use and zeal of the Spanish language, their syncretistic popular religion, and their preferred future. Based on these, the author proposes a methodology that privileges the daily life of Hispanic and Latina women living in the USA and that values their voices.

In privileging the daily lived experience of Latinas, *mujerista* theology challenges traditional classifications in [white] theology. *Mujerista* theology does not start with abstract pre-existing theological categories or universal experience to which Latinas add a perspective. Rather, *mujerista* theology offers some key elements that are closely interrelated. *Lo cotidiano*, *mestizaje/mulatez*, and salvation-liberation are main characteristics of *mujerista* theology.

Lo cotidiano is the source of *mujerista* theology.[9] As theological source, *lo cotidiano* provides a hermeneutical and epistemological framework in which Latinas are not the objects but rather the subjects and agents of *mujerista* theology. *Lo cotidiano* constitutes a liberation praxis. It is not so much a reality into which Latinas are inserted but instead, *lo cotidiano* is the critical thinking exercised each day and the decision-making processes in a daily living that effectively contributes to liberation, rejects essentialism, embraces difference, and works against oppression. *Lo cotidiano* is not a metaphysical category, and it does not exist a priori. It refers to the different way in which Latinas see reality. In *lo cotidiano*, Latinas deliberate between right and wrong, good or bad, using liberation as the criterion for such

8. Isasi-Díaz, *En La Lucha = In the Struggle*, 9.

9. Isasi-Díaz, *En La Lucha = In the Struggle*, x.

deliberations. In *lo cotidiano*, morality means solidarity with the oppressed. *Mujerista* theology is anchored in deep awareness of subjectivity and practices epistemological vigilance as Latinas explain their understanding of the divine. From a *mujerista* perspective, theology is not about God but about what humans know about God.[10]

Mestizaje/mulatez constitutes the social location from which Latinas think, conceive, and express theology. *Mestizaje/mulatez* refers to being racially and culturally mixed people. From such location, *mujerista* theologians consider racism and ethnic prejudice as sin and embrace diversity and difference as virtue. More than a natural or given condition, *mestizaje/ mulatez* as a *locus theologicus* needs to be repeatedly chosen as part of the struggle for peace and justice, which Isasi-Díaz calls, "the cornerstone of the gospel message."[11]

The theology of grassroots Latinas includes the notion of salvation and liberation as two aspects of one process. Salvation refers to having a relationship with God that affects all human reality and all aspects of Latinas' lives. In *mujerista* understanding of salvation, salvation occurs in history, and in the present, intrinsically connected to liberation.[12] In Isasi-Díaz' words, "As in other liberation theologies for us the unfolding of the kin-dom of God does not happen apart from history."[13] The work for liberation, which refers to "establishing justice in concrete ways in our world, is not necessarily different from being good Christians."[14] Latinas are organic intellectuals and theologians who understand theology as praxis, where thinking cannot be separated from acting. In that sense, *mujerista* theology is not reflection upon action, but a liberative action. Theology as praxis results in living one's salvation by struggling for liberation and obtaining liberation as experiencing salvation.

Purposes and Characteristics of Preaching in This Theological Family

The purpose of preaching from a *mujerista* perspective is to provide tools to actively engage in actualizing a vision of justice in which there is liberation for Latinx communities in the USA. This purpose aligns with *mujerista* theology's main task: "our goal is our liberation and the liberation of

10. Isasi-Díaz, *Mujerista Theology*, 71.

11. Isasi-Díaz, *Mujerista Theology*, 66.

12. Isasi-Díaz, *En la Lucha = In the Struggle*, 52–53.

13. Isasi-Díaz, *Mujerista Theology*, 73.

14. Isasi-Díaz, *Mujerista Theology*, 73.

our people."[15] Drawing on the *mujerista* hermeneutic that Isasi-Díaz began to articulate, this essay identifies biblical interpretation for liberation and advancement of Latina's *proyecto histórico* (preferred future) as characteristic of *mujerista* preaching.

Biblical Interpretation for Liberation

Mujeristas interpret the Bible for liberation. While many other preaching traditions do this, *mujeristas* conceive of the Bible as a tool and put biblical interpretation at the service of *la lucha* in such a way that liberation and the lived experience of Latinas has primacy over the Bible. In other words, liberation is more important than the Bible and is both the goal and the critical lens to interpret Scripture.[16] The purpose of biblical interpretation is to provide Latinas with tools to continue struggling.[17] This approach is very different than doing biblical exegesis using historical critical methods of interpretation to determine what the original author tried to communicate to its intended audience. It may be considered reader response criticism, but it goes to a whole new level taking liberties with the biblical text. Isasi-Díaz suggests interpretation, appropriation, and use of the Bible privileging cultural criticism as the preferred method for *mujerista* biblical interpretation and practically redefining what a Bible story is.

In "Communication as Communion," Isasi-Díaz develops cultural criticism as the preferred method for *mujerista* biblical interpretation resulting in interpreting Bible stories from *lo cotidiano*. In the application of the method, the preacher is called to place evidence from the daily-lived experiences of Latinas side-by-side Scripture, looking for tools that will help in the struggle for liberation. Isasi-Díaz shows how the method works by applying it to the story of Jesus' transfiguration. She begins with the lived experience of Latinas who value conversation as a way to know themselves and to be in communion with others. The mixed cultural identity of Latinas and their daily experience is what drives the interpretation of the biblical story.

For Isasi-Díaz the biblical story is not necessarily what is written in Scripture. In her research she found that many Latinas do not read Scripture, rather they have heard the stories from Scripture. Bible stories are in their memory and often times, different stories are mixed into a single story to make a point. Latinas make theirs the stories from the Bible when they use them for liberation. While Isasi-Díaz recognizes that there are

15. Isasi-Díaz, *Mujerista Theology*, 161.

16. Isasi-Díaz, "La Palabra de Dios en Nosotras."

17. Isasi-Díaz, "Communication as Communion," 27.

various approaches to Scripture among Latinas due to multiple Christian traditions influencing their religiosity, what she calls *mestiza/mulata* Christianity, she privileges the lived experience of Latinas who, like her, find that the Bible is not that important. Concerned for those Latinas who are part of traditions where the Bible takes precedence, she rejects such approach for being sometimes fundamentalist and other times individualistic and pietistic and thus, not helpful in advancing salvation-liberation for Latinas and their communities. In *mujerista* theology the need to survive takes precedence. Consequently, in *mujerista* biblical interpretation it is appropriate to mix bible stories, to highlight non-essentials in the text, to interpret, appropriate and use of the Bible for liberation.

Advancement of the *Proyecto Histórico*

Mujerista preaching enhances Latina's moral agency for the advancement of their *proyecto histórico*. Rather than telling them how to live, seeking to shape their behavior to some allegedly ahistorical and universal interpretation of Scripture, *mujerista* preaching further develops the critical thinking skills of Latinas. This kind of preaching augments their capacity to continue in the struggle making real their preferred future, that is, actualizing their own liberation.

Latinas' moral agency is what allows Latinas to actualize their preferred future, their *proyecto histórico*. Latina's moral agency refers to how they understand themselves as agents of their own history, how they create meaning in and through their lives, and how they exercise their agency in spite of their oppression.[18] It also refers to Latina's ability to think critically, to incorporate their religious beliefs into their daily decision-making to improve the living conditions for themselves and their communities. Latina's moral agency is exercised in a *mujerista* theology praxis, which consists in critical reflective action. Latinas analyze the reality in which they live, their historical circumstances. Religion is always part of their analysis as religion is enmeshed in Latinas mixed culture constituting *mestiza/mulata* Christianity. The resulting action is liberative and political action committed to solidarity with Latina's and their communities and seeking to change the socioeconomic oppressive structures in society.[19] Latinas' moral agency is living their Christianity to effectuate salvation-liberation.

When Latinas exercise their moral agency, they advance their *proyecto histórico*. Isasi-Díaz explains that the term *proyecto histórico* refers "to

18. Isasi-Díaz, *En la Lucha = In the Struggle*, 21.

19. Isasi-Díaz, *En la Lucha = In the Struggle*, 176–77.

our liberation and the historical specifics needed to attain it."[20] Liberation is the realization of Latina's *proyecto histórico,* which they actualize daily in *lo cotidiano* using their moral agency. The advancement of Latina's *proyecto histórico* is taking personal responsibility and contributing to the unfolding of God's kin-dom in the present, even knowing that it will not be completely manifested right away. Latinas live into their preferred future questioning and organizing in community to change oppressive structures in society and church, including hierarchies within the church; privileged status of churches and the social and political conditions that keep Latinx communities in poverty.

Preaching to enhance Latinas' moral agency uses the Bible as interpretive key so that Scripture "helps us ask questions instead of insisting that it can provide answers."[21] The preacher weaves the elements that emerge and bring them together to depict a vision of justice that is intrinsic to the task of *mujerista* theology: the liberation of Latinas and their communities. *Mujeristas* use the Bible to learn how to learn. The starting point is always the situation at hand, not the Bible. This kind of preaching allows Latinas to be self-determining, "to be the ones that decide what to do and how to do it."[22]

In "La Palabra de Dios en Nosotras—The Word of God in Us," Isasi-Díaz illustrates the use of the Bible as interpretive with an analysis of the story of Shiphrah and Puah.[23] She uses grammatical analysis to argue the ambiguity of ethnicity of the midwives, and also to define fear of God as reverence for God that leads to help enact God's kin-dom. Isasi-Díaz also uses literary analysis to strengthen the image of midwives as life-givers. She concludes offering many questions that the story raises and that Latinas can apply to their current situation. In offering questions rather than answers, a *mujerista* sermon enables and enhances Latinas' moral agency. Thus, preaching as a *mujerista* interprets, appropriates, and uses the Bible to advance Latina's *proyecto histórico.*

Case Study: Text and a Sermon
(Luke 2:22–40)

Mujerista biblical interpretation seeks liberation of Latina's bodies in the USA highlighting what the text seems to render as non-essential, namely

20. Isasi-Díaz, *En la Lucha = In the Struggle,* 52.

21. Isasi-Díaz, *Mujerista Theology,* 162.

22. Isasi-Díaz, *Mujerista Theology,* 162.

23. Isasi-Díaz, "La Palabra de Dios en Nosotras."

the bodies and their social location, in order to reframe the notion of salvation, and offer questions that enhance critical thinking skills and moral agency.

The following sermon interprets Luke 2:22–40, the story of Jesus' presentation at the temple, when Simeon and Anna encounter him as a newborn.[24] Interpreting the passage from the lived experience of Latinas who have given birth allows to highlight the poor bodies of Mary and Jesus.[25] With this emphasis and using intertextual criticism, the text offers new information about the presence of these bodies in the temple that day. The passage offers implicit references that biblical scholars have exposed. The phrases "to present him"[26] and, "Every firstborn male shall be designated as holy to the Lord,"[27] refer to the law that, according to Exodus 13:2 and 12, God gave Moses, asking for the "redemption of the firstborn."[28] According to *The Jewish Annotated New Testament,* there was no purification ritual required for the father or the baby and there was no law or custom of presenting children at the temple. Similarly, the phrases "When the time came for their purification," and "a pair of turtledoves or two young pigeons" are a reference to Leviticus 12, which prescribes the purification ritual after childbirth, and allows for the presentation of turtledoves or pigeons if the woman cannot afford the presentation of a lamb. This connection reveals the economic situation of Mary as a poor woman.

The body of Jesus is in the temple because his mother, Mary is there for her purification ritual after childbirth. It is the religious and legal regulation over Mary's body that places the holy family in the temple in the first place. *Mujerista* biblical interpretation, highlights the body of Mary as essential to Jesus' arrival into the world, and recovering from the toll that such labor took on her body. It also highlights Jesus' body as that of a forty-day-old infant. Mujerista hermeneutics invites question in relation to this text: What bodies come to your mind when faced with the bodies of Mary and Jesus? What kind of salvation and consolation those bodies need? How may

24. Despite our efforts to let liberation take primacy over the integrity of the Bible text, I am certain that the resulting sermon gives more importance to Scripture than Isasi-Díaz or many of the grassroots Latinas that she interviewed would have given to it.

25. A longer Spanish version was originally published on *WorkingPreacher* (a website). See Valle, "'Cuerpos y salvación'"

26. Luke 2:22.

27. Luke 2:23.

28. Levine and Bretterler, eds., *The Jewish Annotated New Testament* (annotation to Luke 2:22), 637. The phrase "to present him" is a possible allusion to "the redemption of the firstborn." Luke 2:22 may be referring to Exod 13:2, 12, 15; Num 18:15–16; Neh 10:35–36.

a *mujerista* sermon pay attention to those bodies? How does the *proyecto histórico* look like for those bodies?

"Bodies that Cry for Justice"[29]

The body is essential in our religious practices. Why then do we try so hard to eliminate the body in everything we do? Jesus' family was in Jerusalem to perform a ritual obligation, one caused by the body of Mary. It was the time of her purification after childbirth. The lectionary and the narrator attempted to erase the changes in the bodies of Jesus and Mary. The lectionary skipped the verse that tells the story of Jesus' circumcision. The narrator of Luke omits the reason for "them" to need purification.

> *[The introduction announces the body as the hermeneutical key guiding the interpretation of the scriptural text and places at the center of attention Mary's polluted body, a choice consonant with privileging the lived experiences of poor women. The following paragraph will introduce a notion of salvation that goes beyond the soul and includes the body, a choice consonant with mujerista's salvation-liberation.]*

That the lectionary and the narrator of Luke tried to erase the bodies of Jesus and Mary has consequences. It allows us to focus on a spirit-only kind of salvation. Today, I find myself with the people of Israel, and with Simeon and Anna the day before of Mary's purification—waiting for salvation, consolation, redemption of our whole selves.

Because changes in the body are the foundation that makes this story possible, I invite us to pay attention to the stages of body transformation. How does our practice of being aware of our bodies shape our idea of the divine and therefore our interpretation of this text? Let's begin with the reason for Jesus, Mary, and Joseph to be in the temple, in Jerusalem: Mary's childbirth.

---

29. This sermon was recorded on December 17, 2020, for streaming the first Sunday of Christmas, December 27, 2020, for the Presbyterian (PCUSA) churches of the Presbytery of the Twin Cities Area. See, "PTCA December 27, 2020 Worship Service" (https://youtu.be/vCIJOmRlz2E). Most of the sermon's content came from an exercise in communal biblical interpretation held December 6, 2020. During the exercise, Alba Onofrio, Cristian de la Rosa, Lis Valle-Ruiz, and Patricia Bonilla, interpreted Luke 2:22–40, intentionally combining the wisdom from Latina feminist, *mujerista*, and Latina evangelical theologies. We chose to focus on three concepts that all three theologies have in common: lived experience, *lo cotidiano* (everyday life), and *mestizaje / mulatez*.

Exodus 13:3 and 12 call for Israelites to "consecrate the first offspring of every womb." There was no rite at the temple or before a priest associated with such consecration. But Leviticus 12 explains the ritual for the purification of a woman after giving birth. The ritual included bringing a one-year-old lamb to the priest or if she cannot afford a lamb, "she shall take two turtledoves or two pigeons, one for a burnt offering and the other for a sin offering; and the priest shall make atonement on her behalf, and she shall be clean" (Lev 12:8). This was to be done the fortieth day after birth.

The Gospel of Luke places emphasis on Jesus' parents fulfilling the law and on Jesus being fulfillment of the law. In today's passage, this Gospel conveys the special nature of Jesus as salvation and consolation for Israel. This emphasis needed not to result in the erasure of Jesus' and Mary's body. Jesus' body, we believe, makes possible salvation and Mary's body made possible the Incarnation. Without Mary and her birth canal, there is no baby Jesus.

And here we are, with a forty-day-old baby Jesus, accompanying his mama to her purification, thirty-three days after his own circumcision and consecration. And here, we witness two old bodies, one male and one female, who testify to Jesus being the savior. This story is based on changing bodies and tells of many bodies forming a communal body. Many of them "were looking for the redemption of Jerusalem."[30]

> [In what follows, the sermon reveals its own formation, which placed emphasis on community and shared experience, which are important principles for mujerista theology. In the disclosure and use of the sermon's contents produced in community, the sermon not only is based on the principle, it also performs it, brings it to completion, and models it, which allows for future imitation.]

Gathered with a small group of Latinx womyn, we interpreted this text from the perspective of our bodies, from our shared experience of childbirth. We believe that bodies are gifts from God to us. Bodies are divine. As our bodies change and we grow chronologically we understand more God's humanity. We also gain embodied wisdom, wisdom in the body.

The body already has Divine Wisdom, has *Imago Dei*, has the sparkle of God within. Simeon and Anna confirmed what Joseph and Mary already knew about Jesus. To know the body is to know part of God's blessing. And as the text tells us, the body of Jesus was growing and getting full of Divine Wisdom.

---

30. Luke 2:38.

[In what follows, lo cotidiano and Latina's mixed identities and culture are applied to the text. Liberation takes primacy over the content of Bible stories.]

Bodies interrelate. The interaction between Jesus, Joseph, and Mary was essential in Jesus growing up. Jesus must have seen his parents work for the wellbeing of their community. Jesus' body memorized the ways of being of his parents and of his community. Perhaps he saw his mother Mary living into the canticle from just one chapter ago in the Gospel of Luke but almost nine months ago in Mary's life:

> [God's] "mercy extends to those who fear [God],
>> from generation to generation
> He has performed mighty deeds with his arm;
>> he has scattered those who are proud
>> in their inmost thoughts.
> He has brought down rulers from their thrones
>> but has lifted up the humble.
> He has filled the hungry with good things
>> but has sent the rich away empty."[31]

Jesus' small body grew up and became stronger with such teachings. Jesus' body grew and illuminated love and learning and an open heart and open hands and arms to learn from others, always inspired by the Spirit and Grace of God. Jesus noticed that the body was essential matter for daily life (work, food, sex, desire, passion, justice). He lodged himself in the injustices. He put his body in the midst of violence and used his body to defend women who suffered violence. Eventually, his own body suffered violence as well. Jesus' body witnessed suffering and pain. Jesus' body joined other bodies to work for justice. These bodies suffered together and they were setting themselves free.

[The sermon presents Jesus and Mary struggling with their identities. While the words mestizaje o mulatez are not used, the coexistence of multiple identities in Jesus and the particular social consequences for living as womyn rise to the surface from a mujerista theology perspective. The reflection for moral agency is evident and culminates bringing in the embodied experience of a poor Latina womyn living in the USA, raising her children in poverty.]

---

31. Luke 1:50–51 New International Version (NIV).

And perhaps, growing up Jesus felt within him that there was something wrong. Under the Roman Empire he was learning that the spirit is for God but the body is evil. As he worked with people, he also worked within himself, understanding his humanity and divinity mixed together in a single being. Misbehaving, getting close to unclean women, healing the day of Sabbath . . . . He was figuring out what was the best course of action, what way to walk. In everyday life he worked on combining what he learned from society, from his religious community, from his parents, from within himself. All these bodies together cocreated their story. Jesus was working through his own fears and insecurities in community.

As we consider that God incarnated in the body of a poor woman, who gave birth to Jesus' body, and had to go to the priest with two doves or two young pigeons because she had no means to bring a lamb, what was Mary's experience?

In the passage we read today as it was customary in her own historical context, Mary's body was not recognized, even though she gave birth to divinity enfleshed. She gave birth to a hybrid body, a human-divine body. Her body as women in her time, was considered property. Still today, women's bodies are considered property in some contexts.

But women like Mary are *nepantleras*. These womyn create liminal spaces with their own bodies. Her own bodies are bridges in these times of change and struggle. And they give birth to kids like Aiden.

I learned of Aiden's story from the documentary, *A Place at the Table*.[32] In it, Barbie, Aiden's mother, says, "If you don't eat for a day, are you starving? In their (the assistance programs in the United States) eyes no, but in your eyes and in the way you feel, of course."

I see Jesus in Aiden. My church told me to see that way through a worship song that says, "as I go by and I see the smile in a small child's face, right there I see beauty, right there I see my God." Do you see? In Aiden's body there is also the spark of life, the *imago dei*, the presence of the Divine.

When the documentary *A Place at the Table* was produced, there were 50 million "Americans" experiencing food insecurity in the USA. Aiden, his mother Barbie, and his sister were three of them. Barbie cried as she told their story. Her body produced salty water expressing the grief of working hard and not being able to feed her children. She took them to school, she looked for a job but her body was lodged in a system that keeps them all in poverty. Barbie's body joined other bodies in a campaign. They did advocacy, lobbying, they shared their pictures and their stories. Barbie would share that she has dreams for her children too and that she has dreams as well.

---

32. Jacobson and Silverbush, dirs., *A Place at the Table*.

Eventually, they "prevailed." A new law was passed that moved funds from the food stamps to school lunch programs. What this meant for Aiden's family is that the children would have better food in school and less funds in food stamps to eat at home. Finally, Barbie found a job. Her body felt the joy of a goal accomplished but she no longer qualified for food stamps and she was back to not earning enough to feed her family. Malnourishment affected Aden's physical and cognitive development.

In this communal body in which we live, the bodies of many women try with all their might to feed their children every day and many of them cannot succeed, just like Mary could not afford a lamb for her purification ritual. The political body to which we belong keeps crucifying people like Mary and Jesus, and Barbie and Aiden. The Gospels do not tell us much about Jesus' access to food growing up. Luke summarizes the next twelve years of Jesus' life with the phrase, "the child grew and became strong; he was filled with Wisdom, and the grace of God was on him."[33] We might disagree on what the solution might be for the children of this country and of the whole world to not suffer food insecurity. As Christians, we can only hope that Aiden would also, like Jesus, grow in strength, Wisdom and God's Grace. But If we have the power to change the world, what can we do so that every single body in this country may have food? May God give us the strength to do it so. May God give us the dreams that Anna and Simeon had, and allow us to see with our own eyes, whole salvation.

Assessment: Strengths and Limitations in This Theological Family

Mujerista preaching has the strengths of uplifting grassroots theology, actualizing salvation-liberation, and promoting self-determination in spite of oppression. *Mujerista* preaching has the disadvantage of placing preachers at odds with church and society, and of alienating many members of Latinx communities.

Preaching from the perspective of *mujerista* theology has the advantage of bringing to the pulpit the theology produced by grassroots Latinas even if they do not have access to the pulpit themselves, as it is still the case in some Christian traditions to which many Latinas belong.

It also has the advantage of fleshing out what a preferential option for the poor may look like in real life in our time, not so much as charity but as the struggle for salvation-liberation, as action for justice rooted in faith and religion, advancing Latinas' preferred future, which is a present without

33. Luke 2:40 NIV.

the systemic oppression of racism, sexism, and poverty, a present in which Latinxs and allies exercise their agency to change oppressive structures.

Using Bible stories as interpretive key to develop *mujerista* sermons has the advantage of helping parishioners grow in their liberative praxis. It encourages them to actively engage in achieving salvation-liberation in the present as manifestation of the unfolding of God's kin-dom. Preaching from a *mujerista* perspective has the potential to amplify the racial, ethnic, theological, cultural, and religious diversity that *mujerista* theology embraces as part of the *mestiza/mulata* Christianity that shapes *mujerista* sermons. Embracing such diversity requires a secondary location for the Bible and welcoming the syncretic nature of *mujerista* religiosity.

Mujerista preaching has the strength of promoting the self determination of Latinas as oppressed people, and also of Latinx communities as marginalized groups in the USA. This kind of preaching is empowering of grassroots communities, first by listening to the theology that they are already producing, and second by using the pulpit, not to tell them what to do, but to give them more tools to decide what to do and how to do it.

Communities empowered in this way are dangerous for governments that want to maintain the status quo, that want to maintain the social, political, and economic structures that keep Latinxs oppressed in the USA. It is also dangerous for churches as they are called to move out of their sexist, racist, and classist behaviors which are ingrained and sustained in ecclesial structures. Therefore, the strength of recognizing the power that grassroots Latinas already have is also a weakness of *mujerista* preaching. This weakness is consequence of placing oneself at odds with the way things are in church and society. In this sense, *mujerista* preaching shares the advantages and disadvantages of any other kind of prophetic preaching.

Another weakness of *mujerista* preaching is how it places itself at odds with practices in many Latinx churches in the USA. Many of these churches consider the Bible to be the word of God in ways that contradict *mujerista* theology. Many of these churches hold on to fundamentalist, individualistic, and pietistic biblical interpretation that *mujerista* theology critiques. Many of these churches are Pentecostal, non-denominational, charismatic, evangelical, and protestant, in contradistinction to the still too Roman Catholic nature of *mujerista* theology. Mujerista theology is mostly produced and practiced outside of the formal ecclesial institutions or inside, but in the basements, kitchens, and in women's restrooms. To listen to this theological production, to bring out to the open what for decades, even centuries has operated in low-key fashion, almost *clandestinamente* (underground) has the potential of alienating many members of Latinx faith communities who also for decades and centuries have been working towards their after-death salvation by obeying the biblical interpretation that they inherited. This significant part of Latinx religiosity in the USA still needs salvation-liberation. Despite these challenges, we must listen to the theological production of grassroots Latinas in the USA.

For Further Reading

Aquinao, María Pilar, et al., eds. *A Reader in Latina Feminist Theology: Religion and Justice*. Austin: University of Texas Press, 2002.

Isasi-Díaz, Ada María. "Communication as Communion: Elements in a Hermeneutic of *Lo Cotidiano*." In *Engaging the Bible in a Gendered World: An Introduction to Feminist Biblical Interpretation in Honor of Katharine Doob Sakenfeld*, edited by Linda Day and Carolyn Pressler. 27–36. Louisville: Westminster John Knox, 2006.

———. *En La Lucha = In the Struggle: Elaborating a Mujerista Theology*. 10th anniversary ed. Minneapolis, Fortress, 2004.

Martell-Otero, Loida I., et al. *Latina Evangélicas: A Theological Survey from the Margins*. Eugene, OR: Cascade Books, 2013.

13

Preaching in the Asian American Theological Family

Namjoong Kim

Asian American theology emerged from critical reflection on the experience of Asian American groups in the United States. Asian American theologians are primarily American theologians of Asian descent who implement their theological dialogue and participation in the US through their Asian-centric perspectives. These theologians, and the communities from which they come, have diverse ethnic, cultural, philosophical, religious, denominational, and personal backgrounds. Just as there is no universal and normative pan-Asian American identity, so there is no universal, uniform, and monolithic pan-Asian American theology. Each culture and each theology has its own nuances. While we may point to certain shared features among the many Asian communities, it is also important to recognize the distinctive identities not only of each community but of each person. Consequently, this chapter cannot speak for all Asian American theologians but can point to some shared characteristics.

Asian Americans in North America experience cultural conflict between East and West. Asian American communities continue to struggle to define their distinctive ethnic roots and cultural identity as a minority group in North American society. In this respect, an important role of Asian American preaching is to help Asian American congregations develop identity from Asian American theological perspectives.

Circumstances That Gave Rise
to This Theological Family

Asian American theology is a contextual theology that begins with repressive attitudes and policies of the majority culture towards Asian Americans. This theology emerges against the history of Eurocentric peoples in the United States lumping people from Asia into one group and regarding them as foreigners, unassimilable aliens, who need to be kept in check as represented in the Chinese Exclusion Act of 1882, the Immigration Act of 1924, and the Asian Exclusion Act. The Japanese American Internment focused on the Japanese community in the United States during World War II.[1] Even though Eurocentric attitudes towards Asian Americans have begun to be more positive, many Eurocentric people still regard Asian Americans as not-quite-white.

Although people from Asia began immigrating to the United States in relatively large numbers in the 1850s, the numbers have grown exponentially since 1965 as the result of the Immigration and Nationality Act of 1965. Asian Americans are currently the fastest-growing and most diverse racial group in the US. In 2020, there were approximately 20 million Asian Americans in the United States (about 5.6 percent of the national population).[2] Over three-quarters of Asian Americans have a religious faith such as Christianity, Hinduism, Buddhism, Islam, Sikhism, Jainism, Zoroastrianism, and new Japanese religions. Two-thirds of these religious Asian Americans, 42 percent,[3] identify themselves as Christians under the influence of Christianity's rapid growth in the non-European world.[4]

The US Census Bureau institutionalized the term "Asian American" as a name given to United States residents who trace their ancestry to Asia. The expression "Asian American" sounds like a convenient shorthand to categorize all the Americans of Asian ancestry and heritage, with their diverse languages, cultures, religions, and traditions. But, in fact, like a rainbow with multiple colors, each subgroup of Asian Americans has particular histories, different experiences of exclusion and trauma, and interracial/interethnic cultural contact. As pointed out in the introductory paragraph to the chapter, the distinctive characteristics of Asian experiences call for particular interpretations in theology and preaching.

---

1. Park, "Asian American Theology," 115.

2. "World Population Review," https://worldpopulationreview.com/state-rankings/asian-population.

3. Kim and Yang, "Introduction to the Handbook," i.

4. For the full report, see Pew Research Center, *Asian Americans*.

The time line of the emergence of Asian American theologies falls into two broad stages: the first generation and the second and following generations. Black and Latin American liberation theologies inspired early Asian American theological perspectives as Asian Americans sought liberation from oppressive and marginalizing structures.

The first-generation of Asian American theology is dated from the late 1960s through the 1980s.[5] During this period, Asian American theologians were entirely males belonging to the US mainline Protestant traditions. They struggled to define and shape their identities and theological perspectives in response to the entrenched racism and discrimination found not only in US society but also in the Christian denominations. The scholars in this era paid much attention to established social and denominational structures, focusing on issues and debates of race and discrimination, faith and culture, and social justice and liberation. At the same time, this generation of theological leaders paid less attention to the internal tensions of their own ethnic groups.

A significant figure of the first-generation, Roy I. Sano, was an Asian American theologian advocating Asian American liberation theology anticipating radical transformation in the social world. Drawing on biblically liberating sources, Sano elaborates on the importance of the stories of Moses, Esther, and the books of Daniel and Revelation in the service of social justice, especially related to race, discrimination, social justice and liberation.[6]

Sang Hyun Lee developed the pilgrimage image for Korean/Asian American identity in his new theological paradigm. Lee describes the Korean life in the US in particular and the Asian life in the US more broadly as a pilgrimage between two cultures. He highlights the experience of marginality, of living on the boundary in a liminal space between the cultures. While the experience of marginality is sometimes viewed as a negative, Lee shows that reflection can lead to the marginal experience resulting in creative opportunities to cultivate a new and more fulfilling pilgrimage in the future.[7]

The work of Jung Young Lee is also important to the first generation. He developed the theme and theology of marginality as the root experience of Asian Americans and brought it into greater dialogue with East

5. Well-known first-generation Asian American male theological pioneers include Japanese American theologians Roy Isao Sano, Paul M. Nagano, Jitsuo Morikawa, and William Mamoru Shinto; Korean American theologians Jung Young Lee and Sang Hyun Lee; and Chinese American theologians Wesley S. Woo and David Ng. See Tan, *Asian American Theologies*, 85–107.

6. Park, "Asian American Theology," 116–17.

7. Sang Hyun Lee, *From a Liminal Place*.

Asian religious and philosophical heritage than Roy Sano or San Hyung Lee. For instance, Jung Young Lee articulates marginality as the edge that connects two different worlds and cultures, especially the yin and yang cosmology paradigm as holistic both/and thinking, represented in Confucianism and Taoism.[8] Jung Young Lee conceives the balance between yin and yang as one entity of life; they are not mutually exclusive but are ever-present together. In this harmonized respect, Jung Young Lee rejects the paradigms of either/or and neither/nor. For him, people and communities in marginal situations can be centers of life-giving harmony and catalysts of the balance between yin and yang. Drawing on biblical sources, both Sang Hyun Lee and Jung Young Lee identify the marginal experience of Asian Americans with Jesus' story: Jesus was the sacred human being who lived at the margins and transformed the marginalized into his people with transformed identity and social experience.

The second stage emerged during the 1990s and continues into the present.[9] The camp of second and following generations of Asian American theologians is much broader and more diverse than the first generation in ethnic and denominational backgrounds as well as in theological perspectives. The range of the first-generation male Chinese, Korean, and Japanese American theologians extends now to female theologians, biblical scholars, and church historians as well as Catholics, evangelicals, Pentecostals, Vietnamese Americans, Filipino Americans, Asian Indian Americans,[10] and others. The second and multi-generational Asian American theologians actively engage in challenging internal inconsistency and injustice within Asian American communities. They also try to address interracial and interethnic conflicts while reflecting on all aspects of Asian American's racial-ethnic identity, community, gender, and life experiences. The interests of the

8. Jung Young Lee, *Marginality*, 58–170.

9. Prominent second- and multigenerational Asian American theologians include Asian American feminist theologians include Chung Hyun Kyung, Kwok Pui-Lan, Rita Nakashima Brock, and Grace Ji-Sun Kim Greer; Asian American Catholic theologians include Peter C. Phan and Anselm Kyongsuk Min; Asian American evangelical theologians Amos Yong, Young Lee Hertig, Samuel Ling, and Enoch Wan; and Asian American biblical scholars include Sze-kar Wan, Gale Yee, Khiok-Khng Yeo, Tat-siong Benny Liew, Jeffrey Kah-Jin Kuan, Seung-Ai Yang, Uriah Yong-Hwan Kim, Yung Suk Kim, Mary Foskett, and Henry Rietz, who pioneered and developed the field of Asian American biblical hermeneutics. Greer Anne Wenh-In Ng, Russell Moy, Timothy Tseng, Eleazar Fernandez, M. Thomas Thangaraj, Fumitaka Matsuoka, Andrew Sung Park, Namsoon Kang, Eunjoo Mary Kim, HyeRan Kim-Cragg, and Sunggu Yang are also well-known Asian American theologians in the second stage. See Tan, *Asian American Theologies*, 85–107.

10. The US Census Bureau uses the term "Asian Indian" to avoid confusion with "Native Americans."

new generation are wide-ranging, including internal ethnocentrism, racism, gender relations and sexual orientation, along with ecology/environmental issues. They seek to change the status quo within the churches and at broader political, socioeconomic, and cultural levels. These scholars and preachers often take interdisciplinary approaches.

The scope of Asian American theology goes beyond developing ethnocentric theologies. Asian American theology does not narrowly confine itself to the specific racial-ethnic concerns of Asian American communities. Asian American theology engages broader Christian theological traditions and contexts. Indeed, Asian American theology seeks to contribute across racial, ethnic, cultural, and national/global boundaries. The following are among characteristics that are common to many Asian American approaches to theology: social analysis, autobiography, storytelling, apocalyptic hermeneutics, anthropological approaches, eschatological imagination, sociotheological hermeneutics, and paradoxical dialectics. Asian American biblical hermeneutics critically re-examines "the methods and scope of biblical interpretation in mainstream scholarship"[11] and point to approaches to biblical interpretation that take account of Asian-American presuppositions and perspectives.

In *Christianity with an Asian Face: Asian American Theology in the Making*, Peter C. Phan, an Asian American Catholic theologian, defines Asian American theology as "a dual character, neither purely(fully) Asian nor purely(fully) American, yet authentically American and authentically Asian."[12] Phan metaphorically describes Asian American theology as "an offspring of the marriage of two widely divergent cultural and religious heritages . . . it bears all the marks of a mixture of the two traditions."[13] In this sense, he adds, "Asian American theology is by nature an intercultural theology, forged in the cauldron of the encounter between two vastly different cultures."[14]

Although great strides towards establishing life-giving identities have been taken, Asian American theologians keep on asking who we are as Asian, American, and Christian in US society. Asian American theologians have developed their significant perspectives with various sources to retrieve, reflect upon, reformulate, and reshape the varieties of Asian American contexts and their theologies: theologies of liberation, diasporic studies, postcolonial theory, postmodern theory, feminist criticism, sociocultural studies, Asian

---

11. Ho, "The Complex Heterogeneity of Asian American Identity," 1–2.

12. Phan, *Christianity with an Asian Face*, xiii.

13. Kim and Yang, "Introduction to the Handbook," xiii.

14. Kim and Yang, "Introduction to the Handbook," xiv.

religions and worldviews, their own Asian spiritual, philosophical, cultural, and ethnic heritages, and other Asian American studies.

At the risk of oversimplifying, we might say that the second generation of Asian theologians, followed by voices in preaching, seeks to call the community to participate in living together in mutually supportive ways in a multi-cultural and multi-ethnic society by accepting, encouraging, respecting, caring, and appreciating each other in the North American context and beyond. These theologies share two motifs in these respects. The first is to name and resist the community's experience of segregation, racism, marginalization, colonialism, cultural imperialism, and other forms of dehumanizing discrimination. The second is to help the communities move towards healing, hospitality, harmony, solidarity of others, justice, equality and equity, reconciliation, postcolonialism, decolonization, inclusion, humanization, liberation, community building, transformation, mutual well-being, and interdependence. Asian American theology hopes for internal transmutation and external transformation[15] of oppressive structures in US society. Christian preaching in this mode encourages hearers to participate as individuals and communities in bringing about such changes.

Purposes and Characteristics of Preaching in This Theological Family

In *Preaching the Presence of God*, Eunjoo May Kim contends that "one of the major tasks of Asian American homiletics is to develop a new theological perspective for preaching from the particular experience of Asian American congregations." In her perspective, "the theology of Asian American preaching is closely related to the formation and nurture of the congregations' spirituality." She further defines the preaching from an Asian American perspective as holistic-oriented "spiritual preaching" and describes the preacher's image as "a spiritual director."[16]

The typical characteristics of Asian American preaching[17] come from characteristic-but-diverse aspects of Asian cultures discussed in the previous section. Either explicitly or implicitly, the preacher often deals with

15. Park, "Asian American Theology," 124–26. Andrew Sung Park developed his significant transmutation and transformation theology in the early 1990s: internal and natural change/aspect versus external and structural change.

16. Kim, *Preaching the Presence of God*, 48–105.

17. Daniel L. Wong identifies characteristics of Asian North American preaching as follows: the preaching is contextual, intercultural, incarnational, Holy Spirit–led, transformational, narratival, and collaborative (Kim, and Wong, *Finding Our Voice*, chap. 4. Kindle ed.).

issues of identity and racism. Asian American preaching usually includes four dimensions: informing, deforming, reforming, and transforming. The first step is the *informing* stage in which the preacher identifies what the biblical text said to the original hearers. This first step includes exposing an inconvenient truth in the text. This truth may relate to a "heavenly power" or an "earthly power."[18] The second step moves to the *deforming* stage, exploring the positive and negative aspects of the text. The second stage examines whether the text has been interpreted as a tool of oppression or liberation. The second step deconstructs "heavenly powers" and "earthly powers" as they appear in the world of the biblical text, in the context of contemporary US society, and beyond. The third step moves to the *reforming* stage, interpreting the text from Asian American liberation theological perspectives and values. The fourth stage is the *transforming* stage, suggesting how to live together in the light of the Christian message. The sermon below follows this four-stage structure.

Asian Americans join other people who want to live in a safe context marked by healing, peace, and reconciliation. The Bible uses the word "justice" to speak of such a life.[19] The heart of the Bible and the purpose of Asian American preaching are to represent God's desire for justice for Asian American communities, for contemporary US society, and beyond. God calls for the wounds of all communities to be healed, and for all communities reconcile with each other, and live together in love and peace. The idea of community here refers not only to human society but to everything in the cosmos.[20] This justice-oriented direction is the purpose of Asian American preaching.

Eunjoo Mary Kim notes that preaching seeks to name where God's will is revealed and where God is working. In *Preaching in an Age of Globalization*, Kim responds that while such discoveries can happen in the worshiping community, they also take place beyond the worshipping community. God's will is often revealed among the marginalized and powerless

---

18. Hodgson describes inconvenient truths as "heavenly powers," that is, "ideologies: racism, sexism, classism, naturism, homophobia, xenophobia," and he describes "earthly powers as injustice: political, social, economic, and environmental oppression." These characteristics can be an appropriate checklist of inconvenient truths for preaching on social issues, that preachers should cover in each preaching cycle. Hodgson, *Winds of the Spirit*, 225–30.

19. Ottoni-Wilhelm et al., Introduction.

20. Eunjoo Mary Kim's preaching theology of humanization, illuminated by Paul Lehmann's *Ethics in a Christian Context*, is concerned with the liberation of all creatures and the restoration of community "in which all human beings live in solidarity as the image of the Triune God" (Kim, *Preaching in an Age of Globalization*, 54).

in the world.[21] Marginality need not be only a negative experience; it can be a context of creativity in which the perceptions of people on the margins can transform how the congregation understands relationships among communities. These three contexts—the worshipping community, the broad world, and communities on the margins—are not separate but are interconnected. Asian American preachers, agreeing with Kim's perspective, trust that God works through the experience of people on the margins, including their suffering. Consequently, Asian American preachers listen to those experiences with an ear towards how the lessons from the margin can point to healing of all kinds of discrimination.

Kim's theology of humanization for preaching[22] is characteristic of Asian American sermons. This theology seeks the liberation of all creatures and the restoration of community "in which all human beings live in solidarity as the image of the Triune God."[23] In this sense, Asian American preaching seeks to join in God's mission by inviting and guiding Asian American congregations toward true humanization.

To achieve this purpose in preaching, Asian American preachers aim to be intentional about creating a shared identity in which people with differences, aspects of otherness, come together in the full recognition of those differences but aiming to live together in such a way that the members of the congregation recognize "otherness and differences of the people, especially, of the marginalized individually and communally, without denying existential similarity among different people."[24] The shared identity replaces competition or disregard among members of the community with a transcendent sense of appreciation. "This commitment is based on the theological conviction that all human beings are created to live as a community of different people in solidarity with one another." In this community, "others are part of our own true and full humanity."[25]

The role of Asian American preachers includes becoming constructive dialogue partners who seek to create mutual understanding with their congregations for ongoing conversation concerning humanization with a shared

21. Kim, *Preaching in an Age of Globalization*, 20–25.

22. Haslam, "What Is Dehumanization?"; Kim, *Preaching in an Age of Globalization*, 54. Eunjoo Mary Kim articulates that "From the biblical point of view, *humanization* means the liberation of human beings from the present evil age (Gal 1:4), freedom from any kind of slavery or structure that diminishes human dignity or worth, including racism, classism, sexism, ethnocentrism, despotism, even our own devaluation or self-limitations" (Kim, *Preaching in an Age of Globalization*, 54).

23. Kim, *Preaching in an Age of Globalization*, 54.

24. Kim, *Preaching in an Age of Globalization*, 55.

25. Kim, *Preaching in an Age of Globalization*, 55.

identity "through argument, confrontation, endurance, appreciation, challenge, and change on both sides."[26] Kim contends "the formation of a shared identity is possible only through this kind of dialogue approach" that is practiced with civility.[27] In "Hermeneutics and Asian American Preaching," Kim suggests liberation theological perspectives and exegetical methods to help Korean/Asian American preachers interpret the biblical text in a new way as follows: (1) Read the Bible as the source of identity formation; (2) Interpret the text biblically as the voice of the congregation; and, (3) Apply the paschal mystery as a theological foundation.[28]

In "The Abrahamic Pilgrimage Story in Sermons," Sunggu Yang notes that many Asian American theologians have found that "the [various] Abrahamic pilgrimage stor[ies] forming the 'pilgrimage-in-the-wilderness' spirituality have been an ontological-narrative backbone of Asian American faith constructs."[29] As God called Abraham into the land of Canaan through the wilderness, so God calls Korean/Asian Americans into the new country through the experience of marginality, which is their wilderness. Yang categorizes the various Asian American preaching styles as "the allegorical-typological narrative style, the eschatological-symbolic narrative style, and the illustrative narrative style."[30] Asian American preachers read the Bible from the perspective of pilgrims. The pilgrimage motif in Asian American preaching as two dimensions. One dimension is the sorrow and frustration of Asian Americans who find little hope in the existing system. But the other dimension is hopeful. Asian American preaching points towards a new tomorrow of joy and happiness in the Asian American world as it sees itself as an alternative exodus community working liberation from oppressive and marginalizing structures. In this recognition process, the theology of the pilgrim community encourages collective awareness of the things that oppress and collective movement against the vicious manifestations of discrimination dehumanization. Pilgrims can be transformative agents in history who open the way to a new tomorrow in which people live peacefully.

Feminist and womanist theologians try to recover the authentic experiences and stories of women as sources of theological reflection. Asian

---

26. Kim, *Preaching in an Age of Globalization*, 57. In *The Witness of Preaching*, Thomas G. Long suggests the value of "witness" as a master metaphor encompassing the strengths of dominant images of the preacher: *herald*, *pastor*, and *storyteller*. Alongside the images that Long lays out, Kim suggests that witness also means *dialogue partner*. Long, *The Witness of Preaching*, 18–44.

27. Kim, *Preaching in an Age of Globalization*, 57.

28. Kim, "Hermeneutics and Asian American Preaching."

29. Yang, "The Abrahamic Pilgrimage Story in Sermons." 24–25.

30. Yang, "The Abrahamic Pilgrimage Story in Sermons," 35.

American women often reformulate doctrines so that the experiences of women are taken seriously. Regarding Asian American preaching as a way of storytelling, two authors—HyeRann Kim-Cragg, a Korean Canadian scholar of preaching, and EunYoung Choi, a Korean scholar in biblical studies—offer an eye-opening contribution, in *The Encounters: Retelling the Bible from Migration and Intercultural Perspectives*.[31] This resource for Asian American preaching supports the idea of multi-cultural and ethnic communities engaging biblical stories. The authors employ feminist biblical criticism, literary narrative criticism, and reader-response criticism. In terms of postcolonial biblical criticism, Kim-Cragg notes that Scripture can never be value-neutral, universal, or absolute; it must always be understood as value-laden, partial, and contextual, depending on the social location for which the text is interpreted.[32]

Kim-Cragg and Choi take up migration, inter-cultural, and inter-racial/ethnic issues related to women's lives and stories. They use a monologue style when considering women's experiences and stories in the Bible, starting with "I" as a first-person narrative rather than beginning with "she" as the third person point of view. They retell biblical texts as monologues into which they weave interpretive connections to the world today. The retelling of the story is the sermon. This approach encourages Asian American preachers to look at themselves through the eyes of others as well as through the dynamics of migration and multi/inter-cultural living. Asian American storytelling as a form of Asian American preaching is an effective and powerful way to empower the congregation towards becoming an agent of transformation. In the Asian American context, it is often more effective sermons in more Western styles.

Case Study: Text and Sermon
(Mark 4:30–32; Mark 6:34–44)

The following sermon is based on two paradoxical stories: Mark 4:30–32 (the parable of the mustard seed) and Mark 6:34–44 (the story of the five loaves and two fish). The sermon illumines a common theme: the meaning of the realm of God in relationship to Asian values of pilgrimage, marginalization, liberation, and humanization.

This sermon views the "wilderness" as a liminal space that is ambivalent but vital because it is the interspace where gospel messages can empower contemporary listeners to envision a new reality. Wilderness as liminal space

31. Kim-Cragg and Choi, *The Encounters*, 14–22.
32. Kim-Cragg and Choi, *The Encounters*, 16.

presents two possibilities: the wilderness of suffering and the wilderness of awakening to transform the broken world into a more beautiful place.

The sermon encourages listeners to imagine the difference between the extraordinary banquet held in the wilderness by the compassion of Jesus, and a meal characteristic of the old world represented by Herod's banquet. The sermon encourages the Asian American congregation to trust God and invites them to respond to the divine call to share their possessions in ways suggested by the mustard seed and the loaves and fish. The sermon also reminds the listeners that they are mustard seeds and are five loaves and two fish. They represent what the realm of God looks like to those desperately in need in American society and beyond.

"What Does the Realm of God Look Like?"

[Informing Stage. This sermon begins with the preacher's personal experience in Korea. The texts functions as a lens through which the preacher and the listeners can reflect on their communal and individual experiences. Moving between Korea and the biblical worlds of the two texts by sharing stories, the sermon invites listeners to glimpse what the realm of God looks like and it seeks to stimulate their imagination to envision a beautiful world they can live into together. The sermon tells half a story in the introduction and the other half in conclusion.]

"Bring your smallest one!"

What does the realm of God look like? In Mark 4:30–32, Jesus taught a parable about the realm of God to the large crowd gathered by the sea. The realm of God was central to Jesus. In this passage, we can see Jesus teaching that the realm of God is like the smallest mustard seed.

The name of a tree called the *Jungja* tree in Korean can be translated into English as a shade tree or a small pavilion. It stands at an entrance to a village. It is a huge tree that is usually hundreds of years old or even could be a thousand years old. The *Jungja* tree has long branches with abundant leaves that create a large shaded space. It cannot be seen in cities nowadays but is still in rural villages.

In Korean society the *Jungja* is a symbol of community that binds people together. Under that tree, people gathered, chatted, enjoyed themselves, ate together, and rested under. It was an open place where everyone could meet. It was also a shelter for elders, those who passed by, a playground for children, and animals: dogs, cats, and birds. Under the *Jungja* tree, there were always people and animals. There, they told their stories, laughed, and looked back on their memories. It became the space that unified people and animals and gave them a place to get to know one another better.

> *[The sermon now transitions from the preacher's personal experience to the biblical text to help the listeners comprehend the symbolic relationship between the mustard seed and the Jungja tree as an Asian value.]*

The parable of the mustard seed reminds me of the *Jungja* tree in Korean villages and gives me a glimpse of the realm of God. The realm is a place to be with others in the way that people are under the great shade tree. I believe that my existence and life can be more meaningful when I am in a relationship with others. It is a place far from lonely, desolate, and excluded. In fact, the Ream of God is the place of sharing, togetherness, and mutuality in a respectful and nurturing relationship without any discrimination, hostility, and bias.

> *[Deforming Stage: This sermon briefly exposes socioeconomic and political conflicts under the rule of Herod and Caesar in Jesus' time. The sermon invites contemporary listeners to reconsider and reexamine modern imperialistic systems.]*

When Jesus lived, the word "realm" was a political term, and the term "Realm of God" was a political metaphor because there were other realms. Jesus' listeners lived under other empires: the rule of Herod and Caesar. Jesus' listeners understood what those dominions were like, and here is Jesus illustrating the realm of God with a mustard seed.

The rules of Herod and Caesar were oppressive and dominant systems. Ruling elites of power and wealth structured the political and economic systems for their benefits. Imperial Rome structured society to benefit Rome. As a result, in the ancient world, the wealthiest one to two percent of the population possessed approximately two-thirds of the wealth. Jesus posed the realm of God as an alternative to this socioeconomic and political abuse. How about now?

> *[Reforming Stage. At this point, this sermon moves from the deforming stage toward the reforming stage by discovering a Christian message in the biblical text with Asian American liberation theological perspective and purpose. The part of the sermon is intended to generate new perception about the possibilities for the congregation through Asian American theology's vision of sharing.]*

The story of feeding five thousand with five loaves and two fish tells us about the grand feast Jesus offered in a deserted place near the shore of Galilee. Yet, this contrasts with the immediately previous story in Mark 6:14–29. In that earlier story, John the Baptist was an agent for the poor and weak. King Herod beheaded him at a royal banquet. Ironically, Herod's feast was to kill life (Mark 6:14–29). After the murder at King Herod's luxurious feast broke Jesus' heart, Jesus went to a solitary place. People followed him, listened to his teachings and wisdom, and he healed people through compassion. Jesus saw that the great crowd was helpless like sheep without a shepherd; and he had great compassion for them by offering a wonderful banquet to support them. Jesus' banquet contrasts sharply with Herod's.

How could Jesus provide them with food and drink in the wilderness? His disciples suggested that he send the people away to go to the villages and buy some food. However, instead of dismissing the people, he asked the disciples to bring to him what the crowd had: five loaves of bread and two fish. Jesus took them, looked up, blessed and broke the loaves, and gave them to the disciples to offer them to the people. He also shared two fish with them. And when the disciples gave the broken loaves and shared fish to the people, the loaves of bread and fish multiplied enough to feed five thousand men (Mark 6:44) as well as women and children, including twelve basketfuls of leftovers.

Through divine action of grace and Jesus' compassion, five loaves of bread and two fish were more than enough to feed the hungry. These tiny resources were enough for Jesus to provide people with a beautiful feast in a deserted place. Jesus transformed the wilderness of suffering into a wilderness of revelation that included a joyful and fabulous banquet.

Have you ever witnessed people in the wilderness of suffering? Have you seen someone in deep sorrow over losing a loved one to COVID-19 pandemic or some other disease? Have you listened to the desperate voices saying, "I can't breathe?" Have you seen the anxious faces of those who have lost their jobs? Have you felt those who hunger and thirst for God, for justice, meaning, and life? Have you seen the lonely, the disoriented, and the poor in many different ways? Have you listened to those who have been sexually abused?

We may think it is impossible for us to transform the wilderness of suffering into the wilderness of awakening, where everyone can eat, drink, work, and live mutually with one another. We may feel that we have only five loaves of bread and two fish. We may feel we have limited time, energy, financial resources, knowledge, and experience. But, at the same time, we hear the divine voice from Jesus amid the wilderness of suffering to bring our five bread and fish to him. I do not know *how* the wilderness of suffering can be changed into the heavenly banquet. But the more we trust divine power/intervention, the more we share our small amount of bread and fish, then the text says that the wilderness of suffering will turn towards the realm of God, which is entirely different from the domains of Herod, Caesar, and Rome.

[Transforming Stage. The sermon suggests how to live together from the perspective of the gospel. It reminds the listeners that participating in God's vision is the heart of the calling of the Asian American community of faith. In the conclusion, the sermon returns to the other half of the introductory story related to the mustard seed. The sermon provides a direction for the spiritual journey of the congregation through meditative and holistic-centered spiritual hermeneutics.]

Let me go back to the parable of the mustard seed. From the smallest mustard seed, we see the mystery of life as it becomes the tallest tree. How can we explain that creative wonder? There is a life of irresistible energy. There is a life-affirming mystery. The strength of life is buried under the dust. Because the roots of the tree are firmly grounded in the soil, the trees can grow. The more deeply they are rooted in the ground, the stronger the roots and the tree become. The tree stretches its branches farther and farther. Similarly, we have roots that firmly sustain us and strengthen us and allow us to stretch our witness to the realm farther and farther. This root is that God is the fountain of our lives. This root enables us to build the realm of God, to turn the world into a realm of justice and peace. We imagine and dream of the world that has not come yet.

However, the realm of God, the realm of justice and peace, does not come easily and quickly. There must be a growing process. Creating such a world requires effort, and it is a transforming process just as the trees grow slowly and change in all kinds of weather. There are windstorms, cold winters, severe winds, and attacks from insects amid the process of growth. During this process, we need faith, patience, and time. Sometimes we need to struggle with ourselves. There may be the need to abandon our sense of privilege, our selfish ambition, or indifference. We may need to struggle with outside forces that press us down.

However, God is the map in our journey of faith and life. In our every step of growing, God is always God helping us and inviting us to transformation. So, we can dream and hope for the heavenly banquet on this earth. It is a mystery how the smallest mustard seed grows to the tallest tree. It is a mystery that over five thousand people can eat and be satisfied with only five loaves of bread and two fish. Living with mystery is the journey of life and faith. Through the journey, God works *in* us, God works *for* us, and God works *through* us so that we can continuously grow like a tree that willingly puts forth large branches and allows the birds to breathe comfortably, rest, and dwell.

Assessment: Strengths and Limitations in This Theological Family

A strength of this approach is that it offers hope to Asian Americans in marginalizing and dehumanizing places in American society. Drawing on Asian American liberation theology, preachers can speak to the experiences of people on the margins locally and globally and thereby help them identify God's presence and work to make and keep human lives human.

Telling the experiences and stories of those who live on the margins is a particular strength in Asian American preaching.[33] Various experiences and stories from Asian American history into the present not only make the preacher's sermon clear and exciting, but also demonstrate how Christian faith can come to life in particular Asian American social locations.[34] Because such stories illuminate the socioeconomic and political reality of Asian Americans, Asian American preachers can use them to address how God works in history and what God requires of Asian American congregations and others.

Asian American liberation theology encourages preachers to analyze social structures that cause conflict and division. Asian American preaching can help listeners recognize violence and discrimination within Christian institutions and society. Asian American preaching can support the congregation in realizing that social structural repression is contrary to God's purpose and social imagination.

The multiple approaches of Asian American theology encourage the preacher to consider four basic principles conducive to effective Asian American contexts. First, this approach allows preachers to reject social models that are not appropriate to Christian Asian American life: patriarchy, hierarchy, Eurocentrism, anthropocentrism, androcentrism, and similar distortions of life. Second, it encourages preachers and congregations to pay attention to alternative biblical hermeneutics beyond the historical-critical

---

33. For more information regarding the power of storytelling, see Anderson and Foley, *Mighty Stories, Dangerous Rituals*, 3–19; Elkins, *Holy Stuff of Life*; and Elkins, "Holy Stuff of Life."

34. Long, *The Witness of Preaching*, 37.

approach. The expanded approach offers an opportunity to develop a range of interpretive methods for preaching and dialogue between Asian American preachers and congregations: reader-response, narrative, sociocultural, literary, postcolonial, post-structural, autobiographical, and ideological hermeneutics. In *Preaching the Presence of God*, Eunjoo Mary Kim calls this a *spiritual hermeneutic*. It seeks the ongoing critical and comparative hybrid dialogue between Asian ways of communicating, interpreting, and thinking and Western hermeneutics.[35] Third, this approach helps the preacher understand the biblical text's polyphonic voices: especially the powerful and the powerless in biblical texts and in other contexts. Fourth, it leads preachers to understand that when they deal with biblical texts, they approach the biblical material not as value-free and objective texts, containing universal truth, but as ideologically constructed or value-imbued products.

A weakness is a frequent gap between the theology of Asian American preaching and that of the laypeople in many Asian American congregations. Many listeners in local Asian American churches ignore the racial and ethnic liberation movement making it difficult to get collaborative attention and action on the part of the community. Some examples include the Black Lives Matter movement, or solidarity with Native Americans, discrimination against Islamic people, or other discriminatory viewpoints and behaviors. Asian American churches are seldom actively involved. In this regard, Asian American preachers need to call upon inner strength to be disciplined in seeking to empower Asian American individuals and communities to become witnesses, agents in reforming and transforming their cultures and beyond.

There have been few academic or professional resources dealing with Asian American theology and preaching. More resources are becoming available, but the need is great. This is the time to search for new theological perspectives, hermeneutics, and sermon forms.

For Further Reading

Floyd-Thomas, Stacey M., and Anthony B. Pinn, eds. *Liberation Theologies in the United States: An Introduction*. New York: New York University Press, 2010.

Kim, Eunjoo Mary. "Hermeneutics and Asian American Preaching." *Semeia* 90/91 (2002) 269–90.

———. *Preaching the Presence of God: A Homiletic from an Asian American Perspective*. Judson. 1999.

Kim, Matthew D., and Daniel L. Wong. *Finding Our Voice: A Vision for Asian North American Preaching*. Bellingham, WA: Lexham, 2020.

---

35. Kim, *Preaching the Presence of God*, 77–105.

Kim, Uriah Y., and Seung Ai Yang, eds. *T and T Clark Handbook of Asian American Biblical Hermeneutics*. Bloomsbury, 2019.

Kim-Cragg, HyeRan, and EunYoung Choi. *The Encounters: Retelling the Bible from Migration and Intercultural Perspectives*. Daejeon, South Korea: Daejanggan, 2013.

Lee, Sang Hyun. *From a Liminal Place: An Asian American theology*. Minneapolis: Fortress, 2010.

Liew, Tat-Siong Benny. *What Is Asian American Biblical Hermeneutics? Reading the New Testament*. Intersections: Asian and Pacific American Transcultural Studies. Honolulu: University of Hawaii Press, 2007.

Park, Andrew Sung. *Racial Conflict and Healing: An Asian-American Theological Perspective*. 1996. Reprint, Eugene: Wipf & Stock, 2009.

Tajima-Peña, Renee, et al., producers. *Asian Americans* (five-episode miniseries). Public Broadcasting Service (PBS). 2020. https://www.pbs.org/show/asian-americans/.

Tan, Jonathan Y. *Introducing Asian American Theologies*. Maryknoll, NY: Orbis, 2008.

Yang, Sunggu. "The Abrahamic Pilgrimage Story in Sermons: An Ontological-Narrative Foundation of Asian American Life in Faith." *Theology Today* 73 (2016) 24–35.

14

Preaching in the Asian American Feminist Theological Family

Eunjoo Mary Kim

ASIAN AMERICAN FEMINIST THEOLOGY has been claimed and articulated by those who are willing to engage in critical theological discourse in response to Asian American women's unique experiences in North America.[1] It is a relatively new addition to Christian theology and is still at a nascent stage. Its approach and theological concern intersect with those of Asian American theology, feminist theology, and postcolonialism. Like Asian American theology, Asian American feminist theology is concerned with Asian American immigrants and their descendants' social experiences. Yet, it views particularly on Asian American women's lived experiences through the critical lens of feminist and postcolonial theories and responds to them with constructive theological reflection. What is the distinctive theological claim of Asian American feminist theology? How does such a theology influence the purpose and character of Christian preaching? What might a sermon crafted from the Asian American feminist perspective look like? The following discussion focuses on these questions.

---

1. Here the term "Asian American Women" is used "strategically" rather than in an essentialist way. That means, in spite of the danger of generalizing about Asian American women's diverse experiences, the term is used "with the acknowledgement of 'the unavoidable usefulness of something that is very dangerous'" (Nami Kim, "The 'Indigestible' Asian," 37).

Circumstances That Gave Rise
to This Theological Family

Before there was Asian American feminist theology, there were Asian American women's unique experiences. And before theologians reflected on those experiences, Asian American feminist literature and artworks expressed them in creative and provocative ways. What then are the unique experiences of Asian American women in North America? A multitude of issues should be probed in answering this question: Asian American women live in predominantly white North American society as immigrants and the daughters, granddaughters, and great-granddaughters of immigrants. As racial minority people, they experience sociocultural, religious, and generational conflicts over norms and values, language differences, changes in family dynamics and gender roles, and confusion about identity. All these problems are intricately interconnected and have immense impact on daily life.

Along with other racial and ethnic minority people in North America, Asian American women experience systemic racism, tokenism, cultural imperialism, and other forms of discrimination in their workplaces and other sectors of society. They also carry the baggage of the perpetual foreigner syndrome and the model minority stereotype. No matter how many generations of their families have lived in North America as legal citizens, they are frequently asked, "Where are you from?" "Where are you really from?" "Why don't you go back to your country?" These questions suggest that Asian Americans are not fully registered in the collective consciousness of what it means to be American and their distinctive racial and ethnic cultures are not acknowledged as part of North American culture. As Gale Yee, a third-generation Chinese American biblical theologian, states, "The perception of being aliens in their own land is one that Asian Americans find difficult to shake off. They continue to be seen as more Asian than American."[2] A sense of being alien is a traumatic experience for Asian American immigrants, especially for their descendants, who were born and raised in North America.

The model minority stereotype, in terms of which Asian Americans are considered exemplary vis-à-vis other racial minority groups in achieving the "American Dream" and successfully assimilating into white American society, may sound complimentary. But it is in fact a dangerous myth constructed by white Americans from the biased view that Asian Americans are still inferior to whites. Moreover, it creates damaging relationships with other racial minority people in North America by giving

---

2. Yee, "She Stood in Tears amid the Alien Corn," 47.

the false impression that Asian Americans consider themselves superior to other racial minorities. Above all, the model minority stereotype over-generalizes the Asian American population by ignoring its rich tapestry of diversity. Asian American immigrants have come from many countries from the Far East to Southwest Asia and the Pacific islands, through different time periods from the late nineteenth-century to the present. Their native languages, historical and sociopolitical backgrounds, and religious and cultural roots are as diverse as the number of countries found on the continent of Asia and in the Pacific. Their motivations for immigration and current living conditions in North America are as varied as their socioeconomic and educational statuses, as they struggle to fit in white American society. The model minority myth overlooks these disparities among Asian American communities.

In addition to racial and cultural discrimination, sexism is at the core of Asian American women's experiences. Sexism is embedded deeply in both American society and Asian American communities, and functions as a major force in oppressing Asian women with expulsion and exclusion. Sexism subordinates Asian American women to a male-centered hierarchical structure and suppresses them into silence in decision-making at home and in the work place. Sexism also denigrates their bodies and sexuality as exploitable objects. In traditional Asian religious and moral culture, on the one hand, female bodies are regarded as the mere tools for reproduction. In North American white supremacist culture, on the other, numerous films, media, and arts depict Asian American women not simply as unfamiliar, but "as appealingly and invitingly exotic"[3] sexual objects, thereby trivializing them as if they were commodities. These experiences of "dual liminality and marginalization"[4] discourage Asian American women from living as holistic human beings and equal citizens and drive them to abandon too quickly their life-goals in American society. It is so difficult and stressful to overcome racial and sexual discrimination that many retain a sense of powerlessness and fall into self-abasement, despair, and helplessness.

Asian American women's experiences were first voiced through Asian American feminist literature. Maxine Hong Kingston's *The Woman Warrior: Memoirs of a Girlhood among Ghosts* became a landmark when it was published in 1976. It highlights the ambiguity and complexity of being a Chinese American woman in racist and sexist American society.[5] Since then, Asian American feminist writers have made efforts to form a

3. Kim-Kort, *Making Paper Cranes*, 25.

4. Lee, *From a Liminal Place*, 22.

5. Brock, "Cooking without Recipes," 138.

new type of feminism aimed at replacing the negative self-image of Asian American women—which is tainted by racism, cultural imperialism, and sexism—with new images, such as that of the warrior. The edited volume, *Making Waves: An Anthology of Writings By and About Asian American Women,* is a sample of the wide range of Asian American feminist voices reflecting on Asian American women's diverse experiences from new constructivist perspectives.[6]

At this juncture, it is worth noting that in 1984, Letty Russell, Shannon Clarkson, and Kwok Pui-lan, along with a group of Asian and Asian American female seminarians, ministers, and theologians, initiated an organization of Asian and Asian American feminist theologians. They have met together on a regular basis to discuss Asian and Asian American feminist theology and eventually established a network named the Pacific, Asian, and North American Asian Women in Theology and Ministry (PANAAWTM). In 2007, the group contributed to Asian American feminist scholarship by publishing the edited volume, *Off the Menu: Asian and Asian North American Women's Religion and Theology.*[7] In this work, sixteen Asian American female contributors share their feminist theological perspectives constructed around dialogue between their unique experiences in North America and their Asian cultural and religious heritages. PANAAWTM added to its scholarly contribution to Asian American feminist theology by publishing two more edited works, *Leading Wisdom: Asian and Asian North American Women Leaders,*[8] and *Asian and Asian American Women in Theology and Religion: Embodying Knowledge.*[9] These publications respond to Asian American women's sociocultural, religious, and political issues in creative and constructive ways.

Among the members of PANAAWTM, Wonhee Anne Joh, a second-generation Korean American feminist theologian, articulates Asian American women's unique experiences through the Korean concept of *han* and Julia Kristeva's notion of "abjection." *Han* is a Korean term denoting "woundedness of the heart" dominated by "feelings of abandonment and helplessness."[10] Similarly, abjection is a state or feeling of being "rejected from which one does not part."[11] In *Heart of the Cross: A Postcolonial Christology,* Joh not only describes Asian American women's negative experiences

6. Asian Women United of California, *Making Waves.*
7. Brock et al., eds., *Off the Menu.*
8. Pak et al., eds., *Leading Wisdom.*
9. Kwok, *Asian and Asian American Women in Theology and Religion.*
10. Park, *The Wounded Heart of God,* 15.
11. Kristeva, *Powers of Horror,* 4.

in terms of *han* and abjection, but also proposes "a Christology of *Jeong*" as a way of empowering Asian American women to overcome the horror of *han* and abjection. She re-conceptualizes the ordinary Korean word *jeong* (affection, attachment, or goodwill) into a theological term that signifies "a radical form of love," i.e., "compassion, affection, solidarity, relationality, vulnerability, and forgiveness."[12] Through her constructive concept of *jeong*, Joh provides an alternative way of understanding the meaning of the cross in relation to Asian American women's experiences.

The voices of Asian American feminist theologians are not only those affiliated with PANAAWT. During the first two decades of the twenty-first century, a number of Asian American feminist theologians have engaged in critical theological discourse in various areas of theology. They have unceasingly challenged the dominant racist, imperialist, and sexist culture from theological perspectives of globalization, transnationalism, postmodernism, and postcolonialism. Simultaneously, they have worked to construct a newly-envisioned identity for Asian American women through interdisciplinary conversations with sacred texts, religious traditions, spirituality, and social sciences.[13] The present identity of Asian American women, distorted as it is by the dominant culture of racism, cultural imperialism, and sexism, should not be considered permanent or fixed, but should undergo reconstruction that such women might live as full human beings in their new North American home.

Asian American feminist theology therefore aims to provide a creative space or "Third Space" where diverse experiences are critically reflected upon and reconfigured as constructive sources for the formation of a new identity. Homi Bhabha is one of the first postcolonial scholars to use the term "Third Space" to signify a creative force in between two cultures. In his view, the colonized, the immigrants, and the oppressed live in an interstitial space that facilitates the creation of a new hybrid identity.[14] Rita N. Brock, a second-generation Japanese American feminist theologian, affirms the creative force of a Third Space by describing the dynamic process of the formation of a new hybrid identity as "interstitial integrity,"[15] which is "a complex, evolving process over time, captured in moments of self-awareness and self-acceptance." The aim is "to find what is sacred by taking into our lives all that has touched

---

12. Joh, *Heart of the Cross*, xiii.

13. Cf. Choi, *A Postcolonial Leadership*; G. J. Kim, *Embracing the Other*; Kim-Cragg, *Interdependence*; E. M. Kim, "Asian American Women and Renewal of Preaching."

14. Bhabha, The *Location of Culture*, 56.

15. Brock, "Cooking without Recipes," 126.

us."[16] Asian American women and other oppressed people are invited to
such interstitial integrity, through which they untangle the complexities of
lives lived between two cultures and construct new hybrid identities that are
completely different from those constructed in either culture. This process
empowers women with new symbols, images, and stories, so that they might
live as holistic human beings and active agents transforming the status quo
in the country they now claim as their home.

Purposes and Characteristics of Preaching
in This Theological Family

Asian American feminist theologians suggest that Christian preaching has
to do with creating a Third Space and inviting listeners and their communities to interstitial integrity regardless of whether they are marginalized
or privileged in society. More precisely, the purpose of preaching from an
Asian American feminist perspective is to make the preaching moment
a Third Space, in which listeners may construct a new identity as members of the family of God. In so doing, they empower their churches and
communities to function as Third Spaces also, with the creative force to
transform the broader society. The purpose is thus dual dimensional: the
transformation of Asian American churches that have mostly patriarchal
and conservative theological worldviews, values, and practices, and the
transformation of North American society that is deeply rooted in white
supremacy and sexism.

Preaching from the Asian American feminist perspective is, therefore, a prophetic ministry. It challenges listeners to see their past and
present critically, to reconsider who they are from God's point of view,
and to discern their personal and communal calls to participate in creating a new community of equity, justice, and love. Sang Hyun Lee, a
first-generation Korean American theologian, identifies such a visionary
community as "the family of God," which means "an egalitarian and intimate communion."[17] Much like natural human families, Lee explains, the
family of God is imperfect. Yet, it is "the redeemed community on earth,"
a "proleptically real embodiment of the reign of God" where there is no
patriarchal hierarchy or imperialistic oppression.[18]

How, then, might preaching create a Third Space where interstitial
integrity is brought about? Asian American feminist theology suggests

16. Brock, "Cooking without Recipes," 140.

17. Lee, *From a Liminal Place*, 71.

18. Lee, *From a Liminal Place*, 71.

that the preacher should use Asian American women's experiences as the primary sources for preaching. Such diverse experiences should be incorporated in the process of constructing the new identity of the listeners and their communities through dialogues with biblical stories and Christian doctrines. For example, Yee reads the story of Ruth from the point of view of Asian American women's experiences. Although the conventional reading identifies Ruth as a virtuous foreign woman who becomes "an exemplar for the Jewish people," a critical reading of the Book of Ruth depicts her as a "perpetual foreigner" and "model minority convert," similar to the distorted image of Asian American women in North America.[19] Such a reading challenges preachers to create a new meaning for the biblical stories through the lens of Asian American women's experiences and provide listeners with a space for reflecting on their identities in a new way.

Traditional Christian doctrines, such as those of sin, repentance, justification, and reconciliation, should also be reinterpreted in light of Asian American women's experiences. Based on Asian American experiences, Lee defines sin as "what is wrong with humanity . . . in terms of whether or not human beings are in line with what God is doing in history." In other words, sin is "people's resistance to God's end in creation and failure to promote and participate in what God is doing here on earth."[20] For those who are treated as perpetual foreigners, model minorities, and exploitable objects, sin is self-hatred and a lowered self-image of one's racial and gender identity. Such sin often leads women to self-ghettoization, in order to avoid their marginalization and ultimately to ignore their sacred calling to live as holistic human beings created in the image of God. For those who belong to the racially, culturally, and sexually privileged group, sin is a superiority syndrome. This sin encourages people to hubris and, in the worst cases, results in systemic oppression of the marginalized. The superiority syndrome dehumanizes not only the marginalized, but also the privileged, by erasing their identity as members of God's family. By reminding listeners of these sins and helping them repent, the preacher can create a Third Space where listeners may experience justification, i.e., God's redemptive work of "acceptance, belonging, recognition, and inclusion."[21] Through these redemptive experiences, listeners may renew their identity and be empowered to live as agents who in turn transform the world.

When considering Asian American women's experiences as the primary sources of preaching and creating a Third Space, storytelling

19. Yee, "She Stood in Tears amid Alien Corn," 55.

20. Lee, *From a Liminal Place*, 105.

21. Lee, *From a Liminal Place*, 101.

becomes the most effective homiletical tool. Stories, especially biographical stories, are crucial ingredients in preaching from an Asian American feminist perspective. Women's personal and collective experiences and mundane stories carry multiple aspects of their identity formation and have a "narrative quality." Stephen Crites explains that the narrative quality of experience has three dimensions—"the sacred story, the mundane stories, and the temporal form of experience itself"—and these three intersect in storytelling to create meaning.[22]

While a Third Space or the interstices are spatial metaphors, storytelling is a form of temporality, as is preaching. In the story, past, present, and future correlate with one another, and the past and future can be told only from the standpoint of the present. In this way, storytelling bridges "the cleft between remembered past and projected future."[23] It is an art, not "an arbitrary imposition upon remembered experience"[24] or simply recitation of tedious experiences in the chronicle of memory. Stories are "sophisticated activities of consciousness" that recollect the images and symbols that "lodged in memory into new configurations, reordering past experience" to create new meanings[25] In storied preaching, the preacher's role is not simply to reiterate Asian American women' experiences from the past and present or their mundane stories, but it is to reconfigure these into a "sacred story" capable of providing listeners with a meaningful new vision for their future.

Just as storytelling is an art, so too is the storytelling preacher an artist who crafts a sermon in a certain style. While stories can be used as sermon illustration, the entire sermon can be designed as a narrative that follows the basic storyline or narrative plot—a temporal movement from crisis through climax to denouement.[26] Whether using stories as illustrations or crafting the entire sermon as a narrative, the preacher's imagination and narrative skill play a significant role in creating a Third Space. As Flannery O'Connor states, "imagination is the channel of visionary awareness"[27] that links two worlds, those of Asian American women and the listeners. When the preacher tells Asian American women's stories, narrative skills are required to refine the raw material of experience into an artwork that appeals to the listeners' imagination and feelings. Through stories, the preacher shares the hope and vision of Asian American women and other oppressed

---

22. Crites, "Narrative Quality of Experience," 301.

23. Crites, "Narrative Quality of Experience," 302.

24. Crites, "Narrative Quality of Experience," 300.

25. Crites, "Narrative Quality of Experience," 299.

26. Cf., Lowry, *The Homiletical Plot*.

27. Cited in Brueggemann, *The Prophetic Imagination*, xiv.

people, as well as their pain and suffering, and awakens the listener's imagination to a new world of reconciliation and healing.

The art of storytelling also encourages the preacher to consider preaching a performance art. Just as storytelling is an embodied performance, so is preaching. Christian preaching has traditionally been regarded as a monologue or a solo performance of the preacher with the listeners as passive recipients. Yet, preaching based on Asian American women's experiences can be a group performance of sharing stories through singing, acting, dancing, showing pictures, and other artistic performances during the preaching event. Moreover, a sermon can be scripted as a dialogue or a multi-character performance in which Asian American women's diverse voices converge in the process of meaning-making. Preaching as a group performance needs preaching partners. In other words, it should be "an art of shared leadership,"[28] a collaborative work between the pastor/preacher and the congregation. Such a shared ministry of preaching makes it possible for the listeners to participate in creating a Third Space where the Spirit of God is present and at work transforming their identities into those of active agents of God's redeeming work.

Case Study: Text and Sermon
(John 4:4–30, 39–42)

The text for this sermon is John 4:4–30, 39–42, the story of the Samaritan woman who meets Jesus at the well. Here, Jesus breaks the boundaries of gender, ethnicity, and religion when he engages in a lengthy conversation with the woman about her concerns and invites her into a Third Space where she is sufficiently enlightened to find her new self and become a disciple of Jesus, an active agent of transformation in restoring her relationship with God and her fellow villagers.

The dialogue between Jesus and the Samaritan woman is not a story fixed to a particular historical context. In our contemporary world, we see many people like the Samaritan woman, particularly among Asian American women, who are confused by sociocultural and religious teachings about their identities. Like the Samaritan woman, they are thirsty for living water. The sermon invites these contemporary Samaritan women into a conversation with Jesus to share their lived experiences and participate in creating a Third Space for listeners.

The text is divided into three sections—the conversation about living water (vv. 4–14); the Samaritan woman's marital status and her questions

---

28. E. M. Kim, "Preaching as an Art of Shared Leadership," 69.

about worship (vv. 16–26); and the work of the Samaritan woman as an active agent (vv. 27–30, 39–42). This division is reflected in the three parts of the sermon, which follows a narrative plot. Each part begins with a reading of the Scripture section and interprets it from an Asian American woman's point of view. Two female preaching partners are invited to perform the two Asian American women's biographical stories in the first two parts. Their painful and oppressive experiences create the crisis and lead to the climax of the sermon. The third part concludes the sermon with a hopeful vision of the Christian church as a Third Place for the transformation of the world. The entire congregation is invited into the preaching event via a congregational song that is sung as a response at the end of each part. During the delivery of the three parts of the sermon, three different images of wells is projected on the chancel wall as a background scene. The three pictures symbolize the content of each part of the sermon and suggest that the church can be a well of living water, a Third Place where transformation occurs.

"Women at the Well"

Part I

[A picture of a dry well in the desert is projected on the background wall. After the preacher recites the first portion of the text (John 4:4–14), a female preaching partner comes up to the chancel and performs a second-generation Asian American woman's story from a first-person point of view. In her biographical story, the well of the American Dream and the well of living water are contrasted, and she identifies herself with the Samaritan woman who is thirsty for living water.]

I am thirsty.
I come to the well every day to draw water.
Yet I am always thirsty.
I remember my childhood in the United States.
My parents were boat people who left their war-torn country
with corpses and bullet shells,
and crossed the ocean in hope of escaping hunger and death.
They arrived first in a refugee camp,
and then in Little Saigon in Houston, Texas.
Two years later, I was born, and then two of my brothers.
What I remember about my parents is,
they always worked—

twelve hours a day, seven days a week
in a Vietnamese restaurant.
Their dream was to have their own restaurant,
and it finally came true when I was twelve.
Another childhood memory is the aroma of incense
lingering in our small apartment.
My parents were devout Buddhists
and prayed in the living room every day,
lighting incense sticks at the statue of Buddha.
When I entered elementary school,
they began to go to church,
and I could no longer smell incense at home.
It was fun, though, to sing and play games with other Vietnamese kids
every Sunday at church.

When I became a teenager,
my journey of thirst began:
I struggled to fit into the white dominant culture.
I felt inferior to my Caucasian friends
with their white skin, blonde hair, and tall beauty.
I tried to be like them.
But, the more I tried, the more frustrated I felt.
I wished many times that
I had been born to white American parents
who spoke English fluently
and worked white-collar jobs from nine to five.

In my college years,
I focused on study, and left church behind.
I graduated with honors
and a professional job.
My relatives and friends often say
I am one of the "model minority."
A compliment or a tease,
they seem not to care how much I am struggling.

I am still thirsty.
I have drunk the water

from the well of the American dream
that my parents bequeathed me.
Yet, water from that well has never quenched my thirst.
The more I drink, the thirstier I become.
The more I try to be an American,
the more I am hurt by the glass ceiling.

Where can I find the well of living water
that leaves without thirst?
Where can I find that well
that lets me rest as I am
with my Asian roots the gift of God?

Like the Samaritan woman,
I am thirsty.
And I hear Jesus, saying,
"those who drink of the water that I will give them
will never be thirsty.
The water that I will give
will become in them
a spring of water welling up to eternal life." (4:14 NRSV)

[The congregation responds to the woman by singing the hymn "Fill My Cup, Lord."²⁹]

Part II

[After the congregational song, the background picture changes to an empty bucket by a well. The preacher recites the second portion of the text (John 4:16–26), and a female preaching partner comes up to the chancel and performs a first-generation Asian American woman's biographical story from a first-person point of view. The story tells of her experiences in Asian American and European American churches. Like the Samaritan woman, she questions the religious teaching and practices of those churches and draws answers from Jesus' response to the Samaritan woman.]

---

29. Blanchard, "Fill My Cup, Lord," *The United Methodist Hymnal*, hymn 641.

I still remember the day
I arrived at John F. Kennedy in New York City.
In my hand was an admission letter
from a seminary in New Jersey.
I was full of passion to learn about the Bible
and wanted to be an ordained minister
as a long-overdue response to God's calling.
Once I settled in the new land of auspice,
I visited a Korean church near the school,
and their warm-hearted friendship made me feel I was home.
Korean food and speaking Korean in church
helped me endure my homesickness
and overcome my fears about the strange new land.

Yet,
the more I learned about Asian American churches,
the more alien I felt.
They said,
women should obey their husbands
no matter what,
for the Bible says so.
They also said,
women should not be elders or ministers,
for the Bible says that women must be silent in church.
Yet, seminary taught me
feminist theology and the hermeneutics of suspicion.
And I resisted the sexism of Asian American churches.
I talked back,
"I have no husband, but God,
that I should obey!"
After completing the MDiv and PhD. programs,
I was ordained a minister of Word and Sacrament of PCUSA,
and found a full-time teaching job in Colorado.
When I visited a Korean PCUSA church in Denver,
the pastor told me not to return,
"I do not acknowledge women's ordination," he said.

Our family joined a white church nearby,
where the pastor was a woman.
And I enjoyed the equal environment.
Yet, there were few minority families
in that three-hundred member church.
We were always the guest.
We sang their favorite hymns,
prayed in their accustomed style,
and listened to their stories in the sermons.
We were supposed to be thankful
for their spiritual food,
whether we liked it or not.

Twenty years later,
more Asian, African, and Hispanic Americans have joined the church,
as the town becomes a multicultural city.
Yet, the church still follows its white Presbyterian worship.
Like the Samaritan woman,
I question such worship:
Is it right to worship God in racially divided ways?
And I hear Jesus, saying,
"But the hour is coming, and is now here,
when true worshipers will worship [God] in spirit and truth . . . .
God is spirit,
and those who worship [God] must worship
in spirit and truth" (4:23–24).

I am sure that
in true worship
there is no racial and cultural divide.
Instead, our diversity is embraced as the gift of God,
through which we worship God in the Spirit.
In true worship,
our gender and sexuality do not matter.
It's who you are and the way you live that count before God.
Through this way of worship
we can build a beloved community, the family of God.

[The congregation responds to the woman by singing the hymn, "You who are Thirsty."[30]]

Part III

[After the congregational song, the background picture changes to water overflowing from a bucket on a well. The preacher recites the last portion of the text (John 4:27–30, 39–42) and concludes the sermon by encouraging the congregation to be the well of living water, a Third Space, where people can meet Jesus Christ and be transformed into active agents who participate in God's redemptive work.]

Like the Samaritan woman,
millions of Asian Americans are thirsty.
Their daughters and granddaughters, especially, are
in search of a spiritual home,
where their authentic selves can be valued
and nurtured by the water of eternal life.
Where is the well
that can quench their thirst?

The Samaritan woman met Jesus at the well
where she went every day to draw water.
That ordinary place became a sacred space
when she met Jesus there.
She engaged in conversation with him,
discerned the will of God for the people of God,
and became a messenger
bringing her people to Jesus, the source of life.

Like the people in the Samaritan village,
we are searching for the truth.
Racism makes us thirsty;
sexism makes us weary.
But we do not give up on finding the living water
that quenches our thirst
and gives us life-giving energy.

30. Jones, "Fill My Cup," *Glory to God*, hymn 699.

And we will find Jesus there.
Yes, Jesus is already there at the well.
Can our church become a sacred space,
where we can meet Jesus
and drink living water?
I believe so.
For Jesus is right here, in our church.

[The congregation responds by singing the song, "Lord of Light, Your Name Outshining."[31]]

Assessment: Strengths and Limitations in This Theological Family

Asian American women have been considered among the least in racist and sexist North American society as well as in their ethnic communities, and their experiences have been overlooked in the ministry of preaching. As a form of liberation theology, Asian American feminist theology provides a critical lens through which the preacher can see these women's predicament and articulate a vision for the future of the world. The preacher is challenged to pay attention to their oppressed lives within and beyond the church and to use their unique experiences as sources for preaching.

Preaching from an Asian American feminist perspective will make the Christian pulpit more open to diverse stories of racially and sexually marginalized people and empower them by bringing their voices into theological reflection. In other words, Asian American and other ethnic minority women are the subjects of preaching. Their stories are shared, and their burning questions and concerns responded to. In addition to the empowerment of oppressed women, preaching from the perspective of Asian American feminist theology benefits culturally privileged people by evoking and nurturing an "alternative consciousness"[32] amidst the dominant culture. Those who listen to a sermon prepared from an Asian American feminist perspective are encouraged to envision a strange new world in which people are no longer thirsty, because they drink the living water of empathy, compassion, equity, and justice.

31. Lewis, "Lord of Light, Your Name Outshining," hymn number 425 in *The Presbyterian Hymnal*.

32. Brueggemann, *The Prophetic Imagination*, 3.

While the perspective of Asian American feminist theology is effective in preaching to empower Asian American and other ethnic minority women, one of the weaknesses of this approach might be that the uniqueness of Asian American women's experiences does not resonate with racially and sexually different listeners. Racially and sexually privileged people who have never been in a marginalized position and who have no personal relationships with Asian American or other marginalized women may have difficulty relating to their stories. Their unique experiences and particular stories may thus not have universal appeal to general audiences. For this reason, preachers should make an intentional effort to listen to Asian American women's unique experiences empathically and use these experiences in the hermeneutical process of gleaning new meaning from the text. If preachers do not take Asian American women's issues and their predicaments seriously and are unable to preach from the bottom of their hearts, they will not move their listeners' hearts. As well as heart-to-heart communication between the preacher and the listeners, aesthetic approaches to preaching are also necessary to stimulate the imagination of listeners; yet, in reality, many preachers are neither trained in nor exposed to aesthetic approaches to preaching.

Preaching from an Asian American feminist perspective also challenges preachers to develop pastoral leadership. Considering that the purpose of preaching is not only to create a Third Space in the moment of preaching but also to transform the church itself to serve as a Third Space, pastoral leadership must follow preaching. Through the practice of pastoral leadership, the preacher/pastor can help the congregation renew its identity as an active agent of God's redeeming work and participate in building up an egalitarian community. Preaching from an Asian American feminist perspective is, therefore, not only about words, but also actions. It requires the preacher and the congregation to continue to work to transform the church into a worshiping community in spirit and truth and hence become an active agent for the transformation of the larger community.

For Further Reading

Nam Soon Kang. *Diasporic Feminist Theology: Asia and Theopolitical Imagination.* Minneapolis: Fortress, 2014.

Ai Ra Kim. *Women Struggling for a New Life.* Albany: State University of New York Press, 1996.

Jung Ha Kim. *Bridge-Makers and Cross-Bearers: Korean-American Women and the Church.* American Academy of Religion Academy Series 92. Atlanta: Scholars, 1997.

Kim-Cragg, HyeRann. *The Encounters: Retelling the Bible from Migration and Intercultural Perspective.* Daejeon, South Korea: Daejanggan, 2014.

Kwok Pui-lan. *Postcolonial Imagination and Feminist Theology.* Louisville: Westminster John Knox, 2005.

Lee, Unzu. *Coming Home: Asian American Women Doing Theology.* Louisville: PCUSA Women's Ministries Area, 2006.

Pak, Su Yon, et al. *Singing the Lord's Song in a New Land: Korean American Practices of Faith.* Louisville: Westminster John Knox, 2005.

Russell, Letty M. *Just Hospitality: God's Welcome in a World of Difference.* Louisville: Westminster John Knox, 2009.

15

Preaching in the Queer (LGBTQ2SIA+) Theological Family[1]

Karyn L. Wiseman

Gay Liberation Theology emerged from a variety of sources. The Enlightenment sought absolute and universal truth derived from reason and science. However, the Enlightenment project came to be questioned and critiqued in the light of different perspectives and experiences in the human community. Liberation theologies emerged from several highly specific and contextual theologies which exposed the relativity, arbitrariness and even repressive characteristics of many long-assumed beliefs. Gay liberation theology came from this move towards contextualization and seeks to revise, often radically, many traditional beliefs and practices towards the goal of a world that values diversity and provides for freedom, dignity, respect, and security for all members of the human family, and nature, too.

The church has been at the root of the marginalization of the LGBTQ2SIA+ community throughout much of history. The gay liberation movement challenges many traditional interpretations of biblical texts and other theological doctrines that have negatively impacted the gay community. This movement advocates the full inclusion of the gay community in all aspects of church and society, and it works to create safe space for all communities to become allies with persons on the Queer spectrum. This theology has an even deeper opportunity, that of literally saving the lives of members of the gay community from the damaging desire by many to "convert" and "save" them from a life of "sinful" choices.

1. Acronyms for the Queer community vary; however as I use LGBTQ2SIA+ to represent Lesbian, Gay, Bisexual, Transgender, Transsexual, Queer and Questioning, Two-Spirit, Intersex, Asexual, plus people of other non-binary realities.

Circumstances That Gave Rise
to This Theological Family

Liberation theology and poststructural gender studies contributed to the rise of Gay liberation theology.[2] Gustavo Gutiérrez, a Roman Catholic Priest, is thought to be the "parent" of Liberation Theology.[3] The root purpose of this theology is to liberate the marginalized, including the poor, downtrodden, and otherwise oppressed peoples, through participation in public and private actions. The origin is in Latin America and the poor and oppressed communities there. The basic tenets are interpreting and living the gospel from the perspective of "the [person] on the side of the road," as my seminary professor taught me.[4] It is first "interpreting Christian faith out of the perspective of suffering, struggle, and hope of the poor."[5] Second, "through solidarity with the poor theologians of liberation advocate the transcendence from class division to a new type of society."[6] This theology believes that radical love for one's neighbor will bring about such change. And thirdly, it critiques the church in its attitudes and actions for and with the poor.[7]

This theology involves active participation on the part of the oppressed and those who ally with them. It involves theological praxis that calls for and creates transformation. The preacher and congregation cannot just name the evils of injustice and oppression of the poor. The church is empowered by its faith to take concrete actions beyond naming the sinfulness of poverty and oppression. The logical and much needed next step is working for transformation both around the corner and around the world. As said already, liberation theology seeks a world of peace, freedom, justice, dignity, and abundance for all.

Living into freedom and equality for all persons experiencing injustice or oppression has been the hallmark of liberation theology around the world

2. Poststructural gender studies articulate the reality of gender identity and expression along a spectrum. The binary of only male or female is no longer the primary understanding of gender. The Gender Unicorn shows the spectrum of gender identity, gender expression, gender at birth, and physical and emotional attraction. See Figure 1 at the end of this chapter.

3. Gutiérriez, *A Theology of Liberation*.

4. This framing of liberation from the side of the road in the story of the good Samaritan has been transformative for my faith and career. Emilie Townes spoke about this in multiple classes I took with her at Saint Paul School of Theology in Kansas City, Missouri, in the early 1990s.

5. Hillar, "Liberation Theology," 35.

6. Hillar, "Liberation Theology."

7. Hillar, "Liberation Theology."

and has become an ever more significant influence in the United States. The name "liberation theology" did not really emerge until the late 1960s and early 1970s. Yet, even though "liberation theology" had not come into use, the themes of liberation theology resonate with the social justice movements in the 1950s and 1960s, such as those related to civil rights for persons of color, advocating for an end to extreme classism, and protesting against the Vietnam War. A movement for gay rights began to take a more public face with the Stonewall uprising in New York City in 1969.

The first tenet of gay liberation theology is critiquing and interpreting Christian faith from the perspective of the LGBTQ2SIA+ community and its experiences of oppression, discrimination, and prejudice. This tenent is inherited from liberation theology. The second tenet is to speak the truth that Queer persons experience blessedness in their Queerness. This perception will contribute to liberating the gay community from the burdens of judgmental theologies. The third tenent is that through that advocacy and truth-telling, the Church will be held accountable for the ways it has perpetuated and continued oppression, condemnation, and bias against the LGBTQ2SIA+ community. This means countering "anti-gay theology" in the church. The fourth tenent of Gay Liberation Theology is to work toward opportunities for all persons to become allies and advocates for the Queer community in order to transform divisions and judgment into affirming relationships and acceptance.

The life journey of many people in the LGBTQ2SIA+community is similar to my own. Such stories demonstrate the importance of the church taking seriously gay liberation theology. I grew up in West Texas in the 1970s to 80s. During my youth, I never heard the word "gay" in any way other than as a pejorative. People I knew called others they viewed as weak or unimportant a "fag" or "gay." Others sometimes used these expressions for nothing more than a mannerism people exhibited. The meaning of these terms was very clear to me and others. Being gay was not a good thing. Being different meant ostracism, condemnation, and bullying on the part of peers. I knew I was "different" from the time I was four when I told my Mom I was a different kind of girl than my sisters. Nothing I heard or read interpreted homosexuality in any positive light for the entirety of my young life. Watching TV or going to the movies meant only seeing heteronormative characters and stories. The Stonewall Riots, which sparked the Gay Liberation movement, happened in 1969, but that news did not make its way to Andrews, Texas where I grew up. I did not even know another gay person in my high school until my senior year when a student was "outed" and beaten up for who they were. That taught me a lesson I remember to this day: we are not safe.

In the denomination of my birth, the United Methodist Church (UMC), homosexuality was deemed "incompatible with Christian teaching." That decision was made in 1972 at General Conference and still remains in place today. My father, as a pastor in the UMC, never spoke of the decision but I heard about it in my life as a youth leader in our state and in broader church circles. With such fearsome things going on around me, there was no way I would let anyone know who I was during that pivotal time in my life. That meant I never went out with a same-gendered person, or claimed my identity until I was in college and away from home.

This is the reality of many Queer folks from my era. We did not have easy access to positive LGBTQ2SIA+ portrayals. Ellen DeGeneres did not come out until 1997. I did not see a positive portrayal of a loving couple in media until Cam and Mitchell in *Modern Family* in 2009. These are very different times now. And what was the impetus for that change? Most believe that the gay liberation movement owes its origin to the Stonewall Uprising in 1969, and well they should. That was a catalyst for dramatic change in major cities primarily on the two coasts.

However, much of the visibility of the community originated from the AIDS crisis and the way the community "came out" and disclosed their sexuality to their friends and families in order to be public advocates for much needed health care access for gay men and those sick and dying from the disease. Many in the urban coastal cities of the US began protesting against the cruel avoidance and disinterest toward the plight of the Queer community. Most people in my small Texas town knew nothing about AIDS except it was the "gays and fags" who were dying and there was no grief lost for those people, unless a person happened to know and love someone fighting the disease or someone dead because of it. Even then the grief was primarily for the family of the "sinner" and not the death of any individual.

I knew of no one in my hometown with AIDS. I only came to know an AIDS patient when one of my colleagues at my college job became sick and disclosed his status to me. Near the end of his life, I was the only person who came to visit him in the hospital. On the last day of his life, I went to visit him. Kevin asked one thing. He wanted someone to touch him, to hold his hand. I had been required to gown and glove up every time I visited him. That day I removed my glove and held his hand. He said it was the first time anyone had touched him in over 9 months. None of his family came to visit. Not one of his gay friends came to visit out of fear. But that moment of physical connection with him brings tears to my eyes even as I write this.

Visibility and affirmation are two significant parts of gay liberation theology, as well. Knowing an LGBTQSIAA+ person is a significant indicator of one's ability to affirm and welcome them fully into your life. Speaking the realities of the LGBTQSIA+ community did not happen in many families, communities, or churches. That was the reality of my life. Absolute silence ruled the day. That silence spoke so loudly and clearly to me that even talking about my orientation was a risk emotionally, physically, and spiritually. So, silence ruled my life for years. I only "came out" publicly five years ago. That happened with the announcement of and invitations to the wedding my partner of twenty-two years and I were planning.

I know the costs that I paid for the silence while growing up. I know the damage that silence has caused my Queer friends over the years. I have seen the damage it causes younger folks in my life and in the communities where I have served. Seeing and hearing the stories of young Queers being thrown out of their homes, being bullied at school, and literally having a suicide attempt rate that is three times higher than straight youth meant something had to change.[8] Gay liberation theology provides a theological rationale for change and points the church and wider world towards approaches for change.

Purposes and Characteristics of Preaching in This Theological Family

Speaking about and preaching from heteronormative theologies, which assume a straight, cis-gendered reality,[9] around the world has been the norm. Those theologies have dealt with sexual orientation and gender identity and gender expression as a "sinful choice" that Queer persons must have made, which placed them in direct conflict with God's intention and God's word. Gay persons have endured sermon after sermon, lesson after lesson either

---

8. After we did some research, the Trevor Project became a project that my wife and I financially support. It is an advocacy organization helping young Queer folks maintain mental health and avoid the traps of depression and suicidal ideation (https://www.thetrevorproject.org/resources/preventing-suicide/facts-about-suicide).

9. Heteronormative theology assumes that all relationships are between persons who live into their assigned gender at birth, and that all will love and marry a person of the opposite gender living into their assigned gender at birth. This theology at its extreme is seen in protests and proclamations that there is only "Adam and Eve" and not "Adam and Steve" in the creation story of the Hebrew Bible, which also informs the Christian story to this day. This theology is destructive to the LGBTQ2SIA+ community and has meant many have difficult if not nonexistent relationships with God and the church. The Queer community is made up of many different realities around sexuality and gender identity. Gender is more fluid than most people understand. Affirming someone's gender identity or gender expression is a huge part of moving toward inclusion and welcome.

not hearing anything about their lives at all or hearing a drumroll of condemnation and judgment. Many have fled the church all together.

This type of theological badgering and a refusal to engage in meaningful dialogue in many churches is at the root of countless wounds both individually and collectively in the gay community. When the church sees sexuality and gender as a "choice," then "changing behavior" must be the response. Unfortunately, that interpretation of sexuality and gender then becomes a theological weapon to use against the gay community. The stories of our Queer siblings being subjected to conversion therapy, Bible bashing, and more violent means of physical, psychological, and spiritual bombardment are more common than one might expect. These stories are a painful and tragic reminder of the damage Christians have and can inflict on others.

Moving to preach from the perspective of gay liberation theology means critiquing and interpreting the "clobber passages" used against the gay community.[10] It means challenging the belief that sexuality and gender identity are a choice. It means challenging church denominational policies that are exclusive and harmful to the LGBTQ2SIA+ community. It means educating within our congregations to create advocates and allies for our Queer siblings. It means being present alongside, walking with, and even protesting for those siblings to bring about meaningful change. Praxis is at the root of both liberation theology as it relates to poverty and the poor and gay liberation theology. Praxis is doing the hard work of creating, maintaining, and cultivating continued change. A significant part of this work is to deconstruct the binary norms of many theologies, for these norms are the antithesis to liberation theologies generally and gay liberation theologies in particular.[11]

Along with this deconstruction, preachers need to help the congregation acknowledge that all persons are more than their sexuality. We are complex beings who are best seen through the intersectionality of our gender, race, sexuality, and other parts of our lives. This means we are not simply this or that. We are many things. There are more variables and differences that are significant to understanding who we are as human beings beyond our sexuality. Many theologies that perpetuate the oppression of our Queer siblings are formulated in simple binaries, but the world

10. Clobber passages include six texts that the church has used to exclude gay and lesbian people from the church and society. These include: Gen 19:1–9; Lev 18:22; 20:13; Rom 1:26–27; 1 Cor 6:9; and 1 Tim 1:9–10. More contemporary biblical scholars have come to much more contextualized understanding of these texts that are far from the "traditional" interpretations. Guest et al., eds., in *The Queer Bible Commentary* offer revisionary interpretations of biblical passages from LGBTQ2SIA+ perspectives.

11. Lightsey, *Our Lives Matter*, 19–20.

and individual persons are not made of any single elements, much less elements that are always mutually exclusive. The binary ways of thinking posit that, on the one hand, if person is straight, that person is okay. But, on the other, hand if a person is gay, that person is simply not okay. These binaries of rich/poor, black/white, gay/straight, male/female, and all the rest, are incomplete, to say the least. The language of binary theological beliefs have to be challenged and critiqued. This is a substantial part of our work in preaching and teaching.

Becoming acquainted with gay liberation theology along with critical reflection on my life experiences led me to change the way I publicly talked about myself and my marginalized siblings. I had been, as a preacher, very comfortable naming the sins of racism, classism, misogyny, and hate groups. Many preachers feel comfortable with that listing. But I found myself too timid to name homophobia, transphobia, and other issues related to sexuality and gender. I had fallen into the trap of self-preservation over the years. I knew my truth would cost me my career in The United Methodist Church, where I was an ordained preacher, and would potentially cause me to lose connection with friends and even family. But coming out in 2015 so that we could be married, also freed me to speak truth more inclusively and more pointedly.

However, the naming of marginalized folks and inclusion of the Queer community is not enough. I had to advocate with my voice, my online presence, in my preaching, in my public protesting moments, and in my teaching. I have found that this is true of other preachers who are themselves members of the LGBTQ2SIA+ community as well as other preachers who are in solidarity with that community. That change has now helped me become even more of a clear and convicted voice around these issues and a go-to person for many. When the United Lutheran Seminary Chapel Team asked me to preach for their Affirmation Service, I jumped at the chance. Preaching the sermon below on the Wednesday after All Saints' Sunday game me the opportunity to share the stories of multiple Queer leaders who have fought and died for our community.

In sum, then, the characteristics of preaching from this theological framework include naming the LGBTQ2SIA+ community and pointing to its presence in the church and he world. Such preaching must affirm their sacred worth of persons in this community. Preaching will then challenge the ways many in the church have marginalized and ostracized the Queer community. It will challenge the traditional interpretations of texts that inappropriately place the Queer community in opposition to God and the assumed heteronormative standard that is too often assumed in the church and in society. It will create opportunities for others to be allies with the

LGBTQ2SIA+ community. And it will name and claim the blessings of this community boldly and without hesitation.

As I say in all of my preaching classes, preaching is specific to a place and time: the catchphrase is, "Context, context, context." Preaching from this perspective means understanding the context into which preaching will occur and then move to push those contextual boundaries to be a voice for transformational change. This is the hallmark of preaching from a gay liberation framework.

Case Study: Text and Sermon
(Matthew 5:1–12)

The beatitudes in Matthew's Gospel are so well known that many pastors struggle to preach about them. Putting a genuinely authentic take on this text can be daunting. Jesus' Sermon on the Mount declares that groups who might be typically viewed as afflicted are actually blessed. Jesus, here and in other places, turns the norm of typical expectation upside down. He was born to change this world. Jesus' voice speaks to the marginalized and the outcast. When Jesus speaks these words, those who are feeling afflicted are given hope for a new day.

Receiving God's blessing is what the Kindom[12] of God is intended to look like. We are given it freely but we are then called to live into that reality. Unfortunately, that Kindom has not become lived reality for all. There is a moral imperative in these eight Beatitudes. The call is to be more meek, more passionate about striving for justice, more welcoming, more peaceful, and more merciful. This text is a call to action. It is also the epitome of Jesus' active role in the world as the Savior. The beatitudes are basically Jesus' manifesto. And this manifesto echoes the promises from the Hebrew Bible. God is bringing about a transformation through the coming of the Messiah. In Matthew's Beatitudes, Jesus stakes his claim and his intent.

In American culture, being blessed often means being wealthy, healthy, and happy. The Beatitudes offer a different understanding of blessing. Being blessed is more than being content and enjoying life. It means receiving and living into the justice and compassion of God in the midst of a hurting world. To be blessed is to know we are living in harmony with God's purposes and witnessing to those purposes, even when we encounter resistance. We can help in completing transformation from this broken and hurting world into a realm in which everyone has a life

---

12. I intentionally use "kindom" language to counter the male-dominated language of "the kingdom of God."

of dignity, respect, security, and freedom. That is the way we follow Jesus as disciples of the gospel. That is the way to live into blessing and to help to bring about the transformation of the world. That free gift of grace and blessing from God changes us, and thus leads us to help change the world for others. For the Queer community, that change has been painfully slow coming to fruition, and are so many obstacles still need to be addressed. That silence, and the sin of that silence, must end so that our Queer siblings can feel the end of the church's oppression and harmful behavior and can enter into a greater sense of blessing.

Sermon: "All Saints' Means *All* Saints"

[This sermon was preached in he chapel of United Lutheran Seminary on the Wednesday after All Saints' Sunday. I start with a bit of history around the Gospel lesson. I will use this information as a key element later in the sermon around the LGBTQ2SIA+ Saints through history who impacted justice and compassion in our country.]

This story is important to our culture. In Texas we tell stories so often that others just naturally join in the telling and see themselves in the characters. Many ancient cultures kept their legacy, lineage, and history alive by telling stories. The Hebrew Bible is a collection of stories that share the history of the Hebrew people and the struggles they faced throughout history. The Gospels tell the story of Jesus' birth, life, ministry, death, and resurrection. Those stories are profound and powerful. They are also challenging to hear and to live into.

Understanding how the Gospel authors portray Jesus in their stories can be seen from the outset of the ministry of Jesus in all four gospels. Matthew's Gospel begins with the Sermon on the Mount. Mark begins with an exorcism. Luke has the Jesus' sermon at Nazareth, and John tells the story of the water transformed into wine at the wedding at Cana. These stories and images are deep and profound. In each of them, there is a sense of how Jesus will be portrayed in each Gospel.

Matthew portrays Jesus as a teacher who promises to be an advocate of justice and compassion. Mark portrays Jesus as a healer and agitator moving the unclean back into relationship with their community. Luke portrays Jesus as a teacher and powerful storyteller trying to be heard in his hometown. John portrays Jesus as a powerful miracle worker rescuing the wedding party and responding to his mother. These identities are important. They shape how the authors write the Gospel stories and influence the ways we interpret the word today.

Matthew's Sermon on the Mount begins with eight statements that juxtapose the present broken human condition with the affirmation that God seeks to transform that condition into one of blessing. God desires blessing for each of us.

In my graduate studies I was required to take two language courses, choosing two from Latin, German, and French. My Dad took German in College and the language never felt beautiful to me. Latin was obvious as my PhD work was in Liturgy and Preaching. I also did French. Both were gifts to my studies. But, Latin is the more important right now.

> *[The next part of the sermon develops the notion of blessing with the help of a Latin term. I wondered about using a Latin expression since that language was unfamiliar to many in the congregation, but it was fitting for the sermon which was preached at the United Lutheran Seminary where I teach. The use of the phrase as a refrain felt particularly powerful.]*

In Latin, the expression "blessed are" from the Beatitudes is *beati sunt*. That is a beautiful phrase that means more than being blessed with good things in life.

Beati sunt. It is a beautiful phrase that means more than getting good grades and having a nice house and car.

Beati sunt. It is a beautiful phrase that impacts us way down deep in our soul. The blessing is visceral and profound. The message from Jesus in Matthew is not limited to being the teacher. It is a blessing that can be felt into the marrow of our being. It is creating, affirming, and transforming for those in deep need.

Beati sunt. It is a beautiful phrase that for some means their blessings are complete. But it is also speaking to those who are still awaiting to live into or feeling disconnected from that blessing. It is speaking to the moment's need for justice and compassion.

This week we are celebrating and remembering all of the Saints in our lives and in our world. And when I stop to think about those who are the Saints in my life, I come up with family, friends, colleagues, and professors who helped to shape and form me.

But the wider world's Saints have also formed me and probably you and they have to be named. Among them: Sojourner Truth, Martin Luther King, Jr., Susan B. Anthony, John Lewis, Edith Windsor, Bishop Oscar Romero,

Elizabeth Cady Stanton, Fredrick Douglas, Harriet Tubman, Harvey Milk, Mohandas Ghandi, Mother Teresa, and Marsha P. Johnson.

And the deaths of Black and Brown saints at the hands of police have to be named: George Floyd, Breona Taylor, Philando Castille, Michael Brown, and too many more who have been brutalized by a system that is deeply impacted by systemic racism.

And the deaths of Queer saints and siblings have to be named. Some have gone before us, people like:

- Dominique Remmie Fells, a trans woman killed this year along with dozens of other trans persons brutalized and who are rarely mentioned on the news. Their names cannot be lost in the ether.

- Harvey Milk, who was an out politician and the very first openly gay politician elected in California, serving on the City Supervisors' Board in San Francisco in the late 1970s. He was working for full inclusion of the gay community into the wider culture. He was assassinated in 1978 by a homophobic city supervisor.

- Edith Windsor, whose court case, decided by the Supreme Court, ruled that the Defense of Marriage Act was unconstitutional. She fought even after her own partner died to bring these rights to the entire LGBTQ2SIA+ community.

[Next, I move into living saints of the Queer Community. These persons transformed the world for the LGBTQ2SIA+ family by their actions, advocacy, and challenging the legal limitations placed on the community through the court system.]

- James "Jim" Obergefell and John Arthur, whose court case allowed the LGBTQ2SIA+ Community full access to marriage rights in the United States. You may not know these names, but the Queer community does.

- And a name from that first list you may not have known—Marsha P. Johnson was a Trans woman and activist who helped launch the Stonewall Riots in 1969. Every June she is remembered for her acts of courage.

These saints must be named as well. The legacy of their lives impact all of us, even if you did not know who they were or how they changed the course of history.

Beati sunt. It *is* a beautiful phrase but too many of our siblings have not felt it yet. Too many of our black and brown siblings have not felt it. Too many of our trans siblings have not felt it. Too many of our Queer siblings have not felt it. They too often have not felt it from the church or from the culture we all live in.

So today:

- We mourn the sinfulness of refusing to see the divine in all of God's created beings.

- We mourn for our siblings whose bodies and souls are battered, beaten, and belittled.

- We mourn for our nation that is so divided right now with little hope to repair the breech.

- We mourn that affirmation and compassion do not lead us more fully in our relationships with our siblings.

- We mourn for the LGBTQ2SIA+ community that has suffered so much for so long.

- We mourn for the Black, Asian, Latino/a communities that have suffered so much for so long.

- We mourn for the poor and oppressed communities that have suffered so much for so long.

The promise of the Beatitudes is that God sent Jesus and promised the Holy Spirit, to bring justice to an unjust world. God sent Jesus and the Spirit to bring compassion to those who are seen as outsiders or "other." God sent Jesus and the Spirit to flip the realities of the current world. And the Spirit continues to break into the world on behalf of all who are oppressed, bullied, ostracized, beaten, and brutalized.

Beati sunt. It is a beautiful phrase of grace, hope, and love. But part of me believes that we are not living fully into that blessing until our siblings are. We are not living fully into that blessing until justice and compassion are present for all. Although God gifts all with that blessing, living in a world that denies that blessedness because of one's sexual orientation or gender identity and expression is painful for our siblings.

We have to live into the *Beati sunt* of Jesus' promises. We are charged with flipping the realities of the world and work to bring about the promises. We play a part in that blessing. May we be world flippers and may we live more fully into *Beati sunt* for ourselves and help bring about the reality of blessedness for others. Now and always. Amen.

Assessment: Strengths and Limitations in This Theological Family

One of the obvious positives that comes when preaching from this perspective is the simple fact of naming publicly an awareness of LGBTQ2SIA+ realities. Saying the words "gay," "lesbian," "bisexual," or "transgender" from the pulpit or praying out loud for the Queer community during the hour of worship serves notice to all that these individuals share a sacred worth with others. This is a huge first step that can begin a change in both individuals, congregations, and groups. The next step is proclaiming the blessedness of Queer persons and their relationships in a positive light from the pulpit. This can dramatically shift the prevailing sentiments of many in the church and in society.

Speaking these words and dealing with these realities in preaching can literally save the lives of Queer youth grasping for one word of affirmation and acceptance from a God and church who they have mostly experienced as negatively judging their very existence. Speaking these words and dealing with these realities in preaching can help Queer persons reconcile their faith and life in a time when they may be struggling with coming out to their family and friends. Speaking these words and dealing with these realities in preaching can create healthy understandings of both sexuality, gender identity, and gender expression for families of the LGBTQ2SIA+ community. Speaking these words and dealing with these realities in preaching can create a climate for conversation around the Bible, faith, and the gay experience. Speaking these words in preaching can not only create "safe space" where a Queer person would hopefully feel psychologically and physically safe, but also can create "bold space" where they and their allies might speak their own truth in affirmation of the community. Putting positive speech into the world can change it for all.

However, there are also potential negatives that come when preaching from this perspective. There is a long-standing tradition of interpreting Biblical texts and traditional Christian theology in a heteronormative manner. Many in the Queer community see these beliefs as explicitly anti-gay, although the proponents of these traditional theologies would couch the anti-gay sentiment in very different ways. Such traditional biblical and theological understandings have often led persons to do all they can to "protect" heteronormative behavior and to condemn anyone living outside the traditional norms.[13]

---

13. This perspective is often articulated through language such as "protecting traditional marriages" or "maintaining traditional families."

Another potential negative can be backlash the preacher may receive by taking on such a controversial topic from the pulpit. For the gay community, it is not a controversial topic: it is their lives, loves, and their very being. But I also understand the reticence of many preachers to take on the task of preaching from a Gay Liberation perspective. Preachers have been removed from their churches for less than this. Being fired for taking a stand against unjust rules, beliefs, or practices has happened many times. Choosing to refrain from preaching from this perspective can seem like an immediate survival tactic. When salary, pensions, health insurance, and housing are at risk, many preachers choose not to rock the boat. The cost both to themselves and to those in their communities desperately needing a positive word can be significant. Moving beyond such fear by educating and affirming privately and publicly those who are LGBTQ2SIA+ and their families is a goal of this theological perspective. Moving step-by-step in naming, affirming, advocating, and inclusion can take some communities of faith years to achieve. Some communities will move quickly, especially if they have "out" participants and families with "out" members. Some people, unfortunately, will never embrace their Queer siblings, and some Queer folks will never feel comfortable coming to a church where it may be unsafe in the pews.

I believe we have to start somewhere. Maybe the preacher can mention Pride Month in a prayer in June. Maybe the preacher can include homophobia and transphobia in a list of sins to be transformed through faithful discipleship, service, and love. Whatever the starting point, the preacher needs to have a long-term strategy for moving in a pastoral way through a liberating theology towards the transformation of the world, beginning with educating the congregation into praxis, and preaching and praying the new reality into being.

For Further Reading

Askew, Emily and O. Wesley Allen Jr. *Beyond Heterosexism in the Pulpit*. Eugene, OR: Cascade Books, 2015.

Cheng, Patrick S. *Radical Love: Introduction to Queer Theology*. New York: Seabury, 2011.

Downs, Jim. *Stand By Me: The Forgotten History of Gay Liberation*. New York: Basic Books, 2016.

Guest, Deryn, et al., eds. *The Queer Bible Commentary*. London: SCM, 2006.

Hinant, Olive Elaine. *God Comes Out: A Queer Homiletic*. Cleveland, OH: Pilgrim, 2007.

Lightsey, Pamela R. *Our Lives Matter: A Womanist Queer Theology*. Eugene, OR: Pickwick Publications, 2015.

Riggle, Ellen D. B., and Sharon S. Rostosky. *A Positive View of LGBTQ: Embracing Identity and Cultivating Well-Being*. Lanham, MD: Rowman & Littlefield, 2012.

Figure 1

16

Preaching in the Indigenous Theological Families

RAYMOND C. ALDRED

THE CHALLENGE OF PREACHING in a First Nations or Native American context is complicated in the same way the broader relationship of Indigeneous Peoples in North America to newcomers is complicated. The gospel and the practice of preaching was brought into an Indigenous context in the early 1800s by Russian missionaries in Alaska and parts of the North, and by European missionaries in much of North America. The gospel and preaching were foreign concepts that took on a particular shape in Indigenous contexts. This, of course, was not the only complicating factor; it also became clear that missionaries were often being used by governments to try and dislocate Indigenous culture and population with European ideas and even with European people. Yet, despite the complicated nature of the relationship between Indigenous nations and newly arrived states, preaching the gospel has become an essential element of the Indigenous church.

My task in this chapter is to trace my own journey of relearning a way of speaking and communication to my Indigenous brothers and sisters, so that the gospel is highlighted, and people hear the gospel in their heart language. While I tell the story as my story, it is similar to many other stories in and about many other persons and communities. One cannot simply tell "the" story of Indigenous peoples and the gospel because of the great diversity in the stories.

Circumstances That Gave Rise
to These Theological Families

The coming of the Europeans to North America was devastating to Indigenous people and cultures. The devastation included both the influx of disease that previously had not been found in North America and also the devastating colonial policies that Europeans used to attempt to assimilate or exterminate Indigenous peoples. It is an understatement to write that attempted assimilation and attempted extermination are complicating factors for the development of Indigenous North American life, let alone Indigenous Christian Faith. In Canada and in some sense the United States, the ongoing inability of churches to understand Indigenous and Newcomer relationships added another layer of complication to the development of Indigenous Christian faith and thus Indigenous preaching. Despite this complication, or perhaps because of it, Indigenous preaching developed in part to provide assurance for Indigenous people that Christ was active in their lives despite the ongoing colonial oppression. Not only was Indigenous preaching to bring comfort but also to encourage a God-given urge toward self-determination as Indigenous people sought to make the gospel Indigenous.

Indigenous preaching developed as part of an ongoing push toward self-determination. Indigenous people in North America realized that the institutional church was very much in alliance with the political powers of the incoming European peoples. This meant that the motives in any official church teaching on governance, structures, and the order of the church service were always in control of the institutional church and as such were suspect. It was only in places where there were ad hoc meetings and the sharing of honest testimony and teaching that the Indigenous preaching seemed to find room for expression.

Three examples can be examined. First: the objection of the institutional church to the Anglican Church Army among the Nisga which was an exemplar of an egalitarian, emotion- packed expression of Indigenous preaching. Second: an essay by an Indigenous Archbishop of the Indigenous Anglican Church shows tensions between the newcomers and indigenous communities regarding where and when worship should take place spirituality is located in the home rather than in the church building and leans toward spontaneity and communal rather than lead by a church official? Third, the ancient church's figurative approach to finding and Christ in the Hebrew Scriptures is analogous to Indigeneous Peoples finding Jesus in or own stories and rituals.

In my discussion with elders from the Nisga'a, they shared an oral tradition that relayed the story of when the Northern West Coast groups, the Nisga'a and the Tsimshian, heard the gospel; they debated among themselves whether or not they would embrace this new teaching. The Nisga'a in particular, according to this oral tradition, still found in the villages of the Nisga'a, say that on more than one occasion the Nisga debated whether they would receive this teaching. Finally, the Nisga'a decided they would become Christian. They established Gincolx as a Christian village. They first came to faith under the teaching of the Methodists but later, when Methodists would not provide priests and commanded the burning of tradition regalia, they embraced Anglicanism. Another community, in turn, when the Anglican denomination would not provide a priest, embraced the Salvation Army denomination. In an essay entitled, "Mothers of the Empire," the author points out that when they heard about the Anglican Church Army and the Women's Auxiliary, the Nisga'a started these two social groups without any official permission from the Anglican Church.[1] The Nisga'a found that these groups fit the ordering of their own society and they helped advance their new faith. The Church Army, in particular, focused on praise and worship and evangelism through what are referred today as Church Army Rallies. These meetings then as today include a great deal of singing and, of course, preaching.

But the existing institutional church found fault with both of these practices. First, the Institutional Anglican Church believed the Church Army Rally was too "enthusiastic," a euphemism used in the late 1800s and early 1900s for the exhibition of charismatic gifts but also of too much music and singing and too much free form worship behaviors outside of the constraints of the official liturgy, I imagine. The second complaint of the institutional church was that they allowed anyone to speak. This last point adds weight to my observation that Indigenous preaching leans toward personal testimony and free flowing ad hoc approach to preaching. There is an interweaving of one's own story, the story of the community, and the gospel story to encourage living according to spiritual values seeking harmony in all relationships.

Oral tradition goes on to point out, that even though the Nisga'a embraced Christian faith, this did not guarantee that their expressions of Christian faith or human life were appreciated by incoming colonial church officials. One elder told me how a Methodist missionary ordered all the Nisga'a in his village who had embraced Christian faith to burn their button blankets and Nisga'a regalia. The act stripped the community of much of its

---

1. Rutherdale, *Women and the White Man's God*, 144.

history and identity. I mention it here to point out that Indigenization of Christian faith and in turn preaching needed to be owned by Indigenous people themselves. The Christian faith and in turn the proclamation of the gospel message needed to be cast in the categories that already existed within Indigenous cultures. Indigenous evangelists worked to spread the gospel through the rallies of the Church Army and in other ways to create communities in which this could occur. In today's Nisga'a Church, button blankets and regalia are used in the church service.

Turning to the second example mentioned above, Indigenous Archbishop Mark MacDonald has written that Indigenous Christian faith was often expressed through hymn singing in house meetings. In an article entitled, "The Surprising and Improbable Mission of God among the Indigenous Peoples of Canada." MacDonald points out that the practice of going to church on a weekly basis was not and never had been an ideal for Indigenous people.[2] They, however, expressed Christian faith through prayer and hymn singing that occurred within homes. Christian faith was fully expressed in the literal home. Indigenous people often had impromptu home services that occurred as needed. Such a home service often included Scripture reading and hymn singing, as well as praying for the needs of the community. In this setting every person would express, in their turn, what they believed the Scripture was guiding them to do. This was often done through personal testimony. Hans Frei would have agreed that this practice was an example of showing how Indigenous people saw the story of their life taken into the gospel story.[3] The implication, again, for preaching is that the actions of home worship were intimately related to the personal testimony of the speaker as well as expression in extemporaneous settings.

MacDonald also relates how the institutional church of the newcomers continually pressured Indigenous groups to adopt a style of service that was primarily located within the church building. Of course, the newcomers controlled—or tried to control—the church building whereas Indigenous people live out a spirituality located within their entire territory and especially within their homes.

A final expression of the impromptu extemporaneous preaching of Indigenous people includes the figurative preaching of some Charismatic expressions of Indigenous Churches. I must confess that I owe this description, I think, to Ephraim Radner who reported to have identified figurative preaching among some Pentecostal and Charismatic expressions of preaching and

2. MacDonald, "The Surprising and Improbable," 130.

3. Frei, *The Eclipse of Biblical Narrative*, 1.

interpretation.[4] This was a figurative preaching that I observed at different "revival" or "evangelistic" tent meetings or community special Christian "crusades" where the preacher would figuratively interpret primarily passages from the Hebrew Scriptures, pointing out how they could be figuratively interpreted to show the presence of the Christ and church.

This route of interpretation is similar to the interpretive approach described by George Lindbeck in the Christology of the early church. Lindbeck identifies three rules of the language game when making statements about Christ.[5] First, there is only one God. This of course was in keeping with most Indigenous groups in North America, they might have identified many different spiritual entities but there was only one creator. Second, Jesus Christ had come in the flesh. This of course was assumed by Indigenous people because real stories happen in real places to real people. Finally, the maximization of Jesus Christ. This last point meant that for the early church, if they could see Jesus in the Hebrew Scriptures, they did. One only has to peruse the interpretation of Augustine on Genesis to see figurative or allegorical interpretation. Augustine sees Christ in Genesis 1.[6] For Indigenous people, I extend this rule about the figurative maximization of Jesus to include our traditional spiritualities. If our elders could see the figure of Jesus in our traditional spirituality and territories, then we did. Thus, much of Indigenous preaching included situating the gospel in the context of the local people. It meant showing, figuratively, how Jesus was already present not only in the Hebrew Scriptures but also in Indigenous lands as well as Indigenous stories and ceremonies.

The Indigenous Anglican and Episcopal Church sought to produce resources for serves that expressed the religious sentiments of Native Peoples. *A Disciples Prayer Book* provided a minimalist form of group prayer.[7] The sermon, per se, occurs when the Gospel for the day is read three times in the context of a group worship setting. The first time the Gospel for the day is read, people are asked what words, images or ideas come to mind. After the group responds by going around the circle, the Gospel is read again. The second question explores what Jesus or the Gospel is saying to people in the group. Again people express their thoughts, each person taking their turn until it seems everyone has had their say. Finally, a third time, the Gospel is read again and this time the question is what the Gospel or Jesus is telling the people to do? This then is an example of communal extemporaneous

4. Radner, *Time and the Word*, 163–204.
5. Lindbeck, *The Nature of Doctrine*, 94.
6. Augustine, *Confessions* 13.11.
7. *A Disciples Prayerbook*.

preaching. The community is the preacher. They do the work of interpretation and ultimately ask, what should we do? This approach forms the basis of much of what I have practiced in my thirtysome years of Christian Indigenous ministry. In the next section I show how this is the case and identify possible directions for others trying to develop this approach.

Purposes and Characteristics of Preaching in These Theological Families

The above examples point to three characteristics that are found in many forms of Indigenous preaching. First, Indigenous preaching is carried out by Indigenous people in a variety of settings, but within or related to their traditional territories. This can be seen in such things as home hymn sing gatherings, and the Church Army and women's auxiliaries. Second, the charismatic expressions focused upon evangelism and personal testimony and emotion all point out the importance of preaching leaning toward the emotive. This does not mean that Indigenous preaching is only focused on emotion but draws on the fact that feeling is not only emotion but embraces a whole, valid way of understanding. Third, Indigenous preaching includes free-flowing, extemporaneous weaving together the Gospel story and the stories of the communities. These concepts all fit within the rubric of self-determination as the Indigenous Church seeks to embrace their whole world as they embrace all the relationships that make up the world created by the great mystery.

Out of this background come broad concepts that shape my thinking about Indigenous preaching. I am speaking specifically of how I preach as a Cree person. In Canada alone there are over fifty Indigenous languages spoken, and so it would be arrogant to speak as if there is one kind of Indigenous preaching. Also, since I am an English speaker, my preaching is shaped, in part, by the West. I still believe, however, that the generational memory that is handed on to me along with the land and culture where my ancestors and I have lived, is instructional and innovative for the preaching task.

Vine Deloria, in an essay on American Indian Philosophy, identifies three things needed to develop an Indigenous philosophy, or should I say a philosophy that is shaped by Indigenous values.[8] First, one needs to acknowledge that Indigenous ways of knowing and being are different than Western approaches to philosophy. Different does not mean inferior but just different. For example, Western philosophy tends to be abstract. This

8. Deloria, "Philosophy and the Tribal Peoples."

can be helpful in some circumstances like in mathematics, for example, and it may spill over into some forms of preaching in certain streams of society and for theology and religion. Andrew Walls, for example, in an essay on the gospel on the African continent notes that the western church tended to give answers to questions that no one in Africa was asking.[9] As an instructor of theology I understand that the dominant question for much of the modern west was whether God exists or not. This, however, is not a question Indigenous people ask (it may not be a question many in the West ask any longer either). A sermon giving proofs for God's existence would seem rather banal to an Indigenous audience. Delora notes, on the other hand that Indigenous people focus in on real existence and on real stories that happen in real places.

I have noticed other differences as well. Many Eurocentric people in modern North American society tend to begin with the cognitive. Indigenous people begin with the emotive. As I have stated above, this does not mean that the cognitive is unimportant but that the route must pass through the emotions. The modern North American society tends to place greater significance upon a career. This can be seen in how folks introduce themselves by saying what they do. Indigenous people, on the other hand, tend to introduce themselves according to who they are related to which reveals that relationships are primary for significance.

Deloria states that the second concept necessary for an Indigenous philosophy is to embrace or abide by Indigenous boundaries: Indigenous boundaries are related to land to story. That Indigenous people are related to the land seems obvious but perhaps it is not always appreciated. After all, in Canada and the United States, incoming settlers needed to make treaties so they could share the land. The relationship with the land and the boundaries of Indigenous land are defined by Indigenous story. Indigenous Anglican Priest and elder Andrew Wesley told me that the heart of Indigenous spirituality in the Indigenous creation story tells us how we are related to the earth. We Cree understand boundaries by the stories from our elders. The stories tell of our journeying through the land and tell us how we came to be where we are today. The generational memory is handed on through story and is seminal for understanding Indigenous identity and therefore is indispensable for peaching. To preach in an Indigenous context a preacher must abide by Indigenous boundaries, acknowledge the land, and weave the sermon around life in the local place while at the same time acknowledging the whole cosmos.

9. Walls, *The Missionary Movement*, 143–48.

Here is a particularly interesting example of the importance of land. An idiom for land in Cree is the cosmos, and it includes culture and language.[10] The example of the Cree Bible's use of the Cree word *uski*, "land," in John 3:16 yields a back translation into English as "God so loved the *land* God gave his only son." Land is understood to take in all of creation, including people. A sermon on John 3:16 would draw out the importance of all of Creation to the Creator. Needless to say, the importance of creation is important in our time of climate change. Indigenous people have long understood this relationship and it comes out in preaching. Evangelism and mission, then, must be more than winning souls. Evangelism and mission extend to include the restoration of the environment. Creation figures significantly for Indigenous preaching.

The relationship of story to land means that, in my own development as a preacher, narrative has a privileged place in the process of preaching. For exegesis, it means reading the Gospel like a story. It shifts the whole sermon to be story rather than a lecture or deductive sermon. One of the early books that helped me in this process was Ralph Lewis and Gregg Lewis, *Inductive Preaching: Helping People Listen.*[11] I had been trained to preach a deductive sermon but I found that people do not listen to a sermon like a lecture. The congregation where I was preaching wanted to hear a good and meaningful story. Inductive preaching helped me to invert the structure of my sermon from main point, illustration, and then application to something more like application, then illustration, finally leading to a main point.

Of even greater value to my preaching was looking at Scripture with Indigenous eyes. This meant and means, for me, reading the Bible like an Indigenous story. Reading the Scriptures in this way began to make it come alive and it began the process of a developing hermeneutic of love for me, an Indigenous person, taking in the gospel, and the gospel taking in an Indigenous person. This twofold movement became key to embracing Indigenous boundaries and seeing them shape my preaching. For my preaching it also meant a shift toward an exegesis that kept the entire passage in front of the preacher—not just a verse or a phrase or a word—throughout through the whole process.

Let me explain further. Like many, I trained in exegesis using Gordon Fee's, *New Testament Exegesis.*[12] However, in a linear fashion, this book sets out eleven steps toward exegesis with several sub-steps whereby the preacher took the passage apart in several different ways. The preacher often coupled

10. Wolvengrey, "Land."

11. Lewis and Lewis, *Inductive Preaching.*

12. Fee, *New Testament Exegesis.*

this type of exegesis with a deductive preaching approach that reduced the sermon to three significant points. This pattern of exegesis and preaching did not fit my Indigenous orientation. I found that Thomas Long's *Witness of Preaching* set out only five steps (with some sub-steps) but all the time keeping the entire passage before the preacher asking "What is the claim of the text?" Or in the language closer to gospel-based discipleship, what was the Bible or Jesus both offering us and asking us to do?[13]

The significance Indigenous story for my preaching also meant a shift toward focusing primarily upon the gospel as the text for the sermon. Because Matthew, Mark, Luke and John, are primarily narrative, seem to fit better within the story-telling approach of Indigenous life and culture. My concern was also that Indigenous children were not being handed on the gospel story as story but were taught a set of propositional truths resulting from Western theological reduction. I am not saying the Bible is devoid of proposition or principles, but if I accomplished nothing else in my sermon than to hand on the stories of Jesus, I felt this was a success. In this way the pressure to be the most creative preacher so that people would listen, was removed, and all I had to do was tell the story in an Indigenous way. Drawing out the connection to creation or the land, showing how the gospel was really one large story that took in the entire biblical canon.

So, when preaching on biblical passages other than the gospel, I seek to understand its background in the story of Israel or the church within the biblical narrative. For example, if the lesson is from an epistle, I seek to identify how it fits within the narrative of the unfolding early church, usually from Acts. If the passage is from the Hebrew Scriptures, I seek to understand both how the passage fits into the unfolding story of Israel within the Hebrew Scripture and how it continues to show that the promises to the Jewish people are extending to the Gentiles. In this way, we can see Jesus, or the maximization of Jesus, in every place and in every time. Again, focusing primarily on the Gospels allows me to emphasize that God was with Indigenous people, as creator had always been, and the spirituality and harmony we were seeking was being brought to fulfillment through the person of Jesus Christ.

Using the motif of story in preaching not only signals Indigenous people how they are related to the land, but, even more, it tells us how we are related to all things. This highlights Deloria's third concept or value for developing an Indigenous philosophy for an Indigenous preaching approach: the embracing of Indigenous communal identity.

---

13. Long. *The Witness of Preaching.*

The importance of relationship for Indigenous people can be seen in the use of the expression, "all my relatives." This expression captures the idea for Northern plains Indigenous people, that we are related to all things. From Emile Durkheim to Richard Preston, anthropologists have recognized that Indigenous people are more aware of the relationship of everyone in the community. Richard Preston, writing about the Cree of Northern Quebec, around James Bay states that the Cree have an innate understanding of how their individual actions impact every relationship around them.[14] Theirs, according to Preston, is a decentralized form of governance that does not lead to chaos because each Cree person is aware of their relationships.

The Lakota Holy Man, Black Elk, taught that the "making relatives" ceremony was a way to make peace.[15] This ceremony became part of the Indigenous treaty making process when the newcomers came into the territory: the way to achieve harmony was to make relatives of all who came into the land and particularly with those that one had disagreements with. This idea has significance for preaching because it adds to the goal of creation and for salvation, reconciling all things in Christ: everyone is related to everyone else. Indigenous communal identity is always seeking harmony and proper relatedness.

One negative example of early Christian missionaries not understanding communal identity comes from the Tsimshian people. The Christian missionaries wanted the Indigenous Tsimshian people to differentiate who was part of the church and who was not in their villages.[16] The Indigenous people considered this kind of demarcation outside of Indigenous boundaries and outside of Indigenous communal identity. For a people who needs everyone in order for the community to survive and thrive, excluding individuals from the community is not tolerated. The Tsimshian, even when they took in Christian faith, resisted pressure from missionaries to exclude anyone. As one Nisga'a elder told me, the village is the church not the building. The Nisga'a are a cousin language to the Tsimshian. In fact, the Tsimshian would adopt the missionaries into their Tsimshian tribe or family.[17] In so doing, I wonder, if the Tsimshian people hoped to teach the missionaries a better way. In the Tshimshian interpretation the gospel was helpful in not dividing their village but in furthering their Indigenous goal of seeing all things in proper relationship.

---

14. Preston, *Cree narrative*, 78.

15. Black Elk and Brown, *The Sacred Pipe*, 101–15.

16. Neylan, *The Heavens Are Changing*, 251.

17. Neylan, *The Heavens are Changing*, 247.

These concepts then—communal identity as a beginning point, story as the language of the community which functions to illuminate the boundaries of community as well as to form the communal memory as a key element to Indigenous identity—point to several implications for preaching. Remembering that the best way to express these implications are through experience, I will illustrate how embracing Indigenous communal identity through the story of the land impacts preaching. My own approach to a communal narrative homiletics intends to give voice to the community and to further the gospel as our creation story. I know many Indigenous preachers who share similar perspectives.

Communal identity has made me a better preacher by reminding me that my work is always the work of the community. This is not an abstract principle but is a lived reality. The nature of coming to understand who I am as a Cree person and my connection to the earth comes through spending time upon the land and learning the stories of our journey upon the land from the elders. This includes the place of Christian faith within the Indigenous community.

Story is how the communal memory of Indigenous community is handed on from one generation to another. The story takes many different forms. For example the language itself is key to story-telling as my illustration (above) of a Cree translation of John 3:16 and the importance of the land. Story can be a straightforward narrative. It can also take other forms, such as that of a ceremony. The drum songs as well as the dances tell the story of the community. A famous example in Canada is the land claim case of Delgamuukw versus the province of British Columbia that occurred in 1983. The Indigenous people performed their songs and ceremonies in the court room as evidence of their title to their traditional territory.[18] This example is illustrative for preaching in at least two ways. First, the people performing the songs and ceremonies took a traditional story and used it in a different setting to teach others about the connection to the earth. This creative use of a traditional story illustrated how the storyteller, (who, in this case, is the community appointed group) has permission to be creative in the application of the story or song in different kinds of places. Second, the people in 1983 functioned as a kind of author by applying the song and ceremony in a new time. At the same time, they were faithful to how the story has been performed all thee hundred if not thousands of years before. The individuals or group performing the traditional story and song did the work of the community: sharing the communal memory. As such they were both innovative and faithful to a received tradition.

18. McCall, "What the Map Cuts Up, The Story Cuts Across."

The implications for preaching seem obvious but I will expand to make sure it is understood. The preacher as a storyteller is called to tell the story faithfully. The focus, then, is on the story, not primarily on the storyteller. For preaching this means that the task of handing on the gospel story becomes primary. This is supposed to be the focus preaching, but it seems to me that much of the focus on preaching, especially in Eurocentric circles, has been on the creativity of the preacher. From the Indigenous perspective, this is misguided: the job of the preacher is to do the work of the community by faithfully telling the story.

In my own preaching this means, as Eugene Peterson emphasized in *Working the Angles*, paying attention to the act of listening.[19] In fact listening has become a primary skill I have had to develop and it fits in with being an Indigenous elder and preacher. The elder always speaks last. The elder's task is to listen to the whole community and then put into words a consensus that everyone can "buy into." Not that everyone agrees, but they can see how it is the way forward. The preacher in an Indigenous context, then, is tasked with taking the current situations, the traditional stories, including the gospel story, and weaving them together without violating either the stories or the people's boundaries. To be sure, this is probably how all good preachers should think about their roles in their communities. In an Indigenous context, however, the emphasis is upon the story and community, not upon the individual who is preaching.

The importance of land for the Indigenous community also has implication for Indigenous preaching. Land is part of the community and the community is part of the land. Familial relationship has the potential of accentuating the importance of place for story-telling. This aspect of place should play an important role for the preacher or theologian. One of the evidences of the veracity of an Indigenous story is the inclusion of references to specific places on the land.[20] Another component used to verify a story is the relationship of the storyteller to the place where the story being related occurred, and to the people present in the story. This means that if I had a relative at the place where something powerful occurred on the land, then I could tell this story I heard from my relative as if I was there. We can see this same kind of evidence in the gospel story. Names are given to show the connection to a traditional story. Luke for example uses the genealogy of Jesus to explain how Jesus is a new kind of Adam (Luke 3:23–38). Jesus is really human and is really present because he can be located by relatives on the land and in the stories of the communities.

19. Peterson. *Working the Angles*.

20. Ahenakew, *They Knew Both Sides of Medicine*, 147–48.

In addition to being able to see Jesus as part of the human community, the mention of specific places by the Gospel writers means that the stories are true. This affirmation of place and of characters serves as a kind of shorthand for verification that Jesus Christ came in the flesh in the Apostles' Creed as well. At least this is how Dr. Bernie Van De Walle rightly taught the Creed at Ambrose University. He pointed out, and I concur, that the presence of the line, "suffered under Pontius Pilate" shows that the gospel really occurred.[21] As I have mentioned earlier in connection with Indigenous story, real stories happen in real places.

Indigenous people embraced the gospel because they had an experience of Jesus Christ. They were able to see Jesus Christ in line with their understanding of creation or the land. Our elders saw that Christ was present with us. The land is part of our identity, part of our kin along with the people. The land along with our kin form the boundaries of our identity, which is communal. This different approach to creation, land and community enlivens my own preaching. I will turn now to a short sermon around a theology of mother earth.

Case Study: Text and Sermon
(Luke 1:46–55 and 3:23–37)

I come from Northern Alberta, treaty 8 territory. Treaty 8 was signed in 1899 in part because the newcomers were aware of the oil that was present in the territory and they wanted access to the natural resources. First Nations in treaty 8, in turn, sought to enter into a relationship with the newcomers because it is our way to always seek harmony in our territory. As mentioned above, for the First Nations, our nation includes all our relatives, including the earth. We have a kinship relationship with the earth. Our spirituality can be seen in our creation story that tells how we are related to the earth. Our relationship with the earth is complicated.

It would be a understatement to acknowledge that the resource sector of oil and gas has been the object of polarization between the Indigenous community and the newcomers. On the one hand the environmental movement would like to see oil and gas as an industry disappear. At the same time it provides thousands of good paying jobs for many of my relatives. In the end there ends up being much conflict over the land and how we should get food and what our practice should be toward the natural resource industry. I am not going to argue one way or the other, but it is clear that over the next seventy-five years, we will have to temper our use of oil and gas. However,

21. Van De Walle, "Suffered under Pontius Pilate."

instead of vilifying one sector of the economy, it might be better to create an alternative way of looking at the land or creation. If we could embrace the land as our kin, as our family, it could provide a different way of looking at creation and could provide additional resources for making decisions about our uses of natural resources. I want to give you or describe for you my journey to developing a theology of mother earth.

In the sermon, I interpret Luke 1:46–55 and 3:23–37 from the point of view articulated above. I show how the emphasis on relationships in this text become means of verifying the trustworthiness of the text, and consequently, the trustworthiness of the big idea in the sermon.

"Respecting Mother Earth"

1. Mary the Mother of God

I grew up in Northern Alberta and am a bit of redneck. It used to be that when I heard the term "mother earth," I thought it came from some new age ecologist trying to destroy jobs for people. I worked in the lumber industry for 14 years. It was a good union job that provided for my wife and me and our four children.

I eventually went off to seminary because I felt God's call to ministry. I was thinking about the genealogy of Jesus found in Luke 3:23–37. Luke tells the relatives of Jesus right after Jesus baptism. This is significant, but I will pick that up later.

As I read about Jesus family, I was thinking about Jesus' mother, Mary. I was thinking about it this way: "Mary the Mother of God," running it over and over again in my mind. After all, Luke's Gospel also contains Mary's magnificent in Luke 1:46–55. In it Mary sings a song of overflowing praise. She also mentions the ancestors and descendants. This is a song that is recited every evening in the daily office. In Luke, it comes as a response to the news that she will be the mother of God. She will become pregnant and give birth to a son. Mary, is the mother of Jesus.

I was thinking about Mary and a conversation I had with an Indigenous elder. He said to me, I am not sure why some people would say bad things about Mary. This elder had joined a free church tradition whose adherents did not always speak well of Mary. The elder, on the other hand, shared with me that he was raised Roman Catholic and the idea of saying something negative about Mary, was just not a good idea. He said to me, "I wouldn't like it if people said bad things about my mother and, here, Mary is the mother of Jesus and he is God." I chuckled to myself: he was right.

Mary is the mother of God. I was thinking about this reality even as I was reading through the genealogy of Jesus.

2. So Who Is the Mother of Adam?

As I read the names of all the ancestors of Jesus. It reminded me of Cree stories in which you name relatives as proof this is a true story. The ancestors go all the way back to Adam. The genealogy finishes with the phrase in Luke 3:38, "son of Seth, Son of Adam, son of God."

As I read that last line, "Adam, the son of God," I remember thinking, "Who was Adam's mother?" And almost immediately the answer popped into my head: "the earth." Mother earth. As I let the reality of the earth as our mother form in my head, I felt something. I felt an emotional connection to the earth. All the teaching of the elders flooded into my mind. The earth: she provides us with food, and the animals give themselves to us. Our mother the earth: she provides clothing and shelter and way to stay warm in the winter. I thought about the saying of the elder, Chief Seattle, "The earth is our other. Whatever befalls the earth befalls the [children] of earth. If men spit upon the ground they spit upon themselves." It made sense. I had understood this reality before, but I had never felt the emotional connection to mother earth, an emotion similar to how I feel about my birth mother. We Cree do not worship the earth, but we respect her. She is our mother. Our good and her good are wrapped up together.

3. Is This Idea Really Okay?

Of course, I am also a Western-trained theologian and preacher. So you have to check out these things. A good reformation hermeneutical principle is "Scripture interprets Scripture." Am I realistic in thinking that the Bible teaches that the earth is like a mother: Are there other passages of Scripture that give credence to this reality?

How about Rom 8:22? "We know that the whole creation has been groaning in labor pains until now . . . ." The earth groans like a woman in labor waiting for the revealing of the Children of God. Mother earth: her welfare is wrapped up with our welfare.

Of course, as a trained preacher you also have to check out theological sources. Has this theological reality been taught before? Sure enough, Irenaeus wrote, "As Adam came forth from the virgin soil, so Christ came forth from the virgin Mary."[22] The son of Adam, the Son of God, Jesus Christ fully human and fully God.

The earth is our mother and we are all related. These are ideas that are shared among Indigenous peoples, the Bible, and church historians and theologians.

4. Application

I come from Northern Alberta, Treaty 8. For the first nations, our nations are made up of all our relatives. We have a kinship relationship with the earth. When we stand upon the earth, we can feel the land welcome us home. When the newcomers came we made treaty with them, so they could be our relatives. So when we stand upon the earth we can feel her welcome us home.

Jesus Christ came. He was born of a virgin. He was like Adam the son of the virgin soil, the red man from the red earth. Jesus Christ is son of Mary, Son of God. Fully Human, Fully Divine. He is creator and creation in perfect harmony. When he was formed in the womb, when he stood on the earth, he could feel his mother welcome him home. We stand upon the earth; our creation story tells how we are related to the earth. She is our mother; we seek to live out our relationship with the creator and creation in perfect harmony. So when we stand on the earth we feel her welcome us home. When we stand in the presence of Christ, we feel him welcome us home.

If we could come to understand the relationship we have with the earth . . . If we could feel some connection with the earth . . . perhaps those would be additional resources to help us make decisions about how we will live in harmony with the earth.

I am a man born in Northern Alberta, part of treaty 8. I want to live in harmony with all other people, and with our mother, the earth.

Assessment: Strengths and Limitations in These Theological Families

Indigenous preaching is not a different style or genre of preaching. As stated at the outset of this paper, because of the broad variety of Indigenous languages and cultures in North America, for me to attempt to describe *the* Indigenous approach to preaching would continue a colonial or imperial tendency to attempt to erase or minimize the distinctiveness of each

22. Irenaeus, *Against Heresies* 3.22.

community's approach. Therefore, I have focused on my own approach to preaching in a variety of settings. Indigenous preaching, for me has several advantages for presenting the gospel, but there are also some challenges with my approach.

First, since Indigenous identity is intricately entwined with the land or creation, it presents an approach which enhances the relationship of human beings with creation. Since we are in a time of significant climate change, this approach to preaching offers an opportunity to reinvigorate the churches' efforts to work toward the common good. In addition, this approach allows for a greater number of teaching approaches to continue the classic work of early church writers—Irenaeus for example, and Athanasius, for another—who cast salvation within the creation mandate. This in turn could lead to a recasting of evangelism and mission as fitting within our responsibility to draw out from creation that which is best.

In addition, since Indigenous preaching is premised upon a kinship relationship with mother earth, Indigenous preaching creates the possibility of enhancing the emotive connection between human beings and creation. This is in keeping with a Cree cosmology which begins with the understanding that it is a good world. The understanding that our Indigenous territories are part of the family extends to the church, meaning the when the church finally comes to North America, it comes to understand the land is sacred. This perspective enhances emotional resources because when human beings feel the connection to the earth they realize we have greater resources at our disposal when trying to discern what is appropriate development upon the land. An enhanced emotive connection to the land as home might help human beings shift from seeing the land merely as a commodity for exploitation.

This point of view, however, is also a challenge. Since Indigenous preaching is creation centric, it creates the possibility of misunderstanding with regard to some kinds of Christian spirituality which believe that in order to grow in love for God, one must lessen their attachment to created things. Luther resolves this dilemma by noting that if we receive the love of God by faith, this empowers our own love for those things which are created. Luther's approach, of course, does not resolve the problem for many. In addition, many in the past have vilified the Indigenous connection to land by calling it animism and or syncretism, thereby casting derision on Indigenous approaches to understanding our relationship with the earth. The arguments dealing with these kinds of accusations are beyond the purview of this paper, but I want the reader to be aware of the difficulties that one faces as an Indigenous preacher who is open to embracing Indigenous Spirituality and its connection to place.

A second strength of an Indigenous preaching ties Indigenous story with the gospel story. Sermons for Indigenous people are built upon a mutual indwelling of the biblical narrative and Indigenous narrative. The gospel story becomes part of the Indigenous story bundle and is used like a story to help Indigenous peoples navigate our world in a Christian Indigenous spirituality. As part of the story bundle, the gospel could be taken into Indigenous communities as an Indigenous story and no longer primarily a part of colonial oppression. By embracing the gospel and telling the story alongside of Indigenous story, there is the possibility of collaboration.

The gospel as part of the Indigenous story bundle also presents a challenge. Some could think that listing the gospel as an Indigenous story removes the sacredness of the gospel. Some might argue this places the gospel on the same level as any other traditional story. Would this not remove special status from the gospel? This might be the case, if sacredness were considered primarily a term referring to a static standing. Sacred, however, understood from an Indigenous perspective, can be conceived of as "having the potential of being sacred." At any moment the creator could use the gospel story to do something powerful. In this way, the gospel story remains sacred. This, however assumes, that preaching or telling the story is essential to the proclamation of a "sacred story."

Further Reading

Ahenakew, Alice. *Âh-âyîtaw isi ê-kî-kiskêyihtahkik maskihkiy = They Knew Both Sides of Medicine: Cree Tales of Curing and Cursing.* Told by Alice Ahenakew. Edited, translated and with a glossary by H. C. Wolfart and Freda Ahenakew. Publications of the Algonquian Text Society. Winnipeg: University of Manitoba Press, 2000.

Aldred, Raymond. "Us Talking to Us." *Journal of North American Institute for Indigenous Theological Studies* 1 (2003) 79–94.

Archibald, Jo-Ann. *Indigenous Storywork: Educating the Heart, Mind, Body, and Spirit.* Vancouver: University of British Columbia Press, 2008.

King, Thomas. *The Truth about Stories: A Native Narrative.* CBC Massey Lectures Series. Toronto: House of Anansi, 2003.

McCall, Sophie. *First Person Plural: Aboriginal Storytelling and the Ethics of Collaborative Authorship.* Vancouver: University of British Columbia Press, 2012.

Treat, James, ed. *Native and Christian: Indigenous Voices on Religious Identity in the United States and Canada.* New York: Routledge, 1996.

Twiss, Richard. *Rescuing the Gospel from the Cowboys.* Edited by Ray Martell and Sue Martell. Downers Grove, IL: InterVarsity, 2015.

Woodley, Randy. *Shalom and the Community of Creation: An Indigenous Vision.* Prophetic Christianity. Grand Rapids: Eerdmans, 2012.

17

Preaching in the Postcolonial Theological Family

ELIZABETH J. A. SIWO-OKUNDI

COLONIALISM REMAINS THE PUBLIC pride of many countries and institutions, though public statements and actions attempt to mislead the public into believing otherwise. For several centuries, colonial powers systematically and unscrupulously controlled the majority of the world with little exception. Power untethered, privilege undeserved, and superiority presumed over other humans are trademarks of colonialism. Colonialism exhibited human creativity at one of its lowest points, shackled by depravity in its purest evil form. Grabbing hold of every aspect of daily life, colonialism created and crossed boundaries, undermined and coerced local leadership, dismantled cultures, and murdered the maturity of humanity. Evidence of colonialism springs forth in every aspect of religion and politics, family and friendships, finances and aid, healthcare and employment—or lack thereof. The political independence of territories from colonial rulers seemed promising yet could not erase the impact and devastation of colonialism.

The ideology of colonialism remains, continuing to brutalize communities. Scholars disagree on the definition of "postcolonial," but most agree that the definition goes beyond a temporal focus. It cannot refer simply to a time period "after" colonialism or even imperialism. Postcolonial studies examines the ongoing impact and legacy of colonialism. Preaching from a postcolonial perspective critically engages with the colonial past and present, while envisioning the future.

Circumstances That Gave Rise
to This Theological Family

Postcolonial preaching rises from the complexity of colonialism and imperialism, the relationship between colonizers and colonized peoples. Christianity and colonialism cannot be separated, as religion became a key force in controlling and "civilizing" local communities over the centuries. Take for example, the European "Scramble for Africa," which started in the 1880s. European empires more or less looked at a map of Africa and strategically carved out areas to control, instantly determining the fate of millions of people for generations. The decisions separated peoples, destroyed nations, and forced a new way of life, all in the self-interest of those in power. In just a few decades, European empires dominated the entire African continent (with little exception) and controlled natural resources, raw goods, politics, transportation, economics, and nearly every aspect of daily living. Christianity became a useful tool and was at times inseparable from colonialist projects.

A popular saying in Africa is, "When the missionaries arrived, the Africans had the land and the missionaries had the Bible. They taught us how to pray with our eyes closed. When we opened them, they had the land and we had the Bible." The saying speaks volumes about the impact and legacy of colonialism entangled with Christianity. Missiologist Lamin Sanneh (The Gambia) argues for a more nuanced view of mission, particularly in Africa, noting the many contributions of missionaries.[1] It was not until the 1950s and 1960s that African territories became politically independent through a wave of African independence movements. The Scramble for Africa and local resistance to it are but one example of movements and countermovements *worldwide* through various tactics.

Postcolonial preaching rises from such scrambles, taking into account local narratives and voices impacted by imperialist leaders. Postcolonial studies emerges in religious studies as a way to address the past and look to the future. In postcolonial studies, literary and cultural critiques come to the forefront with the writers of modern postcolonial studies examining European imperialism. Four figures have been especially formative in bringing this perspective to wider attention: Frantz Fanon (Martinique), Edward Said (Palestine, USA), Homi K. Bhabha (India), and Gayatri Spivak (India). In the 1950s and 1960s, during the era of African independence and global liberation movements, Fanon—with great inspiration from his mentor Aimé Césaire, also from Martinique—penned works on anti-Black

---

1. Sanneh, *Translating the Message.*

racism, anti-colonialism and visions for a postcolonial society. Fanon was in his late twenties when he managed to publish *Black Skin, White Masks* (1952) based on his experience as a psychiatrist and person of African descent. Like other youth from Martinique, he discovered that he could not fit into white French society simply due to his race. He argued that learning the language and culture of the oppressor does not make one white nor allow one access to the larger culture. Despite his grasp of the language and culture, assimilation proved impossible for him and others like him. He felt and understood explicitly the impact of colonialism and the need to counter it.[2]

Works by African and African diasporic scholars often are minimized in postcolonial studies, with most credit given to Asian and Middle Eastern scholars. Subsequently, conversations on postcolonialism typically begin with Said and Bhabha, both literary critics whose works rose to prominence in the 1970s and 1980s. Said uses the term *orientalism* to describe the way in which the West dominates the East. According to Said, the West elevates itself such that the East becomes inferior and "other." Said's theory became a foundation for postcolonial studies and also offered contrapuntal reading as a lens for interpreting texts.[3] Bhabha builds upon the argument through his concept of "hybridity" and "mimicry" examining the ways in which different cultures interact or mix with each other, most notably how the colonized mimic or copy the colonizers (with hopes to benefit from it) even if they are unaware of doing so.[4] Conversion to Christianity by local people would be considered by some to be a form of religious hybridity, a theme visited by many African writers including Chinua Achebe (Nigeria) and Ngũgĩ wa Thiong'o (Kenya).[5] Alongside Said and Bhabha, Spivak wrote a groundbreaking essay, "Can the Subaltern Speak?" (1988) focusing on male domination over women. For Spivak, the matter of postcolonial critique must extend to include an examination of the burdens placed on non-Western women.[6]

To view postcolonial studies only from the view of literary critics is to limit the scope and impact of colonialism itself. Alongside the establishment of postcolonial studies within literary criticism (in particular), theological voices were noticing similarities in their contexts and taking action to speak

---

2. Fanon, *Black Skin, White Masks*; and Fanon, *The Wretched of the Earth*.

3. Said, *Orientalism*.

4. Bhabha, *The Location of Culture*.

5. Ngũgĩ, *Decolonising the Mind*; and Ngũgĩ, *A Grain of Wheat*. Achebe, *The African Trilogy*.

6. Spivak, "Can the Subaltern Speak?"

for their contexts and voices beyond academia. In 1976,[7] the Ecumenical Dialogue of Third World Theologians met to discuss the state of theology in Africa, Asia, Latin America, and oppressed communities of the First World; their shared marginalization and quest for liberation; concern for the poor, and anti-colonial theology. The conference, hosted in Tanzania by President Julius Nyerere, included theologians James Cone (USA), Gustavo Gutiérrez (Peru), Virginia Fabella (Philippines), and Charles Nyamiti (Tanzania). The meeting resulted in the formation of the Ecumenical Association of Third World Theologians (EATWOT).[8] Women's voices largely were missing from that first meeting but were included in the next year. By 1989, The Circle of Concerned African Women Theologians was founded through the leadership of Mercy Amba Oduyoye (Ghana) and members began engaging Biblical texts and contexts from the perspectives of African women and their lived experiences.[9] The work of EATWOT and The Circle predate the formal recognition of postcolonial studies in theology. The 1980 work by Justo González (Cuba) and Catherine Gunsalus González (USA), also contributed to and challenged existing ideas on perspectives in preaching.[10]

Scholars who focused on theological texts would be among the first to engage postcolonial studies. The strong link between literary criticism and Biblical studies is recognized in the 1990s through the work of Rasiah S. Sugirtharajah (Sri Lanka). Sugirtharajah brought postcolonial studies to the field of Biblical interpretation. He and other scholars who joined him argued that non-Western approaches to Biblical studies do a disservice to those who were colonized. Biblical interpretation should come from the people themselves.[11] In the 1990s and 2000s, Musa Dube (Botswana), Ada María Isasi-Díaz (Cuban-American), Chung Hyun Kyung (South Korea), and scholars worldwide offered new ways of examining the Bible, with particular attention to people of the Third World.[12]

The 2000s saw the emergence of scholarship on postcolonial preaching, from the greater field of religion, to practical studies, to the field of homiletics (a subdiscipline of practical theology). In 2001, Societas Homiletica (an international, though mainly European guild) held a conference focusing

---

7. Torres and Fabella, *The Emergent Gospel*; and Appiah-Kubi and Torres, eds., *African Theology En Route*.

8. Joseph, *Theologies of the Non-Person*. Also https://eatwotglobal.com/

9. Oduyoye, "The Story of a Circle."

10. González and González, *Liberation Preaching*.

11. Sugirtharajah, *Voices from the Margin*.

12. Dube, ed., *Other Ways of Reading*; and Dube, *Postcolonial Feminist Interpretation*; and Dube, ed., *Postcolonial Perspectives*. Isasi-Díaz, *Mujerista Theology*; and *En la lucha*. Chung, *Struggle to Be the Sun Again*. Sugirtharajah, *Postcolonial Biblical Reader*.

on "Creating Perspective" and included diverse cultural perspectives with subsequent conferences on global conflict.[13] Globally, more and more focus appeared about colonialism and preaching. Homiletician Luke Powery's (USA) 2008 overview on "Preaching under the Postcolonial Influence" often is overlooked in present-day histories on postcolonial preaching.[14] He cautions that preachers are not exempt from colonialism's influences. In 2011, Kwok Pui-lan's (Hong Kong) presidential keynote address to the American Academy of Religion (AAR) focused on "Empire and the Study of Religion"—a critical topic given that AAR includes nearly 8,000 members worldwide, though mainly in North America. Kwok argues,

> The origin and development of our field have been shaped by imperialism in the past and Empire in the present. Some scholars in the field have supported the status quo, served imperial interests, and shown inertia and resistance to change. The study of religion has been marginalized in the humanities and in American higher education. Seminaries and divinity schools have seen dwindling financial support. Our field risks becoming irrelevant in the global demand for change.[15]

Kwok has one clear goal: "to offer some suggestions for the field to change so that it can be a positive force against Empire and for human flourishing."[16] In closing her address, perhaps as a hint to homileticians, Kwok advocates:

> What our world desperately needs are communicators, people who have a deep knowledge of the subject and can speak to the lawyers, doctors, social policy makers, government officials, and ordinary people on the street about why religion matters. In the name of God and religion, racism, bigotry, violence, and colonialism have been perpetrated. Yet religion has also inspired people to fight for justice, search for the common good, save the environment, and speak out for the 99 percent.[17]

Two years later, the International Academy of Practical Theology in Canada met and used as its theme "Complex Identities in a Shifting World." Postcolonial studies took center stage.[18] The following year, practical/pastoral

13. Immink and Stark, eds., *Preaching Creating Perspective.*

14. Powery, "Postcolonial Criticism," 159–61.

15. Kwok, "Empire and the Study of Religion," 286.

16. Kwok, "Empire and the Study of Religion," 287.

17. Kwok, "Empire and the Study of Religion," 296–97.

18. For a summary of the conference essays, art, and music, refer to Couture et al., eds., *Complex Identities.* In particular, Kwok provides a range of perspectives in her article, "Changing Identities and Narratives."

theologian Emmanuel Lartey (Ghana) published *Postcolonializing God: New Perspectives on Pastoral and Practical Theology.* Lartey offers seven "postcolonializing activities," among them is the insistence on being polyvocal—numerous voices are encouraged to speak regardless of educational level or background.[19] In 2014, North American homileticians formally entered the conversation when The Center for Practical Theology at Boston University hosted a consultation on postcolonial preaching and the papers later were published in *Homiletic* (the scholarly journal of homiletics and religious communication).[20] The current year, 2021, began with a new work by HyeRan Kim-Cragg: *Postcolonial Preaching: Creating a Ripple Effect.*[21]

It is critical to keep in mind that many homiletical works from a postcolonial perspective have not appeared in academic conferences nor taken center stage on a global scale. Local communities engage in postcolonial preaching. Doctoral students are producing more and more research. At times, postcolonial preaching can be considered just one of the descriptions for a range of preaching, such as the works of scholars in South Africa (for example) where there is a strong focus on anti-apartheid and prophetic preaching. Context matters for naming and framing.

Purposes and Characteristics of Preaching in This Theological Family

Postcolonial preaching does not aim for a return to life before colonialism nor does it paint current life with a board all-encompassing brush. For some people, colonialism conveniently remains a topic buried in the archives of history and history books. The page flipped, sins of the past disappeared, and a new progressive era of human dignity emerged. For other people, colonialism effortlessly parades itself in daily life. On a leisurely stroll through the streets of one's own neighborhood or country, one bumps into colonialism as though colonialism were a living and breathing being—for indeed, it is living and breathing, even in the very language that is spoken, the food eaten, the names given, the scholarships offered, the education provided, and the version of history told and untold. Evidence of colonial powers carved in stone and righteously erected in public spaces abound, as reminders of a history that never ended. To speak of "post" colonial perspective in preaching is to imagine and to invoke and to hope.

19. Lartey, *Postcolonializing God.*

20. Go et al., "Introduction to the Essays of the Consultation on Preaching and Postcolonial Theology."

21. Kim-Cragg, *Postcolonial Preaching.*

But is that not the very essence of preaching? Hence, postcolonial preaching moves forward while also looking back realistically.

Postcolonial preaching begins with self-reflection on the preacher's part. Sarah Travis (Canada) argues, "Postcolonial preaching cannot happen unless preachers are willing to acknowledge to themselves and to their listeners complicity with imperial systems, the first step in bringing to consciousness the reality that all inhabit colonial spaces."[22] Travis writes from the perspective of being white and privileged, shares her own limitations, and points to the work of Kwok as an invitation for everyone to participate in postcolonial preaching.

Kim-Cragg (Canada) identifies the role of the preacher as an important starting place. She argues for six principles in postcolonial preaching through the acronym RIPPLE: Rehearsal, Imagination, Place, Pattern, Language, and Exegesis. Kim-Cragg posits that postcolonial preaching is similar to a pebble in a lake: there is a ripple effect that touches many dimensions. For Kim-Cragg, "postcolonial preaching is a circular multidimensional movement, with the purpose of creating a ripple effect in people's hearts and minds for the sake of the Kin-dom"[23] The six principles of RIPPLE guide the preacher beyond revealing sins and realities into what the world should be based on God's vision for the world. For example, exegesis must include a postcolonial interpretation of the Bible. The identity of the preacher and the preacher's social location contribute to the way in which the preacher examines texts. Kim-Cragg makes an important contribution regarding language: "The postcolonial preacher would do well to tap into linguistic wisdom embedded in languages other than English and cultures other than those that are dominant in their community. Other languages and cultures will only expand the imagination of postcolonial preaching."[24] I believe that we can learn much from Achebe and Ngũgĩ, regarding the impact of colonialism on culture and language (Ngũgĩ writes primarily in Gĩkũyũ).

Postcolonial preaching is "multilingual, multicultural, and ecumenical," according to homiletician Pablo Jiménez (USA, Puerto Rico, and St. Crois).[25] We should examine the way in which preaching is taught and not taught. In reflecting on a sermon that took place within a Caribbean context, Jiménez observes the conflict between colonialism and postcolonialism. He witnessed the "three points and a poem" sermon style popularized in many theological settings. He notes that the formula is

22. Travis, "Troubled Gospel," 50.

23. Kim-Cragg, *Postcolonial Preaching*, 6.

24. Kim-Cragg, *Postcolonial Preaching*, 33.

25. Jiménez, "If You Just Close Your Eyes," 28.

deductive, monological (with the preacher as the sole and scholarly expert), rationalistic, individualistic, and authoritarian (reflecting colonial days). He concludes, "In short, traditional deductive preaching is colonial preaching."[26] We need new models of preaching. For Jiménez, understanding colonial history, using pastoral theology, and relying on sound Biblical hermeneutics can help remedy the situation.

Postcolonial preaching relies heavily on imagination, which is a central theme. Kwok defines postcolonial preaching as "a locally rooted and globally conscious performance that seeks to create a Third Space so that the faith community can imagine new ways of being in the world and encountering God's salvific action for the oppressed and marginalized," and "it challenges Eurocentric styles of worship and preaching methods."[27] Citing African-American, Asian-American and Hispanic preaching, Kwok emphasizes the artistic aspects of postcolonial preaching. Such art can extent to biblical criticism, evident in the storytelling methods used by Dube.

Postcolonial preaching examines the selective authority placed upon preachers and brings in the voices of the community, while reading and rereading the Bible. Much of postcolonial preaching depends on the preacher's position. Here, Powery's observations are poignant:

> Preachers could be viewed as colonialists in that they have the power to speak while others sit, listen, and obey, without a voice. Postcolonial critics realize that someone in authority gives power to particular people to become preachers while others may not be given the same opportunities (e.g., women of color), portraying the preaching enterprise as an imperial and patriarchal educational tool, as evident in the past. Postcolonialism could be a force to destroy preaching, even criticizing the Bible as a colonial resource to perpetuate imperial domination and abuse.[28]

Powery raises concern regarding the power and position of preachers. In the academy and in pulpits, the majority of preachers are male; and the majority of ordained persons are male. Such a limitation brings with it a limitation in the pulpit space. Hence, the importance of diverse voices in the pulpit.[29]

26. Jiménez, "If You Just Close Your Eyes," 24.

27. Kwok, "Postcolonial Preaching in Intercultural Contexts," 10, 14.

28. Powery, "Postcolonial Criticism," 160.

29. My PhD dissertation, Siwo-Okundi, "Listening to and Learning from the 'Small Voice,'" included an examination of preaching from the perspective of African women and youth preachers. Many of them are not ordained ministers due to power dynamics in church structures and leadership. Yet, the preachers emphasize that they are "called" by God to preach. They preach on topics that others dare not, to people who are overlooked, and in places that are neglected by other preachers.

Case Study: Text and Sermon
(Exodus 3:1–14)

The most dangerous preacher (and leader) is one who lives an unexamined life and lacks humility for the magnitude of one's call-in service to God and God's people. The following sermon is based on Exodus 3:1–14, a popular story which details the prophet Moses' encounter with God at a burning bush. I believe Moses to be a pivotal figure for preaching from a postcolonial perspective, because Moses represents both power and powerlessness. Moses is a key figure for marginalized communities, because his life as a Hebrew boy adopted and raised in privilege by the oppressive ruling party, involves hardship and suffering even while he was in his mother's womb. Born into an enslaved family, Moses' life is threatened by political forces determined to kill Hebrew boys and oppress Hebrew people. His mother and sister find a way to protect him, resulting in Moses adoption by the elite ruling class and royal family. He leads a privileged life until the day he rescues a Hebrew from beatings. He then becomes a fugitive, running to escape the death penalty.

Moses was raised in a world of privilege yet has the cultural identity of a marginalized being. His life is a clash of identity! Moses has mastered the language and culture of the oppressor but cannot escape his identity— the very situation that Fanon discovers about Africans who have mastered the language and culture of the oppressed. Having examined the problems of authority and power raised by postcolonial perspectives, there is a desire to move away from authority. Doing so is impossible in homiletics, because the preacher is a figure of authority. Rather than shy away from authority, the following sermon goes directly into dealing with one of the most significant and powerful (and even problematic) Biblical figures: Moses.

A key aspect of interpretation is the self-examination of the preacher. When listening to the sermon, one must move away from the expectation of three points and a poem. One must also be open to understanding that the story about Moses essentially is a story about self—thought that is not always explicitly stated. One must resist the urge to wonder, "Where is this sermon going?" and focus instead on the moment.

"On an Ordinary Day"

[This sermon begins with questions that many of us have raised regarding whether or not to take action on justice matters. The focus highlights an ordinary day of life.]

Why involve ourselves in justice issues? The risks are too many, the support too little, the situations unpredictable, and the time too consuming. Friends disappear, enemies increase, and allies prove less than amicable. When one takes a stand, one often stands alone being ridiculed, humiliated, shamed, and questioned with no promise of a positive outcome and rarely a word of encouragement. Why bother being involved?[30]

The Exodus 3:1–14 story of Moses—a fugitive, hiding in a foreign land—highlights the internal questions many of us wrestle with regarding our purpose in life. While tending to his father-in-law's sheep, Moses witnesses the odd sight of a bush, burning bright but "not consumed" with fire. The oddity draws him away from his routine task, on an otherwise ordinary day.[31] As Moses attempts to investigate the odd sight, God sees him and twice calls his name. Moses responds, "Here I am." Wasting no time, God moves to the point of this remarkable encounter and engages Moses: "I have observed the misery of my people . . . I have heard their cry . . . I know their sufferings . . ." God concludes by telling Moses, "Now I am sending *you*" to help those who are suffering (emphasis mine).

Moses does not argue with God, nor does he say "No" to God. However, the same Moses who initially responded "Here I am," now asks "Who am I?" God reassures Moses, promising, to "be with" Moses. In turn, Moses asks God what he should tell the people "if" *they* ask him the name of the god/one who has sent him. God responds, "I AM WHO I AM . . . [Tell them] I am has sent me to you."

[The sermon transitions to focus on the preacher. The significance of the preacher's self-examination cannot be understated, particularly in preaching from a postcolonial perspective. Moses' self-examination reveals his past weaknesses and reckless inclinations.]

Preachers, scholars, and truth-seekers long have wrestled with God's "I am who I am" response to Moses. The overwhelming attention given to God's response overshadows Moses' question. Most people assume that Moses' question concerns the name or nature of God. However, a "small voice"[32] examination of the text, reveals something else: When Moses asks God "who shall he say is sending him," Moses is *not* asking God about God's name!

---

30. I thank The One I Run To, for continued support. Thank you to Rev. J. B. Blue and Ms. Nicole S. Johnson for their feedback and attention to clarity.

31. Unless otherwise stated, biblical references are from the New Revised Standard Version of the Bible (NRSV).

32. I define the "small voice" as the unnoticed, unnamed, silenced, and marginalized voices in biblical texts and social contexts. To learn more about the "small voice," refer to Siwo-Okundi, "Listening to the Small Voice."

Rather, Moses is asking a question about *himself*: "Of all the people You [God] could send to do this particular task, why are You sending *me*?"

God's famous "I am who I am" response must be interpreted not as a matter of the name or nature of God, but rather in relation to Moses' self-doubt. The seed of that self-doubt was planted long before this burning bush encounter with God and was shaped by two incidents in particular. The first time Moses witnesses the suffering of his people, he secretly and recklessly intervenes. The results are fatal (Exod 2:11–12). The second time he intervenes, someone asks him, "Who made you a ruler and judge over us?" (2:14). Moses' confidence seems to shatter under the weight of being questioned.[33] Rather than wrestling with the person's question at this point, Moses runs away, dodges threats against his life, settles elsewhere, marries, and becomes a father. Running away does not erase the sufferings of Moses' people nor suppress their cries (2:23–25). Their cries meet him unexpectedly at a burning bush, on an ordinary day (3:7–10).

The incidents leading to the burning bush recall Moses' experience with his own suffering and the suffering of others. The incidents also illustrate Moses' willingness—however flawed—to become involved. Yet when God tells Moses that *he* is the one to lead the people out of their suffering, seeds of self-doubt re-emerge and begin to grow. Moses wonders, "Who am I?" (3:11)—meaning, "I have tried twice to intervene on behalf of others, but I failed. Who am I that I should be the one to return to the very place from which I ran away? What qualifies me to intervene on behalf of others?" Disguising his concerns under the voices of past and potential doubters who ask, "Why *you*, Moses?" Moses essentially asks, "Why *me*, God?"[34]

Perhaps Moses would have found comfort in hearing God say something like, "Moses, I surveyed the land and interviewed everyone on earth. Based on this and that, you obviously are the best one for this work. Do not worry, everything will be fine." That kind of answer would have given Moses some validation and even a boost of confidence! While Moses sinks deeper into the pit of self-doubt, God comes forward and tells Moses

---

33. Moses rightly recognizes that being involved in justice means that one will be questioned. One will be questioned directly, through gossip, through serious concern, or even through curiosity. When Jesus returned to his hometown to be involved in the lives of people who are suffering, those around him pose endless questions: "'Where did this man get this wisdom and these deeds of power? Is not this the carpenter's son? Is not his mother called Mary? And are not his brothers James and Joseph and Simon and Judas? And are not all his sisters with us? Where then did this man get all this?' And they took offense at him" (Matt 13:54–57). See also Mark 6:2–3 and Luke 4:22.

34. Moses's internal question of "Why me?" mirrors the earlier external question of "Who made you a ruler and judge over us?" (2:14).

something that each of us needs to know at some point or another (even again and again): "I am with you."

What follows is Moses' exhaustive disclosure of his limitations, faults, and reasons why he cannot be the one God has in mind for helping others. Moses wonders aloud, "Suppose [the people] do not believe me or listen to me . . . " (4:1). He reaches the point of desperation, begging God, "Please send someone else" (4:13). He even points to his past and his inadequacies: "I have never been eloquent, neither in the past nor even now . . . I am slow of speech and slow of tongue" (4:10). Despite the heated conversation, God does not waver (4:10–16). God promises over and over again to "be with" Moses and offer guidance on what to say and what to do (3:12, 4:12, 4:15).[35] Moses somehow gathers the courage to go forth and begin his ministry, though his self-doubt lingers well past the burning bush.[36]

> [Moses's self-doubt remains an important aspect of his leadership. Even Jesus hesitated before turning water into wine. No leader should ever be above self-interrogation. Self-doubt should remind us that we are in service to God and community. Having explored Moses' past and disclosed his weaknesses, the sermon transitions to Moses' actions and our actions.]

God comes to us on otherwise ordinary days in the midst of our routine tasks, reminding us of issues in our world and calling our attention to neglected people and matters. No matter our experience, we tend to rehearse the numerous reasons why we are unable or even unprepared to participate in liberating lives, sit with those who are suffering, or stand against stupidity and oppressive powers. *What ifs* fill our minds. We wonder, *Suppose I go to help others and they question me about my role, then what shall I say or do?*[37] But God reassures us, promising to *be with* us. We may feel alone and inadequate, but the God who sends us to intervene, to help, to support, does not send us alone. That same God promises to *be with* us. We need not go alone, secretly, or desperately.

I recall an ordinary day, when I had escorted a friend to the hospital. After hours of waiting in long lines under the scorching heat of the East African sun and attending to my friend's needs, I now desperately needed

35. Other biblical examples of God promising to "be with" include Isa 41:9–10 (God speaking to Israel); Isa 7:14 and Matt 1: 23 (prophecy concerning the birth of Emmanuel, "God [is] with us"); Matt 28:20 (Jesus speaking to his disciples); and Acts 18:9–10 (God speaking to Paul).

36. Refer also to Exod 5:22–23; 6:12; and 6:30.

37. Here I am borrowing the New International Version's (NIV's) wording of Exod 3:13.

to attend to my own ordinary needs. I hurried to the small, outdoor facility just a few steps behind the women's ward. Soft, piercing screams grabbed my attention while I was entering the women's restroom.

When I heard the screams, I stopped, listened, and looked ahead, trying to find the origin of the painful cries. Of the two or three wooden toilet room doors squeezed side-by-side on the slightly raised concrete platform, one door remained wide open. There stood a skinny little girl with even skinnier legs. Rather than squatting comfortably over the rectangular hole in the ground—a typical toilet for our area—she stood almost straight with her back bent at a strange angle. Her elbows held her skirt to her thighs and her hands dangled over her bony knees, which awkwardly knocked against each other. Her bowed head allowed her tears to fall easily onto the concrete floor, barely missing her feet on either side of the rectangular hole in the ground.

I gently asked her if she needed help and if there was someone I could call for her. Surely, she was in the hospital with her mother or another loved one. She managed to raise her head. Staring at me were red, tear-filled eyes, wondering, perhaps, why I was there, wondering whether or not she could trust me. Me, a stranger. Her brief stare did not stop her tears from flowing nor her voice from uttering the soft, piercing screams. I listened more closely.

"I can't . . . I can't . . . ," she cried.

I was puzzled, not knowing what she meant. Over and over again, she cried and sobbed, still standing in her awkward position. Her painful cries of "I can't" filled the area, while the noise of the hospital all but disappeared behind us.

"I can't . . ." What did she mean? "I can't . . . I can't . . . but the doctor . . . I can't . . . says I must . . ." Her awkward position coupled with her painful cries allowed me finally to understand: she was trying to relieve herself, but the pain of doing so was too much for her to bear. Not able to leave her, but also not certain what to do or say, I stood there.

"I can't . . . I can't . . . ," she said, over and over again through tears.

Her cries demanded something of me. But what? I had no idea what to say or what to do. Suppose I said the wrong thing? Suppose others thought me to be the cause of her cries? So many questions ran through my mind.

Clumsily, I whispered, "You can. You can do it." My words seemed inadequate.

"I can't . . . I can't . . . ," she cried.

"You can . . . you can. . . ," I said.

Back and forth we continued, until she wailed steadily, tearfully, loudly as she relieved herself. She was finished. Only my silence mixed with her sniffles of relief and pain stood between us. She gave me a slight smile. I, too, smiled.

She then realized that I was a stranger with whom she had shared a very intimate, painful, and embarrassing moment. She cleaned herself, put her skirt in place, and wiped her wet face. I hoped she would run off, giggling as children do. Instead, she walked away at an uncomfortably slow pace. Her skinny legs pressed close together, her frail body hunched over, as though leaning on a walking stick.

I returned to the women's ward of the hospital—in the big room where patients and visitors stayed in one large room. I returned, somehow forgetting what had brought me to the restroom in the first place. Over the next few days of visiting my friend in the women's ward, I learned that this little girl's condition was not an illness or the result of an accident. Rather, her condition was due to an attack against her. An adult man, known to the community, had raped her while she was returning home from her mother's funeral. The man ripped and tore the inside of this little girl, leaving her delicate parts painfully held together with stitches. The man who had raped her was enjoying the freedoms of community life, while this little girl struggled to relieve herself at the toilet and mourn the death of her mother. Trauma upon trauma. When it came time for her to return home, I heard her wail again. All of us heard her wail again. Even if you did not know her situation, her wail would grab your heart.

Cries of pain reach us on ordinary days at a burning bush or even a bathroom. My role that day was small. Is it possible to state which part of my identity stood with her that day? No. *I* am who *I* am. Justice begins with ordinary encounters set against the backdrop of routine aspects of life. "I am with you," says God, over and over again. "Now, go and *be with* someone else."

Assessment: Strengths and Limitations in This Theological Family

Preaching from a postcolonial perspective encourages human engagement, Biblical exegesis, critical thinking, and knowledge of the historical and current lived experiences of colonial legacies, congregations, and communities. Culturally specific examples must abound. Further, this preaching tradition encourages creativity. If three points and a poem is the formula familiar to most preachers, the current preaching style requires that one not settle for a predictable formulaic recipe.

A challenge of preaching from postcolonial perspectives is the role of preachers from privileged positions and non-marginalized positions. Their desire to preach must be balanced by a willingness to examine their own privilege and listen to marginalized voices. Travis, a practical theologian who studies postcolonial preaching reflects on the role of non-marginalized communities. She examines her own experience noting, "most of our household income stems from organizations that have been complicit in colonial/imperial projects."[38] As such, she admits her fears: "The task of decolonizing the mind is as essential to the colonizer as it is to the colonized. I tread these postcolonial pathways with care, recognizing that some will wonder at my audacity to speak against a system from which I benefit."[39] Postcolonial preaching challenges us to reconsider the ways in which we benefit from and contribute to the pain of others. It challenges us to truthfully and lovingly reconfigure, reimagine, and reconstruct the present and future.

For Further Reading

Dube, Musa W. *Postcolonial Feminist Interpretation of the Bible*. St. Louis: Chalice, 2000.

González, Justo, and Catherine Gunsalus González. *Liberation Preaching: The Pulpit and the Oppressed*. Abingdon Preacher's Library. Nashville: Abingdon, 1980.

———. *Liberation Preaching: The Pulpit and the Oppressed*. 1980. Eugene, OR: Wipf and Stock, 2000.

Go, Yohan, et al. "Introduction to the Essays of the Consultation on Preaching and Postcolonial Theology." *Homiletic* 40 (2015) 3–7.

Jiménez, Pablo A. "If You Just Close Your Eyes: Postcolonial Perspectives on Preaching from the Caribbean." *Homiletic* 40 (2015) 22–28.

———. "A Presentation Offering Caribbean Perspectives on Postcolonial Preaching." https://soundcloud.com/drpablojimenez/if-you-just-close-your-eyes (2014). Also available as an oral presentation at https://drpablojimenez.net/2014/11/25/if-you-just-close-your-eyes-caribbean-perspectives-on-postcolonial-preaching/)

Joseph, M. P. *Theologies of the Non-Person: The Formative Years of EATWOT*. Christianities of the World. London: Palgrave Macmillan, 2015. Available online as a free ebook. Also refer to https://eatwotglobal.com/

Kim, Eunjoo Mary. *Preaching in an Age of Globalization*. Louisville: Westminster John Knox, 2010.

Kim-Cragg, HyeRan. *Postcolonial Preaching: Creating a Ripple Effect*. Postcolonial and Decolonial Studies. Lanham, MD: Lexington 2021.

Lartey, Emmanuel Y. *Postcolonializing God: New Perspectives on Pastoral and Practical Theology*. London: SCM, 2013.

Powery, Luke. "Postcolonial Criticism." In *The New Interpreter's Bible Handbook of Preaching*, edited by Paul Scott Wilson et al., 159–61. Nashville: Abingdon, 2008.

Sugirtharajah, R. S., ed. *The Postcolonial Biblical Reader*. Malden, MA: Blackwell, 2006.

38. Travis, *Decolonizing Preaching*, 6.
39. Travis, *Decolonizing Preaching*, 6.

————, ed. *Voices from the Margin: Interpreting the Bible in the Third World*. 25th anniversary ed. Maryknoll, NY: Orbis, 2016.

Travis, Sarah. *Decolonizing Preaching: The Pulpit as Postcolonial Space*. Lloyd John Ogilvie Institute of Preaching Series. Eugene, OR: Cascade Books, 2014.

18

Preaching in the Process
Theological Family

Casey T. Sigmon

AT FIRST GLANCE, IT may be surprising that process philosophy is a post-modern framework for viewing God and the world that is picking up steam in many theological circles (not just in the ivory tower, either). One need only to look at the vocabulary associated with process to be surprised at this development, e.g., causal efficacy, superject, nexus, objective datum, corpuscular societies, prehension. While these words may not "preach" in and of themselves, the ideas behind them do. Process theology resonates with a life lived in actuality and mutuality for creatures great and small.

Process theology challenges many Christian notions of *how* God is—e.g., omnipotent, omniscient, unchanging, and unmoved—and instead proposes God's relationality as dynamic, shared among all living things, omnipresent and omni-compassionate. Preachers in the process family lean into this relationality and demonstrate concern for all of God's creation–beyond the church and humanity to include animals, amoebas, and ecosystems. Preaching as a process theologian is a practice of amplifying God's living word in worship so that more of us can be in tune with God's range of liberating possibilities within the grasp of every living thing at any given moment.

Circumstances That Gave Rise
to This Theological Family

The neologisms listed above originated with Alfred North Whitehead (1861–1947), the "intellectual ancestor" of process philosophy.[1] Whitehead was both a mathematician (his focus of study from 1885 to 1914) and philosopher, first of natural science, theoretical physics in particular (from 1914 to 1924) and then metaphysics (from 1925 to 1947).[2] Born in England, Whitehead began teaching at Trinity College, then University College, finally bringing his academic career to Harvard in 1924. Whitehead's eclectic intellectual career is the source of what would become process philosophy, or as he termed it, "the philosophy of organism."

Rather than considering these fields of study as separate silos, Whitehead engaged the ideas of each and began to see connections that helped to understand reality. He also began to question the limits of any one field of study on its own to answer the questions of existence—its origin, purpose, and design. Whitehead became convinced in these academic endeavors that philosophy had lost touch with reality. If idea systems are found incongruent with lived experience, "the metaphysics is inadequate and requires revision," for "Whatever is found in 'practice' must lie within the scope" of philosophy."[3] Whitehead's analogy of an airplane illustrates this notion. According to Whitehead, the process of discovery "is like the flight of an aeroplane. It starts from the ground of particular observation; it takes flight in the thin air of imaginative generalization; and it again lands for renewed observation."[4] Here is a pattern, a hermeneutic of knowing born out of experience and applied through lived experience, that emerged around the same time as Martin Heidegger, who described the hermeneutic circle in 1927. This prioritization of experience over systems of thought resonates with other theologies that would emerge in the twentieth century: liberation theology, feminist theology, and practical theology, to name a few.

Whitehead's acclaimed book, *Process and Reality*, was first published in 1929. In this set of lectures, Whitehead lays the groundwork for revisions needed in the field of philosophy in order for a cohesive metaphysic to emerge and resonate with experience. *Process and Reality* dances across traditionally established boundaries for fields of study to propose a cosmology grounded in reality and open to exploring God's function in the

---

1. Bowman, "God for Us," 4.
2. Dorrien, "The Lure and Necessity of Process Theology," 316.
3. Whitehead, *Process and Reality*, 13.
4. Whitehead, *Process and Reality*, 5.

complex matrix of reality.[5] Process thought was born in an attempt to "frame a coherent, logical, necessary system of general ideas in terms of which every element of our experience can be interpreted."[6] While process philosophy is original in many ways, including Whitehead's vocabulary, Whitehead clarifies that the philosophy of organism creeps into these previous philosophical systems from Descartes to Hume. Whitehead brings these ideas into conversation with American pragmatists such as William James and John Dewey and Einstein's theory of relativity, which challenged Newtonian physics.

For Whitehead, science, philosophy, and theology are partners in the process of interpreting experience. Whitehead articulated a hope that theologians would eventually "rethink his cosmological system in the categories of theological" universals.[7] Whitehead goes so far as to critique Christianity in the final chapter of *Process and Reality* for casting God in the image of Caesar, resulting in the worship of God's "raw power," rather than concluding who and how God is from the "brief Galilean vision of humility" seen in Jesus.[8] According to Whitehead, God as an unmoved mover is a misconception. God is not exempt from the relational nature of biology and physics. Instead, God is moving and moved by all actual entities, feeling their becoming and becoming along with them. God is the poet of the world, not Caesar barking orders to his subjects. God is the unity of all of these changing events and actualities. God is with them all and seeks to save the world of events and actualities, "with tender patience leading it by his vision of truth, beauty, and goodness."[9]

Theologians in the neo-orthodox lineage of the 20th century were uncomfortable with Whitehead and what appeared to be another foray into natural theology. Chief among the critics of natural theology was Karl Barth (1886–1968). For Barth, God cannot be known "from below," rather revelation comes "from above," chiefly through Jesus Christ.[10] Moreover, this knowledge can only be ours by the grace of God to reveal Godself. For Barth and others in the theological lineage of neo-orthodoxy, human reason and experience cannot be trusted.

Nonetheless, some theologians were quick to engage the philosophy of Whitehead. Back in England, Lionel Thornton and William Temple

---

5. Bowman, "God for Us," 12.

6. Whitehead, *Process and Reality*, 3.

7. Dorrien, "The Lure and Necessity of Process Theology," 319.

8. Whitehead, *Process and Reality*, 343.

9. Whitehead, *Process and Reality*, 346.

10. Bowman, "God for Us," 13.

appropriated Whitehead. However, process theology did not thrive in England, where neo-orthodox theology would take root. The Chicago School of Theology was the first greenhouse for process theology, though Whitehead did not sow the seeds. When Chicago theologians first picked up Whitehead's *Religion in the Making* in 1926, they "dismissed the book as completely unintelligible."[11] However, by the late 1920s, Chicago theologians were articulating process theology before the term "process theology" existed.[12] This shift emerged from adopting a "radical version" of William James's empiricism.[13] They challenged the notion that ideas referred to a pure Platonic realm of unchanging forms. Instead, influenced by the pragmatism of James and John Dewey, ideas were tools for action in the world of experience. They turned mostly to the realm of history for evidence. According to these theologians, experience is profoundly relational, not atomistic. Life flows in an accumulation of experiences, and the boundaries are not firm. It would take a lecture from Henry Nelson Wieman to translate Whitehead's philosophy and render it relatable to American theology's emerging ideas.

Among the first so-called process theologians to adopt Whitehead was Bernard MacDougall Loomer (1912–1985). Loomer earned his PhD at the University of Chicago in 1942. His dissertation, "The Theological Significance of the Method of Empirical Analysis in the Philosophy of A. N. Whitehead," is considered one of the first and most influential process theology documents.[14] Loomer himself dubbed the theology he proposed out of Whitehead's thought "process-relational" theology. Among the distinctions of this theology from neo-orthodox theology was Loomer's differentiation between understanding God's power as "unilateral" rather than "relational."[15] According to Loomer, linear or unidirectional power is the capacity of someone to influence and shape another "to advance one's purposes . . . while being minimally influenced by the other."[16] In the classic Western theological schema, linear power dominates. God influences all, but we do not influence God. In this conception of power, the aim is self-sufficiency. Others (people, animals, plants) become objects, their subjectivity erased in the quest for a greater expression of the self on the dominant side of the power equation.

11. Dorrien, "The Lure and Necessity of Process Theology," 320.
12. Dorrien, "The Lure and Necessity of Process Theology," 320.
13. Dorrien, "The Lure and Necessity of Process Theology," 320.
14. Towne. "Empirical Naturalism," 255.
15. Loomer, "Two Conceptions of Power."
16. Loomer, "Two Conceptions of Power," 8.

There is an alternative to the linear conception of power that domi-nates Western politics, religion, and society. This alternative is what Loomer simply calls "relational power." It is the power to both "influence and be influenced by others," to give as well as to receive.[17] God's power, in process thought, is relational. God can influence *and be influenced* by every single event and occasion taking place throughout the world, and throughout time. Divine power in process thought is God's power to be tenderhearted enough to feel *everything*, every event, however minuscule or massive, and to be informed by and through that feeling.

For decades, the influence of process thinkers including Loomer, as well as Charles Hartshorne, Daniel Day Williams, and Bernard Meland, at Chicago would help process theology and philosophy gain notoriety in the academy. Hartshorne in particular challenged the traditional omnipotent view of God's power. He advised arguably the most significant contributor to process theology emerged from the Divinity School at Chicago during this era: John B. Cobb Jr. (b. 1925). In 1958, Cobb moved the greenhouse for process theology from Chicago to Claremont, where he cofounded the Center for Process Studies with David Ray Griffin in 1973 and the jour-nal *Process Studies* in 1971. Cobb is still the predominant voice in process theology today, drawing an international audience through books as well as podcasts.

Embodying the transdisciplinary nature of Whitehead, Cobb inte-grated a growing concern for environmentalism into process theology. Cobb critiqued how constructive theology had siloed itself from ethical concern for the world, resulting in a mind-matter dualism that concerned Christian-ity with soul salvation rather than care for the world. Cobb's ecological model of living things "pictures the organism as inseparably connected with its environment."[18] All beings are becoming as a result of past experiences, de-fining the context of what is possible in the present and what we in freedom choose to do in light of these inherited realities. There is no level of analysis below the ecological system, for each element behaves as it does because of its relationships to every other element. Thus process theology, in Cobb and others, is a theoethical framework for understanding our responsibility as being part of the system. One particular legacy of Cobb endures through theologies of creation care amid the climate crisis.

Another legacy of Cobb is the resistance to theologizing in traditional silos of academic disciplines. The intersectionality of process thinking endures. Various disciplines offer propositions to theologians about God.

17. Loomer, "Two Conceptions of Power," 17.
18. Birch and Cobb, *The Liberation of Life*, 80.

Monica A. Coleman is a process thinker who weaves womanist theology, science fiction,[19] mental illness, and Yoruba-based African religions into her process propositions.[20] Nancy R. Howell is a feminist process theologian integrating genetics, ecology and primatology into her work.[21] Process, as a speculative and open-ended system, will continue its creative transformation as new fields are engaged as propositions for knowing and encountering God. Some of the most significant theologians of the 20th and 21st century have embedded and/or explicit echoes of process-relational thought, including Rosemary Radford Ruether, Catherine E. Keller, Rita Nakashima Brock, Sallie McFague, and Thomas Jay Oord.

Purposes and Characteristics of Preaching in This Theological Family

No other homiletician has probed as deeply into the potentialities of process thought for the field of preaching as Ronald J. Allen. For over two decades, Allen has engaged the potentialities of process theology for the practice of preaching and Christian worship.

In *A Credible and Timely Word,* Allen and his colleague Clark Williamson see in process-relational theology an undeniable push toward Christian living rooted in tangible acts of love and justice. The book opens with a brief but convincing proposition that traditional theism and classic Christian theology with its unmoved Mover of a God has rendered churches apathetic to or incapable of engaging in the realities of systemic injustice (in their case sexism, classism, racism, and environmental degradation specifically). With its emphasis on a relational and compassionate God, process theology paints the portrait of an embodied and active theology of the *Imago dei* that requires humans to practice care and compassion for the whole world, which is God's own body. The image of the world being God's own body originated in process theologian Charles Hartshorne and continues to be developed in the theology of Sallie McFague, "in ways that are particularly helpful for Christians seeking to think and act responsibly in our nuclear-ecological

19. In particular, Coleman has ongoing engagement with the 1990s science fiction of the late Octavia Butler. Butler's series of *Parables* centers on the new religion of a young black girl in a pre-apocalyptic California in the early 2020s. Her religion, "earth seed," brings the people back to earth and into an embrace of change, resonating profoundly with process philosophy. For example, "All that you touch, You change. All that you Change, Changes you. The only lasting truth is Change. God is Change." Butler. *Parable of the Sower,* 79.

20. See for example Coleman, *Making a Way out of No Way*; Coleman, *Bipolar Faith.*

21. See for example Howell, "Embodied Transcendence."

age."[22] As the title of their book suggests, Allen and Williamson emphasize the role of process hermeneutics in preaching to "shed much helpful light on how texts can be reinterpreted in ways appropriate not only to the Christian faith but to the human situation in our time."[23]

In sermon preparation and delivery, the corresponding quality for the process preacher is that of conversation and relationality. She is ever in conversation with the text as it was and has been used. She is also in conversation with the context, that is, where her community has been and is in the present moment. Finally, she is in conversation with God, intentionally cultivating a spirituality sensitive to the pull and presence of the companioning Spirit in every given moment. Williamson and Allen highlight the "deep roots" of these conversational postures in preaching in the world "homily" itself: "a transliteration of a Greek term for conversation."[24] Preaching then has embedded within it the notion of "companionship."[25] The preacher and congregation are companions on a discipleship journey with no predetermined road map but an ever-present Guide.

Whitehead's theory of propositions is another foundational piece to Allen's homiletic. According to the theory of propositions, propositions are deemed either true or false but must most importantly be a "lure for feeling" that paves the path to novel actualities.[26] Applied to preaching a sermon must lure the listener, wake them from unconscious behavior and patterns to introduce novel transformative possibility. The preaching should make the congregation feel something, not just think about an idea. Preaching is always a proposition to the listener to decide for themselves if what the preacher offers is true or false to how they constitute a life shaped by the gospel of Jesus Christ in their situation.[27] Allen and Williamson deem this proposition to live in the manner of Jesus a "confrontation."[28]

Another significant contribution to process preaching is from Marjorie Suchocki. Unlike Allen, Suchocki is not a teacher of preaching. Instead, her focus has been on systematic and practical theology as a process theologian. She is deeply involved in the Center for Process Studies at Claremont. She has applied her process theology to ecclesiology in *God, Christ, Church: A Practical Guide to Process Theology* and preaching in *The*

---

22. Williamson and Allen, *A Credible and Timely Word*, 28.

23. Williamson and Allen, *A Credible and Timely Word*, 4.

24. Williamson and Allen, *Adventures of the Spirit*, 143.

25. Williamson and Allen, *Adventures of the Spirit*, 145.

26. Williamson and Allen, *A Credible and Timely Word*, 82.

27. Williamson and Allen, *A Credible and Timely Word*, 6.

28. Williamson and Allen, *A Credible and Timely Word*, 5.

Whispered Word: A Theology of Preaching. Like Allen and Williamson, the core of Suchocki's theology is a non-static, dynamic God, revealed in the growth of Christ in his moment in time. God is omni-compassionate, present in every occasion's becoming, but in a non-preferential way. All events and actualities are of equal value in God's whisper.

Suchocki's foundational claim from process philosophy into her theology of preaching is that to exist is to be receiving a word from God. The "whispered word" is God's "initial aim" for every moment.[29] In process theology, God instigates each moment with possibilities catered to the value, experience, and feelings particular to every particular subject in its becoming.[30]

Jesus is the word of God revealed and "proclaimed" in time and history. Jesus shows us what we can be and leads us to live into the kin-dom of God. Jesus judges and enables us to begin creative transformation, akin to the confrontation described in Allen and Williamson.[31] Jesus is the norm of appropriateness for Christian practice. Thus, in Suchocki's theology of preaching, our ministry is pivotal to the ongoing "re-presentation of Jesus the Christ."[32] Preaching pariticiaptes in God's ongoing redemptive work as it norms Christian activity by bringing God's hidden word to consciousness.

Suchocki lists four core process principles in her theology of preaching:

1. All of God's words are contextual to every being in the process of becoming; circumstances matter; change is incremental in each circumstance; "It is clothed in the past even as it bespeaks a future" and leads to ordinary faithfulness[33]

2. There is never a moment when God is not offering a formative word, we just need to become aware and break out of our habituation

3. The word is the initial aim operating in every moment and it becomes subjective once it comes to consciousness, thus our autonomy is involved as well as responsibility.

4. The aim is targeting communal good in this world[34]

Notice that the gift of God's whispered word is not reserved for the preacher in process theology, including Suchocki's own word. The preacher must

---

29. Suchocki, *The Whispered Word*, 7.

30. Whitehead, *Process and Reality*, 244.

31. Suchocki, *The Whispered Word*, 17.

32. Suchocki, *The Whispered Word*, 21.

33. Suchocki, *The Whispered Word*, 6.

34. Suchocki, *The Whispered Word*, 10.

amplify the whispered word in their own life and in others' lives, for God is creating through that word in every moment. We are all responsible for responding to this present, empowering word. Every occasion, including the preaching event, is an occasion for becoming.

What is sin in a process relational world? Suchocki addresses this question in *God, Christ, Church*. Sin is an accumulated quality of relationship between entities that does violence to another rather than enriching life. Sin is individual and it is systemic in process theology, and the "degree to which individuals/societies reflect inclusive well-being is the degree to which they reflect the image of God" or fail to do so.[35] Sin is "a distortion of existence" that leads to assent to the demonic rather than assent to the whispered wisdom and creativity of God.[36] For Suchocki, the "power of the demonic can be seen in any situation in which the cumulative weight of the past denies a richness of well-being to anyone."[37] Process theologians such as Cobb would expand the "anyone" to "any living thing," noting the demonic egocentric nature of human treatment of the fragile environment and ecosystem of our planet. Preachers in the process family will at times preach concretely about distorted existence between men and women, white people and people of color, rich and poor, and also distortions about consumption of earth's resources, and stewardship as well.

How can life come from this death? What is the good news process preachers proclaim? That by listening to an ever-present God who feels the whole of this universe we can be empowered to transform demonic habits, and living into the power of the future to transform past patterns into a new way of being in relation to God, self, neighbor, and planet.

How does process preaching move the congregation toward God? Linear power is resisted in practice in favor of relational. Preaching is the art of persuasion toward feeling, not coercion. The use of the preacher's power and privilege impacts the theology of and in process preaching. She does not preach as a superior Christian. Rather, she preaches as one still growing and changing through an active spirituality.

Creativity, story, conversational delivery are all markers of process preaching. Emphasis is on relational connection within the web of creation in the content of the sermon, both when exegeting Scripture and the present moment of the particular congregation. Process preaching seeks not to win an argument with domination and manipulation, but to propose a story to dwell in, a window to peek through, a song to hum, a holy transformational

35. Suchocki, *God, Christ, Church*, 70.

36. Suchocki,. *God, Christ, Church*, 25.

37. Suchocki,. *God, Christ, Church*, 18.

moment through the sermon event for the congregation to enter into and encounter a living, speaking word for our own brief moment on earth.

But that word must act, for it is not merely an idea. Preaching as a process theologian about the "interdependence of life challenges us to consider the impact of our actions on the non-human and human future, as well as on our lives and the lives of our immediate companions."[38] The purpose of the sermon is to bring the congregation to feeling the lure of God toward beauty, goodness, and justice for all creatures great and small.

Finally, if God is the unity energizing and adventuring with all that lives, then no field of study, nor field of wildflowers, is out of the realm for process theologians to discover God and uncover where our actions do harm to God's body. The libraries of process preachers need not only be stocked with Christian theology study guides to be faithful and in tune with God's teaching. Fiction, poetry, music, trees, and microbiology are all avenues for sermonic illustration and exploration of God's will and way for us and with us as well.

Case Study: Text and Sermon
(Matthew 15:10–28)

The sermon is based on Matthew's account of Jesus' encounter with a Canaanite woman, Matt 15:10–28 (CEB). This is a complicated text for preachers with a high conception of Christology and of God's omnipotence and omniscience. But there is beauty and wisdom in its complexity.

Looking at the whole of Matthew's Gospel leading up to this point in chapter 15, the mission of Jesus and the twelve disciples was limited to Israel. This is explicit in the tenth chapter of Matthew, verse 5, when Jesus sent the disciples out with the following instructions: "Go nowhere among the Gentiles and enter no town of the Samaritans." Thus, the tension is heightened in this moment for the preacher tuned into land and identity in the time this event takes place. The pericope opens with Jesus and the disciples leaving Gennesaret (14:34) for Tyre and Sidon. Gennesaret is located beside the Sea of Galilee. This is familiar land for Jesus and his crew. This is the land of Israel, far from the gentiles and towns of the Samaritans.

Nonetheless, Jesus leads the twelve north, on the other side of the tracks, into gentile territory when they leave for Tyre and Sidon. This is the only time Jesus goes outside of the boundaries of Palestine. This would not be a quick trip by foot, nor do these towns seem to be the most direct route to any of the lost sheep of Israel. Tyre is roughly 50 miles from Gennesaret.

38. Epperly, *Process Theology*, 104.

And while this knowledge would not be embedded in my congregation in the United States, it certainly would be common to those first hearing Matthew's account, thus heightening the tension.

Further heightening of tension is Matthew's use of the word "Canaanite" to describe this woman's identity. The original audience would be triggered to remember a complicated history between Canaan and Israel. The term "Canaanite" draws out her "otherness" in ways more provocative than "Syrophoenician" would.[39] This highlights for me a purpose within the author's account that coincides with a broader aim to open up the gospel of Jesus Christ to more than the house of Israel. This thesis will come up in the sermon when I highlight the addition of the Canaanite prostitute Rahab in Mathew's genealogy of Jesus. For those reading closely, the woman then is described not only as "other" but also as Jesus' "kin."[40]

Ultimately, Matthew's Gospel closes with a Gentile mission mandate in 28:19–20. The journey to this radical openness is crucial to the sharing of the gospel. Encounters and adventures with holy others, including the unnamed Canaanite woman, prepared the way for Jesus' message to be shared with all. The disciples, even Jesus, at one point are not open to expanding the mission. But they change. The mission changes along with them. Matthew highlights this in his Gospel account and deems it good news. In this pericope, we see Jesus begin with an exclusivist posture and open into inclusion through the faith and courage of this foreign woman. She is rewarded with full standing as a child of God—as a woman and a gentile. But the mission of Jesus, from a process perspective, is also richly rewarded as it grows into diversity and complexity. The kin-dom of God is being realized.

I decided to focus on the text as an encounter that opened up an opportunity to increase the complexity and beauty of Jesus' ministry. I did not go so far in this sermon as to say that Jesus was speaking truly from his heart in ways counter to the welcome and kindness of God. Jesus is holding a mirror up to the narrowness of the disciples concerning gender and ethnicity. Why else would Jesus map out a journey into Tyre and Sidon? The woman is an agent of God's lure toward justice and beauty. Process theologians do not have one shared Christology. It is important to keep that in mind, but not important to bog the sermon down with these points when the aim is proposing a new way of hearing God's whispered word through Scripture and proclamation.

The sermon links structural evil born of fear of the other in the time of the of the pericope to structural evils born of this same fear in our present

39. Gullotta. "Among Dogs and Disciples," 331–32.
40. Gullotta, "Among Dogs and Disciples," 331.

time. Preached in the midst of pandemic and the Summer of George Floyd, Breonna Taylor, and too many other black and brown children of God (summer 2020), this sermon asks a predominately white church if we are so dull (unfeeling even more than unthinking) and weak of faith to see the full humanity of our siblings in the United States as they cry out for healing and justice from the church—the body of Christ in the world now.

One final word about the sermon—in this preaching event that challenges to feel the congregation I preached to was great. Like so many preachers in 2020, I was tasked to preach to my laptop, imagine the congregational response, and post the video into a worship service video edited for Sunday rather than preaching synchronously. According to Allen, "a sermon is not fully a sermon until it is spoken in the presence of the congregation."[41] But these are novel times and God is offering new ways for preachers in this pandemic time to preach the living word. In delivery then, the sermon recording had many spaces for pause in an effort to embody the conversational nature of preaching that is at the core of a process homiletic.

"Words That Defile. Hearts That Defy"

[The sermon begins by naming a feeling of discomfort that occurred upon initially reading the text.]

This is, no doubt, an uncomfortable text to come across. Not just about the washing of hands in a time of pandemic, no, it's the encounter between Jesus and this woman that is uncomfortable. We, or let me speak for myself, I believe that all lives matter to Jesus because he is the Son of a God who created all life. So I don't like this event. I don't like it when Jesus is silent in the face of her cries for her daughter.

[Now I turn to investigate this feeling and why it is stirred by this pericope.]

Why? Because my Jesus would get down on his knees with her, hold her, rush to heal a child in suffering. So no, I don't like it when she persists and begs for a crumb of mercy and Jesus seems to call her a dog while a group of men look on at this helpless woman.

But in context . . . I wonder if there is more to the story. After all, when we dig in to the text, it is Jesus who has led his disciples across a boundary as the stage is set for this encounter. Jesus goes out of the way to bring his cohort to the other side of the tracks in land that Jews should not venture to.

41. Allen, "Preaching as Conversation," 85.

Knowing that Jesus has led them across a boundary, into another's land, after calling the disciples dull for not grasping what really defiles a person and what actions and words define who a person follows, I wonder if Jesus is trying to break through to his cohort about the limits of their vision for what this new way of life could be, and for whom it applies. I wonder if Jesus is actually trying to break the gospel out of a boundary.

The Canaanite woman cries out, "Lord Son of David . . . " and in a flash, a lineage is lifted up from the very first passage of Matthew's Gospel. She knows who he is. And perhaps more than the disciples know . . . As Dr. Mitzi Smith points out, with her initial words, this woman may be claiming an ancestral relationship to Jesus. After all, three women in Jesus' genealogy are Canaanite women: Rahab, Tamar, and Ruth (Matt 1:3, 5).

Huh. Makes you wonder . . . did Matthew know, did I catch before that the "The anonymous woman's foremothers are Jesus' kinfolk?"[42] Boundaries broken from the start of the gospel.

[This move in the sermon intentionally steps to the side of the sermon flow to embody the ways in which Scripture reveals new insight over time. I anticipate others noticing this idea with me and invite them to ponder anew the narrow understanding of who Jesus' people are.]

I wonder if what we see here is Jesus preaching as public theater, beyond the pulpit, as he embodies the prejudice and silence of his disciples toward those outside of Israel. We are made to feel uncomfortable and they are made to feel uncomfortable as well and to question then the limitations placed on God's mission. Consider how this passage confronts us today.

After all, Jesus knew where he was: on her turf. He and his disciples were not journeying within their proper boundaries. Tyre and Sidon? That's the land of the gentile, the land of the Canaanites. Not the land of Israel, a nation that once obliterated Canaanites long ago under the rule of King David.

And yet, she greets him, "Lord, Son of David," without fear, full of faith.

[The confidence of the woman stands in juxtaposition to Peter's attempt at walking on water when fear overwhelms him. The Canaanite woman then will model the power of faith to bring about healing for Matthew's Gospel instead.]

A woman approaching a man at this time? Another purity boundary broken. A Canaanite to an Israelite? More rules broken.

42. Smith, "Commentary."

Hence the words of the disciples to Jesus, "Send her away; she keeps shouting out after us." Followed by Jesus leaning into the disciple's stereotypes and boundaries . . . his sermon in action for the onlookers begins: "This is what I meant about making false distinctions about things, including histories or cultural identities that defile."

But she is not a "thing." Jesus reveals this. She is a child of God. She is planted by God and is a part of the story being written through Jesus' time on earth. Her being as a woman and a Canaanite do not defile her nor define her. Her heart defies the boundaries and defends in action a God-given notion that all lives matter in the face of silence that perpetuates a notion that only Israelite lives matter.

Consider Possible Meanings for Today

But what does this riddle mean for us today? Are we so dull? Jesus asks his disciples this question not long after asking Peter why he has such little faith. Though she is not given a name, (lingering prejudice of the author of this Gospel against women), the presence of the Canaanite woman in the Gospel speaks volumes of the impact this exchange had on the spread of Jesus' message and mission. Not just for a special, select group defined by ethnicity, class, or gender, but for all.

Jesus voices the prejudices of the onlookers, and I believe she gets what he is up to, just as she gets the power of faith in his gospel love. They are the insiders—Jesus and this anonymous woman—luring the onlookers into a deeper, more complex, robust faith.

> [The lure to the complex, and the notion that complexity is God's will are both process ideas. In this moment, I see the next chapter of Christianity beginning through the testimony of this Canaanite woman who will faithfully embody the gospel for her unique context.]

She gets it, she knows, as Jesus knows, that in order for all lives to matter Jesus and all who call themselves followers of him must say and show this: that her life . . . her Canaanite. Gentile, female life . . . matters to God, to followers of Jesus.

We are known by our actions. We are known by our silence.

> [Process theology is not content with Christians holding right ideas about God. Rather, as Cobb, Allen, and Suchocki make clear, we are known as Christians when we consistently make choices to act in line with the Imago dei revealed in Jesus Christ.]

The good news here is that Jesus hears the cries of persistent mothers advocating for the well-being of their children and he heals them. The invitation is for the Body of Christ now on earth to go and do likewise: To have defiant hearts that beat in tune with mothers crying out for the healing of their children, and to resist silence when the cries make the church uncomfortable.

(singing) "Savior, Savior, Hear my humble cry! While on others thou are calling, do not pass me by!"[43]

> *[Because process preaching is influenced by the poet of the world, I prefer to weave in elements of song and art throughout the sermon in order to amplify feeling in the congregation. Preaching in the process family is not about winning an argument. Rather, process preaching aims at inviting the community into the palpable presence of God in the sermon, in the text, and in all those in need of our attention.]*

Assessment: Strengths and Limitations in This Theological Family

> When process theology is truly experienced—and lived—by its practitioners, it fulfills its promise as an experience-based, open-ended, and spiritually-transformational theological movement.[44]

A process hermeneutic for interpretation and a process theology of preaching cultivates a particular spirituality that is both inward and outward. What I mean by this is that in order to break free of accumulated habits that seem to determine our actions in the moment, one must discern the novel invitation to creative transformation by listening deeply for the whisper of God. God is always ever speaking and offering adventures to us, according to process theology. But because these offerings are relational in nature, they are not merely for the benefit of one. This means that at times we may feel pain as we wake from apathy into empathy for those who suffer in the world. God does not abandon us in suffering. The other pole of process-relational theology is that we are empowered to act in the world in ways that facilitate the good, beautiful, just ways of becoming that God wills for all of creation. This dipolar spirituality is a strength of process theology.

Another strength is the capacity to let go of abstracted notions of church, preaching, worship, evangelism, etc., that no longer "work" in the

---

43. This is the chorus from Fanny J. Crosby's 1868 hymn "Pass Me Not, O Gentle Savior"; the tune, from 1870, is by William Howard Doane (https://www.hymnary.org/).

44. Epperly, *Process Theology*, 156.

idiom and circumstance of the present moment. God is not locked in a static tradition. God is with us in the becoming of each person and institution. So when circumstances change (such as a pandemic that spreads rapidly in the ordinary space and practice of worship), the Body of Christ can lean into its spirituality and trust that God will present a novel way for the preacher to amplify the whispered word (such as Zoom, Facebook Live, Drive-In theaters, etc.)

The critique of Barthians about revelation coming from below challenges process preachers. What sort of God is worthy of worship if that God is not all-powerful and can be "deduced from observation" of human condition?[45] Isn't God better than, more beautiful and loving and just, than what we see in actuality? Process preaching may slip into sentimentality if the experience of human subjects, science, and art shape theological discourse without any conversation with the unique person and revelation of Jesus Christ. Depending upon your theological anthropology, a process hermeneutic may not fit if the fallen nature of human condition occludes the presence of God in humanity.

Process preaching is challenged by accounts of the miraculous in holy Scriptures as well. How does one preach about the relational God who collaborates and creates within the universe and its laws when manna falls from the sky? When rivers part for safe passage? When an earthquake releases prisoners? Or, perhaps most challenging of all, when Jesus cures someone of a lifelong disease?

In times of crisis, the God of process theology may come across as too weak to turn to for salvation. This is an echo of the Barthian, neo-orthodox critique of revelation from below. When everything below seems fallen, broken, and devoid of God, the temptation of the process preacher may be to slide into other-worldly theological systems of God sovereignty. When doctors say *only a miracle will remove this cancer*. When the environment turns hostile to life and scientists say *if only we could reset the system and remove the human destruction of our ecosystem*. When racism continues to rear its ugly head . . . wouldn't you want to pray to God to exorcise humanity of the demon of white supremacy or remove the carbon warming our planet or remove every single cancerous cell from a loved ones' body? How can process theology's God—without the power to coerce creation—save us from the time of trial?

A (I would be in error to claim it as 'the') process answer is that God is actively pursuing us with new possibilities for wholeness and justice in every moment and through every channel of life. Salvation may not come in any way we can yet imagine. Death is coming for us all just as it does for plants, butterflies, and pets. Nonetheless, process is not closed off to the mystery

45. Bowman, "God for Us," 13.

that lies beyond this one unique life. In the meantime, process preachers remind the congregation to pursue a sort of heaven on earth with their being and through their becoming. God needs partnership from us. And even when we are numb or apathetic to that invitation for partnership, God never withdraws from the world. God is steadfast, insistent and persistent with an aim for what could be if we would only listen.

Though he may not be a household name, Whitehead's process proposals are woven into a great many authors today who are more approachable: Diana Butler Bass and her horizontal grounded theology for example, which has taken off in evangelical and mainline areas,[46] and organic church models that focus on the local and particular rather than general institutional church programs abstracted from reality.[47] If one's preaching is drawn to relational, interdependent categories for God and the world, they just might be a process theologian without realizing it.

For Further Reading

Allen, Ronald J. "Preaching as Conversation among Proposals." In *Handbook of Process Theology,* edited by Jay McDaniel and Donna Bowman, 78–90. St. Louis: Chalice, 2006.

———. *You Never Step into the Same Pulpit Twice: A Process Approach to Preaching.* Eugene: Cascade, 2022.

Cobb, John B., Jr. *A Christian Natural Theology Based on the Thought of Alfred North Whitehead.* 2nd ed. Louisville: Westminster John Knox, 2007.

Coleman, Monica A., et al., eds. *Creating Women's Theology: A Movement Engaging Process Thought.* Eugene, OR: Pickwick Publications, 2011.

Epperly, Bruce. *Process Theology: A Guide for the Perplexed.* Guides for the Perplexed. London: T & T Clark, 2011.

McDaniel, Jay, and Donna Bowman, eds. *Handbook of Process Theology.* St. Louis: Chalice, 2006.

Suchocki, Marjorie. *The Whispered Word: A Theology of Preaching.* St. Louis: Chalice, 1999.

Whitehead, Alfred North. *Process and Reality.* Corrected ed. Edited by David Ray Griffin and Donald W. Sherburne. New York: Free Press, 1978.

Williamson, Clark M., and Ronald J. Allen. *Adventures of the Spirit.* Lanham, MD: University Press of America, 1997.

———. *A Credible and Timely Word.* St. Louis: Chalice 1991.

46. See Bass, *Grounded.*

47. See for example: Cole, *Organic Church*; Ingram, *Organic Student Ministry*; Simson, *The House Church Book*; Suttle, *Shrink.*

APPENDIX A

A Note on Mutual Critical Correlation

RONALD J. ALLEN

SEVERAL OF THE THEOLOGICAL families discussed in this volume grow out of the liberal and progressive spirits. Although these families differ in important respects, many share the goal of seeking to translate the ancient significance of a text into contemporary terms, an essentially liberal project. In the broad sense, such preachers seek to find ancient ideas, feelings, and behaviors that correspond with contemporary ones. This work is often broadly associated with notion of correlation.[1] At the same time, preachers in liberal and progressive movements recognize that texts sometimes contain theological ideas or moral prescriptions that are problematic for many in today's world. I think many such preachers have instincts for mutual critical correlation even if they are not specifically familiar with it.[2]

---

1. Paul Tillich proposes a specific method of correlation discussed in the next section of this appendix. However, many theologians and preachers who are not Tillichian nonetheless employ a correlative structure of relating yesterday and today that is not tied to Tillich's philosophical theology. The structure of correlations is similar, although the theological terms of the correlation differ from Tillich's. This appendix details Tillich's approach because Tracy developed mutual critical correlation in response to it.

2. This is especially true of theological families and preachers, such as the various liberation theologies, that practice versions of the hermeneutic of suspicion. This hermeneutic seeks to expose implicit assumptions of power and meaning that serve to keep people with less power in their place and to reinforce the positions of those who have power. For example, the household codes in the Gospels and Letters instruct women and slaves to be submissive to husbands and masters (e.g., Eph 5:22–6:9; Col 3:18–4:1). My colleague Helene Tallon Rusell asks, "Would a slave or a woman have written this? Who does a text benefit and how have such passages have been used (and misused) over the centuries?" (personal communication). A classic statement of the hermeneutic of suspicion is Ricoeur, *Freud and Philosophy*.

Mutual critical correlation is particularly associated with the work of David Tracy. Although Tracy seldom turns his gaze directly upon preaching, mutual critical correlation offers a vital theological method to preachers. This brief appendix introduces the background and development of the method of mutual critical correlation and draws attention to both a hermeneutics of retrieval identifying positive meaning from texts and a hermeneutics of suspicion which confronts theological, social and moral difficulties associated with texts themselves as well as with how the church and world have interpreted texts.

Tillich and the Theological Method of Correlation

A philosophical theologian, much of Tillich's thought is related to the theological family of existentialism.[3] Yet, while Tillich employed certain existentialist perspectives, as a theologian he argued that the meaning of life could not be sufficiently explained by philosophy alone but could only be grasped through theological commitment.[4] Tillich articulated the notion of correlation as a way of relating Christian tradition to the contemporary situation.

On the one hand, Tillich's work is in the spirit of the liberal theological family in the sense that he recognizes tensions in worldview and cultural forms between elements of older Christian tradition (especially the Bible) and elements in the contemporary setting. Tillich seeks to resolve those tensions by interpreting Christian faith in the worldviews and cultural forms of modernity.[5] Like others in the liberal theological tradition, Tillich accords authority to reason and science as well as to the Bible and traditional Christian doctrine.

On the other hand, Tillich joined the neo-orthodox theologians in concluding that modern theology of the late eighteenth, nineteenth, and early twentieth centuries went too far in accommodating Christian theology to culture.[6] However, Tillich was not truly neo-orthodox. Mainstream neo-orthodox theologians rejected the idea that the human family could learn

---

3. On existentialism, in this volume see Allen, "Preaching in the Existentialist Theological Family," 59–73.

4. Still valuable as a guide to Tillich's thought: Kegley, ed., *The Theology of Paul Tillich.*

5. The liberal project is described more fully in this volume in Greenhaw, "Preaching in the Liberal Theological Family," 14–27; and in Allen, "Preaching in the Existentialist Theological Family," 52–73.

6. On neo-orthodoxy, in this volume, see Allen, "Preaching in the Neo-Orthodox Theological Family," 27–46.

anything about God from culture or nature. For the neo-orthodox thinkers, the knowledge of God can come only from revelation; Christian faith and culture are in fundamental opposition. By contrast, Tillich believed that contemporary culture provided resources that could help the contemporary community make theological sense of God and of the situation of the world. Tillich's project is apologetic: he wanted to show that Christian faith can be a reasonable stance in the modern world.[7]

"The method of correlation explains the contents of the Christian faith through theological existential questions and theological answers in mutual interdependence."[8] Tillich expands on how the theologian and preacher make the correlation: "In using the method of correlation, systematic theology proceeds in the following way: it makes an analysis of the human situation out of which existential questions arise, and it demonstrates that the symbols used in the Christian message are the answer to these questions.[9]

The theologian and preacher aim to formulate the deep questions that the contemporary community is asking. To bring these questions into expression, the theologian pays attention to the issues that are raised by human "self-interpretation in all realms of culture," including philosophy, "poetry, drama, the novel, therapeutic psychology and sociology."[10] The theologian and preacher then turn to the Bible and Christian tradition for satisfactory answers to these questions.

This process is not something that occurs once and is then finished. The church needs to continue naming the deep questions and searching for appropriate answers because the questions can change from one time and place to another.

This correlation is not, however, simply a matter of asking a question and looking to the Bible verses for answers, as is commonplace in some Christian circles.[11] The questions Tillich has in mind are the most probing questions of life. The questions are "we ourselves." Indeed, "Being human means asking the questions of one's own being and living under the impact

7. On the apologetic motif in contemporary theology and preaching, see Allen and Allen, *The Sermon without End*, 2–12, 26–40.

8. Tillich, *Systematic Theology*, 1:60. Tillich discusses the method of correlation in his *Systematic Theology*, vol. 1, 59–66. Tillich contends that systematic theology (and presumably preaching) has always used a version of the method of correlation, "sometimes more, sometimes less, consciously." (60).

9. Tillich, *Systematic Theology*, 1:62.

10. Tillich, *Systematic Theology*, 1:63.

11. Helene Tallon Russell compares the practice of correlation to juggling. "It is true that one ring is in the air before the other one, but it is very brief, and once the process gets going, it is hard to tell which ring is which and which one is first" (personal communication).

of the answers given to this question." Not surprisingly, "Conversely, being human means receiving answers to the questions of one's own being and asking questions under the impact of the answers."[12] These "answers" seldom consist of one word but come from complex analyses of value and meaning.

The call of the preacher is to articulate the questions and to correlate responses from the Bible and Christian theology with them. While world views and cultural forms often differ between antiquity and today, *human experience* is often similar, though named in different language. An important part of the work of the preacher is to identify the experience described by the language of the Bible with a comparable experience of people today. To use a simple analogy, when translating a passage from one language to another, a translator renders the meaning of the first language into the meaning of the second language. Since languages are often structured differently and contain many idioms, the translator cannot move from one language to the other in a one-to-one fashion but must use structures and expressions in the new language that capture the intent of the original. In a similar way, the preacher translates the experience named by the language of the Bible to the cultural forms and language through which people have similar experience today. The preacher helps the congregation see how something from the Bible or Christian tradition can speak a meaningful, even life-shaping, word for today when its meaning is unpacked in today's terms and experience.

One of Tillich's most well-known correlations occurs in the sermon "You are Accepted."[13] Tillich correlates sin with separation, estrangement. To feel estranged is to experience sin. Sin is not simply an act but is a state of being. We can feel separated from ourselves, from other creatures and from God. Estrangement occurs in division between communities, in competing interests, and in the horrific suffering of human existence. God, however, responds to this separation with grace: a divine gift that brings into relationship those things that have been estranged. This act is truly a work of unmerited favor, something God does for us that we cannot do for ourselves. Grace points towards reconciliation, reunion, unification. In an elevated homiletical moment, Tillich relates grace to the experience of acceptance.

---

12. Tillich, *Systematic Theology*, 1:62.

13. The sermon appears in Tillich, *The Shaking of the Foundations*, 153–61. The scriptural text for its basis is Rom 5:20. "Moreover, the law entered that the offense might abound. But where sin abounded, grace did much more." However, while Tillich deals with the notions of sin and grace and refers to the life of the apostle Paul in the course of the sermon, Tillich does not engage the text in a serious exegetical way. He uses the text as a springboard towards the ideas of sin and grace. Tillich published three volumes of sermons in which the reader can easily see his theological method at work. In addition to *The Shaking of the Foundations*, note *The New Being* and *The Eternal Now*.

> Grace strikes us when we are in great pain and restlessness. It
> strikes us when we walk through the dark valley of a meaning-
> less and empty life. It strikes us when we feel that our separation
> is deeper than usual because we have violated another life, a life
> which we loved, or from which we were estranged. It strikes us
> when our disgust for our own being, our indifference, our weak-
> ness, our hostility and our lack of direction and composure have
> become intolerable to us. It strikes us when, year after year, the
> longed-for perfection of life does not appear, when the old com-
> pulsions reign within us as they have for decades, when despair
> destroys all joy and courage. Sometimes at that moment a wave
> of light breaks into our darkness, and it was as though a voice
> were saying: "You are accepted. *You are accepted,* accepted by
> that which is greater than you, and the name of which you do
> not know. Do not ask for that name now; perhaps you will find
> it later. Do not try to do anything now; perhaps later you will do
> much Do not seek for anything; do not perform anything; do not
> intend anything. *Simply accept the fact that you are accepted.*![14]

Tillich then points to some of the possible effects of grace. By accepting the
fact that we are accepted by God, the Ground of Being, we can have renewed
relationships with others. We can accept ourselves which, in turn, leads to
the capacity to accept others.

As noted, the content of Tillich's own theology flows in the stream of
existentialism refracted through Christian theology. However, a preacher
can employ the method of correlation with a different theological content.
For example, a preacher who belongs to a liberation theology family could
use a hermeneutic that correlates God's liberating work in the Bible with
situations in need of liberation today.

Tracy and the Theological Method
of Mutual Critical Correlation

In the method of correlation, the traffic of meaning usually moves one way
on the bridge over the gap between the ancient and contemporary communities.[15] Preachers typically assume that they can carry something from the
Bible across the bridge that should shape aspects of what we believe and do

---

14. Tillich, "You Are Accepted," 159–60.

15. A comprehensive guide to the work of David Tracy is Okey, *A Theology of Conversation.*

today.[16] Figuratively speaking, the preacher crosses the bridge and makes a delivery. By contrast, mutual critical correlation thinks of hermeneutics less as a one-way bridge and more as a conversation that takes place between then and now. Conversations often take on a life of their own. The outcomes of conversations cannot be predicted in advance; they may come to a powerful affirmation, raise important questions and leave them hanging in the air, or turn some participants away from something they had long assumed but never considered in the light of what came up in the conversation.[17]

Tracy sees two factors shaping the situation in the latter part of the twentieth century and the beginning of the twenty-first century, especially in Eurocentric cultures. One is the direct descendent of modernity: "the emergence of historical consciousness into Western consciousness and the resultant problematic status of all classical traditions and authorities," including, of course, the Bible and traditional Christian theology.[18] The second is the "new pluralism" in theology, that is, the appearance of a remarkable number of new and renewed approaches to doing theology. Henceforth, each way of doing theology must "attempt to articulate and defend an explicit method of inquiry and use that method to interpret the symbols and texts of our common life and of Christianity."[19]

In many contexts today, the preacher can no longer simply invoke long-standing authorities such as the Bible or church doctrine as the authority in and for the sermon. The preacher needs to think critically about the nature of authority itself, what functions authoritatively, why, and how to bring the congregation into the discussion.

As a way of moving forward in this complex ethos, Tracy explicitly seeks to go beyond Tillich. Indeed, Tracy contends, "Tillich's method of correlation is crucially inadequate," for it does not develop real criteria for "correlating the questions and the answers."[20]

16. The one-way movement of meaning is true even when the preacher begins with a contemporary question and then goes to the tradition for an answer. The preacher ordinarily assumes that the answer—the meaning that can inform current life—comes back across the bridge with the authority to inform what people believe and do today. The message travels only one way on the bridge. When it reaches the near side of the bridge, the preacher's task is to show how it applies to today.

17. For trenchant criticism of the bridge paradigm, see Farley, *Practicing Gospel*, 71–92.

18. Tracy, "Why Orthodoxy in a Personalist Age?," 81.

19. Tracy, *Blessed Rage for Order*, 3. At the time Tracy first made this observation, he identified five basic approaches to theology: orthodox, liberal, neo-orthodox, radical, and revisionist (*Blessed Rage for Order*, 22–32). Tracy expands especially on these discussions in *The Analogical Imagination*.

20. Tracy *Blessed Rage for Order*, 46. According to Tracy, "The fact is that Tillich's

Tracy unfolds his model for a genuine critical correlation, a "revision-ary theology," by naming five principles creating a theological method that intends to go beyond Tillich's model of correlation. (1) Tracy identifies two sources for this theological method: (a) Christian texts (both the Bible and traditions beyond the Bible) as well as (b) "common human experience and language."[21] The latter includes not only specifically religious experience but all experience. Indeed, for Tracy religious experience is not one kind of ex-perience alongside other kinds; rather, all experience has religious character.

(2) Tracy identifies broadly what happens in the revisionist approach to theology: the essential work is critical correlation between "the results of the investigation of the two sources of theology."[22] In the next steps, Tracy points to the crucial perspectives that theologians and preachers must bring to the investigation of the two sources.[23]

(3) The preacher and theologian explore "common human experience and language." That is, preacher and theologian study lived experience as people say they perceive that experience.[24] In a sense, the preacher conducts an exegesis of lived experience to identify how people perceive their experi-ence and how they interpret the world. The investigator tries to name what people apprehend as really happening to them, searching along the way for both the conscious and the unconscious dimensions of apprehension. It aims to describe the *Gestalt*. In crude terms, theologian and preacher want to clarify what people believe really happens.

method does not call for a critical correlation of the results of one's investigations of the "situation" and the "message." Rather, his method affirms the need for a correla-tion of the "questions" expressed in "the situation" with the "answers" provided by the Christian message. Such a correlation, in fact, is one between "questions" from one source and "answers" from the other" (Tracy, *Blessed Rage for Order*, 46). Nevertheless, a preacher can "accept Tillich's articulation of the need for a method of correlation but . . . cannot accept Tillich's own model for theology as one which actually correlates" (Tracy, *Blessed Rage for Order*, 46).

21. Tracy, *Blessed Rage for Order*, 43–45. By "common human experience," Tracy means more than sense data. He means "that immediate experience of the self-as-self which can be reflectively mediated though such disciplines as art, history, cultural analysis, scientific analysis, and philosophical analysis" (*Blessed Rage for Order*, 69).

22. Tracy, *Blessed Rage for Order*, 45–46.

23. It is important to note that in order to effect a correlation between the past and the present, the preacher must have a substantial theology, similar to the theo-logical families discussed in the two volumes of this work. Tracy has concentrated on theological *method* and has never written a systematic theology. His own theology is reminiscent of process thought, but he is not a doctrinaire process theologian. For his criticism of classical theology, see *Blessed Rage for Order*, 180).

24. Tracy, *Blessed Rage for Order*, 47–49. Tracy turns to phenomenology as a guide to exploring "common human experience and language." An accessible explanation off phenomenology is Smith, "Phenomenology."

(4) Preachers investigate sources emanating from the Christian tradition. The preacher turns to historical criticism, literary criticism, and
other methods to interpret the Bible and other texts. The investigation
aims to uncover the "religious referent" of the Scripture text or other theological statement from the past. To run the risk of oversimplification, the
preacher employs the methods of biblical exegesis to understand what text
proposed that people in the past believe.[25]

(5) With the results in hand from the studies of contemporary experience (and language) and Christian texts, theologians and preachers
can move forward with the correlation.[26] The preacher seeks to help the
congregation come to as much clarity as possible regarding what they can
believe and do, and why.

According to Tracy, preacher and theologian employ a "transcendental" mode of analysis when considering the relationship between Christian
text and contemporary experience. The word "transcendental" here refers
to the theologian or preacher transcending—insofar as possible—the assumptions and claims of both traditional Christian sources and our perceptions of experience and looking at the claims of each source in depth
and in light of how they compare and contrast with one another.[27] The
preacher and theologian should initially investigate the two sources independently and in such a way as to honor the integrity of each source. Tracy
calls for an in-depth understanding of the sources. Insofar as possible, a
preacher seeks to come to a responsible understanding of a source that
"overcomes the strangeness of another horizon not by empathizing with
the psychic state or cultural situation of the author but rather by understanding the basic vision of the author implied by the text and the mode-
of-being-in-the-world referred to by the text."[28]

Tracy elucidates the goal of this process. "The results of these investigations should be correlated to determine their significant similarities and
differences and their truth-value."[29] The preacher aims to help the congre-

25. Tracy, *Blessed Rage for Order*, 49–51.

26. Tracy, *Blessed Rage for Order*, 51–56.

27. Long ago, Rudolf Bultmann pointed out that exegesis without presuppositions
is impossible (Bultmann, "Is Exegesis without Presuppositions Possible?"). Because of
human finitude we can likely never fully name the assumptions that blind us to viewing
texts in fresh ways. That is an important reason for interpreting in community. Others
in the circle of conversation may help us see things we have difficulty seeing.

28. Tracy, *Blessed Rage for Order*, 78. Interpreters can never achieve pure, completely
objective perception of a text. Elements of the preacher's subjectivity are always present.
Preachers can become as aware and as critical as possible of such things, recognizing
the continuing importance of monitoring one's interpretive lenses.

29. Tracy, *Blessed Rage for Order*, 53.

gation articulate both what the Christian source(s) invited people in other times and places to believe and do, and what contemporary worldviews and experience invite people to believe and do today. Through the correlation, the preacher then helps the congregation sort out what they might (and might not) believe today.

Tracy suggests two criteria that the interpreting community can employ when considering the adequacy of each source. Preachers can use these criteria to evaluate the adequacy of particular possibilities that come forward in mutual critical correlation. Each of these criteria can be formulated as a question that the community can ask of a theological source and of the experience of the community in the world.

1. Appropriateness to "the Christian understanding of existence."[30] To be acceptable in the Christian house, a claim must be consistent with the core of Christian conviction. To be sure this is not a simple criterion in that each theological family (and, often, groups and individuals within a family) sets out their own core convictions with nuances distinctive to each family. In light of the preacher's own theological family, where appropriate, the preacher can ask of each source and of each possible correlation, "Is what this source asks us to believe appropriate to the core of my Christian conviction?"

2. Consistent with our experience. "There must be a necessary and a sufficient ground in our common experience for such claims."[31] That is, the theological formulation that comes out of the correlation needs to be true to what we can actually expect to happen in the world. A preacher can ask, "Is the worldview and experience this source asks us to believe adequate to the way in which we the world and our experience today?"[32]

30. Tracy, *Blessed Rage for Order*, 72–73.

31. Tracy, *Blessed Rage for Order*, 55.

32. Clark M. Williamson reformulated these criteria as (1) Appropriateness to the gospel, (2) Intelligibility, and (3) Moral plausibility. In this reformulation, appropriateness to the gospel and intelligibility function in the same way as above. For Williamson, the gospel is the news of God's unconditional love for each and all and God's will for justice (the social form of love) for each and all. Moral plausibility refers to the moral treatment of all involved in a text or situation. The criterion of moral plausibility is implied in the criterion of appropriateness to the gospel but is expressed separately in the current fractious age in order to call attention to the concern of Christian faith for social relationships to manifest justice (per above: the social form of love). I join Williamson in this structure of formulation, although since the word "gospel" is often interpreted in ways that are christologically limited, I now express the first criterion as "appropriateness to our deepest convictions about God and God's purposes of unrelenting love and justice for all entities" See Williamson and Allen, *A Credible and Timely*

Tracy consequently summarizes, "Any such claims must have a coherence both internally and with other essential categories of our knowledge and belief."[33]

The theologian or preacher applies the criteria above to both sources: the Christian text and the experience of the community. In the course of engaging in the critical correlation, "the meanings discovered as adequate to our common human experience must be compared to the meanings disclosed as appropriate to the Christian tradition in order to discover how similar, different, or identical the former meanings are in relationship to the latter."[34] The results of a critical correlation usually result in one of four possible relationships between the text and contemporary community.

- The text may be appropriate to a Christian understanding of existence and assume an experience consistent with the community's experience. In this case, the preacher can directly help the congregation explore how the text can enrich their life and witness.

- The text be may partly appropriate to a Christian understanding of existence and consistent with the experience of the contemporary community. In this case, the preacher needs to help the congregation sort through which aspects of the text to embrace and which aspects to leave behind, and, perhaps to help the congregation identify additional elements to leave on the shelf for further consideration.

- The text may be appropriate to a Christian understanding of existence, but the experience assumed by the text may be inconsistent with the experience of the contemporary community. In this case, the preacher needs to help the congregation sort through which aspects of the experience assumed by the text to embrace and which parts to leave behind. The preacher may also need to help the congregation articulate clearly how to bring the Christian understanding of the text to life in contemporary experience

- The text may be mostly or altogether inappropriate to a Christian understanding of existence and assume an experience that is inconsistent with that of the contemporary community. In this case, the preacher needs to help the congregation identify the distance between the text and today, and the preacher needs to help the congregation move towards what it can believe. Of course, different theological families can come to different conclusion regarding what

---

Word, 71–135.

33. Tracy, *Blessed Rage for Order*, 55.

34. Tracy, *Blessed Rage for Order*, 79.

they believe. These different conclusions sometimes to beyond disagreement to active conflict.

The process of mutual correlation may not yield a simple statement of the utterly confident truthfulness or falsehood of the perspective of either source or of a third perspective that results from engaging the two sources in critical correlation. A transcendental methodology includes the constant awareness of the relativity of one's own perceptions, awareness that can change in response to fresh data. In such a methodology, preachers should be constantly aware that their own processes of thought and feeling are always involved in the course of making an interpretation.

The process seeks to articulate a point of view that is "adequate" to both the heart of the tradition and the lived experience of the community.[35] To be adequate is to maintain continuity with key aspects of Christian identity and to be believable with respect to contemporary sensibility. The adequate interpretation is not completely comprehensive, covering every detail, but gives the interpreting community "enough to go on" (my expression) until more perspective becomes available.

The practical work of making the critical correlation takes place through conversation among the Christian source, experience as viewed then and now, the preacher and the preacher's contemporary theological viewpoint.[36]

> Conversation in its primary form is an exploration of possibilities in the search for truth. In following the track of any question, we must allow for difference and otherness. At the same time, as the question takes over, we notice that to attend to the other as other, the different as different, is also to understand the different *as* possible.[37]

35. Tracy typically applies the word "adequate" to the source "common human understanding," but it can also describe the source "Christian texts" and the perspective of the eventual mutual critical correlation. A text can be relatively adequate (or inadequate) to the core of Christian conviction, and a statement of critical correlation can likewise be relatively adequate (or inadequate). D. W. Winnicott says that a mother needs to be adequate, not perfect. I think the same is true of theology (Winnicott, e.g., *Playing and Reality*, 10).

36. Mutual critical correlation is a stream of thought contributing to the movement in preaching that interprets preaching as conversation. See Rose, *Sharing the Word*; Allen, *The Homiletic of All Believers*; and Allen and Allen, *The Sermon without End*. I developed a textbook on preaching with a conversational approach at its heart but did not follow the conversational implications into the whole of preaching; see Allen, *Interpreting the Gospel*. For understanding conversation as paradigmatic many aspects of the life of the church see Allen et al., *Under the Oak Tree*.

37. Tracy, *Plurality and Ambiguity*, 20.

The preacher encourages the congregation to consider the possibilities offered by the text and by experience and to find points of similarity and points of difference. On the one hand, "the good interpreter is willing to put [his or her] preunderstanding at risk by allow the classic [e.g., a text] to question the interpreter's present expectations and standards."[38] In this role, the Christian source might offer the preacher enriching ways of viewing the world. On the other hand, the good interpreter also puts questions to the text to ascertain the degree to which text is appropriate to the preacher's core beliefs about God and the preacher's understanding of experience.

Tracy points out that conversation comes "with some hard rules."

> Say only what you mean; say it as accurately as you can; listen to and respect what the other says, however different or other; be willing to correct or defend your opinions if challenged by the conversation partner; be willing to argue, if necessary, to confront if demanded, to endure necessary conflict, to change your mind if the evidence suggests it.[39]

While these rules are easy to apply in give-and-take with another person, they can also apply in conversation with a text, as long as interpreters are willing to listen to the text as other by doing their best not to impose their perspectives on the text.

The preacher identifies what a biblical text (or other expression) asked people to believe about God, the world, and the human response in its own time and place. The preacher then brings that perspective into the contemporary setting and explores the degree to which the perspective of the text offers the contemporary community the opportunity to enrich its life by embracing the text (or aspects of it). and/or the degree to which the text (or aspects of it) is not believable in light of the ways in which experience of the contemporary community and its world view. The "critical" dimension of the correlation does not simply assume that the text puts forward a word that *should* shape the life of the community but examines the text for elements of worldview, theological affirmation, or ethical guidance that may run against the grain of the preacher's deepest convictions about God or what happens in experience and in the world.

The conversation does not settle the issue. The result of the conversation is a road marker. It identifies how far the participants have come. The result of the conversation is thus the beginning point for a new conversation.[40]

38. Tracy, *Plurality and Ambiguity*, 16.

39. Tracy, *Plurality and Ambiguity*, 1–16.

40. Tracy notes that conversations can be ambiguous and can even reach erroneous conclusions. Grant and Tracy, *A Short History of the Interpretation of the Bible*, 160–64.

Preparing to preach from Mark 13:1–37 provides an illustration of the conversational approach to mutual critical correlation using process theology as the contemporary theological voice.[41] Consideration of the Christian source, the text, begins with the recognition that it is apocalyptic, that is, a text that expects God to destroy the present, broken world and replace it with a new one, the realm of God, an age of love, peace, justice, and abundance. For Mark, Jesus is God's agent in the transformation from the old to the new. Mark 13 believes that the Roman destruction of the temple is a sign that the apocalyptic return of Jesus is to occur soon. This passage is part of Mark's larger project which is to offer the congregation hope and to encourage the congregation a hopeful reason it should continue to witness to the coming of the realm even in the midst of the social chaos following the destruction of the temple.

When thinking about the relationship of the text to my perception (and that of many of my contemporaries) of the experience of the contemporary world, I note a great distance from aspects of the world view of the text as well as aspects of its theology. We no longer share the apocalyptic view of a three-story universe in which it would be possible for God to come from "up there" on the kind of mission described in apocalyptic literature. Moreover, the core of my theology is a God who loves unrelentingly and wills everlastingly for people to live in relationships of love (justice). Such a God would not actively initiate the suffering associated with the transition of the ages in apocalyptic literature.

Nevertheless, distinguishing between the surface meaning of the text (the expectation of an imminent apocalypse) and the deeper meaning of the text helps bring a dimension of retrieval into view.[42] The text makes a deep theological point that is not imprisoned by apocalypticism. That point is that God is dissatisfied with the way the world is in its present attitudes and behaviors and is resolved to offer the world opportunities to manifest more of the qualities associated with the realm of God—love, peace, justice, and abundance (to name just four).

Moreover, I share a conviction with some other Christians that God is ever present in the world, inviting human beings and other entities in the world to live together in the manner of the realm of God. This way of thinking is not a version of the old but mistaken adage that "the world gets better and better every day." Human beings and other parts of creation sometimes turn away from God's invitations and cling, instead, to familiar but broken

41. On process theology, see in this volume, Sigmon, "Preaching in the Process Theological Family," 274–290.

42. On distinguishing between surface and deeper meanings, see Bultmann, "The New Testament and Mythology."

patterns of relationship. The revised perspective does not offer the satisfaction of a singular moment of transformation from the broken present to the restored realm, but it does offer the hope that God never gives up but, in every situation, invites the community towards qualities of love, peace, justice, and abundance that are possible in the circumstance at hand. There never is a moment when God is not present and actively inviting all members of a community towards the realm.

With respect to its perspective on Christian existence, then, the text is partly inappropriate but partly appropriate. With respect to its perspective on common experience, the same is true.

A major strength of the method of mutual critical correlation is that it offers preacher and congregation the opportunity to articulate a faith that they can truly believe. It articulates a faith that is genuinely at home in a contemporary world view, and it faces the most difficult theological questions arising from biblical texts and from the tradition. Another strength is that it can take account of changing perceptions while maintaining essential core Christian identity. At the same time, preachers and congregations can easily misuse this approach and embody the criticism with which liberals are sometimes charged: creating a God and faith that is little more than a human being "writ large."

APPENDIX B

Bringing Historical and Contemporary Theological Families into Dialogue

	Orthodox	Roman Catholic	Lutheran	Reformed	Anabaptistt	Anglican/Episcopal
Evangelical						
Liberal						
Neo-Orthodox						
Postliberal						
Existential						
Radical Orthodox						
Deconstructioonist						
Feminist						
Black Liberation						
Womanist						
Latinx Liberation						
Mujuerista						
Asian American						
Asian American Feminist						
Queer (LGBTQAI+)						
Indigenous						
Postcolonial						
Process						

This table points to possible ways in which preachers relate historical and contemporary theological families. A preacher with roots in a historical theological family might interpret that family in conversation with a contemporary theological family, and vice versa.

Wesleyan	Baptist	African American	Friends	Stone-Campbell	Pentcostal	
						Evangelical
						Liberal
						Neo-Orthodox
						Postliberal
						Existential
						Radical Orthodox
						Deconstructioonist
						Feminist
						Black Liberation
						Womanist
						Latinx Liberation
						Mujuerista
						Asian American
						Asian American Feminist
						Queer (LGBTQAI+)
						Indigenous
						Postcolonial
						Process

Bibliography

Achebe, Chinua. *The African Trilogy: "Things Fall Apart"; "No Longer at Ease"; and "Arrow of God."* Everyman's Library 237. New York: Knopf, 2010.

Achtemeier, Elizabeth. *The Old Testament and the Proclamation of the Gospel.* Philadelphia: Westminster, 1973.

Ahenakew, Alice. *Âh-âyîtaw isi ê-kî-kiskêyihtahkik maskihkiy = They Knew Both Sides of Medicine: Cree Tales of Curing and Cursing.* Told by Alice Ahenakew. Edited, translated and with a glossary by H. C. Wolfart and Freda Ahenakew. Publications of the Algonquian Text Society. Winnipeg: University of Manitoba Press, 2000.

Alcántara, Jared. *The Practices of Christian Preaching.* Grand Rapids: Baker Academic, 2019.

Aldred, Raymond. "Us Talking to Us." *Journal of North American Institute for Indigenous Theological Studies* 1 (2003) 70–94.

Allen, Donna E. *Toward a Womanist Homiletic: Katie Cannon, Alice Walker, and Emancipatory Proclamation.* Martin Luther King, Jr. Memorial Studies in Religion, Culture, and Social Development 13. New York: Lang, 2013.

Allen, O. Wesley, Jr. *The Homiletic of All Believers: A Conversational Approach.* Louisville: Westminster John Knox, 2005.

———. *Preaching and the Human Condition.* Nashville: Abingdon, 2016.

Allen, O. Wesley, Jr., and Ronald J. Allen. *The Sermon without End: A Conversational Approach to Preaching.* Nashville: Abingdon, 2015.

Allen, Ronald J. *Preaching and the Other: Studies of Postmodern Insights.* St. Louis: Chalice, 2009.

———. "Preaching as Conversation among Proposals." In *Handbook of Process Theology,* edited by Jay McDaniel and Donna Bowman, 78–90. St. Louis: Chalice, 2006.

———. "Preaching as Mutual Critical Correlation through Conversation." In *Purposes of Preaching,* edited by Jana Childers, 1–22. St. Louis: Chalice, 2004.

Allen, Ronald J., et al., eds. *Preaching God's Transforming Justice: A Lectionary Commentary for Year B, Featuring 22 New Holy Days for Justice.* Louisville: Westminster John Knox, 2011.

———, eds. *Under the Oak Tree: The Church as Community of Conversation in a Conflicted and Pluralistic World.* Eugene, OR: Cascade Books, 2013.

Alves, Rubem A. *A Theology of Human Hope.* St. Meinrad, IN: Abbey 1972.

Ambrosino, Brandon. "Jesus' Radical Politics." *Boston Globe,* April 1, 2015. https://www.bostonglobe.com/opinion/2015/04/01/jesus-radical-politics/txdjkQSMn3BWPBgciEbgZP/story.html.

Anderson, Herbert, and Edward Foley. *Mighty Stories, Dangerous Rituals: Weaving Together the Human and the Divine*. Minneapolis: Fortress, 2019.

Andrews, Dale. "Response to Narrative Renewed by Eugene Lowry." In *The Renewed Homiletic*, edited by O. Wesley Allen, Jr. 96–100. Minneapolis: Fortress, 2010.

Appiah-Kubi, Kofi, and Sergio Torres, eds. *African Theology En Route: Papers from the Pan African Conference of Third World Theologians, December 17-23, 1977, Accra, Ghana*. Maryknoll, NY: Orbis, 1979.

Aquinas Thomas. *Summa Theologica*. Translated by Fathers of the English Dominican Province. 2nd ed. London: Burns Oates and Washbourne, 1941.

Aquino, Maria Pilar, et al., eds. *A Reader in Latina Feminist Theology: Religion and Justice*. Austin: University of Texas Press, 2002.

Archibald, Jo-Ann. *Indigenous Storywork: Educating the Heart, Mind, Body, and Spirit*. Vancouver, University of British Columbia Press, 2008.

Ashcroft, Bill et al., eds. *Key Concepts in Post-colonial Studies*. Key Concepts Series. New York: Routledge, 1998.

———. "Liminality." In *Key Concepts in Post-colonial Studies*, 130–33. Key Concepts Series. New York: Routledge, 1998.

———. "Place." In *Key Concepts in Post-colonial Studies*, 177–83. Key Concepts Series. New York: Routledge, 1998.

"Asian Americans." https://www.pbs.org/show/asian-americans/.

Asian Women United of California. *Making Waves: An Anthology of Writings By and About Asian American Women*. Boston: Beacon: 1989.

Askew, Emily, and O. Wesley Allen Jr. *Beyond Heterosexism in the Pulpit*. Eugene, OR: Cascade Books, 2015.

Augustine of Hippo. *Sermons (20-50) on the Old Testament*. Translated with notes by Edmund Hill, OP. Edited by John E. Rotelle, OA. Sermons 2. Works of Saint Augustine: A Translation for the 21st Century. New York: New City, 1990.

Bain, Paul G., et al., eds. *Humanness and Dehumanization*. New York: Taylor & Francis, 2014.

Baker-Fletcher, Karen. "Anna Julia Cooper and Sojourner Truth: Two Nineteenth Century Black Feminist Interpreters of Scripture." In *Searching the Scriptures: A Feminist Introduction*, edited by Elisabeth Schüssler Fiorenza, 1:41–51. New York: Crossroad, 1993.

———. "'Soprano Obligato:' The Voices of Black Women and American Conflict in the Thought of Anna Julia Cooper." In *A Troubling in My Soul: Womanist Perspectives on Evil and Suffering*, edited by Emilie M. Towne, 172–83. The Bishop Henry McNeal Turner Studies in North American Black Religion 8. Maryknoll, NY: Orbis, 1993.

Barth, Karl "Biblical Insights, Questions, and Vistas." In *The Word of God and the Word of Man*. Translated by Douglas Horton, 51–96. New York: Harper & Row, 1957.

———. *Church Dogmatics*. 13 vols. Translated by Geoffrey W. Bromiley. Edinburgh: T. & T. Clark, 1932–1967.

———. *Deliverance to the Captives*. Translated by Marguerite Wieser. 1978. Reprint, Eugene, OR: Wipf & Stock, 2010.

———. *Dogmatics in Outline*. Translated by G. T. Thompson. New York: Philosophical Library, 1949.

———. *The Epistle to the Romans*. Translated by Edwyn C. Hoskins. New York: Oxford University Press, 1968.

————. *Homiletics*. Translated by Geoffrey W. Bromiley and Donald E. Daniels. Louisville: Westminster John Knox, 1991.

————. "The Humanity of God." In *The Humanity of God*, 35–65. Translated by John Newman Thomas. Atlanta: John Knox, 1960.

————. *The Preaching of the Gospel*. Translated by B. E. Hooke. Philadelphia: Westminster, 1963.

————. "The Strange New World within the Bible." In *The Word of God and the Word of Man*, 28–50. Translated by Douglas Horton. New York: Harper & Row, 1957.

————. "The Word of God and the Task of the Ministry." In *The Word of God and the Word of Man*, 183–217. Translated by Douglas Horton. New York: Harper & Row, 1957.

Barth, Karl, and Eduard Thurneysen. *God's Search for Man: Sermons*. Translated by G. W. Richards et al. New York: Round Table, 1935.

Bass, Diana Butler. *Grounded: Finding God in the World. A Spiritual Revolution*. San Francisco: HarperOne, 2017.

Bebbington, D. W. *The Dominance of Evangelicalism: The Age of Spurgeon and Moody*. A History of Evangelicalism 3. Downers Grove, IL: InterVarsity, 2005.

————. *Evangelicalism in Modern Britain: A History from the 1730s to the 1890s*. London: Routledge, 1989.

Bentley, William H. "Bible Believers in the Black Community." *The Evangelicals: What They Believe, Who They Are, Where They Are Changing*, edited by David F. Wells and John D. Woodbridge, 108–21. Nashville: Abingdon, 1975.

Bhabha, Homi K. *The Location of Culture*. London: Routledge, 1994.

Bialik, Hayim Nahman, and Yehoshua Hana Ravnitzky, eds. *The Book of Legends: Legends from the Talmud and Midrash = Sefer Ha-Aggadah*. Translated by William Gordon Braude. New York: Schocken, 1992.

Birch, Charles, and John B. Cobb Jr. *The Liberation of Life: From the Cell to the Community*. Cambridge: Cambridge University Press, 1981.

Black Elk, and Joseph Epes Brown. *The Sacred Pipe: Black Elk's Account of the Seven Rites of the Oglala Sioux*. Penguin Metaphysical Library. Baltimore: Penguin, 1971.

Blanchard, Richard. "Fill My Cup, Lord." In *The United Methodist Hymnal*, hymn 641. Nashville: Abingdon, 1989.

Boers, Hendrikus. "Gabler, Johann Philip." In *Dictionary of Biblical Interpretation*, edited by John H. Hayes, 1:425–26. 2 vols. Nashville: Abingdon, 1999.

Boff, Leonardo. "Como Pregar a Cruz Hoje numa Sociedade de Crucificados?" *Revista Eclesiástica Brasileira* 44 (1984) 58–72.

————. *Passion of Christ, Passion of the World*. Translated by Robert R. Barr. Maryknoll, NY: Orbis, 2011.

————. *Teología desde el lugar del pobre*. Translated by Jesús García-Abril. Santander, Spain: Sal Terrae, 1986.

Boring, M. Eugene, and Fred B. Craddock. *The People's New Testament Commentary*. Louisville: Westminster John Knox, 2004.

Bowman, Donna. "God for Us: A Process View of the Divine-Human Relationship." In *Handbook of Process Theology*, edited by Jay McDaniel and Donna Bowman. 11–24. St. Louis: Chalice, 2006.

Brekus, Catherine A. *Strangers & Pilgrims: Female Preaching in America, 1740–1845*. Gender & American Culture. Chapel Hill: University of North Carolina Press, 1998.

Brock, Rita Nakashima. "Cooking without Recipes: Interstitial Integrity." In *Off the Menu: Asian and Asian North American Women's Religion and Theology*, edited by Rita Nakashima Brock et al., 125–43. Louisville: Westminster John Knox, 2007.

Brock, Rita Nakashima, et al., eds. *Off the Menu: Asian and Asian North American Women's Religion and Theology*. Louisville: Westminster John Knox, 2007.

Brown, James, performer, with backing accompaniment. "It's a Man's Man's World." Track 5 on *The Best of James Brown*. Polydor 314 547 719-2. 1999. CD. Originally released in 1966.

Brown, Sally. *Cross Talk: Preaching Redemption Here and Now*. Louisville: Westminster John Knox, 2008.

Brown, Teresa L. Fry. "Prophetic Truth-Telling in a Season of Fatigue and Fragmentation." In *Questions Preachers Ask: Essays in Honor of Thomas G. Long*, edited by Scott Black Johnston et al., 126–39. Louisville: Westminster John Knox, 2016.

———. "A Womanist Model for Proclamation of the Good News." *African American Lectionary*. 11pp. http://www.theafricanamericanlectionary.org/pdf/preaching/WomanistPreaching_TeresaBrown.pdf/.

Brueggemann, Walter. *The Practice of Prophetic Imagination: Preaching an Emancipating Word*. Minneapolis: Fortress, 2012.

———. *The Prophetic Imagination*. 2nd ed. Minneapolis: Fortress, 2001.

Brunner, Emil, and Karl Barth. *Natural Theology Comprising "Nature and Grace" by Professor Dr. Emil Brunner and the Reply No! by Dr. Karl Barth*. Translated by Peter Fraenkel. 1946. Reprint, Eugene, OR: Wipf & Stock, 2002.

Buechner, Frederick. *Preaching the Story Telling Secrets: A Memoir*. New York: Harper-Collins, 1991.

Bultmann, Rudolf. "Is Exegesis without Presuppositions Possible?" In *The New Testament and Mythology and Other Basic Writings*. Translated and edited by Schubert M. Ogden, 145–54. Philadelphia: Fortress, 1984.

———. *Jesus Christ and Mythology*. New York: Scribner, 1958.

———. "The New Testament and Mythology." In *The New Testament and Mythology and Other Basic Writings*. Translated and edited by Schubert M. Ogden, 1–44. Philadelphia: Fortress, 1984.

———. *This World and Beyond: Marburg Sermons*. Translated by Harold Knight. New York: Scribner, 1960.

Burrell, David. "Radical Orthodoxy: An Appreciation." *Philosophy and Theology* 16 (2004) 73–76.

Butler, Octavia E. *Parable of the Sower*. New York: Grand Central, 2019.

Buttrick, David G. Foreword to *Homiletics*, by Karl Barth. Translated by Geoffrey W. Bromiley and Donald E. Daniels, 7–12. Louisville: Westminster John Knox, 1991.

———. *Homiletic: Moves and Structures*. Philadelphia: Fortress, 1987.

Campbell-Reed, Eileen. "State of the Clergywomen in the U.S.A.: A Statistical Update. October 2018." Posted on Campbell-Reed's website: www.eileencampbellreed.org/.

Campbell, Charles L. *Preaching Jesus: New Directions for Homiletics in Hans Frei's Postliberal Theology*. 1997. Reprint, Eugene, OR: Wipf & Stock, 2005.

Cannon, Katie G. *Black Womanist Ethics*. American Academy of Religion Acad-emy Series 60. Atlanta: Scholars, 1988.

———. *Katie's Canon: Womanism and the Soul of the Black Community*. New York: Continuum, 1996.

———. "Structured Academic Amnesia: As If This Womanist Story Never Happened." In *Deeper Shades of Purple: Womanism in Religion and Society*, edited by Stacy M. Floyd-Thomas, 17–38. Religion, Race, and Ethnicity. New York: New York University Press, 2006.

Caputo, John D. *Cross and Cosmos: A Theology of Difficult Glory*. Indiana Series in the Philosophy of Religion. Bloomington: Indiana University Press, 2020.

———. *Deconstruction In a Nutshell: A Conversation with Jacques Derrida*. Perspectives in Continental Philosophy. New York: Fordham University Press, 1997.

———. *In Search of Radical Theology: Expositions, Explorations, Exhortations*. Perspectives in Continental Philosophy. New York: Fordham University Press, 2020.

———. "Jacques Derrida (1930–2004)." *Journal for Cultural and Religious Theory* 6 (2004) 6–9. https://jcrt.org/archives/06.1/caputo.pdf.

———. *On Religion*. 2nd ed. New York: Routledge, 2019.

———. *The Insistence of God: A Theology of Perhaps*. Indiana Series in the Philosophy of Religion. Bloomington: Indiana University Press, 2013.

———. "The Return of Anti-Religion: From Radical Atheism to Radical Theology." *Journal for Religious and Cultural Theory* 11 (2011) 22–35.

———. *The Weakness of God: A Theology of the Event*. Indiana Series in the Philosophy of Religion. Bloomington: Indiana University Press, 2006.

———. *What Would Jesus Deconstruct? The Good News of Postmodernity for the Church*. The Church and Postmodern Culture. Grand Rapids: Baker Academic, 2007.

Caputo, John D., and Gianni Vattimo. *After the Death of God*. New York: Columbia University Press, 2007.

Caputo, John D., and Michael J. Scanlon, eds. *God, the Gift, and Postmodernism*. Indiana Series in the Philosophy of Religion. Bloomington: Indiana University Press, 1999.

Carpenter, Delores C. *A Time for Honor: A Portrait of African American Clergywomen*. St. Louis: Chalice, 2001.

Chapell, Bryan. *Christ-Centered Preaching: Redeeming the Expository Sermon*. 3rd ed. Grand Rapids: Baker Academic, 2018.

Cheng, Patrick S. *Radical Love: An Introduction to Queer Theology*. New York: Seabury, 2011.

———. *Rainbow Theology: Bridging Race, Sexuality, and Spirit*. New York: Seabury, 2013.

Chesterton, G. K. *Orthodoxy*. London: Bodley Head, 1957.

Childers, Jana, ed. *Birthing the Sermon: Women Preachers on the Creative Process*. St. Louis: Chalice, 2001.

Childs, Brevard S. *Biblical Theology in Crisis*. Philadelphia: Westminster, 1970.

Choi, Hee An. *A Postcolonial Leadership: Asian Immigrant Christian Leadership and Its Challenges*. Albany: State University of New York Press, 2020.

Chung, Hyun Kyung. *Struggle to Be the Sun Again: Introducing Asian Women's Theology*. Maryknoll, NY: Orbis, 1990.

Clayton, Philip D. *God and Contemporary Science*. Edinburgh Studies in Constructive Theology 79. Cambridge: International Society for Science and Religion, 2007.

Cobb, John B., Jr. *A Christian Natural Theology Based on the Thought of Alfred North Whitehead*. 2nd ed. Louisville: Westminster John Knox, 2007.

Cole, Neil. *Organic Church: Growing Faith Where Life Happens*. San Francisco: Jossey-Bass, 2005.

Coleman, Monica A. *Bipolar Faith: A Black Woman's Journey with Depression and Faith.* Minneapolis: Fortress, 2016.

———. *Making a Way out of No Way: A Womanist Theology.* Minneapolis: Fortress, 2009.

———, ed. *Ain't I a Womanist, Too? Third-Wave Womanist Religious Thought.* Minneapolis: Fortress, 2013.

Coleman, Monica A., Nancy R. Howell, and Helene Tallon Russell, eds. *Creating Women's Theology: A Movement Engaging Process Thought.* Eugene, OR: Pickwick Publications, 2011.

Cone, James H. *The Cross and the Lynching Tree.* Maryknoll, NY: Orbis, 2013.

Consultation on Common Texts. *Revised Common Lectionary.* Nashville: Abingdon, 1992.

Copeland, M. Shawn, "A Thinking Margin: The Womanist Movement as Cognitive Critical Praxis." In *Deeper Shades of Purple: Womanism in Religion and Society,* edited by Stacy M. Thomas. Religion, Race, and Ethnicity. 226–35. New York: New York University Press, 2006.

Costas, Orlando, ed. *Predicación evangélica y Teología Hispana.* San Diego: Publicaciones de Las Américas, 1982.

Couture, Pamela, et al., eds. *Complex Identities in a Shifting World: Practical Theological Perspectives.* International Practical Theology 17. Zurich: Lit, 2015.

Craddock, Fred B. *Tell It.* (DVD). General Assembly of the Christian Church (Disciples of Christ), 2011.

———. *As One without Authority: Revised and with New Sermons.* 4th ed. St. Louis: Chalice, 2001.

Crawford, A. Elaine Brown. *Hope in the Holler: A Womanist Theology.* Louisville: Westminster John Knox, 2002.

Crawford, Evans E., with Thomas H. Troeger. *The Hum: Call and Response in African American Preaching.* Nashville: Abingdon, 1995.

Crites, Stephen. "Narrative Quality of Experience." *Journal of the American Academy of Religion* 39 (1971) 291–311.

Davison, Andrew. *Participation in God: A Study in Christian Doctrine and Metaphysics.* Cambridge: Cambridge University Press, 2019.

Davison, Lisa Wilson. *Preaching the Women of the Bible.* St. Louis: Chalice, 2006. Kindle ed.

Dayton, Donald W., and Robert K. Johnson. *The Variety of American Evangelicalism.* Downers Grove, IL: InterVarsity, 1991.

Dean, William D. "Can Liberal Theology Recover?" *American Journal of Theology and Philosophy* 30 (2010) 24–47.

Deloria, Vine, Jr. "Philosophy and the Tribal Peoples." In *American Indian Thought,* edited by Anne Waters, 3–11. Malden, MA: Blackwell, 2004.

Derrida, Jacques. "The Force of Law." In *Deconstruction and the Possibility of Justice,* edited by Drucilla Cornell et al., 3–69. New York: Rutledge, 1992.

———. *Points . . . Interviews, 1974–1994.* Edited by Elisabeth Weber. Translated by Peggy Kamuf et al. Crossing Aesthetics. Stanford: Stanford University Press, 1995.

A Disciples Prayerbook. Minneapolis: Indigenous Theological Training Institute. ND.

Dorrien, Gary J. *The Barthian Revolt in Modern Theology: Theology without Weapons.* Louisville: Westminster John Knox, 2000.

———. "The Lure and Necessity of Process Theology." *Crosscurrents* 58 (2008) 316–36.

————. *The Making of American Liberal Theology.* Vol. 1, *Imagining Progressive Religion, 1805–1900.* Louisville: Westminster John Knox, 2001.

————. *The Making of American Liberal Theology.* Vol. 2, *Idealism, Realism, and Modernity, 1900–1950.* Louisville: Westminster John Knox, 2003.

————. *The Making of American Liberal Theology.* Vol. 3, *Crisis, Irony & Postmodernity, 1950–2005.* Louisville: Westminster John Knox, 2006.

Downs, Jim. *Stand By Me: The Forgotten History of Gay Liberation.* New York: Basic Books, 2016.

Du Bois, W. E. B. *The Souls of Black Folk.* New York: Millennium, 2014.

Dube, Musa W., ed. *Other Ways of Reading: African Women and the Bible.* Global Perspectives on Biblical Scholarship 2. Atlanta: Society of Biblical Literature, 2001.

————. *Postcolonial Feminist Interpretation of the Bible.* St. Louis: Chalice, 2000.

Dube, Musa W., et al., eds. *Postcolonial Perspectives in African Biblical Interpretations.* Atlanta: Society of Biblical Literature, 2012.

Duncan, Carol B. "From 'Force-Ripe' to 'Womanish/ist': Black Girlhood and the African Diasporan Feminine Consciousness." In *Deeper Shades of Purple: Womanism in Religion and Society,* edited by Stacy M. Floyd-Thomas. 29–37. Religion, Race, and Ethnicity. New York: New York University Press, 2006.

Ehrman, Bart D. *The New Testament: A Historical Introduction to the Early Christian Writings.* 3rd ed. New York: Oxford University Press, 2004.

Elkins, Heather Murray. "Holy Stuff of Life." https://www.youtube.com/channel/UC3ff_PeRKKX4B0Bq8EN_eJQ.

————. *Holy Stuff of Life: Stories; Poems and Prayers about Human Things.* Cleveland: Pilgrim, 2006.

Emerson, Ralph Waldo. "Divinity School Address." https://emersoncentral.com/ebook/Divinity-School-Address.pdf/.

Epperly, Bruce G. *Process Theology: A Guide for the Perplexed.* Guides for the Perplexed. London: T. & T. Clark, 2011.

Fanon, Frantz. *Black Skin, White Masks.* Translated by Richard Philcox. New York: Grove, 2008.

————. *The Wretched of the Earth.* Translated by Richard Philcox. Commentary by Jean-Paul Sartre and Homi K. Bhabha. New York: Grove, 2005.

Fant, Clyde E. *Preaching for Today.* New York: Harper & Row, 1975.

Farley, Edward. *Practicing Gospel: Unconventional Thoughts on the Church's Ministry.* Louisville: Westminster John Knox, 2003.

Farmer, Herbert. H. *The Servant of the Word.* Preachers Paperback Library. Philadelphia: Fortress, 1964.

Fee, Gordon. *New Testament Exegesis: A Handbook for Beginners.* 3rd ed. Louisville: Westminster John Knox, 2002.

Florence, Anna Carter. *Preaching as Testimony.* Louisville: Westminster John Knox, 2007.

Floyd-Thomas Stacey M., ed. *Deeper Shades of Purple: Womanism in Religion and Society.* Religion, Race, and Ethnicity. New York: New York University Press, 2006.

————. "Introduction: Writing for Our Lives—Womanism as an Epistemological Revolution." In *Deeper Shades of Purple: Womanism in Religion and Society,* edited by Stacy M. Flooyd-Thomas. 1–16. Religion, Race, and Ethnicity. New York: New York University Press. 2006.

Floyd-Thomas Stacey M., and Anthony B. Pinn, eds. *Liberation Theologies in the United States: An Introduction*. New York: New York University Press, 2010.

Fosdick, Harry Emerson. "Shall the Fundamentalists Win?" https://teachingamerican-history.org/library/document/shall-the-fundamentalists-win/.

Fox, Ruth. "Women in the Bible and Lectionary." https://www.futurechurch.org/women-in-church-leadership/women-and-word/women-in-bible-and-lectionary.

Frei, Hans W. *The Eclipse of Biblical Narrative: A Study in Eighteenth and Nineteenth Century Hermeneutics*. New Haven: Yale University Press, 1974.

———. Response to 'Narrative Theology: An Evangelical Appraisal.'" In *Theology and Narrative: Selected Essays*, edited by George Hunsinger and William C. Placher, 207–12. New York: Oxford University Press, 1993.

Freire, Paulo. *Pedagogy of the Oppressed*. Translated by Myra Bergman Ramos. 30th anniversary ed. New York: Continuum, 2000.

Gerstner, John H. "The Theological Boundaries of Evangelical Faith." In T*he Evangelicals: What They Believe, Who They Are, Where They Are Changing*, edited by David F. Wells and John D. Woodbridge, 21–37. Nashville: Abingdon, 1975.

Gibson, Scott M., ed. *On the Teaching of Preaching: The Use of Educational Theory and Christian Theology in Homiletics*. Wooster, OH: Weaver, 2018.

———, ed. *Training Preachers: A Guide to Teaching Homiletics*. Bellingham, WA: Lexham, 2018.

Gilbert, Kenyatta R. *The Journey and Promise of African American Preaching*. Minneapolis: Fortress, 2011.

Go, Yohan, et al. "Introduction to the Essays of the Consultation on Preaching and Postcolonial Theology." *Homiletic* 40 (2015) 3–7.

González, Justo L. *The Liberating Pulpit*. 1994. Reprint, Eugene, OR: Wipf & Stock, 2003.

González, Justo L., and Catherine Gunsalus González. "Liberation Preaching." In *Concise Encyclopedia of Preaching*, edited by William H. Willimon and Richard Lischer, 307–9. Louisville: Westminster John Knox, 1995.

———. *Liberation Preaching: The Pulpit and the Oppressed*. Abingdon Preacher's Library. Nashville: Abingdon, 1980.

González, Justo L., and Pablo A. Jiménez. *Púlpito: An Introduction to Hispanic Preaching*. Nashville: Abingdon , 2005.

Grant, Jacquelyn. *White Women's Christ and Black Women's Jesus: Feminist Christology and Womanist Response*. American Academy of Religion Academy Series 64. Atlanta: Scholars, 1989.

Grant, Robert M., and David Tracy, *A Short History of the Interpretation of the Bible*. 2nd ed. Philadelphia: Fortress, 1984.

Guest, Deryn, et al., eds. *The Queer Bible Commentary*. London: SCM, 2006.

Gullotta, Daniel. "Among Dogs and Disciples: An Examination of the Story of the Canaanite Woman (Matthew 15:21–28) and the Question of the Gentile Mission within the Matthean Community." *Neotestamentica* 48 (2014) 325–40.

Gutiérrez, Gustavo. *Hacia una teología de la liberación*. Bogotá, Colombia: Indo-American, 1971.

———. *A Theology of Liberation*. Translated by Sister Caridad Inda and John Eagleson. Fifteenth anniversary ed. Maryknoll, NY: Orbis, 1988.

Hall, Douglas John. *Remembered Voices: Reclaiming the Legacy of "Neo-Orthodoxy."* Louisville: Westminster John Knox, 1998.

Harris, James Henry. *Beyond the Tyranny of the Text: Preaching in Front of the Bible to Create a New World*. Nashville: Abingdon, 2019.

———. *Black Suffering: Silent Pain, Hidden Hope*. Minneapolis: Fortress, 2020.

———. *No Longer Bound: A Theology of Reading and Preaching*. Eugene, OR: Cascade Books, 2013.

———. *Pastoral Theology: A Black-Church Perspective*. Minneapolis: Fortress, 1991.

———. *Preaching Liberation*. Fortress Resources for Preaching. Minneapolis: Fortress, 1995.

———. *The Word Made Plain: The Power and Promise of Preaching*. Minneapolis: Fortress, 2004.

Haslam, Nick. "What Is Dehumanization?" In *Humanness and Dehumanization*, edited by Paul G. Bain et al., 34–48. New York: Routledge, 2014.

Hayes, Diana L. "Standing in the Shoes My Mother Made: A Catholic Womanist Theologian." In *Deeper Shades of Purple: Womanism in Religion and Society*, edited by Stacy M. Floyd-Thomas, 54–79. Religion, Race, and Ethnicity. New York: New York University Press, 2006.

Haykin, Michael A. G., and Kenneth J. Stewart, eds., *The Advent of Evangelicalism: Exploring Historical Continuities*. Nashville: Broadman & Holman, 2008.

Hegel, Georg Wilhelm Friedrich. *Phenomenology of Spirit*. Translated by A. V. Miller, and John N. Findlay. Oxford Paperbacks. Oxford: Oxford University Press, 2013.

Hillar, Marian. "Liberation Theology: Religious Response to Social Problems. A Survey." *Humanism and Social Issues: Anthology of Essays*, edited by Marian Hillar and H. Richard Leuchtag, 35–52. Houston: Humanists Involved in Greater Houston, Chapter of the American Humanists Association, 1993.

Hinton, Olive Elaine. *God Comes Out: A Queer Homiletic*. Center for Lesbian and Gay Studies in Religion and Ministry. Cleveland, OH: Pilgrim, 2007.

Ho, Tamara C. "The Complex Heterogeneity of Asian American Identity." In *T. & T. Clark Handbook of Asian American Biblical Hermeneutics*, edited by Uriah Y. Kim and Seung Ai Yang, 1–32. T. & T. Clark Handbooks. London: Bloomsbury, 2019.

Hodgson, Peter C. *Winds of the Spirit: A Constructive Christian Theology*. Louisville: Westminster John Knox, 1994.

Hopkins. Dwight N. *Down, Up, and Over: Slave Religion and Black Theology*. Minneapolis: Fortress, 1999.

Howell, Nancy R. "Embodied Transcendence: Bonobos and Humans in Community." *Zygon: Journal of Religion and Science* 44 (2009) 601–12.

Hudson, Mary Lin, and Mary Donovan Turner. *Saved from Silence: Finding Women's Voice in Preaching*. St Louis: Chalice, 1999.

Hutchinson, Mark, and John Wolffe. *A Short History of Global Evangelicalism*. Cambridge: Cambridge University Press, 2012.

Immink, Gerrit, and Ciska Stark, eds. *Preaching: Creating Perspective*. Studia Homiletica 4. Utrecht, the Netherlands: Societas Homiletica, 2002.

Ingram, Stephen. *Organic Student Ministry: Trash the Pre-Packaged Programs and Transform Your Youth Group*. St. Louis: Chalice, 2015.

Irenaeus. *Against Heresies*. In *Ante-Nicene Fathers*. Translated by Alexander Roberts, et. al. Volume 1. Edinburgh: T. & T. Clark, 1867.

Isasi-Díaz, Ada María. "Communication as Communion: Elements in a Hermeneutic of *Lo Cotidiano*." In *Engaging the Bible in a Gendered World: An Introduction to Feminist Biblical Interpretation in Honor of Katharine Doob Sakenfeld*, edited by Linda Day and Carolyn Pressler, 27–36. Louisville: Westminster John Knox, 2006.

———. *En La Lucha = In the Struggle: Elaborating a Mujerista Theology.* 10th anniversary ed. Minneapolis: Fortress, 2004

———. *Mujerista Theology: A Theology for the Twenty-First Century.* Mayknoll, NY: Orbis, 1996.

———. "La Palabra de Dios en Nosotras—The Word of God in Us." In *Searching the Scriptures.* Vol. 1, *A Feminist Introduction,* edited by Elisabeth Schüssler Fiorenza, 148–69. New York: Crossroad, 1994.

———. "Womanists and *Mujeristas*: Sisters in the Struggle; A *Mujerista* Response. In *Deeper Shades of Purple: Womanism in Religion and Society,* edited by Stacy M. Thomas. 265–69. Religion, Race, and Ethnicity. New York: New York University Press, 2006.

Isasi-Díaz, Ada María, and Fernando F. Segovia, eds. *Hispanic/Latino Theology: Challenge and Promise.* Minneapolis: Fortress, 1992.

Isasi-Díaz, Ada María, and Yolanda Tarango. *Hispanic Women, Prophetic Voice in the Church: Toward a Hispanic Women's Liberation Theology = Mujer hispana, voz profética en la iglesia: hacia una teología de liberación de la mujer Hispana.* San Francisco: Harper & Row, 1988.

———. *Hispanic Women, Prophetic Voice in the Church = Mujer hispana, Voz Profética en la iglesia.* Minneapolis: Fortress, 1992.

Isbouts, Jean-Pierre. *Women of the Bible.* National Geographic Partners. New York: Meredith Corporation, 2020.

Jacobsen, David Schnasa, ed. "Essays on Preaching on the Consultation on Preaching and Postcolonial Theology." *Homiletic* 40 (2015) 3–61.

———, ed. *Homiletical Theology in Action: The Unfinished Task of Preaching.* Eugene, OR: Cascade Books, 2015

Jacobson, Kristi, and Lori Silverbush, dirs. *A Place at the Table.* Starring Jeff Bridges et al. Produced by Participant Media, 2013. DVD. New York: Magnolia Pictures, 2013. Distributed by Ro*co Films Educational, 2021.

Jameson, Fredric. "Postmodernism, or the Cultural Logic of Late Capitalism." In *Postmodernism: A Reader,* edited by Thomas Docherty, 62–92. New York: Columbia University Press, 1993.

Jiménez, Pablo A. "If You Just Close Your Eyes: Postcolonial Perspectives on Preaching from the Caribbean." *Homiletic* 40 (2015) 22–27.

———. "In Search of a Hispanic Model of Biblical Interpretation." *Journal of Latino/ Hispanic Theology* 3/2 (1995) 44–64.

———. *La predicación en el siglo XXI.* Barcelona, Spain: CLIE, 2009.

———. "A Presentation Offering Caribbean Perspectives on Postcolonial Preaching." https://soundcloud.com/drpablojimenez/if-you-just-close-your-eyes (2014). Also available at https://drpablojimenez.net/2014/11/25/if-you-just-close-your-eyes-caribbean-perspectives-on-postcolonial-preaching/.

———. "Toward a Postcolonial Homiletic: Justo L. González's Contribution to Homiletics." In *Hispanic Christian Thought at the Dawn of the Twenty-First Century: Apuntes in Honor of Justo L. González,* edited by Alvin Padilla et al., 159–67. Nashville: Abingdon, 2006

Joh, Wonhee Anne. *Heart of the Cross: A Postcolonial Christology.* Louisville: Westminster John Knox, 2006.

Johnson, Kimberly P. *The Womanist Preacher: Proclaiming Womanist Rhetoric from the Pulpit.* Rhetoric, Race, and Religion. Lanham, MD: Lexington, 2019.

Johnston, Scott Black, Ted A. Smith, and Leonora Tubbs Tisdale, eds. *Questions Preachers Ask: Essays in Honor of Thomas G. Long*. Louisville: Westminster John Knox, 2016.

Jones, Isaiah, Jr. "Fill My Cup." In *Glory to God: Hymns, Psalms, and Spiritual Songs*, hymn 699. Louisville: Westminster John Knox, 2013.

Joseph, M. P. *Theologies of the Non-Person: The Formative Years of EATWOT*. Christianities of the World. London: Palgrave Macmillan, 2015. Also refer to https://eatwotglobal.com/.

Kang, Nam Soon. *Diasporic Feminist Theology: Asia and Theopolitical Imagination*. Minneapolis: Fortress, 2014.

Kearney, Richard. "Desire of God." In *God, the Gift, and Postmodernism*, edited by John D. Caputo and Michael J. Scanlon, 112–45. Indiana Series in the Philosophy of Religion. Bloomington: Indiana University Press, 1999.

———. *The God Who May Be: A Hermeneutics of Religion*. Indiana Series in the Philosophy of Religion. Bloomington: Indiana University Press, 2009.

Kegley, Charles W., ed. *The Theology of Paul Tillich*. 2nd ed. New York: Pilgrim, 1982.

Kierkegaard, Søren. *Training in Christianity and the Edifying Discourse Which "Accompanied" It*. Translated by Walter Lowrie. London: Oxford University Press, 1944.

Kim-Cragg, HyeRan. *Interdependence: A Postcolonial Feminist Practical Theology*. Eugene, OR: Pickwick Publications, 2018.

———. *Postcolonial Preaching: Creating a Ripple Effect*. Postcolonial and Decolonial Studies in Religion and Theology. Lanham, MD: Lexington, 2021.

Kim-Cragg, HyeRan, and EunYoung Choi. *The Encounters: Retelling the Bible from Migration and Intercultural Perspectives*. Daejeon, South Korea: Daejanggan, 2013.

Kim-Kort, Mihee. *Making Paper Cranes: Toward an Asian American Feminist Theology*. St. Louis: Chalice, 2012.

Kim, Eunjoo Mary. "Asian American Women and Renewal of Preaching." In *New Feminist Christianity: Many Voices, Many Views*, edited by Mary E. Hunt and Diann Neu, 245–53. Woodstock, VT: SkyLight Paths, 2010.

———. "Hermeneutics and Asian American Preaching." *Semeia* 90/91 (2002) 269–90.

———. "Preaching as an Art of Shared Leadership." In *Women, Church, and Leadership: New Paradigms, In Honor of Jean Miller Schmidt*, edited by Eunjoo Mary Kim and Debora Creamer, 69–88. Eugene, OR: Wipf & Stock, 2012.

———. *Preaching in an Age of Globalization*. Louisville: Westminster John Knox, 2010.

———. *Preaching the Presence of God: A Homiletic from an Asian American Perspective*. Valley Forge, PA: Judson 1999.

Kim, Grace Ji-Sun. *Embracing the Other: The Transformative Spirit of Love*. Prophetic Christianity. Grand Rapids: Eerdmans, 2015.

Kim, Jung Ha. *Bridge-Makers and Cross-Bearers: Korean-American Women and the Church*. American Academy of Religion Academy Series 92. Atlanta: Scholars, 1997.

Kim, Matthew D., and Daniel L. Wong. *Finding Our Voice: A Vision for Asian North American Preaching*. Bellingham, WA: Lexham, 2020. Kindle ed.

Kim, Nami. "The 'Indigestible' Asian." In *Off the Menu: Asian and Asian North America Women's Religion and Theology*, edited by Rita Nakashima Brock et al., 3–43. Louisville Westminster John Knox 2007.

Kim, Uriah Y., and Seung Ai Yang, eds. *T. & T. Clark Handbook of Asian American Biblical Hermeneutics*. T. & T. Clark Handbooks. London: Bloomsbury, 2019.

Kim, Uriah Y., and Seung Ai Yang. "Introduction to the Handbook." In *T. & T. Clark Handbook of Asian American Biblical Hermeneutics*, edited by Uriah Y. Kim and Seung Ai Yang, i–xxiv. T. & T. Clark Handbooks. London: Bloomsbury, 2019.

Kim., Ai Ra. *Women Struggling for a New Life*. Albany: State University of New York Press, 1996.

King, Martin Luther, Jr. "Letter from Birmingham City Jail." In *A Testament of Hope: The Essential Writings and Speeches of Martin Luther King, Jr.*, 289–308. San Francisco: HarperSanFrancisco, 1991.

King, Thomas. *The Truth about Stories: A Native Narrative*. CBC Massey Lectures Series. Toronto: House of Anansi Press, 2003.

Kristeva, Julia. *Powers of Horror: An Essay on Abjection*. European Perspectives. New York: Columbia University Press, 1982.

Kwok, Pui-lan, ed. *Asian and Asian American Women in Theology and Religion: Embodying Knowledge*. Asian Christianity in the Diaspora. Cham, Switzerland: Palgrave Macmillan, 2020.

———. "Changing Identities and Narrativities: Postcolonial Theologies." In *Complex Identities in a Shifting World: Practical Theological Perspecfives*, edited by Pamela Cotoure et al., 115–26. Zurich: Lit, 2015.

———. "Empire and the Study of Religion." *Journal of the American Academy of Religion* 80 (2012) 285–303.

———. "Postcolonial Preaching in Intercultural Contexts." *Homiletic* 40 (2015) 8–21.

———. *Postcolonial Imagination and Feminist Theology*. Louisville: Westminster John Knox, 2005.

———. "Postcolonial Preaching in Intercultural Contexts." *Homiletic* 40 (2015) 8–21.

Larsen, David L. *The Company of the Preachers: A History of Biblical Preaching from the Old Testament to the Modern Era*. Grand Rapids: Kregel, 1998.

Larson, Rebecca. *Daughters of Light: Quaker Women Preaching and Prophesying in the Colonies and Abroad, 1700–1775*. Chapel Hill: University of North Carolina Press, 2000.

Lartey, Emmanuel Y. *Postcolonializing God: New Perspectives on Pastoral and Practical Theology*. London: SCM, 2013.

Lee, Jarena. *The Religious Experiences and Journal of Mrs. Jarena Lee "A Preach'in Woman."* Nashville: AMEC Sunday School Union/Legacy, 1849.

Lee, Jung Young. *Marginality: The Key to Multicultural Theology*. Fortress, 1995.

Lee, Sang Hyun. *From a Liminal Place: An Asian American Theology*. Minneapolis: Fortress, 2010.

Lee, Unzu, and Presbyterian Church (U.S.A.). *Coming Home: Asian American Women Doing Theology*. Louisville: PCUSA Women's Ministries Area, 2006.

Lehmann, Paul L. *Ethics in a Christian Context*. New York: Harper & Row, 1963.

Levinas, Emmanuel. *Of God Who Comes to Mind*. Translated by Bettina Bergo. Crossing Aesthetics. Stanford: Stanford University Press, 1998.

Levine, Amy-Jill, and Marc Zvi Bretterler, eds. *The Jewish Annotated New Testament*. 2nd ed. Oxford: Oxford University Press, 2017.

Lewis, Donald M., and Richard V. Pierard. *Global Evangelicalism: Theology, History and Culture in Regional Perspective*. Downers Grove, IL: IVP Academic, 2014.

Lewis, Howell Elvet. "Lord of Light, Your Name Outshining." *The Presbyterian Hymnal*, hymn number 425. Louisville: Westminster John Knox, 1990.

Lewis, Ralph H., and Gregg Lewis. *Inductive Preaching: Helping People Listen*. Wheaton, IL: Crossway, 1983.

Liew, Tat-Siong Benny. *What Is Asian American Biblical Hermeneutics? Reading the New Testament*. Intersections: Asian and Pacific American Transcultural Studies. Honolulu: University of Hawaii Press, 2007.

Lightsey, Pamela R. *Our Lives Matter: A Womanist Queer Theology*. Eugene, OR: Pickwick Publications, 2015.

Lindbeck, George A. *The Nature of Doctrine: Religion and Theology in a Post-Liberal Age*. Philadelphia: Westminster, 1984.

Lindner, Robert D. "The Resurgence of Evangelical Social Concern (1925–75)." In *The Evangelicals: What They Believe, Who They Are, Where They Are Changing*, edited by David F. Wells and John D. Woodbridge, 189–210. Nashville: Abingdon, 1975.

Livingston, James C., et al. *Modern Christian Thought*. Vol. 2, *The Twentieth Century*. 2 vols. 2nd ed. Minneapolis: Fortress, 2006.

Lloyd, Vincent. "Thick or Thin?" *Journal of Religious Ethics* 42 (2014) 335–56. https://doi.org/10.1111/jore.12059/.

Long, Thomas G. *Preaching from Memory to Hope*. Louisville: Westminster John Knox, 2009.

———. *The Witness of Preaching*. 3rd ed. Louisville: Westminster John Knox, 2005.

Loomer, Bernard. "Two Conceptions of Power." *Process Studies* 6 (1976) 5–32.

Lorensen, Marlene Ringgaard. "Carnivalized Preaching: In Dialogue with Bakhtin and Other- Wise Homiletics." *Homiletic* 36 (2011). file:///Users/Admin/Downloads/3438-Article%20Text-13217-1-10-20110613%20(1).pdf.

Loritts, Bryan, and John Ortberg. *Insider Outsider: My Journey as a Stranger in White Evangelicalism and My Hope for Us All*. Grand Rapids: Zondervan, 2018.

Lowry, Eugene. *The Homiletical Plot: The Sermon as Narrative Art Form*. Exp. ed. Louisville: Westminster John Knox, 2001.

MacDonald, Mark. "The Surprising and Improbable Mission of God among the Indigenous Peoples of Canada." In *Green Shoots Our of Dry Ground*, edited by John P. Bowen, 127–41. Eugene, OR: Wipf & Stock, 2013.

Magnuson, Norris. *Salvation in the Slums: Evangelical Social Work, 1865–1920*. ATLA Monograph Series 10. Metuchen, NJ: Scarecrow, 1977.

Majeed, Debra Mubashshir. "Womanism Encounters Islam: A Muslim Scholar Considers the Efficacy of a Method Rooted in the Academy and the Church." In *Deeper Shades of Purple: Womanism in Religion and Society*, edited by Stacy M. Floyd-Thomas, 38–53. Religion, Race, and Ethnicity. New York: New York University Press, 2006.

Marsden, George M. *Fundamentalism and American Culture*. New ed. New York: Oxford University Press, 2006.

———. *Reforming Fundamentalism: Fuller Seminary and the New Evangelicalism*. Grand Rapids: Eerdmans, 1995.

———. *Understanding Fundamentalism and Evangelicalism*. Grand Rapids: Eerdmans, 1991.

Martell-Otero, Loida I., et al. *Latina Evangélicas: A Theological Survey from the Margins*. Eugene, OR: Cascade Books, 2013.

McCall, Sophie. *First Person Plural: Aboriginal Storytelling and the Ethics of Collaborative Authorship*. Vancouver: University of British Columbia Press, 2012.

———. "What the Map Cuts Up, the Story Cuts Across: Translating Oral Traditions and Aboriginal Land Title." *Essays on Canadian Writing* 80 (2003) 305–28.

McAuley, James Philip. *Collected Poems 1936–70*. Sydney, Austrailia: Angus & Robertson, 1971.

McClure, John S. "Deconstruction." In *The New Interpreter's Handbook of Preaching*, edited by Paul Scott Wilson, 146–49. Nashville: Abingdon 2008.

———. *Other-wise Preaching: A Postmodern Ethic for Homiletics*. St. Louis: Chalice, 2001.

McDaniel, Jay, and Donna Bowman, eds. *Handbook of Process Theology*. St. Louis: Chalice, 2006.

McDermott, Gerald R., ed. *The Oxford Handbook of Evangelical Theology*. Oxford: Oxford University Press, 2010.

McFague, Sallie. *Metaphorical Theology: Models of God in Religious Language*. Philadelphia: Fortress, 1982.

Medina, Lara, and Martha R. Gonzales. Introdcution to *Voices from the Ancestors: Xicanx and Latinx Spiritual Expressions and Healing Practices*, edited by Lara Medina and Martha R. Gonzales, 3–20. Tucson: University of Arizona Press, 2019.

Meyers. Robin R. *Saving God from Religion: A Minister's Search for Faith in a Skeptical Age*. New York: Crown, 2020.

Milbank, Alison, et al., eds. *Preaching Radical and Orthodox*. London: SCM, 2017.

Milbank, John. *Theology and Social Theory: Beyond Secular Reason*. 2nd ed. Oxford: Wiley Blackwell, 2006.

———. *The Word Made Strange: Theology, Language, Culture*. Cambridge, MA: Wiley Blackwell, 1997.

Milbank, John, and Simon Oliver, eds. *The Radical Orthodoxy Reader*. Radical Orthodoxy Series. London: Routledge, 2009.

Milbank, John, et al., eds. *Radical Orthodoxy: A New Theology*. London: Routledge, 1999.

Mitchell, Ella Pearson, and Valerie Bridgeman Davis. *Those Preaching Women: A Multicultural Collection*. Valley Forge, PA: Judson, 2008.

Mitchell, Henry H. *Black Preaching: The Recovery of a Powerful Art*. Nashville: Abingdon, 1990.

Mitchem, Stephanie Y. *Introducing Womanist Theology*. Maryknoll, NY: Orbis, 2002.

Moltmann Jürgen. *The Crucified God: The Cross of Christ as the Foundation and Criticism of Christian Theology*. Translated by R. A. Wilson and John Bowden. San Francisco: HarperSanFrancisco, 1991.

Montag, John. "Radical Orthodoxy and Christian Theology." *Philosophy and Theology* 16 (2004) 89–100.

Moody, Katharine Sarah. *Radical Theology and Emerging Christianity: Deconstruction, Materialism and Religious Practices*. Intensities: Contemporary Continental Philosophy of Religion. New York: Routledge, 2016.

Morton, Nelle. *The Journey Is Home*. Boston: Beacon, 1985.

Myers, Jacob D. *Preaching Must Die! Troubling Homiletical Theology*. Minneapolis: Fortress 2017.

Naselli, Andrew David, and Collin Hansen, gen. eds. *Four Views on the Spectrum of Evangelicalism*. Counterpoints. Bible & Theology. Grand Rapids: Zondervan, 2011.

Newsom, Carol A., and Sharon H. Ringe. "Introduction." In *The Women's Bible Commentary*, edited by Carol A. Newsom and Sharon H. Ringe, xiii–xix. 1st ed., Louisville: Westminster John Knox Press, 1992.

———, eds. *The Women's Bible Commentary*. 1st ed. Louisville: Westminster John Knox, 1992.

Neylan, Susan. *The Heavens Are Changing: Nineteenth-Century Protestant Missions and Tsimshian Christianity*. McGill-Queen's Native and Northern Series 31. Montreal: McGill-Queen's University Press, 2003.

Ngũgĩ wa Thiong'o. *Decolonising the Mind: The Politics of Language in African Literature*. Studies in African Literature. London: Currey, 1986.

———. *A Grain of Wheat*. African Writers Series. London: Heinemann, 1968.

Niebuhr, Reinhold. *An Interpretation of Christian Ethics*. New York: Scribner, 1935.

———. *Moral Man and Immoral Society: A Study in Ethics and Politics*. New York: Scribner, 1932.

———. *The Nature and Destiny of Man*. 2 vols. New York: Scribner, 1941, 1943.

Noll, Mark A. *The Rise of Evangelicalism: The Age of Edwards, Whitefield and the Wesleys*. A History of Evangelicalism 1. Downers Grove, IL: InterVaristy, 2003.

O'Connor, Flannery. "The Catholic Novelist in the Protestant South." In *Collected Works*, edited by Sally Fitzgerald, 853–64. Library of America 39. New York: Library of America, 1988.

Oduyoye, Mercy Amba. "The Story of a Circle" [Circle of Concerned African Women Theologians]. *The Ecumenical Review* 53 (2001) 97–100.

Okey, Stephen. *A Theology of Conversation: An Introduction to David Tracy*. Collegeville, MN: Liturgical Press Academic, 2018.

Old, Hughes Oliphant. *The Reading and Preaching of the Scriptures in the Worship of the Christian Church*. Vol. 7, *Our Own Time*. 7 vols. Grand Rapids: Eerdmans, 1998–2010.

Ottoni-Wilhelm, Dawn, et al. Introduction to *Preaching God's Transforming Justice: A Lectionary Commentary: Year A; Featuring 22 New Holy Days for Justice*, edited by Dawn Ottoni-Wilhelm et al., ix–xxv. Louisville: Westminster John Knox, 2013.

Pabst, Adrian, and Christoph Schneider, eds. *Encounter between Eastern Orthodoxy and Radical Orthodoxy: Transfiguring the World through the Word*. Farnham, England: Ashgate, 2009.

Painter, Nell Irvin. *Sojourner Truth: A Life, A Symbol*. Rev. ed. New York: Norton, 1997.

Pak, Su Yon, and Jung Ha Kim, eds. *Leading Wisdom: Asian and Asian North American Women Leaders*. Louisville: Westminster John Knox, 2017.

Pak, Su Yon, et al. *Singing the Lord's Song in a New Land: Korean American Practices of Faith*. Louisville: Westminster John Knox, 2005.

Pannell, William. "The Religious Heritage of Blacks." *The Evangelicals: What They Believe, Who They Are, Where They Are Changing*, edited by David F. Wells and John D. Woodbridge, 96–107. Nashville: Abingdon, 1975.

Pape, Lance B. *The Scandal of Having Something to Say: Ricoeur and the Possibility of Postliberal Preaching*. Baylor: Baylor University Press, 2013.

Park, Andrew Sung. "Asian American Theology." In *Liberation Theologies in the United States: An Introduction*, edited by Stacy M. Floyd-Thomas and Anthony B. Pinn, 115–30. New York: New York University Press, 2010.

————. *Racial Conflict and Healing: An Asian-American Theological Perspective.* 1996. Reprint, Eugene, OR: Wipf & Stock, 2009.

————. *The Wounded Heart of God: The Asian Concept of Han and the Christian Doctrine of Sin.* Nashville: Abingdon, 1993.

Parker, Theodore. "Of Justice and the Conscience." In Ten Sermons on Religion by Theodore Parker Farris. 66–101. New York: Francis, 1853.

Peterson, Eugene H. *Working the Angles: The Shape of Pastoral Integrity.* Grand Rapids: Eerdmans, 1987.

Phan, Peter C. *Christianity with an Asian Face: Asian American Theology in the Making.* Kindle ed. Maryknoll, NY: Orbis, 2015.

Pickstock, Catherine. "Duns Scotus." In *The Radical Orthodoxy Reader,* edited by John Milbank and Simon Oliver, 116–46. Radical Orthodoxy Series. London: Routledge, 2009.

————. *Repetition and Identity: The Literary Agenda.* Oxford: Oxford University Press, 2014.

Pew Research Center. *Asian Americans: A Mosaic of Faiths.* July 19, 2012. https://www.pewforum.org/2012/07/19/asian-americans-a-mosaic-of-faiths-overview/

Pool, Jeff B. "Liberal Theology." In *The New and Enlarged Handbook of Christian Theology,* edited by Donald W. Musser and Joseph L. Price, 297–99. New and rev. ed. Nashville: Abingdon, 2003.

Powery, Luke. "Postcolonial Criticism." In *New Interpreter's Bible Handbook of Preaching,* edited by Paul Scott Wilson et al., 159–61. Nashville: Abingdon, 2008.

Preston, Richard J. *Cree Narrative: Expressing the Personal Meanings of Events.* Carleton Library Series. 2nd ed. Montreal: McGill-Queen's University Press, 2002.

Procter-Smith, Marjorie. "Feminist Interpretation and Liturgical Proclamation." In *Searching the Scriptures,* edited by Elisabeth Schüssler Fiorenza with the assistance of Shelly Matthews, 1:313–25. 2 vols. New York: Crossroad, 1993–1994.

Pseudo-Dionysius. *Pseudo-Dionysius: The Complete Works.* Translated by Colm Luibheid. Classics of Western Spirituality. New York: Paulist, 1987.

Putnam, Robert D. et al. *American Grace: How Religion Divides and Unites Us.* New York: Simon & Schuster, 2012.

Radner, Ephraim. *Time and the Word: Figural Reading of the Christian Scriptures.* Grand Rapids: Eerdmans, 2016.

Rauschenbush, Walter. *A Theology for the Social Gospel.* New York: Macmillan, 1922.

Reddie, Anthony. *Working against the Grain: Re-Imaging Black Theology in the 21st Century.* Cross Cultural Theologies. London: Equinox, 2008.

Rice, Charles L. *Interpretation and Imagination: The Preacher and Contemporary Literature* Philadelphia: Fortress, 1970.

Ricoeur, Paul *Freud and Philosophy. An Essay on Interpretation.* Translated by Denis Savage. New Haven: Yale University Press, 1970.

————. "The Hermeneutics of Testimony." In Essays on Biblical Interpretation, edited by Lewis S. Mudge, 119–54. Philadelphia: Fortress, 1980.

————. *Interpretation Theory: Discourse and the Surplus of Meaning.* Fort Worth: Texas Christian University Press, 1976.

————. *The Symbolism of Evil.* Translated by Emerson Buchanan. Boston: Beacon, 1986.

Riggle, Ellen D. B., and Sharon S. Rostosky. *A Positive View of LGBTQ: Embracing Identity and Cultivating Well-Being.* Lanham, MD: Rowman & Littlefield, 2012.

Rivera Pagán, Luis N. *A Violent Evangelism: The Political and Religious Conquest of the Americas*. Louisville: Westminster John Knox 1992.

Robinson, Haddon. *Biblical Preaching: The Development and Delivery of Expository Messages*. 3rd ed. Grand Rapids: Baker Academic, 2014.

Rose, Lucy Atkinson. *Sharing the Word: Preaching in the Roundtable Church*. Louisville: Westminster John Knox, 1997.

Rosell, Garth M. *Boston's Historic Park Street Church: The Story of an Evangelical Landmark*. Grand Rapids: Kregel, 2009.

———. *A Charge to Keep: Gordon-Conwell Theological Seminary and the Renewal of Evangelicalism*. Eugene, OR: Wipf & Stock, 2020.

———. *The Surprising Work of God: Harold John Ockenga, Billy Graham, and the Rebirth of Evangelicalism*. Grand Rapids: Baker Academic, 2008.

Ross, Barbara, "You Who Are Thirsty." In *The Faith We Sing*, edited by Gary Alan Smith, hymn number 2132. Nashville: Abingdon, 2011.

Rubenstein, Mary-Jane. "Unknow Thyself: Apophaticism, Deconstruction, and Theology after Ontotheology." *Modern Theology* 19 (2003) 387–417.

Ruether, Rosemary Radford. *Sexism and God-Talk: Towards a Feminist Theology*. London: SCM, 1983.

Russell, Letty M. *Just Hospitality: God's Welcome in a World of Difference*. Louisville: Westminster John Knox, 2009.

Rutherdale, Myra. *Women and the White Man's God: Gender and Race in the Canadian Mission Field*. Vancouver: University of British Columbia Press, 2002.

Said, Edward. *Orientalism*. New York: Pantheon, 1978.

Salinas, Daniel. *Taking Up the Mantle: Latin American Evangelical Theology in the 20th Century*. Global Perspectives Series. Carlisle, Englad: Langham Global Library, 2017.

Sandberg, Sheryl. *Lean In: Women, Work, and the Will to Lead*. New York: Knopf, 2013.

Sanneh, Lamin. *Translating the Message: The Missionary Impact on Culture*. American Society of Missiology Series 13. Maryknoll, NY: Orbis, 1989.

Saiving, Valerie. "The Human Situation: A Feminine View." *Journal of Religion* 40 (1961) 100–112.

Scarry, Elaine. *On Beauty and Being Just*. Princeton: Princeton University Press, 1999.

Scherer, Paul. "Reinhold Niebuhr–Preacher." In *Reinhold Niebuhr: His Religious, Political and Social Thought*, edited by Charles W. Kegley, 387–408. 2001. Reprint, Eugene, OR: Wipf & Stock, 2009.

Schleiermacher, Friedrich. *On Religion: Addresses in Response to Its Cultured Critics*. Translated, with introduction and notes, by Terrence N. Tice. Research in Theology. Richmond: John Knox, 1969.

———. *The Christian Faith*. Translated by H. R. Mackintosh and J. S. Stewart. Philadelphia: Fortress, 1976.

Schrekneringer, Ben. "The Home of FOMO." *Boston Magazine*. July 29, 2014. https://www.bostonmagazine.com/news/2014/07/29/fomo-history/.

Schüssler Fiorenza, Elisabeth. "A Feminist Introduction." In *Searching the Scriptures*, edited by Elisabeth Schüssler Fiorenza with the assistance of Shelly Matthews, 1:i–xx. 2 vols. New York: Crossroad, 1993.

———. "Preface: Rethinking *The Women's Bible*." In *Searching the Scriptures*, edited by Elisabeth Schüssler Fiorenza with the assistance of Shelly Matthews, 1:1–23. 2 vols. New York: Crossroad, 1993.

Schüssler Fiorenza, Elisabeth, with the assistance of Shelly Matthews. *Searching the Scriptures*. 2 vols. New York: Crossroad, 1993–1994.

Segovia, Fernando. "Two Places and No Place on Which to Stand: Mixture and Otherness in Hispanic American Theology." *Listening* 1 (1992) 31.

Shelley, Bruce, and Marshall Shelley. *The Consumer Church: Can Evangelicals Win the World Without Losing Their Souls?* Downers Grove, IL: InterVarsity, 1992.

Simmons, Martha, and Frank A. Thomas, eds. *Preaching with Sacred Fire: An Anthology of African American Sermons, 1750 to the Present*. New York: Norton, 2010.

Simpson, Christopher Ben. *Modern Christian Theology*. New York: T. & T. Clark, 2016.

Simson, Wolfgang. *The House Church Book: Rediscover the Dynamic, Organic, Relational, Viral Community Jesus Started*. Carol Stream, IL: Barna Books, 2009.

Siwo-Okundi, Elizabeth J. A. "Listening to and Learning from the 'Small Voice' of African Preachers: A Practical Theological Examination of African Preaching in Kenya." PhD diss., Boston University, 2018.

———. "Listening to the Small Voice: Toward an Orphan Theology." *Harvard Divinity Bulletin* 37 (2009) 33–43.

Smith, Christine M. *Preaching as Weeping, Confession, and Resistance: Radical Responses to Radical Evil*. Louisville: Westminster John Knox, 1992.

———. *Preaching Justice*. 1998. Reprint, Eugene, OR: Wipf & Stock, 2008.

———. *Weaving the Sermon: Preaching in a Feminist Perspective*. Louisville: Westminster John Knox, 1989.

Smith, David W. "Phenomenology." In *Stanford Encyclopedia of Philosophy*. https://plato.stanford.edu/entries/phenomenology/.

Smith, James K. A. *Introducing Radical Orthodoxy: Mapping a Post-Secular Theology*. Grand Rapids: Baker Academic, 2005.

Smith, Mitzi J. "Commentary on Matthew 15:[10–20] 21–28." Eleventh Sunday after Pentecost (August 16, 2020). Working Preacher (website). https://www.workingpreacher.org/commentaries/revised-common-lectionary/ordinary-20/commentary-on-matthew-1510-20-21-28.

Smith, Timothy Lawrence. *Revivalism and Social Reform: American Protestantism on the Eve of the Civil War*. Baltimore: Johns Hopkins University Press, 1980.

———. "A Shared Evangelical Heritage." In *Evangelicalism: Surviving Its Success; Conference, June 1986*. Vol. 2, *The Evangelical Round Table*, edited by David A. Fraser, 12–28. St. Davids, PA: Eastern College and Eastern Baptist Theological Seminary, 1987.

Spain, Rufus B. *At Ease in Zion: Social History of Southern Baptists, 1865–1900*. Nashville: Vanderbilt University Press, 1967.

Spivak, Gayatri, "Can the Subaltern Speak?" In *Marxism and the Interpretation of Culture*, edited by Carey Nelson and Lawrence Grossberg, 271–313. Communications and Culture. Basingstoke, England: Macmillan Education, 1988.

Stanley, Brian. *The Global Diffusion of Evangelicalism: The Age of Billy Graham and John Stott*. A History of Evangelicalism 5. Downers Grove, IL: IVP Academic, 2013.

Stanton, Elizabeth Cady. *The Woman's Bible*. New York: European Publishing Company, 1895, as found in *The Original Feminist Attack on the Bible*. Introduction by Barbara Welter. New York: Arno, 1974.

Steimle, Edmund A., et al. *Preaching the Story*. 1980. Reprint, Eugene, OR: Wipf & Stock, 2003.

Stewart, Gina M. "God Is Doing A New Thing." Sermon preached for the installation of the Reverend Jacqueline A. Thompson, at Allen Temple Baptist Church, Oakland, California, on December 8, 2019.

Stone, Ronald H., and Matthew Lon Weaver, eds. *Against the Third Reich: Paul Tillich's Wartime Addresses to Nazi Germany*. Translated by Matthew Lon Weaver. Louisville: Westminster John Knox, 1998.

Stott, John. *Between Two Worlds: The Challenge of Preaching Today*. Grand Rapids: Eerdmans, 2017.

Suchocki, Marjorie Hewitt. *God, Christ, Church: A Practical Guide to Process Theology*. New, rev. ed. New York: Crossroad, 1989.

———. *The Whispered Word: A Theology of Preaching*. St. Louis: Chalice, 1999.

Sugirtharajah, R. S., ed. *The Postcolonial Biblical Reader*. Malden, MA: Blackwell, 2006.

———, ed. *Voices from the Margin: Interpreting the Bible in the Third World*. Revised and expanded 3rd ed. Maryknoll, NY: Orbis, 2006.

———, ed. *Voices from the Margin: Interpreting the Bible in the Third World*. 25th anniversary ed. Maryknoll, NY: Orbis, 2016.

Suttle, Tim. *Shrink: Faithful Ministry in a Church-Growth Culture*. Grand Rapids: Zondervan, 2014.

Sweeney, Douglas A. *The American Evangelical Story: A History of the Movement*. Grand Rapids: Baker Academic, 2005.

Sweet, Leonard I., ed. *The Evangelical Tradition in America*. Macon: Mercer University Press, 1984.

Tan, Jonathan Y. *Introducing Asian American Theologies*. Maryknoll, NY: Orbis, 2008.

Taylor, Charles. *A Secular Age*. Cambridge: Harvard University Press, 2007.

Taylor, Mark C. "What Derrida Really Meant." Opinion. *New York Times*, October 14, 2004. https://www.nytimes.com/2004/10/14/opinion/what-derrida-really-meant.html.

Thomas, Frank A. *Introduction to the Practice of African American Preaching*. Nashville: Abingdon, 2016.

Throckmorton, Burton H., Jr. "Language and the Bible." *Religious Education* 80 (1985) 523–38. https://doi.org/10.1080/0034408850800403.

———. "Why the Inclusive Language Lectionary?" *Christian Century* 101 (1984) 742–45.

Thurman, Howard. *Jesus and the Disinherited*. Boston: Beacon, 1996.

Tidball, Derek. *Who Are the Evangelicals? Tracing the Roots of the Modern Movements*. London: Marshall Prickering, 1994.

Tillich, Paul. *Systematic Theology*. 3 vols. Chicago: University of Chicago Press, 1967.

———. *The Eternal Now*. New York: Scribner, 1963.

———. *The New Being*. New York: Scribner, 1955.

———. *The Shaking of the Foundations*. New York: Scribner, 1948.

———. "You Are Accepted." In *The Shaking of the Foundations*, 153–63. New York: Scribner, 1948

Tisdale, Leonora Tubbs, ed. *The Abingdon Women's Preaching Annual*. Nashville: Abingdon, 2001.

———. *How Women Transform Preaching*. Nashville: Abingdon, 2021

Torres, Sergio, and Virginia Fabella. *The Emergent Gospel: Theology from the Underside of History: Papers from the Ecumenical Dialogue of Third World Theologians, Dar Es Salaam, August 5–12, 1976*. Maryknoll, NY: Orbis, 1978.

Towne, Edgar A. "Empirical Naturalism: Bernard M. Loomer's Interpretation of Whitehead's Philosophy." *American Journal of Theology & Philosophy* 32 (2011) 255–66.

Townes, Emilie M. "The Womanist Dancing Mind: Speaking to the Expansiveness of Womanist Discourse." In *Deeper Shades of Purple: Womanism in Religion and Society*, edited by Stacy M. Thomas, 236–50. Religion, Race, and Ethnicity. New York: New York University Press, 2006.

———. *Womanist Ethics and the Cultural Production of Evil*. Black Religion, Womanist Thought, Social Justice. New York: Palgrave Macmillan, 2006.

Tracy, David. *The Analogical Imagination: Christian Theology and the Culture of Pluralism*. New York: Crossroad, 1981.

———. *Blessed Rage for Order: The New Pluralism in Theology*. New York: Winston Seabury, 1975.

———. *On Naming the Present: Reflections on God, Hermeneutics and Church*. Concilium. Maryknoll, NY: Orbis, 1994.

———. *Plurality and Ambiguity: Reflections on God, Religion, Hope*. San Francisco: Harper & Row, 1987.

———. "Why Orthodoxy in a Personalist Age?" *Proceedings of the Catholic Theological Society of America* 25 (1970) 78–110.

Travis, Sarah. *Decolonizing Preaching: The Pulpit as Postcolonial Space*. Lloyd John Ogilvie Institute of Preaching Series. Eugene, OR: Cascade Books, 2014.

———. "Troubled Gospel: Postcolonial Preaching for the Colonized, Colonizer, and Everyone in Between." *Homiletic* 40 (2015) 46–54.

Treat, James, ed. *Native and Christian: Indigenous Voices on Religious Identity in the United States and Canada*. New York: Routledge, 1996.

Trevor Project. https://www.thetrevorproject.org/resources/preventing-suicide/facts-about-suicide/.

Turner, Mary Donovan. "Disrupting a Ruptured World." In *Purposes of Preaching*, edited by Jana Childers, 131–40. St. Louis: Chalice, 2004.

Twiss, Richard. *Rescuing the Gospel from the Cowboys*. Edited by Ray Martell and Sue Martell. Downers Grove, IL: InterVarsity, 2015.

Turner Mary Donovaan, and Mary Lin Hudson, *Saved from Silence: Finding Women's Voice in Preaching*. St. Louis: Chalice, 1999.

Valle, Lis. "'Cuerpos y salvación,' Comentario del San Lucas 2:22–40 para el Primer domingo de la Navidad." *Working Preacher*. https://www.workingpreacher.org/commentaries/revised-common-lectionary/first-sunday-of-christmas-2/comentario-del-san-lucas-222-40.

———. "PTCA December 27, 2020 Worship Service." Presbytery of the Twin Cities Area. https://youtu.be/vCIJOmRlz2E.

Van De Walle, Bernard. "Suffered under Pontius Pilate: The Humanity of Christ." Lecture Notes from "The Christian Faith Class." Calgary: Ambrose University, circa, 2007.

Van Dyk, Leanne. "The Church in Evangelical Theology and Practice." *Cambridge Companion to Evangelical Theology*, edited by Timothy Larsen and Daniel J. Treier, 125–42. Cambridge Companions to Religion. Cambridge: Cambridge University Press, 2007.

Walker, Alice. "Alice Walker's Womanism." In *The Womanist Reader*, edited by Layli Phillips, 3–20. New York: Routledge, 2006.

———. *In Search of Our Mothers' Gardens: Womanist Prose*. New York; Harcourt, 1983.

Wallace, Mark. *The Second Naiveté: Barth, Ricoeur, and the New Yale Theology*. 2nd ed. Studies in American Biblical Hermeneutics. Macon: Mercer University Press, 1995.

Walls, Andrew F. *The Missionary Movement in Christian History: Studies in the Transmission of Faith*. Maryknoll, NY: Orbis, 1996.

Waltke, Bruce K. "Biblical Authority: How Firm a Foundation." *In Evangelicalism: Surviving Its Success; Conference, June 1986*. Vol. 2, *The Evangelical Round Table*, edited by David A. Fraser, 84–96. St. Davids, PA: Eastern College and Eastern Baptist Theological Seminary, 1987.

———. "Biblical Authority: How Firm a Foundation." In *The Dance between God and Humanity: Reading the Bible Today as the People of God*, 212–26. Grand Rapids: Eerdmans, 2013.

Ware, Frederick L. *Methodologies of Black Theology*. 2002. Reprint, Eugene, OR: Wipf & Stock, 2012.

Weil, Simone. *Gravity and Grace*. Translated by Marion Crawford and Marion von der Ruhr. New York: Routledge, 1999.

Wells, David F. *God in the Wasteland: The Reality of Truth in a World of Fading Dreams*. Grand Rapids: Eerdmans, 1994.

West, Cornel, and Eddie S. Glaude, eds. *African American Religious Thought: An Anthology*, Louisville: Westminster John Knox, 2003.

Westfield, Nancy Lynne. "'Mama Why . . . ?'A Womanist Epistemology of Hope." In *Deeper Shades of Purple: Womanism in Religion and Society*, edited by Stacy M. Thomas. 128–42. Religion, Race, and Ethnicity. New York: New York University Press, 2006.

Whitehead, Alfred North. *Process and Reality*. Corrected ed. Edited by David Ray Griffin and Donald W. Sherburne. New York: Free Press, 1978.

Wilcox, Ashley M. *The Women's Lectionary: Preaching the Women of the Bible throughout the Year*. Louisville: Westminster John Knox Press, 2021.

Wilkens, Steve, and Don Thorsen. *Everything You Know about Evangelicals Is Wrong (Well, Almost Everything): An Insider's Look at Myths & Realities*. Grand Rapids: Baker, 2010.

Willard, Frances E. *Woman in the Pulpit*. New York: Lothrop, 1889.

Williams, Delores S. *Sisters in the Wilderness: The Challenge of Womanist God-Talk*. Maryknoll, NY: Orbis, 1993.

Williamson, Clark M. *Way of Blessing/Way of Life: A Christian Theology*. St. Louis: Chalice,1999.

Williamson, Clark M., and Ronald J. Allen. *Adventures of the Spirit: A Guide to Worship from the Perspective of Process Theology*. Lanham, MD: University Press of America, 1997.

———. *A Credible and Timely Word: Process Theology and Preaching*. St. Louis: Chalice, 1991.

Willimon, William H. "Barth on Preaching." In *The Wiley Blackwell Companion to Karl Barth*, edited by George Hunsinger and Keith L. Johnson, 1:253–64. 2 vols. Wiley-Blackwell Companions to Religion. London: Wiley, 2020.

———. *Conversations with Barth on Preaching*. Nashville: Abingdon, 2016.

Wilson, Paul Scott. *Preaching as Poetry: Beauty, Goodness, and Truth in Every Sermon*. Nashville: Abingdon, 2014.

Winnicott, D. W. *Playing and Reality*. London: Tavistock, 1971.

Winter, Miriam Therese. *Woman Word: A Feminist Lectionary and Psalter*. New York: Crossroad, 1990.

Wolterstorff, Nicholas. "Why Care about Justice?" In *Evangelicalism: Surviving Its Success; Conference, June 1986*. Vol. 2, *The Evangelical Round Table*, edited by David A. Fraser, 156–67. St. Davids, PA: Eastern College and Eastern Baptist Theological Seminary, 1987.

Wolvengrey, Arok. "Land." In *nehiyawewin itwewina: Cree words*, edited by Freda Ahenakew et al., 1:10, 2:419–20. 2 vols. Regina SK: Canadian Plains Research Centre, 2001.

Woodley, Randy. *Shalom and the Community of Creation: An Indigenous Vision*. Prophetic Christianity. Grand Rapids: Eerdmans, 2012.

Woosley, Louisa M. *Shall Women Preach? On the Question Answered*. Memphis: Frontier, 1989.

"World Population Review." https://worldpopulationreview.com/state-rankings/asian-population.

Wright, G. Ernest. *God Who Acts: Biblical Theology as Recital*. Studies in Biblical Theology 1/8. Chicago: Regnery, 1952.

Wright, G. Ernest, and Reginald H. Fuller. *The Book of the Acts of God: Christian Scholarship Interprets the Bible*. Garden City, NY: Doubleday, 1957.

Yang, Sunggu. "The Abrahamic Pilgrimage Story in Sermons: An Ontological-Narrative Foundation of Asian American Life in Faith." *Theology Today* 73 (2016) 24–35.

Yee, Gale A. "She Stood in Tears amid the Alien Corn: Ruth, the Perpetual Foreigner and Model Minority." In *Off the Menu: Asian and Asian North American Women's Religion & Theology*, edited by Rita Nakashima Brock et al., 45–65. Louisville: Westminster John Knox, 2007.

Yong, Amos. *The Future of Evangelical Theology: Soundings from the Asian American Diaspora*. Downers Grove, IL: IVP Academic, 2014.

Zikmund, Barbara Brown, et al. *Clergy Women: An Uphill Calling*. Louisville: Westminster John Knox, 1998.

Zink-Sawyer, Beverly. *From Preachers to Suffragists: Women's Rights and Religious Connections in the Lives of Three Nineteenth-Century American Clergywomen*. Louisville: Westminster John Knox, 2003.

Ingram Content Group UK Ltd.
Milton Keynes UK
UKHW012235170423
420333UK00003B/104